# XI JINPING
## China's Third New Era

# XI JINPING
## China's Third New Era

JAYADEVA RANADE

KW Publishers Pvt Ltd
New Delhi

ISBN 978-93-91490-52-2 Hardback
ISBN 978-93-91490-20-1 ebook

Published in India by Kalpana Shukla

KW Publishers Pvt Ltd
4676/21, First Floor, Ansari Road
Daryaganj, New Delhi 110002
Phone: +91 11 43528107
Marketing: kw@kwpub.in
Editorial: production@kwpub.in
Website: www.kwpub.in

Printed and Bound in India

# Contents

# Preface

Observing China is an interesting, albeit arcane, pursuit. Reading Chinese tea leaves has always been difficult, but since Xi Jinping came to power and stricter and more restrictive controls have been placed on media and society, it has become even more so. This book seeks to pierce through this opacity in an attempt to decipher China's internal developments, its foreign policy agenda and, of course, its attitude and policy towards India.

Since 2013, changes in China have been fast-paced and definitive, reflecting Xi Jinping's character and growing self-confidence. From the time of Mao Zedong, no Chinese leader has consolidated more power into his own hands than Xi, who has assumed the chairmanship of at least nineteen Central Small Leading Groups—the most powerful bodies in China. Xi now exercises control over a broad sweep of subjects, ranging from the modernization and control of the People's Liberation Army (PLA), the direction of economic reform, the shaping of foreign policy and security affairs, as well as the leadership of Chinese Communist Party (CCP)'s United Front—its arm for liaising, influencing and winning over political parties and individuals the world over, in addition to China's ethnic minorities. It is no surprise, then, that Xi is often referred to as the 'Chairman of Everything'!

The briefs selected for this book cover the period from mid-June 2017 till the end of 2020, an important phase in China's contemporary history. It marks China's reversion to communist orthodoxy, but one overlaid with the soft overtones of cosmetic window dressing to distinguish it from the harsh decade of the Cultural Revolution. The period has been marked by Xi consistently fanning nationalist sentiment and ensuring that the CCP's ideology and control permeates all sections of State and society. Furthermore, in an attempt to consolidate his grip on power and fortify his position, Xi has strengthened China's security apparatus thus preparing the way for his indefinite continuance at the helm of China's affairs. Incidentally, Xi's acolytes had observed as early as 2013, that 'China under Xi Jinping has embarked on a third new, thirty-year era like that of Mao and Deng before him'!

At the same time, the resentment simmering at all levels of Chinese society has become noticeable. In 2017-18 and again between late 2019 and mid-2020, there was an outpouring of criticism levelled personally against the CCP and its "leader", Xi Jinping—an outburst not witnessed since the Tiananmen Square incident in 1989. This resentment was first sparked by Xi's decision to abolish the informal term limits that denied cadres more than two terms in office and governed their elevation to senior positions. Resentment was rekindled after the perceived mishandling of the initial stages of the Covid pandemic. Nonetheless, Xi Jinping appears for now to have successfully suppressed dissent by imposing progressively tougher security controls and punitive measures.

The book examines these and other important issues that have far reaching consequences for China's neighbours. The deterioration of China-US relations—regarded by Chinese as the most crucial of China's relationships and which many senior CCP cadres and Chinese analysts privately say has been mishandled by Xi Jinping -- has been dealt with in detail. It looks at Sino-Pakistan relations, the China Pakistan Economic Corridor (CPEC) and the recent developments in Tibet. Xi's aggressive goal of "rejuvenation of the great Chinese nation"—code for "recovering" territories that China lays claim to—as well as his uncompromising stance on foreign policy has left China's neighbours wary. India is directly affected.

Special attention has been paid to India-China relations since China's attitude towards India has altered significantly since Xi came to power. The new hostile posture became particularly evident during the 73-day face-off at Doklam in 2017, followed by the ongoing Chinese incursions in Ladakh and massing of troops along the entire Line of Actual Control (LAC) since May 2020—an act of aggression that was anticipated by this author as early as 2016. The writing on the wall is clear. With trust having been demolished, India-China relations will for many years be marked by wariness and suspicion. There is a high probability of armed clashes in the coming decade.

A fair amount of detail has been provided in the book so that it interests not only the general reader, but also the more serious China watchers. Footnotes and references have deliberately been omitted to avoid distracting the reader, but the sources for the data are incorporated in the text where considered necessary.

I hope the book succeeds in providing some clarity and useful insights into China's internal developments, its leadership's thinking and foreign and strategic policies. Each of these have a direct impact on India and, with an aggressive 'rising' China, are becoming increasingly important for the world at large. The period till 2030 is crucial.

New Delhi **Jayadeva Ranade**
October 2021

# 1. Xi Jinping Prepares to Lead China into New Thirty-Year Era

Last week there was a major, though anticipated, development in China's internal politics with the announcement that term limits on the posts of China's President and Vice President would be abolished. Removing the limitation on these tenures establishes Xi Jinping's preeminent stature and allows him to continue interminably, subject to his health. It removes the possibility of any perceived depletion of authority in case he is compelled to step down as President on the completion of two terms in 2023. In reality, Xi Jinping and the 'princelings' or 'Red Descendants' have effected a coup to achieve the dreams of their forebears and restore China to what they perceive is its former greatness. The decision potentially has immense implications and long-term repercussions.

On February 25, 2018, the Chinese Communist Party's (CCP's) Central Committee (CC) convened a special plenary session to recommend an amendment to the Constitution of the People's Republic of China (PRC). A 4,457-character communiqué issued after the plenum proposed abolition of the two-term—10-year—limit on the tenures of China's President and Vice President. The amendments will be incorporated into the PRC's Constitution when the 2,980 newly elected Deputies of the National People's Congress (NPC)—China's version of a Parliament—meet in Beijing for its first session on March 5, 2018.

This will be the first amendment to China's Constitution in 14 years. Another ten amendments of varying importance will also be deliberated upon, with at least two further adding to Xi Jinping's authority. One will establish the State Supervisory Commission, a body that will exercise authority over even the Party's powerful Central Discipline Inspection Commission (CDIC). Another amendment to the Constitution, but unlike others, significantly asserts, "CCP leadership is the most substantive feature of socialism with Chinese characteristics". The amendment amplifies the thrust of Xi Jinping's report to the 19th Party Congress—that the Party will pervade every sphere of endeavour of the state—and, in doing so, effectively dispenses with the, albeit cosmetic superficial, separation of the Party and state that Deng Xiaoping sought to usher in.

The time limit on the tenures of China's President and Vice President was brought in by Deng Xiaoping in 1982, who was determined to guard against the reemergence of a personality cult like that of Mao Zedong. Deng Xiaoping was also keen that there be no repetition of the one-man authoritarian rule that China witnessed during Mao's almost 30-year regime and during which many Party cadres and members had suffered. Many senior cadres, including Deng Xiaoping and Xi Jinping's father, Xi Zhongxun, had personally suffered and been purged for questioning Mao's judgement or because Mao felt they were not complying with his instructions. By discarding these provisions, Xi Jinping has effectively closed the door on Deng Xiaoping's era.

Xi Jinping, who has used nationalism and ideology to promote political stability and ensure the Party's monopoly on power, began to quickly concentrate greater power soon after his appointment to China's three top posts of CCP CC General Secretary, Chairman of the Central Military Commission (CMC) and President of China. By September 2017, Xi Jinping was overseeing crucial aspects of the state and exercised direct control over the security apparatus, military, cyber security and the economy. He holds fifteen formal positions, more than any CCP leader, including Mao Zedong or Deng Xiaoping! He has taken care to simultaneously build his credentials as a Chinese Communist ideologue, and in June 2014, the CCP's theoretical fortnightly journal *Qiu Shi (Seeking Truth)* described Xi Jinping as "one of China's greatest Communist leaders". The 19th Party Congress incorporated "Xi Jinping's Thought on Socialism with Chinese Characteristics in the New Era" into the Party Constitution and, after the first Politburo meeting a couple of days later, the term *lingxiu* (respected leader) is being used for Xi Jinping. The term *lingxiu* was last used for Mao. Xi Jinping has used the media effectively too and is regularly the lead news item in the *People's Daily* and China Central Television (CCTV). In contrast to his predecessors Jiang Zemin and Hu Jintao, who received media coverage 3,000 and 2,000 times a year respectively, there are more than 5,000 news items on Xi Jinping each year!

Quite aside from the symbolic value of the amendment, it is interesting that the post of China's President is the least important of Xi Jinping's three posts and that of the PRC Vice President even less so, with neither exercising any substantive power. Real power vests in the post of General Secretary of the CCP CC, which has no formal fixed tenure. Since the 17th Party Congress in 2007, however, the CCP has observed an informal rule that no individual shall hold the post of CCP CC General Secretary for more than two terms of five years each. The next most important post in China, that of Chairman of the Central Military Commission (CMC) also has no such limitation. In fact, since 1987, the Chairman of the CMC need not be the CCP CC General Secretary or a member of the Politburo or even a member of the CC. Jiang Zemin, for instance, continued as Chairman of the CMC for one and a half years after Hu Jintao had taken over as CCP CC General Secretary.

On the surface, Xi Jinping's move to abolish limits on the terms of China's President and Vice President does not appear to materially affect him except that he would have to give up the post of President in case he continues beyond his second term. Speculation is rife in Beijing that the amendment paves the way for the appointment of Wang Qishan, till recently Politburo Standing Committee (PBSC) member and Xi Jinping's trusted friend and lieutenant, as Vice President of China. Wang Qishan could possibly concurrently be appointed Chairman of the powerful State Supervisory Commission that will be formally established by the upcoming NPC session, allowing him to continue the work he began while chairing the Party's CDIC, but from a more powerful vantage perch. This move nonetheless implies that the 'informal' limit on the term for a General Secretary of the CCP CC can easily be dispensed with. Similarly, observance of the 'informal' rule that Party cadres aged 68 years or more are ineligible for entry to the Politburo (PB) or Politburo Standing Committee (PBSC) is now at risk. The amendments could open the doors for Xi Jinping for promoting his followers and loyalists to higher Party bodies as well retaining loyal cadres, like 67-year old PBSC member Li Zhanshu and 66-year old Harvard-trained economist Liu He, in the PB and PBSC, regardless of age.

While quite predictably the People's Liberation Army (PLA) expressed "resolute support" to the amendments on February 27, there are hints of opposition to the lifting of limits on the terms of the President and Vice President.

The sequence of meetings to deliberate upon, and approve, the decision is an indication. On January 18-19, 2018, the 2nd Plenum Communiqué announced a constitutional amendment along with a summary in the communiqué but did not mention the removal of term limits. According to a Reuters report, there were differing views and no consensus at this plenum attended by 204 CC members; the date inscribed at the bottom of the constitutional amendment draft published on February 26 is "signed" by the Central Committee on January 26—however, there is no record of a Central Committee Plenum on January 26 or of a Politburo meeting; a Politburo meeting was held on January 30; the NPC Standing Committee which met on February 22-23, is said to have decided on the submission of proposals to a full NPC; on February 24, there was a PB meeting and 'study session' on constitutional matters; on February 25, the text of the constitutional amendment (and an announcement on the term limit) dated January 26 and signed "Central Committee" was published; and a 3rd CC Plenum was held on February 26-27.

There is an important indication of the nervousness in the central Party leadership on this issue. A Reuters report that filtered out of Hong Kong on February 28 stated that Xinhua has been blamed by the leadership for releasing a single message in English titled "CPC Proposes Change on Chinese President's term in Constitution" at 3:55 pm on February 25. The Chinese version was released two hours later with the full text from the CCP CC. No report for the term limits in Chinese was released. According to the report, this was considered to be severe political misconduct: the relevant editors were dismissed and the leader of Xinhua was required to write a self-critical piece.

Public articulation of anger on February 25 flooded Wechat, Weibo and Sina—which together account for hundreds of millions of users—with criticism, satire and satirical cartoons of Xi Jinping. The same day, the Party's Central Propaganda Department ordered the blocking of at least 28 words and phrases deemed critical of either Xi Jinping or the decision. Sixty Six-year-old Li Datong, a former editor of the state-run *China Youth Daily*, issued a statement addressed to Beijing's 55 Deputies to the NPC on WeChat on February 25, asking them to oppose the bill. Asserting that "he is old and has nothing to fear", Li Datong said lifting term limits would "sow the seeds of chaos and that if there are no term limits on a country's highest leader, then we are returning to an imperial regime. My generation has lived through Mao. That era is over. How can we possibly go back to it?" Separately, Wang Ying, a businesswoman who has advocated government reforms, on WeChat described the Communist Party's proposal as "an outright betrayal" and "against the tides." She said, "I know that you (the government) will dare to do anything and one ordinary person's voice is certainly useless. But I am a Chinese citizen, and I don't plan on leaving. This is my motherland too!" The state-run *Global Times,* on February 25, indirectly acknowledged the opposition when it said, "There has been a related statement in the Preamble to the Constitution, but this has been challenged by some who are supported and instigated by overseas forces. In this sense, stressing the CPC leadership in the constitutional amendment proposal was essential."

Of interest too is the appearance since November 2017 in commentaries in the *PLA Daily* and military media of new phraseology emphasising the need to "protect" Xi Jinping as the core of the leadership. The phrases include: "we must ... keep a close watch on our awareness and resolutely safeguard Chairman Xi's core position in the Party Central Committee and the whole Party"; "Chairman Xi as the core of the Party Central Committee, ... and the whole Army sincerely supports and resolutely safeguards it ..."; "safeguarding Chairman Xi's position is at the core of the Party Central Committee"; and "ensure that the whole Army is absolutely loyal, absolutely pure and absolutely reliable. It resolutely listens to the Chairman's command, ... and makes President Xi reassured." This emphasis on 'protecting' and 'safeguarding' Xi Jinping's position is new and worth noting. It coincides with a usually informed but unconfirmed report of an attempt on Xi Jinping's life towards the end of last year.

The amendments solidify Xi Jinping's position as China's preeminent leader and will have an impact on China's domestic policies and relations with other countries. There will now be no restraints domestically on Xi Jinping pursuing his goals. However, having taken charge of economic policy,

Xi Jinping will be responsible for any slowdown in growth and the people's living standards not keeping pace with their aspirations. In the nearer term, China's effort to establish sovereignty over the South China Sea and effect reunification with Taiwan will be redoubled. China will pursue Xi Jinping's flagship projects of the 'Belt and Road Initiative' (BRI) and 'China Dream' —both incorporated in the Party Constitution—along with his ambition of achieving the "rejuvenation of the great Chinese nation" with greater vigour. There will be increased pressure on countries to acquiesce to the BRI. The timetable spelt out in Xi Jinping's report to the 19th Congress, of making China a strong developed nation having "pioneering global influence" by 2050, will now acquire increased emphasis. China can be expected to adopt a tougher stance and negotiate harder to realise the 'China Dream' by 2021. There is little prospect of any softening in China's stance on issues of sovereignty and territory. It is anticipated that China will be even more assertive now that Xi Jinping is its sole leader.

*(This article was published by the Centre for China Analysis and Strategy, New Delhi, on March 1, 2018.)*

# 2. China's Internal Situation before the 19th Party Congress: An Overview

Especially since the 18th Party Congress in November 2012 and as China moves to convene the 19th Party Congress in November 2017, there has been a steady hardening of the Chinese state. Political stability and regime survival have been on top on the Party agenda, and to ensure this, Xi Jinping has introduced progressively restrictive domestic measures and promoted the rise in nationalism.

The first sign of the toughening stance was the Party conferring on Xi Jinping China's three top positions of General Secretary of the Chinese Communist Party (CCP) Central Committee (CC), Chairman of the Central Military Commission (CMC) and President of the People's Republic of China (PRC), simultaneously for the first time in thirty years! The other was the installation in a now reduced 7-member Politburo Standing Committee (PBSC) of stolid, doctrinaire apparatchiks. The backdrop to this was the unprecedented domestic political scrabbling for top positions by senior CCP cadres witnessed through 2011-12 when Politburo (PB) member Bo Xilai attempted to usurp the top position. The failed bid by Wang Lijun, Bo Xilai's chief of public security in the Chongqing municipality—a position equivalent to a central Vice Minister—to defect to the US, also severely jolted the Party's top echelons as it revealed that the CCP 'nomenklatura' had been penetrated by the West.

The 18th Party Congress —a watershed in contemporary Chinese politics —consequently hammered out the unequivocal message of stability, assertive policies, Party supremacy and the 'China Dream'.

Xi Jinping has used nationalism and ideology to promote political stability and regime survival. He has consolidated his position and today chairs thirteen central leading groups overseeing all crucial aspects of the state, including direct control over the security apparatus, military, cyber security and the economy. Xi Jinping's titles are: General Secretary of the Central Committee (CC) of the CCP; Chairman of the Central Military Commission (CMC); President of the People's Republic of China (PRC); Leader of the Central Leading Group for Foreign Affairs; Leader of the Central Leading Group for Taiwan Affairs; Head of the Central Leading Group for Comprehensively Deepening Reforms; Chairman of the Central National Security Commission; Head of the Central Leading Group for Internet Security and Informatisation; Leader of the Central Leading Group for National Defence and Military Reform; Head of the Central Leading Group for Financial and Economic Affairs; Commander-in-Chief of the Joint Battle Command of the People's Liberation Army (PLA); and since January 2017, Chairman of the Central Commission for Integrated Military and Civilian Development. He now holds more formal positions than any CCP leader including Mao Zedong or Deng Xiaoping!

Xi Jinping has paid special attention to the PLA. Among the main reasons are the rampant corruption in the PLA wherein ranks were purchased and officers operated 'illegal' businesses; the existence of lobbies owing loyalty to retired veteran leaders; ousted PB member Bo Xilai's success in creating a lobby in the PLA to support his personal ambitions; and persistent propaganda by outside 'foreign forces' and 'liberal' elements inside China that the PLA is an Army of the state and not the Party.

Attention was buttressed by Xi Jinping's conviction that the Soviet Union had actually "disarmed" the Communist Party of the Soviet Union (CPSU) by designating the Soviet Army as a national Army. Within a day of being appointed Chairman of the CMC, Xi Jinping moved to tighten the Party's grip on the PLA and discipline it. At an enlarged meeting of the CMC, he declared that political reliability would be the key determining criterion for promotions.

At the 3rd Party Plenum convened in October 2013, Xi Jinping brought the PLA within the ambit of the Party's watchdog anti-corruption body, the Central Discipline Inspection Commission (CDIC), as part of his effort to discipline the PLA and eliminate resistance to its restructuring and reform. CDIC investigators soon uncovered instances of corruption in the PLA and the arrests of senior officers followed. Many PLA officers of and above the rank of Major General/Rear Admiral committed suicide while under investigation to ensure that their families received the benefits due. By September 2016, official reports stated that 86 PLA officers of the rank of Major General or above had been dismissed on charges of corruption. An additional 50 PLA officers of the rank of

Major General or above were retired in January 2017. By the end of 2016, a total of 4,300 PLA officers, or over 30 per cent of the PLA officer corps, were under investigation for corruption. In March 2017, the official news agency Xinhua publicised that a total of 4,885 PLA officers had been 'punished' for graft. There is a high degree of popular support inside China for Xi Jinping in his campaign against corruption in the PLA. The campaign additionally allows Xi Jinping to build a loyal band of at least 135 PLA officers whom he will promote to the rank of Major General and above, strengthens the Party's grip on the PLA, and ensures that PLA officers unquestioningly obey Xi Jinping and the CCP.

Party control on the PLA was stressed again most recently on April 27, 2017, when Xi Jinping visited the Southern Theatre Command and asked the PLA to strengthen ideology and ensure that it "resolutely follows the command of the CCP CC". He pointedly asked officers to "eliminate the impact" of Guo Boxiong and Xu Caihou. Such references almost five years after Guo Boxiong and Xu Caihou were punished suggest that their influence and that of their mentor, former CCP CC General Secretary Jiang Zemin, along with effects of their corrupt practices continue to linger. The continuing existence of problems in the PLA were highlighted by a *PLA Daily* commentary in March 2017, which asserted that "malpractice, including spreading political rumors, reckless comments on the Party's theories and policies, and participation of illegal associations should all be prohibited and punished"! Nonetheless, Xi Jinping has been successfully pushing through the most extensive and far-reaching reforms to streamline and restructure the PLA since its founding!

Within days of the Party Congress, Xi Jinping began tackling problems within the Party, including corruption, a lazy work-style and ostentation. He introduced the practice of obtaining feedback from the people and colleagues to assess the potential of a cadre. Standards for admission to the Party were sought to be enhanced and Xi Jinping told Party cadres that the emphasis should be on better quality and not on increasing numbers. In October 2016, the government announced that more than a million of the 88 million Party members had been investigated in the past three years during an intense campaign against corruption. By early this year, 176 Party cadres of the rank of Vice Minister and above had been dismissed on charges of corruption. The Party mouthpiece *People's Daily* complained in October 2016 against "lazy, foot-dragging officials" who were too "scared to do their jobs for fear of being accused of taking bribes, while others were unwilling to act unless the kickbacks resumed". It added "... those who complain or are nostalgic for the good old days? Well, they are just 'rotten with corruption!'" Xi Jinping also cut the budget of the Communist Youth League (CYL) and initiated a programme to reduce its membership. At the same time, he initiated an austerity campaign to tackle corruption and ostentation in the Party and mandated a regime of 'one soup, four dishes' at banquets. A large number of restaurants and hotels have consequently closed down, but the austerity measures remain in place despite the estimated annual 2-4 per cent adverse impact on the Gross Domestic Product (GDP).

The economy is a major factor affecting society and China's internal situation. The slowdown in growth has been faster than anticipated and the forecast for economic growth in 2017 is now officially pegged at 6.5 per cent, described by Premier Li Keqiang as the minimum essential for job creation. Very few of the 300 reforms decided upon at the 3rd Party Plenum in 2013 have progressed. The 106 central State owned Enterprises (SoEs) have been particularly resistant to reform, not least because most are headed by 'princelings'. For example, while the rules recommended a cap on the salaries of senior SoE executives, the SoEs were permitted to themselves determine the salaries. The shutting down of 'zombie' enterprises, often owned by SoEs, has also made tardy progress, with pilot projects being undertaken in Shanghai. Some major decisions have, however, been taken such as to lay off 5-6 million workers in the coal, steel and mining industries between 2016-18. Official Chinese media reports say that protests by workers have increased by an estimated 30 per cent over the 210,000 reported officially in 2010. Unemployment of graduates is up by 30 per cent, adding to the levels of popular dissatisfaction. Early this year, responding to complaints by graduates of the lack of jobs, officials said there were adequate jobs but not of the kind the graduates wanted!

Reports of regular protests by veteran demobilised soldiers have surfaced and with 300,000 more demobilised soldiers likely to soon join their ranks the number of protests could increase. Hundreds of Chinese military veterans demonstrated in mid-February 2017, outside the Central Discipline Inspection Commission (CDIC) in central Beijing for two days, demanding unpaid retirement benefits. A smaller number protested outside the Ministry of Civil Affairs the following day. In October 2016, more than 1,000 veterans demonstrated outside the Defence Ministry headquarters in Beijing.

Income inequality is also growing. Latest official Chinese figures state that while disparity between provinces is gradually reducing, the gap between the poor and rich is widening. As publicised during the National People's Congress (NPC) session in March 2017, one-third of China's wealth is owned by the top one per cent households. There is also a lack of confidence in the country's economy as evidenced by the continuing flight of capital. The People's Bank of China (PBoC) has estimated that US$ 1 trillion has fled the country since 2015!

Poverty is causing considerable concern. At the Politburo meeting on February 22, 2017, President Xi Jinping underscored the importance of "precision in the battle against poverty, saying that poverty relief targets should be accomplished as scheduled". Poverty alleviation was the focus again at the Politburo meeting on March 31, 2017, as well as the NPC session that month. To highlight the leadership's concern, Xi Jinping has nominated himself as a delegate to the 19th Congress from Guizhou, China's poorest province.

Very high on the list of concerns of the CCP's higher echelons are the perceived destabilisation efforts, or 'colour revolution', by the West. Early in April 2013, the CCP CC issued Document No. 9, which quoted Xi Jinping as saying "regime dissatisfaction often begins in the realm of ideas". He complained of an intensification of Western cultural and ideological infiltration. The CCP launched a campaign to counter such elements. In January 2015, the CCP CC issued Document No. 30 strengthening Party control over primary and secondary schools and universities. Also, in January 2015, the PRC Education Minister prohibited the use of Western sources for teaching, and Western books began being weeded out of university and college libraries.

In the third week of December 2016, a seven-and-a-half-minute video issued by the CCP CC Propaganda Department focussed on the dangers of a 'colour revolution' of which, it said, "Embassies in China are the forward command, combining forces to promote street politics". The video, which has no title, was propagated online under the head "Who Most Wants to Overthrow China". The theme was highlighted in a high-level conference in December 2016 to discuss strengthening of ideological controls in universities.

During the conference, China's Minister of Education, Chen Baosheng observed that "the first option for hostile forces infiltrating us is our education system". He added, "To wreck your future, first of all, they wreck your schools". Hong Kong was singled out as a "bridgehead" for subversion. The video ended with the assertion, "Thoroughly expelling 'colour revolution' will be a long war, but if there is war, we will answer the call".

Reflecting the CCP leadership's concern, the 442,000 foreign students studying in China have also—for the first time—been formally brought within the purview of the Party's controls. On June 5, 2017, China's Ministries of Education, Foreign Affairs and Public Security jointly issued new regulations which mandate that foreign students pursuing higher education diplomas in China will have to take compulsory courses in Chinese. They require universities and colleges to teach international students about China's laws and regulations, plus its institutions and traditional Chinese culture and customs, and require international students majoring in philosophy and politics to take compulsory political theories courses. The regulations state that they were made to "regulate schools' admission, the cultivation and management of international students and for the convenience of international students studying in schools in China". The regulations ban any form of religious activities on campus, such as preaching or religious gatherings and say that schools should respect the customs and religious beliefs of foreign students, but are not allowed to provide any venue for their religious activities. International students who do not live in school dormitories are required to register their address with the police in the neighbourhood. Universities and colleges are now also required to have "instructors" for foreign students, following a similar practice of employing "political instructors" for Chinese students. University political instructors have long been tasked with political education and overseeing Chinese students' ideological teaching. The Social Credit Management system, which ensures total monitoring of all residents in China, is planned to be implemented across China by 2018.

These measures are reinforced by the National Security Education Campaign launched in August 2016 amidst accusations of "hostile foreign forces" meddling in China and fanning of domestic discontent. In April 2017, Beijing announced incentives of up to US$ 72,000 for people providing information on suspected spies. On May 16, 2017, China issued its first public draft of an Intelligence Law that is expansive and allows the detention and monitoring of suspects as well as search of their premises, seizure of vehicles and devices, and investigation of individuals and groups. Chinese citizens and foreigners are within the ambit of this law. There has also been a crackdown on human rights lawyers, with almost 300 arrested till May 2017. There is also apprehension that Buddhist monks, especially Tibetan Buddhist monks, have the potential of being guided and controlled from "outside". Consequently, since March 2017, controls are being enforced on the movements of monks and they have been directed to take prior permission for their 'teachings'.

Additionally, there is an arc of vulnerability developing around China. The Tibet Autonomous Region (TAR) remains restive despite the implementation of progressively restrictive security measures. While the 'iron grid' system ensures a response to an incident by the security forces within 3-5 minutes of the occurrence of an incident, the authorities introduced additional measures in early May 2017. The TAR Public Security Bureau (PSB) enhanced its surveillance and rapid deployment capability across counties. The PSB budget which was US$ 1 billion in 2014 was increased by 54 per cent in 2016 over the previous year. However, the number of medical teams visiting the PLA and People's Armed Police (PAP) personnel deployed in the TAR to treat them for post-traumatic stress disorders has increased from one to three each year. Simultaneously, Party surveillance has been expanded, with efforts to recruit one Party member in each village in the TAR each year; 21,000 Party cadres also fanned out to each of the TAR's over 5,000 villages. Monks and monasteries continue to be specially targeted, with Party cadres deployed in each monastery. Tibetans still do not accept the China-appointed Gyaltsen Norbu as the Panchen Lama, but only as a "learned monk". There is also a divide between the Hans and Tibetans, with China's provincial media often reporting fights between Han and Tibetan students. The issue of recognition of the Dalai Lama's reincarnation is an additional complication. China's strong reaction to the Dalai Lama's visit to Arunachal Pradesh reflects these tensions in the TAR.

There is also no sign of the tension and violence in the Xinjiang-Uyghur Autonomous Region (XUAR) abating. The public security budget in Xinjiang too was enhanced this year by 54 per cent from the US$ 1.05 billion last year. A report issued last year by the Chinese Academy of Social Sciences (CASS) highlighted that incidents of terrorist violence by the Uyghurs were spreading to other parts of the country with substantive Muslim populations. It said that some countries, like Turkey were providing travel documents to the Uyghurs to help them escape or enter Xinjiang through Southeast Asia, and that China should not expect assistance from foreign countries. In the past few years, provincial Communist cadres and delegates to the National People's Congress (NPC) have, unusually, named Pakistan as the source of support to the Uyghurs. In May 2017, China expressed concern about the potential danger from the Rohingyas in Myanmar being trained by the Islamic State. There are other tensions developing on China's periphery. Since Tsai Ing-wen of the Democratic Progressive Party (DPP) took over as Taiwan's President, tension has risen across the Taiwan Strait, with Beijing insisting that she has plans to "sneakily" make a bid for independence. The telephone call between then US President designate Trump and Tsai Ing-wen aroused deep suspicion in Beijing, with Chinese analysts stating that "with the ruling DPP moving faster toward de facto independence, China is now preparing for a final solution by non-peaceful means, which is the last resort China would prefer to turn to".

While political tensions in Hong Kong have seemingly settled for now, it was not before Beijing cracked down hard on the advocates of 'independence'. Beijing has also preempted any bid by Hong Kong residents to interpret the Basic Law, declaring that Beijing's would be the final word. Differences between Hong Kong 'independence' groups and Beijing, however, remain.

When the 19th Party Congress reviews the achievements since the last Congress, it can be expected to positively evaluate the measures implemented by Xi Jinping to ensure social stability and the CCP's primacy. Despite the pools of dissatisfaction comprising those adversely impacted, Xi Jinping has initiated substantive steps to 'professionalise' the PLA and cleanse the Party. As Xi Jinping begins his second term at the end of this year and advances the 'China Dream' and 'One Belt, One Road', the hardening of the Chinese state will continue. The ensuant inflexibility will mean that negotiations are unlikely to yield concessions. This will be evident as China pursues its claims in the South China Sea and in China's relations with India and its neighbours.

*(This article was published by the Centre for China Analysis and Strategy, New Delhi, on June 11, 2017.)*

# 3. China's Internal Situation: Is Xi Jinping under Pressure?

Social stability is a topmost concern for China's leadership as they see it as essential for the perpetuation of the Chinese Communist Party (CCP)'s monopoly on power. To achieve this, they play, to an extent, on the fears of the Chinese people of *dongluang*, or upheaval/chaos.

Despite the efforts of the CCP leadership, especially under Xi Jinping, there is noticeable resentment and dissatisfaction. This has particularly marked his second term since the 19th Party Congress in October 2017. The trigger for the dissatisfaction was the abolition by Xi Jinping at the 19th Party Congress of the term limits on the top posts as well as his ignoring the informally agreed upon age limits for the elevation of cadres to top positions like in the Politburo (PB) and Politburo Standing Committee (PBSC). These were set by Deng Xiaoping with the precise objective of preventing a recurrence of a situation wherein too much power is concentrated in the hands of a single leader, or avoiding one-man rule. CCP members, including retired veteran leaders, protested and posted open letters on the social media stating, "No return to Mao's one-man rule"! At least a couple of letters urged Deputies to the National People's Congress (NPC) to reject the proposal. Many Party members, including in the CCP Central Committee, still retain unpleasant memories of the Cultural Revolution.

Independently, the economy was slowing and unemployment was rising. Economic reforms had seen the closure of tens of thousands of small coal and iron ore mines, rendering tens of millions jobless. The move to shift from an export-led economy to a domestic-led one, which is taking considerably longer than anticipated, further slowed the economy as has the CCP's preference for the State-owned Enterprises (SoEs). Unemployment grew to around 17-20 million by the end of 2019.

Meanwhile, the military reforms had kicked in, adding to the number of unemployed. The demobilised and retired military veterans complained that measures for their rehabilitation were unsatisfactory and their pensions and allowances inadequate. They staged some major protests, prompting the leadership to address their grievances and set up the Ministry of Veterans Affairs to pacify them. Apprehensive that this discontent could spread to the People's Liberation Army (PLA), steps were taken to get them 'respect' in society and arrange jobs on a preferential basis.

But these pressures were exacerbated by two more events: the US-China trade war and the coronavirus (COVID-19) epidemic.

Xi Jinping's bold enunciation of a roadmap for China's future ambitions was the trigger for the US-China trade war. During the 19th Party Congress, Chinese President Xi Jinping announced that he would achieve the 'China Dream' by 2021, 'Made in China' by 2025, modernisation of the PLA by 2035, and make China a "major power with global pioneering influence" by 2049! With this announcement, he effectively put the US on notice that China would be a 'rival'. Additionally, he underscored China's potential global leadership role when he reiterated his proposal of a "Community of Common Destiny" and offered the Chinese system of governance as an alternative to the world's democracies.

The US identified technology as the key driver of China's modernisation efforts and ambitions and targeted that. The first sanctions were applied on China's telecommunications company ZTE which, with access to US markets and critical components blocked, became virtually bankrupt. The second company to be targeted was China's leading technology and telecommunications company, Huawei. Meng Wangzhou, Chief Financial Officer (CFO) and daughter of Huawei's founder Ren Zhengfei , was charged with violations of US sanctions on Iran and falsification of accounts, and proceedings to extradite her to the US were started in Canada. US companies were banned from selling Huawei and ZTE micro-chips, wafers, imaging laser chips, etc. After the initial bluster that it had adequate reserves of these specialised micro-chips, wafers, etc., Huawei had to finally admit that it was in serious trouble and was stopping the manufacture of smart phones from mid-September 2020. There was simultaneously a pushback on Huawei's flagship fifth generation (5G) project, with the roll out of which Huawei expected to become a world leader of telecom and set global standards for the international market. All this severely hit China's technology sector and stocks plummeted further, contributing to China's economic slowdown. Meanwhile, the US expanded the scope of sanctions and said it would issue a letter to warn chip suppliers like Taiwan's SMIC to stop exports to China and Huawei. SMIC's shares have subsequently dropped.

The US also began pushing back on China's Belt and Road Initiative (BRI) following India's lead.

COVID-19 (coronavirus) has severely impacted China. Unemployment soared in March-April 2020 to 80-90 million from the 17-20 million at the end of 2019. Factories, shops, restaurants and small businesses closed, rendering millions jobless. More than 300 million workers who had returned to their villages have not yet come back for work. Agriculture too has been impacted, with grain and pork prices registering sharp increases.

At the same time, COVID-19 fuelled a huge surge in anti-China sentiment across the world. The China Institutes of Contemporary International Relations (CICIR), a think-tank of China's Ministry of State Security, in its briefing to a meeting of the Politburo chaired by Xi Jinping in April 2020, reported that anti-China sentiment was globally at an all-time high. The same month, the Chinese Academy of Social Sciences (CASS), in a separate assessment, concurred and proposed recommendations on how to change the mood among opinion-makers in the US. A *PLA Daily* editorial similarly highlighted China's tense domestic situation and warned that the US could use this to fan social upheaval and provoke social conflict. Hu Xijin, the Editor-in-Chief of the CCP-owned *Global Times* lamented in an article earlier in September that "China has been left friendless"!

Professor Xu Xiaonian, a well-known Chinese economist, said at a conference that "so long as the pandemic continues in Europe and US, Chinese export companies will have no orders, workers will have no wages, and there will be no consumption and a recession is inevitable". He pointed out that China's Gross Domestic Product (GDP) is one-fifth that of the US and one-fourth that of Europe. Ma Jun, an academician and member of the People's Bank of China's (PBoC's) monetary policy committee, endorsed these remarks and said Chinese "growth will largely depend on how the pandemic develops in Europe and the US".

Despite protestations to the contrary, the economic prospects are not bright, if not bleak. Prominent Chinese businessmen, including Jack Ma of Alibaba and Li Chuanzhi of Lenovo signed a letter addressed to Xi Jinping calling for urgent reforms and handed it over to Chinese Premier Li Keqiang at a conference in March 2020. There is serious concern about economic growth and there was considerable debate on whether the Chinese government should mention a growth rate target in its Work Report to the National People's Congress (NPC) plenary session in March 2020. Finally, for the first time in the history of the People's Republic of China (PRC), it was decided not to mention it. Further reflecting the economic distress caused by the COVID-19 pandemic, the budgets of all Central Ministries, except notably the Ministry of Public Security, were cut by 50 per cent.

Continuing through 2018 till date, there has been a steady stream of criticism of the CCP and Xi Jinping. Reputed academics, intellectuals, economists, senior Party members and, importantly, 'princelings' posted their criticism on China's social media. These included persons like Tsinghua Professors Xu Zhangrun and Xu Zhiyou, former Central Party School senior faculty Cai Xia, etc. Their posts remained on social media for days and even longer despite claims by China's internet security administrators that they can remove "offending posts" within minutes. This suggests tacit connivance.

Unprecedented in these posts was the direct criticism of the CCP and personal criticism by name of Xi Jinping. Among the few that were especially scathing in their criticism were the reputed Tsinghua University Professor Xu Zhangrun, who authored a 6,246-word essay on February 5, captioned "Angry People No Longer Fear", which went viral on China's social media. It accused China's leaders and specifically Xi Jinping of being out of touch with the people's needs. On March 2, and February 23, 2020, Zhao Shilin, a retired Professor of China's Minzu University, Deputy Director of the Culture and Arts Commission and former member of the CCP CC, posted two open letters to President Xi Jinping, both of which were scathing in their criticism. In an interview to the *Guardian* in August, Cai Xia, former senior Professor of the Central Party School, stated that Xi Jinping had "killed the Party and country"! She added that he seeks to divert the attention of the Chinese public by provoking conflict with other countries—and that examples include encouraging anti-American sentiment as well as the recent clashes with India. On March 23, Ren Zhiqiang, a princeling and Chinese realty tycoon wrote an opinion piece, in which he called Xi Jinping a "clown".

The Chinese authorities cracked down on these critics. Xu Zhangrun, known for his scathing and public criticisms of Xi Jinping, was detained in July this year. After publishing several public attacks on the Chinese leadership, Xu Zhiyou was placed under house arrest earlier this year. Former Central Party School Professor Cai Xia, who has settled in the US, was deprived of her pension and all financial benefits.

Xi Jinping is under definite immense pressure, but true to character, he is not stepping down or yielding ground: he is fighting back and has cracked down on dissidents. Security measures have been made even more restrictive. For example, Ren Zhiqiang, despite being a 'princeling' and the pleas for his release, was arrested and finally awarded an exceptionally lengthy prison sentence. The message that Xi Jinping is sending is that he will spare no one.

Meanwhile, the US has decided to place sanctions on those CCP leaders who take active part in formulating or implementing harsh policies against the people. Sanctions have been imposed on the cadres in Xinjiang and Hong Kong, including Xinjiang Party Secretary Chen Quanguo and Hong Kong Chief Executive Carrie Lam. This will render vulnerable any assets they might have abroad. US Secretary of State Pompeo additionally proposed that Chinese Communist Party members and their families could be banned from getting US visas. This sent shockwaves through the CCP as it will directly impact many Party cadres who have assets illegally stashed in the US or abroad, or have close relatives studying there. Almost 70 per cent of Communist Party members at and above the department level have children studying in the US, UK, Canada and Australia, and all of them could face problems.

In the wake of steadily increasing US pressure on China in recent months, escalated by the imposition of sanctions against CCP cadres and the proposal to ban US visas to members of the CCP, Xi Jinping has not yielded ground. Instead, he has launched a number of new ideological campaigns to strengthen adherence by the Party's 92 million members to the CCP's policies and principles and ensure that they do not waver. These campaigns stress the 'four consciousnesses', consolidate the 'four confidences', and particularly emphasise the 'two safeguards' or 'two maintenances'. The two maintenances are "maintaining the core position of General Secretary Xi Jinping means maintaining the authority of the Party Central Committee and centralised and unified leadership; maintaining the authority of the Party Central Committee and centralised and unified leadership must first maintain the core position of General Secretary Xi Jinping." These are accompanied by efforts to advance global 'understanding' and 'appeal' of the Chinese system.

On the economic front too, Xi Jinping is pushing ahead with plans to achieve China's long-term goals. Work has begun on the next Five-Year-Plan (2020-25) but Xi Jinping has also directed the Politburo to work out goals for 2035!

For China, the road ahead seems difficult and if the US pressure continues, there will be a pronounced economic downturn, hampering China's global ambitions. This will affect Xi Jinping's position. For him to remain in power, a lot depends on how many cadres are opposed to him and if their number increases to a critical mass, it can result in his being compelled to step down. Within the Politburo, all the members are not of his faction, for example, Li Keqiang, Han Zheng and Wang Yang. Security for Xi Jinping has also been increased. One can assess that there is continuing uncertainty in China, including of Xi Jinping's future.

*(Text of speech at the CCAS-KAS Diginar on "China's Internal Situation: Is Xi Jinping Under Pressure", on September 15, 2020.)*

# 4. The China Dream

An idea never dies and the Chinese elite understood that centuries ago!

The 'China Dream' or the idea of making China great again has been espoused by Chinese leaders for more than a couple of centuries and it continues to resonate with the Chinese people. The first popular expression of this sentiment was the Boxer Rebellion (1889-1901), which was anti-imperialist, anti-foreign and anti-Christian—together crystalising into resentment against the colonial powers who had divided China, as the Chinese say, "like an over-ripe pomegranate"! The narrative being propagated by the Chinese Communist Party (CCP) leadership of "a hundred years of humiliation" is part of this. Chinese leaders, including Mao Zedong and the founders of the CCP in 1921, have articulated this with varying intensity. One reason why it is called the 'China Dream' and not the Chinese Dream is that this is an idea that has inspired Chinese leaders and the leadership elite, and not the Chinese masses.

Formulated in its present form initially by People's Liberation Army (PLA) Col Liu Mingfu, the idea gained wide traction in China—particularly among children of veteran Party leaders and Communist cadres—after he published it as a book entitled *The China Dream* in 2010. The book became a bestseller in China. Xi Jinping, within days of taking over as General Secretary of the CCP and Chairman of the Central Military Commission (CMC) in November 2012, quoted from the book on quite a few occasions, thereby according its contents legitimacy. Though now retired from the PLA, Liu Mingfu continues to be a Professor in the prestigious PLA National Defence University (NDU).

Xi Jinping referred to the 'China Dream' at the 18th Party Congress in November 2012, when he was appointed General Secretary of the CCP, Chairman of the Central Military Commission (CMC) and President of China. At the Congress, he declared that he would achieve the 'China Dream' by 2021 — the centenary year of the CCP! He elaborated on this concept at the 19th Party Congress held in October 2017, when he presented a bold timetable for China's rise and announced: the 'China Dream'—2021; 'Made in China'-2025; and that China would become a "major world power with pioneering global influence" by 2049!

It is important to understand the formulations. The 'China Dream', to be achieved by 2021 includes making the Chinese people prosperous—or abolition of poverty; making the Chinese nation wealthy; and "the rejuvenation of the great Chinese nation". The last promise includes the "recovery of sovereignty over Chinese territory lost through the imposition of unequal treaties by hostile foreign powers". This last reference is to the "hundred years of humiliation" that the Chinese Communist Party (CCP) repeats consistently in its narratives.

In December 2012, after the 18th Party Congress, members of the top advisory body, the Chinese People's Political Consultative Conference (CPPCC), fanned out across the world to brief governments, strategic communities and opinion-makers on the 18th Party Congress and the 'China Dream'. In Delhi, one CPPCC Vice Chairman quite candidly said, in reply to a question about whether China would take back territories which are now within the sovereign possession of other countries, "We studied what is China's in our school history and geography books. We will get it back!"

At the 19th Party Congress in October 2017, Xi Jinping spelt out all the components of the 'China Dream' and gave the target dates for achieving each. The dates are important: 2021, for example, is the centenary year of the CCP and 2049 is the hundredth year of the founding of the People's Republic of China (PRC). For the CCP, both dates are very important to its legitimacy and its monopoly on power as China's sole ruling party. In other words, the 'China Dream' is welded to the Party's existence and continuance as the sole ruling Party.

The 'China Dream' is not just a military ambition, but encompasses a whole range of national aspirations. Most importantly, it includes the idea of 'Community of Common Destiny', or China's alternative to the current system of democracies and values. A few examples to illustrate the scope of China's ambitions are briefly mentioned below.

- **Culture and 'Soft Power':** Xi Jinping's predecessor, Hu Jintao, had decided that the time had come for China to push its viewpoint across the world and project a positive image. China initially invested US$ 6.6 billion in the effort. The state-owned China Central Television's (CCTV's) international channel was revamped as China Global Television Network (CGTN), editions of Chinese newspapers like the *People's Daily* began being published abroad, and a boost was given to spreading the Chinese language, culture, food, etc. It was felt that the negative image of China and the Chinese being projected by Hollywood needed to change and Chinese State-owned Enterprises (SoEs) began investing in Hollywood films and well-known foreign directors, with instructions to portray China and the Chinese in a positive light. Hollywood is attracted also by the rich pickings at China's box office.
- **Chinese Language and 'Influence Operations':** China has been setting up Confucius Institutes in higher educational institutes and Confucius Classrooms in schools of various countries ostensibly to facilitate the spread of the Chinese language and culture. The Director of the Confucius Institute is selected by them as are the teachers, and the subjects taught conform with China's approved version. For example, on Tibet, Taiwan, the Sino-Indian War of 1962, India-China relations, etc. it will be the Chinese official version that is taught. Also, they decide which subjects and topics can be discussed. China had set up at least 100 Confucius Institutes in the US before the colleges/universities began shutting them down in the past some months. China had spent approximately US$ 200 million on these institutes till 2016. It has been making consistent efforts to try and set them up in India too. China has additionally stepped up 'influence operations' in the past 2-3 years, including in India. The focus is on academics, journalists, younger politicians, opinion-makers et al, who are enticed by visits, scholarships, cash, etc.
- **Diplomatic Constituency:** China has used its US$ 14 trillion economy to build a constituency of support in world organisations, including the UN, and make inroads into the resource rich African continent, the Middle East, divide the European Union (EU) and drive a wedge between Europe and the US. In Africa, it spent US$ 631 million in 2003, increasing to

US$ 3 billion in 2015, and still rising, and invested Euros 37.2 billion in the EU. It has made substantial investments in countries within India's strategic space namely Pakistan, Nepal, Bangladesh, Myanmar, Sri Lanka and Maldives. It continues to be unyielding in its efforts with Bhutan. The Belt and Road Initiative (BRI) is a prime geostrategic initiative which facilitates this.

- **Artificial Intelligence (AI):** Recognising AI as the technology of the future, China initially invested Yuan 500 billion for Research and Development (R&D), etc. and US$ 1 billion each year since 2013 in government funding for start-ups, augmented by an equal amount brought by private venture capital. The Digital Silk Road announced by Chinese President Xi Jinping to complement the BRI has been quickly exploited by Chinese information and telecommunication companies like Huawei and ZTE. Huawei is now already present in 30 countries along the BRI and has set up AI and cyber nodes in some places. China's aim is to be the global leader in AI and cyber, and write the rules governing them.
- **Quantum Technologies:** China has recognised the potential of quantum science and technology to enhance the economic and military dimensions of national power and is positioning itself to be a leader in the "second quantum revolution". China's leadership has provided extensive funding to this sector and actively cultivated top talent. The Civil-Military Fusion programme is a major contributor. Chinese researchers have made major advances in basic research and development of quantum technologies, including quantum cryptography, communications, and computing, and have made progress in quantum radar, sensing, imaging, meteorology, and navigation. China is making extensive use of secure quantum cryptography and quantum communications. It exhibited its prowess in quantum science in August 2016 with the launch of the world's first quantum satellite, Micius (or Mozi, 墨子) and, since then, the launch of new national 'megaprojects' in quantum communications. China's quantum ambitions are part of its national strategic objective to become a science and technology superpower.
- **Landing on Mars:** Zhang Yulin, former chief of the China Manned Space Engineering Office (CMSEO), was quoted by the *Science and Technology*

*Daily* as saying that Beijing plans to launch a Mars exploration mission in 2020 and a Mars landing in 2021—the centenary year of the founding of the CCP! China's annual investment in space projects is as high as US$ 8 billion, second only to the United States.

- **Earth-Moon Economic Zone:** Bao Weimin, Director of the Science and Technology Commission of the China Aerospace Science and Technology Corporation (CASC), the main state-owned contractor for China's space programme, has disclosed that China is planning to establish an Earth-Moon economic zone by 2050. Experts predict that China's annual output in the zone may reach US$10 trillion. Bao Weimin added that China should develop a reliable and low-cost space transportation system between the Earth and the Moon. According to its plan, China will accomplish the basic technology development by 2030 and the manufacture of key transportation technologies by 2040. China hopes to successfully establish a space economic zone by the middle of this century—the hundredth year of the founding of the PRC!
- **Domestic Campaign:** Aware that domestic support is imperative, Xi Jinping has sought to reinforce the ideological and 'political education' campaigns begun since November 2012. Two years ago, Xi Jinping initiated a vigorous 'Red Genes' campaign throughout the Party and PLA, which is continuing. Its objective is to instill in the cadres the same aspirations as those of the 'Red Descendants', or children of Communist cadres, so that they will carry forward the torch of the 'China Dream'. China's Ministry of Education issued a document in 2018, asserting "the need to nurture a new man of the era, who will take up the great responsibility of national rejuvenation"!

In other words, the 'China Dream' is a programme intended to build national power, and China into a rival of the US or capable of overtaking it. Chinese leaders, starting from former Chinese President Hu Jintao, have proposed a "new type of big power relationship" with the US so that the two could be partners in managing global affairs. The US has declined to respond. Beijing, however, now feels its time has come. With the 'China Dream', it feels that by 2049 it will overtake the US in AI, cyber, fifth generation (5G) information and telecommunications technology, have a larger diplomatic constituency supporting it, be bigger militarily—the PLA Navy already matches the US Navy in tonnage—and dominate the South China Sea, and effect the 'recovery' of Taiwan!

The PLA has an important role and China has definite plans to realise the modernisation of the PLA and its territorial ambitions. In addition to streamlining and downsizing the personnel strength of the PLA and making it a hi-tech force—the Strategic Support Force and PLA Rocket Force are examples—China aims to fully mechanise it by 2020; modernise it by 2035; and make it a "world class military by the mid-21st century or 2049". The declared objective is to make AI an integral part of the PLA and shift the PLA from 'informationisation' to 'intelligentisation'. China's leaders have invested a lot in new capabilities and technologies. This is evidenced by China's third aircraft carrier going for its ninth sea trials; modern Aegis class frigates being produced at the rate of one every three months; China inducting the J-20, its indigenous fifth generation 'stealth' fighter jet into the PLA Air Force (PLAAF) while commencing work on the sixth generation fighter; and commencing work on unmanned, or 'autonomous', battlefield platforms like tanks. The unwavering focus on making the military a world class force capable of "fighting and winning" a war, suggests that China's leaders are preparing the PLA for a potentially muscular role in realising their objectives.

In this context, an interview given by PLA Col Liu Mingfu (Retd) to the *Asahi Shimbun* in May 2019 is pertinent, especially for India. Asked about China's territorial ambitions and what its limits would be, Liu Mingfu replied that the map used by "the current Chinese government is the clear standard for national sovereignty and territory". This implicitly refers to the East Sea or Sea of Japan, the Senkaku Islands or Diaoyu Islands, South China Sea, Taiwan, and India's Ladakh, Jammu and Kashmir (J&K) and Arunachal Pradesh. Liu Mingfu also hinted at the possible use of force, probably in the context of Taiwan, by stating that "as time passes, the gap in national power with China will become less for the US".

Finally, the 'China Dream' has thus far progressed well with China's US$ 14 trillion economy smoothening the way. But difficulties are now beginning to surface. To list a few: there is growing concern about the BRI; the US has targeted China's technology sector or 'Made in China' and has begun to restrict its access to the US market; Europe is apprehensive about the BRI, the Maritime Silk Road and Digital Silk Route and has begun to examine ways to restrict the flow of hi-tech to China; India, Japan, Indonesia and Australia will, at least, not accept China's dominance; the restive minority-dominated Autonomous Regions of Xinjiang and Tibet are not likely to be calmed any time soon; and the troubles in Hong Kong, now entering their sixth month, are an indicator of the limits of the CCP's power and potential for disturbances to spread inside China. The road ahead for the China Dream is difficult, but attempts to frustrate its realisation would require sustained efforts as China's leaders have noticeably energised diverse nationalist aspirations to converge into making China a leading global power.

*(This article was published by the Centre for China Analysis and Strategy, New Delhi, on November 22, 2019.)*

# 5. China: Path to Hi-Technology

The world is on the threshold of major technology advances that will translate what has so far been in the realm of science fiction into everyday reality. There is clear promise of transformational changes, with the next couple of decades being witness to technology driving almost every aspect of life.

Signs of this are already visible in robotics; artificial intelligence; telecommunications, especially voice and data transmission; Internet of Things; seamless linkage of public utilities and items of everyday use; machine-to-machine communications; unmanned automobiles; biomedicine; and treatment of serious injuries to humans on the battlefield. In the race not to be left behind in a world of advanced technologies, the US, Russia, some European countries and China have been working on different aspects of these technologies for a while. Taiwan, South Korea and Vietnam too have been getting ready to compete globally in fifth generation (5G) communications.

China is striving to progress in hi-tech research areas like organelles to build tissue for soldiers injured in war and 3-D printing to build weapons on the battlefield. It finalised a Civil-Military Fusion Programme so that hi-tech advances made by the military and civilian private industry could be pooled and optimised. China has made huge capital investment in Artificial Intelligence (AI), already crafted an AI policy and holds more patents than the US. Its People's Liberation Army (PLA)-affiliated information and telecommunications companies like Huawei and ZTE are exerting to roll out 5G networks across the world—Huawei is already present in fifty countries! China has also made great strides in quantum communications. Interestingly, though, Beijing has chosen to go in for the 5G networks of Ericsson and Nokia inside China!

Cognisant that advanced technology is the future, China has made clear that it is willing to suffer short-term pain to become a leading global power in technology. Despite its huge surplus manpower, China chose to train and upgrade manpower skills and opted for robotics in its factories. In 2017, China bought 36 per cent of all factory robots in the world, more than any other country, including the US, with the aim of boosting its own production of robots to become the preeminent technological superpower. By 2019, China had the largest number of factories using robotics. A consideration would have been the longer-term challenge that China faces of its working age population declining. China's workforce started to drop in 2012, with the slide gathering pace in the 2020s and predicted to fall by over 20 per cent, or around 210 million, by 2050. In other words, against the present about 7 workers for each retiree, by the 2040s, this will have fallen to 2.5 workers!

China's leadership was prescient in recognising the importance of advanced technology and its potential for varied applications. The 'Long March' era of Chinese leaders understood that without technology, China could again be subject to 'bullying' by the major powers, with Mao Zedong himself harbouring apprehensions about the US and Soviet Union with their atom bombs. There have been three factors that put China on the track of acquiring and developing advanced technology. These were: (i) Mao's vision of the future China; (ii) dominance of the military in China's politics; and (iii) the wave of nationalist sentiment in the wake of China's 'liberation' and leadership-led programme which combined to persuade Chinese scientists to return to serve the Mainland.

This is reinforced by the substantive presence of senior Party cadres with scientific backgrounds. There are 14 members in the new 19th Central Committee (CC) of the Chinese Communist Party (CCP) who have a background in academics and universities, especially in aeronautical sciences indicating a focus on Research and Development (R&D) and scientific research.

Three key areas will help provide a clear idea of China's ambitions and goals. These are Civil-Military Fusion, also called Civil-Military Integration and which is the foundation for China's Science and Technology (S&T) effort; Artificial Intelligence; and 5G S&T information and communications technology.

**Civil-Military Fusion (军民融合/Civil-Military Integration**

Civil-military fusion (军民融合)—also called 'civil-military integration'—is an important policy enunciated, with some variations, by Mao Zedong, Deng Xiaoping, Hu Jintao and Xi Jinping, and is inextricably intertwined with China becoming an advanced world technology power as envisaged in 'Made in China-2025'. The "China Military-Civilian Integration Development Report 2014" issued by the National Defence Economic Research Centre of the PLA National Defence University revealed that China's military-civilian integration is around 30 per cent. Xi Jinping acknowledged that many private high-tech enterprises in China are technologically advanced, have great potential for development and can tie up with traditional defense military enterprises to mutual advantage. On March 12, 2015, at the plenary meeting of the PLA delegation of the Third Session of the 12th National People's Congress of China, Xi Jinping, for the first time, stressed on the need for "improving the integration of military and civilian development into a national strategy". In January 2017, the Chinese Communist Party (CCP) Central Committee (CC) Political Bureau (PB) established a Central Military-Civilian Integration Development Committee, with Xi Jinping as its Chairman. The Central Military-Civilian Integration Development Committee is responsible for the in-depth development of military and civilian integration.

The CCP CC, with "Xi Jinping as its core", closely links the development of military-civilian integration with the "realization of the great rejuvenation of the Chinese nation". It promotes interaction between China's national defence construction and economic construction as the only way to realise the dream of strengthening the country and strengthening the military and, in effect, blends guarding national sovereignty, security, and development interests. Civil-military fusion has been backed by the heads of prominent Chinese military State-owned Enterprises (SoEs). In March 2017, Peng Jianwei, President of the Beijing Modern Industrial Planning Research Institute, told *China Enterprise News* that the integration of military and civilian development as a national strategy is related to the overall situation of national security and economic development, and the enthusiasm of social capital to participate in the military industry is constantly rising. He assessed that with more social capital participation, China's military-civilian integration process will continue to accelerate. He added, however, "It is undeniable that the current development of military-civilian integration in China is still facing a series of challenges such as insufficient channels, inadequate institutional barriers, and inadequate transformation of ideas and concepts, which has greatly affected the pace of military-civilian integration". Gao Hongwei, Chairman of the military industrial enterprise Aerospace Science and Technology, anticipated, "In 2017, the revenue of the military-civilian integration industry of the group company will reach 147 billion yuan" and collaborative research and development of the military-civilian integration industry will gradually improve the R&D capabilities and combine innovation with entrepreneurship. More forthcoming was Lu Guangshan, Chairman of AVIC Aerospace, who said the military industry is a priority area for cutting-edge technology and a gathering place for disruptive innovation. "From the current point of view, China's military-civilian integration industry has a very broad prospect, such as general aviation, Beidou satellite navigation, commercial space launch, and network security. Every industry has a market scale of trillions." Guo Zhengbiao, Chief Executive Officer (CEO) of the Nanjing World-based Space-Based Communication Technology Co., Ltd., who is a founder of a start-up and a serial entrepreneur, said that there were many entrepreneurs who are willing to participate in the "military and civilian integration." He observed that there are, however, many obstacles impeding such integration, including mindsets of discrimination against private enterprises, small size of private enterprises that lack adequate funds, technology, equipment, etc., and unwillingness of some central enterprises to take risks and cooperate with small and medium-sized enterprises.

The Chinese authorities, including in the provinces, were quick to initiate efforts to promote civil-military fusion and persuade private companies to participate in the joint development and manufacture of military equipment and systems. In September 2017, for example, Beijing held its third Integrated Military and Civilian Development Technology and Equipment Exhibition, at which 354 companies from across China displayed 422 new logistics and defence technologies. Guancha.cn, a privately run news and commentary website that is usually enthusiastic about the Party line, headlined its report (in Chinese) on the one-week exhibition of the "Third Military-Civilian

Integration Development High-Tech Equipment Achievements Forum" in Beijing. It observed that all 422 exhibits were "blackware" or "black technology" (黑科技/hēi kējì)—a slang term that refers to very advanced 'alien' weapons and technology. On April 9, 2018, Xi Jiayin, Chairman of the Board of Directors of the Evergrande Group, announced the official entry of the group into the high-technology industry and signed a contract with the Chinese Academy of Sciences. He declared that in the next ten years, Evergrande will invest Yuan 100 billion in the hi-tech areas of life sciences, aerospace, integrated circuit, quantum science and technology, new power sources, artificial intelligence, robotics and modern agricultural science and technology.

Other examples include the Beijing Civil-Military Integration Expo 2019 held in Beijing from May 6 to 8, 2019, to promote military-civil trade, especially between China and countries involved in the Belt and Road Initiative. It displayed a wide range of dual-use military and civil products such as marine equipment, unmanned vehicles, communications systems, and network security products. The China Electronics International Exhibition Advertising Co Ltd, China National Electronics Import & Export Corp, CETC International Co Ltd, and Poly Defense Research Centre hosted the Expo which was held at the China International Exhibition Centre (Jing'anzhuang Mansion).

Xinhua reported on February 26, 2019, that the PLA and Chengyang district in Qingdao are creating a Model for Deep Development of Military and Civil Integration. The person in charge of Chengyang district, said that the "Chengyang Military-Civilian Integration Industrial Park Project" would have a total investment of about Yuan 2.34 billion to create a modernisation integrating technology R&D centre, business incubation, industrial agglomeration, academic exchange, and technology finance. It said a technical team of Professors and PhDs has undertaken the transformation of advanced technological achievements and market expansion of the PLA Information Engineering University and Qingdao Ocean University. Latest statistics showed that Chengyang district has 20 military-civilian integration enterprises such as radar, electronic information and special vehicles, and the national high-speed train technology innovation centre. The integration development demonstration project library has a total investment of Yuan 1.5 billion. The city of Chongqing has proposed developing a model 5G network and applications demonstration with involvement from China Telecom, China Mobile and China Aerospace Science and Technology Corporation, a major defence industry conglomerate. Similarly, Sichuan plans to promote partnerships for military-civil fusion in 5G as Beijing develops the Zhongguonancun Science Park. At least 36 national-level industrial zones to promote civil-military fusion have opened across China.

AI is another priority area for civil-military fusion. The *Financial Times* last year published a photograph of Mao Yongqing, head of the 28th Research Institute of China Electronics Technology Group, which develops electronic warfare technology for the PLA, and Yin Shiming, Vice President of Cloud Computing at Baidu, one of China's privately owned internet groups, at a conference in Nanjing. Mao Yongqing is one of a small group of state cadres entrusted by Chinese President Xi Jinping with the task of pushing the military into the era of Artificial Intelligence. Yin Shiming is an engineer who built his expertise at some of the most important Western tech companies, including Apple. At the ceremony, Mao Yongqing and Yin Shiming declared China Electronics Technology Group Corporation (CETC) and Baidu to be partners in a "joint lab for intelligent command and control technology"—the facilities that are used to direct military operations. Mao Yongqing lauded the deal as an example of "military-civil fusion". Yin Shiming said CETC and Baidu should "work hand-in-hand to link up computing, data and logic resources to further advance the application of new generation AI technologies in the area of defence."

Reporting on civil-military fusion, the *PLA Daily* (March 2, 2019), said that in the past 40 years of reform and opening up, China's private enterprises have accumulated a large number of advanced technologies and products through introduction, absorption, transformation and independent research and development. It said that they have become the main force in national economic construction and a new force in the construction of national defence forces. It said that by the end of 2017, nearly 10,000 private enterprises of the 27.72 million private enterprises in the country had entered national defence and military construction. Thousands of private enterprises are deeply involved in the research, production, maintenance and technical services of weapons and equipment. Regrettably, the speed of the "civilians' participation in the Army" and "military and civil integration" is still slow. In local areas and for a certain period of time, there is even a phenomenon of slowing down or stagnation. The door of the "civilians' participation in the Army" has been fully opened, and the barriers of "military-civil integration" have been basically dismantled, it said. On why the above-mentioned phenomena occur in the integration of the military and the civilians, the *PLA Daily* said it is due to the special nature of military characteristics and market rules. Weapons and equipment are special products exported by the military industry. It has inherent attributes such as monopoly production, targeted sales, complicated technology, difficult development, and high quality standards. This determines the characteristics of the military market with a relatively small volume, strict control of plans, large changes in demand, long procurement cycle, and slow return on profits. Private enterprises have long been away from the military environment, the foundation is relatively weak, the products are relatively single, and the management is relatively loose, lacking competitive experience. It is imperative that we work hard and streamline procedures without reducing standards the *PLA Daily* said.

Pointing to the potential for civil-military fusion, official Chinese statistics state that there were more than 80,000 high-tech private enterprises in China in 2017, with the output value of more than 1,500 exceeding Yuan 100 million. Some enterprises have reached or exceeded the military standard in the fields of new materials, electronics, information and other fields. The statistics, however, disclosed that less than 1 per cent can presently participate in equipment research and production.

### Artificial Intelligence (AI)

The "13th Five-Year Plan for Developing National Strategic and Emerging Industries" (2016-20) identified AI development as the 6th among 69 major tasks for the central government to pursue. It received impetus after the 19th Party Congress in October 2017, when Chinese President Xi Jinping declared that he would like to see China as "a scientific and technology power superpower".

China sees AI as one of the leading technologies of the next decade with its predictive capabilities ensuring its application in maintaining social stability (predicting social unrest), military (graduating from *informationisation* to *intelligentisation*), medicine, etc. The State Council has formulated an AI superpower strategy (人工智能强国战略) which envisages an ambitious three-stage process aimed at China leading the world in AI. It outlines that by 2020, China's AI industry will be "in line" with that of the most advanced countries, with a core AI industry gross output exceeding RMB 150 billion (US$ 22.5 billion) and AI-related industry gross output exceeding RMB 1 trillion (US$ 150.8 billion); by 2025, China should reach a "world-leading" level in some AI fields, with a core AI industry gross output exceeding RMB 400 billion (US$ 60.3 billion) and AI-related industry gross output exceeding RMB 5 trillion (US$ 754.0 billion); by 2030, China is likely to become the world's "primary" AI innovation centre, with a core AI industry gross output exceeding RMB 1 trillion (US$ 150.8 billion) and AI-related gross output exceeding RMB 10 trillion (US$ 1.5 trillion). In other words, its three strategic phases of AI development are: (a) catching up with the most advanced AI powers; (b) becoming a world leader in AI; and (c) achieving primacy in AI innovation.

China has a limited talent pool of around 39,000 AI researchers, less than half the size of the US pool of over 78,000 researchers. With AI as a priority, the Chinese government has encouraged development of AI start-ups and enhanced efforts to bring back researchers from abroad under its "Thousand Talents Programme" begun in 2008. The *South China Morning Post* reported on November 8, 2018, that the Beijing Institute of Technology, breaking new ground, has recruited 31 'patriotic' youngsters straight from high school to begin training as the world's youngest AI weapons scientists in a new AI weapons development programme. The 27 boys and four girls, all aged 18 and under, have been selected for the four-year "experimental programme for intelligent weapons systems" at the Beijing Institute of Technology (BIT) from more than 5,000 candidates. BIT is one of China's top weapons research institutes, and the launch of the new programme underscores the importance China accords to the development of AI technology for military use. According to a BIT Professor, "These kids are all exceptionally bright, but being bright is not enough. We are looking for other qualities such as creative thinking, willingness to fight, a persistence when facing challenges. A passion for developing new weapons is a must … and they must also be patriots." Each student will be mentored by two senior weapons scientists, one from an academic background and the other from the defence industry. After completing a short programme of course work in the first semester, the students will be asked to choose a speciality field, such as mechanical engineering, electronics or overall weapon design. They will then be assigned to a relevant defence laboratory where they will be able to develop their skills through hands-on experience. BIT launched the programme at the headquarters of Norinco, one of China's biggest defence contractors, on October 28, 2018. After completing the four-year course, the students are expected to enrol in a PhD programme and become the next leaders of China's AI weapons programme.

At the same time, China began funding AI start-ups through "Government Guidance Funds" (GGFs) set up by local governments and state-owned companies. In two years since 2016, the Chinese government has invested more than US$ 1 billion on domestic start-ups. The Hong Kong-headquartered Sun Hung Kai Financial has forecast that the quantum of funding flowing from GGFs is likely to eclipse China's private Venture Capital (VC) investments. It cited as example that for the year 2016, GGFs set a total fund-raising target of RMB 3.3 trillion (US$ 500 billion) vs. a RMB 2.2 trillion (US$ 330 billion) total raised by private funds. A report said that in parallel with accelerating AI development, this would help tech companies incorporate Party committees, thereby promoting the Party's goals. In the past few years, more than 35 tech companies, including Baidu and Sina, have created company Party committees.

A Wuzhen Institute report said that between 2012 to 2016, Chinese AI firms received US$ 2.6 billion in investment funding. Another report from IT Juzi and Tencent Institute, however, offered a different estimation and said that Chinese AI companies received 33.18 per cent (US$ 9.6 billion) of the world's AI funding. Global funding received by Chinese AI start-ups in 2017, jumped up and they received 48 per cent of the total global funding. The report assessed the growth in China's AI scene over the past year alone as astronomical. Xinhua on December 9, 2018, quoted the latest report by

Bloomberg Intelligence (BI), which said that China's core AI industry could exceed US$ 145 billion by 2030 and with the AI-enabled industries, more than Yuan 10 trillion. The Bloomberg report titled "China's Great Tech Leap Forward", said that China's push to commercialise AI technologies, supported by the rollout of the world's biggest 5G network, could position the country as a global leader for technology and innovation. The report said, "China may overtake the US in global technology-patents share by 2025". AI-related industries may exceed 6 per cent of China's Gross Domestic Product (GDP) by 2030. According to Tsinghua University, private funding for Chinese AI-related companies in 2017 totalled US$ 27.7 billion, equivalent to 70 per cent of global investments in the industry. Data showed that China's cumulative venture-capital investments in AI start-ups had already caught up with the United States by 2016.

Tsinghua University is the lead university for AI in China and is ranked second in the world in the number of high-level papers published in the field of AI in the past decade, indicating that it is among the world's advanced institutes in AI basic theory and methods. An authoritative report released by it in 2018, revealed that it has established a number of AI research bases, most with military related research. Among these are the State Key Laboratory of Intelligent Technology and Systems (智能技术与系统"国家重点实验室) established in 1990; the Intelligent Microsystems Ministry of Education Key Laboratory (智能微系统教育部重点实验室) of the CMC Science and Technology Commission National Defence Frontier Innovation Special Zone (国防前沿创新特区); the CMC Science and Technology Commission's High-End Laboratory for Military Intelligence (军事智能高端实验室); Tsinghua Brain and Intelligence Laboratory (清华脑与智能实验室) established in 2017; and an interdisciplinary research centre, the Tsinghua University Intelligent Unmanned Systems Research Centre.

In the commercial AI ecosystem, the Chinese government actively picks winners in the AI space. For example, in November 2017, it designated Baidu, Alibaba, Tencent, and iFlyTek to lead the development of national AI innovation platforms in self-driving cars, smart cities, computer vision for medical diagnosis, and voice intelligence, respectively. Later, in August 29, the *South China Morning Post* disclosed that China has named Huawei

Technologies and Hikvision Digital Technology as new 'national champions' in AI. The two are the latest batch of ten companies tasked to spearhead efforts in that field, with the others including Xiaomi, JD.com, Qihoo 360, Megvii and Yitu.

Much of China's research on AI is focussed on its military applications. Chinese military experts refer to changing the PLA's goal from *informationisation* to *intelligentisation*. The predictive aspect of AI appears to be of special interest with its application in, what China euphemistically describes as, 'stability maintenance' to anticipate social unrest. The establishment of the Tsinghua Brain and Intelligence Laboratory in 2017 confirms that research is underway on predicting the behaviour of military adversaries.

The US think-tank Jamestown Foundation reported that in early 2019, PLA Senior Col Li Minghai, Director of the National Security Studies Institute at the National Defence University (NDU) and Deputy Secretary of NDU's Communist Party Committee, published a pair of articles that offered a new set of terms and theoretical ideas related to the incorporation and operationalisation of AI by the PLA. Li Minghai introduced a new term: the "algorithm game" (*suanfa boyi*, 算法博弈), which was presented in the context of conflict between first-tier military forces in a dawning age of "intelligentized warfare" (*zhinenghua zhanzheng*, 智能化战争). The author pointed out that the terms have been used since 2017, including by Professor An Bo of Nanyang Engineering University, who discussed how AI and algorithmic game theory will allow the more efficient deployment of resources for a broad range of domestic security missions. Discussions of "intelligentized" warfare have also been used with increasing frequency by PLA writers in recent years, suggesting a nascent effort to develop a doctrinal framework for how AI and game theory could be integrated into future military operations by the PLA. This would connect to PLA ambitions to seek battlefield information and command superiority, as well as effectively control escalation in a future armed conflict. Separately, Adam Ni, China researcher from Macquarie University in Sydney, said that China has set up two major research organisations focussed on AI unmanned systems, and China's pursuit of artificial intelligence for the PLA aims at leveraging the emerging technology to enhance national power. He added that the *PLA Daily* in November carried a description of a swarm of drones, operated by a cloud "brain", that could detect a target enemy and automatically attack it. He said future "intelligent" wars will be fought with smart weapons and systems, supported by AI and capable of analysing situations, undertaking tasks and missions on their own.

### 5G Communications Technology

The fifth generation of information and communications technology, or 5G, is viewed in the West as the next big change after the industrial revolution. According to a report issued by the Asia Studies Centre in the UK in May this year, the fifth generation (5G) of wireless networks will deliver a profound change in latency, data speed and volume, allowing for new technologies such as agricultural or delivery drones, self-driving vehicles, and other data-driven tech. The 5G equipment is complicated and will play a major part in the economic and national security of nations. Concerns about security arise because it is much faster than the 4G, with huge numbers of channels, and will link literally millions of pieces of equipment in the world. China's Huawei has emerged as a leader in this sector with a presence in over 50 countries. It is presently establishing AI nodes in approximately 30 countries along the Digital Belt and Road Initiative.

Two main considerations weighing with prospective buyers of 5G are expense and national security. Additionally, there are very few providers in the market. Ericsson and Nokia are the two European companies and China's Huawei is the other. South Korea with Samsung, and Taiwan and Vietnam are about to ready their systems. However, the 5G equipment supplied by Ericsson and Nokia costs twice as much as that of Huawei. Countries, therefore, have three choices: pay almost double the cost for ensuring national security, especially since the European companies can be expected to resist government pressure to tap communications; try and upgrade their existing 4G system, which is feasible but will not give the same speed and capabilities as 5G; and opt to continue with the present system till they develop one indigenously or purchase a lower priced 5G from South Korea, Taiwan or Vietnam. Countries like India that are unlikely to need 5G, except for limited data and voice communications, for the next 3-4 years, can consider the third option.

Unlike the old 4G where antennae were on the periphery, away from the core, the 5G network relies upon a complicated series of active advanced Multiple-Input/Multiple-Output (MIMO) antennae closely integrated with the hardware and software required for transmission and reception of radio signals, and signal processing algorithms to support the execution of the entire system. The antennae control the radiation pattern, gain, bandwidth, polarisation, and frequency range and power across the network. The key to MIMO and the ability to control multiple data streams using the same time and frequency resource is the 'antenna'. Whoever controls the antenna, controls the network. Experts say it is possible for the systems provider, like Huawei, for example, to insert a 'backdoor' within the antennae and allow it to stay dormant till required. It is very unlikely to be detected by even technically advanced and proficient agencies. Worth noting is that certain antennae and microwave equipment for Huawei's 5G are produced by the China Electronics Technology Group Corporation (CETC), a state-owned defence conglomerate.

A British "Risk Analysis of Huawei 5G" by Nicholas Weaver (April 17, 2019) states that Huawei uses, like much of the rest of the world, a complex code, but written in an "unsafe" manner, using "unsafe" languages. He assessed that the scale and complexity make it impossible to analyse the code to look for new bugs, let alone efforts at sabotage. Sabotage itself can be very hard to detect even when one does have the source code, and even if discovered, it can also be almost indistinguishable from a "mistake." A former senior officer of an American intelligence agency confided that Britain's Government Communications Headquarters (GCHQ), after examining Huawei's 5G network systems, had informed him that in addition to other concerns, the engineering of its system was poor.

While evaluating 5G network systems, India needs to give prime consideration to national security and the fact that the 5G system will expose and render vulnerable the entire communications traffic, whether it is civil or military. Depending on the provider, the communications of officials, senior leaders and politicians will be vulnerable to interception. China has an adversarial relationship and a 4,057-km-long border with India. Its comprehensive relationship, including intelligence sharing, with its "iron brother" Pakistan adds to India's concerns. Huawei itself has very close documented links with China's military and security establishments and receives 'preferential' treatment. The 'Civil-Military Fusion Programme' has blurred even the thin line that might have existed. Its bonds with the CCP are evident from its founder Chairman Ren Zhengfei being a CCP member and Huawei having 12,000 CCP members among its employees and 300 CCP branches by 2007. Huawei's Chairwoman from 1999 to 2018, was Sun Yafang, who previously held senior posts in the Ministry of State Security as well as Chinese government research centres.

As China works towards developing AI for 'predictive' battlefield capability and upgrading the PLA from an "informationised' force to an 'intelligentised' force, Huawei will play an important contributory role. Already the ingress by Chinese companies like Huawei and ZTE and products like PayPal, Xiaomi and Tik-Tok into the Indian telecommunications market facilitates collection of huge volumes of personal data on Indians. China can well use this for building AI's predictive capability for military or strategic use. It is clear that China's Ministry of State Security (MSS) is interested in large data sets of government officials for refining predictive capability. An example was the MSS hacking into the US Office of Personnel Management (OPM) and stealing more than 22 million records of US government officials. Using AI and big data sets, China has begun to develop smart city technologies to track and shape the political behaviour of its population.

As briefly illustrated, China has made rapid advances in future advanced technologies. These, like AI and 5G networks, are mainly dual-use technologies. While China's effort is driven primarily by domestic security and strategic military considerations, commercial factors play an important role. Noticeable is how China's leadership has entrusted policy-making and implementation to experts, specialised universities and high powered government bodies. It has also broken new ground, for example, by recruiting candidates directly from schools for moulding them into weapons experts. As China narrows the gap, its effort to reach the level of the world's advanced technology powers has met obstacles. The US trade war has specifically targeted China's technology sector, or 'Made in China-2025' programme. China which has been dependent on four foreign companies for its supply of graphic semi-conductors and laser micro-chips vital for AI and 5G, is now scrambling to develop its own capability. Tighter controls by the West on these supply chains will hamper China's efforts which can mean delays in meeting target deadlines.

**References**

1. "Tsinghua's Approach to Military - Civil Fusion in AI", May 2018 (in Chinese).
2. Jayadeva Ranade, "China: Emerging Cyber Power" in *China Unveiled: Insights into Chinese Strategic Thinking* (2013).
3. Bob Seely MP, Dr Peter Varnish OBE, Dr John Hemmings, "Defending our Data: Huawei, 5G and the Five Eyes", Asia Studies Centre, Henry Jackson Society, May 2019.
4. Nicholas Weaver and forward by Sir Richard Deerlove, former Head of SIS, "Risk Analysis of Huawei 5G", April 2019.
5. Guancha.cn military affairs, September 22, 2017.

*(This article was published as a book chapter for Vivekanand India Foundation, New Delhi, December 2019, and as an article by the Centre for China Analysis and Strategy, New Delhi, on October 28, 2019.*

# 6. China's Maritime Challenge in the Indo-Pacific

## Overview

With the status quo under challenge and competition for strategic space intensifying, especially among the major regional powers in the Indo-Pacific, the region has seen an increase in tensions. China's 'rise' has fuelled its ambition to become a global power. The perceived decline of the US, its reduced interest in the region and its reluctance to back even treaty allies like Japan and the Philippines, has encouraged China and exacerbated the situation. Central to China's ambition to become the preeminent regional power are maritime dominance and reunification with Taiwan. China has so far moved with prudence in its effort to advance its maritime territorial claims and held back from asserting itself in the East Sea to avoid antagonising Japan, but it has moved with greater assertion in the South China Sea—including by ignoring the decision of the Permanent Court of Arbitration—where it has incrementally acquired a dominant position. It has shown little hesitation in clashing with the Philippines or Vietnam. While it has not yet declared the South China Sea as a "core national interest", it depicts the area as part of its sovereign territory in official maps, and the People's Liberation Army Navy (PLAN) has vowed in its recruitment 'anthem' to recover all the three million square kilometres of the South China Sea that Beijing claims. At the same time, China is working towards realising the goal of extending its 'reach' across the Indian Ocean and the 'far seas'.

## PLAN: The Rise of a Global Naval Power

The 19th Party Congress held in Beijing from October 17–24, 2017, reiterated China's aspiration to become a global maritime power and stressed that by 2050, the People's Liberation Army (PLA) will be a "world class force". By then, the PLAN was already projecting power and had been maintaining a sustained presence in the Indian Ocean, with warships and a submarine sailing in waters off the Gulf of Aden for anti-piracy operations. By 2015-16, all captains of PLAN vessels had familiarised themselves with the Indian Ocean by completing a tour of duty there. Since 2015, the PLAN has been sailing in the Baltic and Bering Seas, South China Sea, East Sea, Indian Ocean and the Mediterranean Sea and calling on ports in Europe and the African continent. Establishing a substantive near permanent presence in the Indian Ocean is a major Chinese objective and China seems well on the way to achieving this. China has begun strengthening its Navy for larger tasks.

In fact, months before the 19th Party Congress in January 2017, Chinese President and Chairman of the Central Military Commission (CMC) Xi Jinping, for the first time ever, appointed a PLAN officer to head the important PLA Southern Theatre Command, which exercises operational jurisdiction over the South China Sea and Indian Ocean. It is among the more important commands and exercises jurisdiction over China's first, and so far only, overseas base of Djibouti, and at least two aircraft carriers have already been earmarked for this Command. The appointment indicates that China's leadership felt the PLA had acquired sufficient competence in Integrated Joint Operations (IJ0), to which it had given priority since 2007. PLAN Vice Admiral Yuan Yunbai a graduate of the PLAN Qingdao Submarine Academy and the first Navy officer to be appointed a Theatre Commander, is familiar with the Gulf of Aden, Indian Ocean and the PLAN's North Sea Fleet. Interestingly, Vice Admiral Yuan Yunbai had, at the Shangri La Dialogue in 2015, observed that the "South China Sea, as the name indicates, is an area that belongs to China. And the sea, from the Han dynasty a long time ago, is where the Chinese people have been working and producing from the sea".

As part of its plans to acquire blue sea capability and meet its obligation of ensuring the security of Chinese interests, investments and personnel in any part of the world, a continuing consideration for the PLAN has been acquiring bases for its global operations. Chinese Navy strategists have identified Karachi and Gwadar as a "base" and "logistics base" respectively, and Chinese warships and submarines, including a nuclear submarine, have already paid visits there. Recent reports claim that China has shown interest in the port of Jiwani, also in Pakistan. A study of July 2017 reported that

China had doubled investments in acquiring overseas bases in 2016-17 to US$ 20 billion. Chinese companies have announced plans to buy or invest in nine overseas ports with discussions underway for several other ports. Some of the planned investments are: Melaka Gateway US$ 7.2 billion; Kuala Linggi Port US$ 2.84 billion; Penang Port US$ 1.4 billion; Kuentan Port US$ 177 million; and investments are planned in Indonesia's Kalibaru project to expand Tanjung Priok, and in Arkhangelsk (Russia), Klaipeda (Lithuania), Kirkenes (Norway) and two ports in Iceland.

While subsequent to the 19th Party Congress there has been a noticeable increase in reporting on developments relating to the PLAN and China's assertions of sovereignty over the South China Sea, the strengthening of the PLAN has been underway for years. Reports in the Chinese official media and official and 'informed' blog sites reveal the rapid progress being made and the focus on building the PLAN's power projection capability. China's stated objective is to have 350 surface warships and 100 submarines by 2030. China is, by all accounts, well on the way to this.

**PLAN: Current Status of Equipment**

By 2000, China had built 19 large surface combatants and 63 small surface combatants like frigates and corvettes. The speed of construction has been stepped up, and in 2016 alone, the PLAN commissioned 18 warships including destroyers, corvettes and guided missile frigates. In November 2017, the PLAN commissioned new Type 056/056A corvettes. Described as "light missile frigates", the PLAN already has 37 of the Type 056/056A Jiangduo class corvettes and wants to build a fleet of 60 corvettes, with one new ship to be launched every three weeks. In 2017, the PLAN commissioned 7 Jiangduo class corvettes, with four to be inducted in December 2017 and January 2018. Anti-Submarine Warfare (ASW) capability is a priority for the PLAN.

At present, China has six large naval vessels shipyards, namely, Dalian shipyard, Huludao shipyard, Jiangnan shipyard, Zhonghua dockyard, Huangpu dockyard and Wuchang dockyard. Among these, Dalian shipyard and Jiangnan shipyard are the main players and are held up as models of China's construction abilities. Jiangnan shipyard is going to finish construction work of 10 warships of four different kinds. Dalian shipyard is also going to complete the construction of eight warships of three different kinds. These two shipbuilding groups are mainly responsible for construction of the Navy's aircraft carrier, guided missile destroyer, Air-Independent Propulsion (AIP) powered submarine, landing craft, etc. These two shipyards have also undertaken the task of constructing 054A type and 056type corvettes, which will be used in coastal defence and aircraft carrier formation. Jiangnan shipyard is going to build the 039B type AIP powered submarine, which has been developed after years of research.

Underlining its determination to continue reclaiming land and building 'islands' in the South China Sea to 'recover' sovereignty, China's military media publicised the launch at Jiangsu shipyard on November 3, 2017, of the *Tiankun*, described as "the biggest dredger in Asia". The launch was timed for the eve of US President Trump's visit. The Marine Design and Research Centre in Shanghai, which built the *Tiankun*, describes it as "a magical island maker".

**Supplements to PLAN: Aviation**

A very important part of China's naval ambition is aircraft carriers, which have been described as essential to China's status as a major global power. Their construction has been given national priority and work has begun on China's fourth aircraft carrier which it hopes to operationalise by 2024. It has been described as the largest of the aircraft carriers and is likely to have the latest electro-magnetic launcher system for carrier-based aircraft. Meanwhile, the indigenously built type 001A aircraft carrier is likely to commence sea trials in early 2018. To accelerate construction of aircraft carriers, China has constituted a contingent of 5,000 personnel drawn from different shipyards with experience in building aircraft carriers.

To enhance its 'far seas' operations capability, the PLAN is developing its aviation arm. Chinese Navy strategists have justified this on the ground that training required for aircraft carrier pilots is different from that for land-based pilots. At the same time, it is observed that the PLA Air Force (PLAAF) and PLA Army (PLAA) pilots are carrying out training exercises with PLAN pilots. As part of the effort to strengthen its aviation arm, the PLAN established the Naval Aeronautical University in 2017. In its first year it recruited 450 pilots and commenced their first round of training on the JL-10 H Navy trainer jets. This year, it is planned to recruit another 400 pilots. The PLAN estimates that it will have 40 jets aboard each aircraft carrier and should have at least two pilots for each aircraft.

After the PLAAF, the PLAN Aviation forces have also recently received the naval retrofit of the H-6KH bomber aircraft, photographs of which appeared on the internet. The H6KH bomber aircraft is said to be a new type of bomber developed for the PLAN Aviation force. Reports suggest that it may already be in active service. The H6KH bomber will significantly increase the PLAN's sea combat capability.

There are clear indications that with this build-up in capacity, the PLAN is preparing for operations in distant seas. The PLAN's destroyer *Haikou*, guided missile corvette *Yueyang* and comprehensive supply ship *Qinghai*, for the first time conducted a 4-day combat training in the Gulf of Guinea, which the PLA Navy described as a test for the Navy's long-term missions overseas and to examine its ability in the "distant, strange battlefield environment". China's response to the crisis in Maldives, including cautioning India against unilateral action, when viewed with the official statement that a 4-ship flotilla of "warships entered the East Indian Ocean at the time when the situation in Maldives was tense, follow up of the situation was needed" is a pointer.

*(This article was published by the Centre for China Analysis and Strategy, New Delhi, on May 10, 2018.)*

# 7. Belt and Road Initiative and its Future Implications

When we look at the Belt and Road Initiative (BRI), it is important to look at it from a broader perspective. Over the last decade or so, there has been a flux in global geopolitics. The older established powers are being challenged by other emerging centres of power, especially in Asia. It is in this context that we have to look at the BRI, the evolution of which coincides with this flux. In addition, there is an attempt by China to reshape the world order as we know it.

Since 2008, China has made successive bids to place itself on par with the US or to at least be recognised as its equal. In the course of time, China wants to gradually surpass the US in the exercise of global power. For this, it came up with a new formulation: 'a new type of big power relations', which envisaged precisely that the US and China would be joint arbitrators on global issues. However, the US has declined to give China that status. At the 19th Party Congress in October 2017, Xi Jinping spelt out China's ambitions very clearly. He said that by 2049—that is the anniversary of the founding of the People's Republic of China (PRC)—"China will be a major world power with pioneering global influence". The term "world power with pioneering global influence" implies that China will have the influence to create or reshape international organisations like the UN, World Bank, World Trade Organisation (WTO), etc. More recently on April 3, Yan Xuetong, a well-known Chinese scholar and strategist who is close to Xi Jinping, expressed confidence in China's rise by saying he hoped "that the US and China will work together to provide progressive leadership to the world".

There are major implications for the region too. China's rise has been assertive, and some would even say aggressive, as evidenced by its activities in the South China Sea (SCS), air violations over Japan, with Taiwan, and along the borders with India. With the BRI, China is effectively squeezing the strategic space of its neighbours and also bending international borders. The China–Pakistan Economic Corridor (CPEC) brings this out clearly. China has shed its decades-long ambiguity over PoK (Pakistan occupied Kashmir), Gilgit and Baltistan and has now openly backed Pakistan's claims. To protect Chinese investments, it has asked Pakistan to further integrate these regions into the federal structure of Pakistan and the Pakistan government is carrying out elections in these areas. With the flow of Chinese economic, diplomatic and military power into Pakistan, we can see the military implications of the CPEC.

The Bangladesh-China-India-Myanmar Corridor (BCIM) is the last leg of the BRI and is similarly not acceptable to India. Both Myanmar, and Bangladesh don't really manufacture any goods that India needs and it is Chinese goods and people that will come through the BCIM and flood the northeast. More Chinese products and immigrants will flow into the sensitive and vulnerable areas, like our northeast, where our businessmen already have problems transporting goods to the region, and we have problems with identification of the population. The problem is magnified with China coveting Arunachal Pradesh.

The BRI is a geostrategic economic initiative, which will expand China's economic, diplomatic, and military power across the globe. It has already begun to do so regionally, which fits into its declared ambition of achieving the 'China Dream', which includes the 'rejuvenation of the great Chinese nation' by 2021 which is the centenary of the Chinese Communist Party and includes the 'recovery' of territories said to have been lost by the imposition of unequal treaties by foreign powers.

What actually does the BRI imply? It covers 55 per cent of the world Gross National Product (GNP), 70 per cent of the total population, and 75 per cent of the world's known energy reserves. I define it simply, "The US$ 1.4 trillion BRI is to connect production centres in China with natural resources centres and markets around the world over a China-built communications artery. It has rail, road, sea, aerospace and cyber components" and is multi-dimensional. The BRI will put to use China's surplus manpower, idling financial resources, and the unused infrastructure and technological capabilities of China's huge State-owned Enterprises (SoEs). The best part is that the recipient countries will be paying for it since the projects are mostly financed by loans, with very few grants except in cases like Gwadar!

In this context, worth noting is the fact that the SoEs have gained 28 per cent in profitability since 2014. A European Union (EU) study showed that 89 per cent of the contracts awarded under the BRI are to Chinese SoEs. The rates of interest charged by Chinese banks are around 7 per cent, with reportedly additional hidden costs.

The BRI, incidentally, is a collection of projects, with some begun almost 10 years before 2013, that have been stitched together and put under this umbrella. It is a China-conceived and China-led project. To underscore the point, last year China's Supreme Court set up special BRI courts in China where all matters relating to the BRI and all arbitration relating to the BRI are to be decided. These are in Beijing, Xi'an, and Shenzhen.

Over the past 18 months, there has been a burgeoning pushback to the BRI. India's refusal to join the initiative, which lacks transparency and violates its territorial integrity and sovereignty, has contributed to the difficulties of the BRI. Many countries have begun reviewing the BRI projects following India's assertion that it is a 'debt trap', and the example of Hambantota in Sri Lanka. These include China's "iron brother" Pakistan, who hosts the BRI flagship of the CPEC. Pakistan is reviewing 50 per cent of the BRI projects, but has already given Gwadar to China on a 50-year lease. There are also conflicting figures of China's actual investment in the CPEC, with Pakistan mentioning a figure of US$ 19 billion. Thailand and Malaysia are also reviewing the BRI projects, and Malaysian Prime Minister Mahathir accused China of being a new imperialist power soon after his meeting with the Chinese Premier and has successfully brought down the cost of a BRI rail project by 30 per cent, showing the high margins in costs. But the BRI was incorporated into China's Constitution at the 19th Party Congress and Xi Jinping is personally backing the project, thereby putting the state's might behind the BRI. Also, Premier Li Keqiang, in his report to the second session of the 13th National People's Congress (NPC), which concluded on March 15, said that China "continues to have a window of strategic opportunity", implying that it will continue to push ahead with the BRI despite the obstacles that it faces.

Closely associated with the BRI and to which little attention is paid is the acceleration in build-up of the muscle power, or armed forces, of China along with its economic and diplomatic power. The PLA Navy (PLAN), the second largest Navy in the world today, which is celebrating its 70th founding anniversary in Qingdao today, plans to have five aircraft carriers and is rapidly building a number of warships. By 2030 or 2035, China intends to have a Navy which has 350 surface warships and 100 submarines. That's a very large Navy. China has also started building or upgrading 75 ports around the world along with coastal infrastructure. Its Ministry of Transportation in May claimed that "they are building 42 ports in 34 countries". Many of these will be bases or logistics bases. Chinese military literature already mentions Gwadar as a "logistics naval base", and Karachi as "a regular Navy base". China clearly intends to back its commercial and diplomatic initiatives with military muscle.

The digital BRI also expands China's cyber capabilities with digital espionage hubs detected in some countries on the BRI.

Closer home, the CPEC highlights the military overtones of the BRI. The secure fibre optic cable that has been laid from Kashgar, namely the headquarters of the South Xinjiang Military District which is just north of and across Ladakh, connects with the Pakistan General Headquarters (GHQ) in Rawalpindi, bypassing the political capital of Islamabad. And there are a number of PLA personnel deployed in Pakistan, especially in Gwadar. Chinese security companies are now operating in Pakistan as much as they are operating in Africa. There is a clear expanding Chinese military presence in Pakistan and these are factors India has to contend with.

But it's not all smooth sailing and the pushback to the BRI will grow unless the Chinese are able to fund it in a manner that is much more attractive and transparent. But China's economy is slowing down and is in difficulty, as suggested by the Chinese banks' meeting in last April when they said that they would have to look for diverse sources of funding—indicating that China does not have the capacity or willingness to pump huge sums into the BRI. China's Exim Bank, in fact, said on April 22 that it has Yuan 1 trillion stuck in outstanding loans which it has not been able to recover. Also the areas through which the BRI will pass such as Pakistan, Turkey and the Central Asian Republics are troubled areas. There is also growing resentment due to the huge influx of Chinese people. These issues are further compounded by the Chinese advancing formulas like 'creating a community of common destiny' and suggesting it and their system as an alternative to the world's democracies. Given the direction the situation inside China is moving in and the 'social credit management system' that seeks to regulate the actions and possibly even thoughts of people, all this is troubling for those asked to subscribe to it. There are hidden worries for virtually all countries and, as far as India is concerned, there are no tangible benefits in opting for the project.

*(Text of talk by Mr Jayadeva Ranade at a seminar on "The Implications and Future of the Belt and Road Initiative"' at India International Centre (IIC) on April 23, 2019.)*

# 8. China's 19th Party Congress: New Leaders to Steer China to the China Dream

The week long (October 18-24, 2017) 19th Congress of the Chinese Communist Party (CCP), which was held in Beijing, concluded as anticipated with Xi Jinping emerging considerably stronger. His contribution to Chinese Communist ideology was recognised and unanimously approved for incorporation into the Party Constitution as the "Xi Jinping Thought on Socialism with Chinese Characteristics for a New Era". He is the first CCP leader to have his contribution, attached to his name, enshrined in the Party Constitution while still alive. This places it next in heft to those of Mao Zedong and Deng Xiaoping, especially with the Chinese media already having begun to headline it as "Xi Jinping Thought"!

The approval by the 19th Party Congress to the appointment of many Xi Jinping loyalists, who now constitute the majority of the membership of the Politburo Standing Committee (PBSC), Politburo (PB), CCP Central Committee's (CC's) Secretariat and Central Military Commission (CMC), underscores the unmistakable—and anticipated—enhancement of Xi Jinping's authority and influence. Pertinent in this context are the revelations by China's official media in the weeks before the 19th Party Congress of the successes achieved by the campaign against corruption and, on the sidelines of the Congress on October 20, by Liu Shiyu, Chairman of the China Securities Regulatory Commission, who said that "Xi Jinping had saved socialism by bringing down high-ranking officials who intended to "usurp the Party leadership and seize state power" and described Xi Jinping as a saviour of the Communist Party. Liu Shiyu has since been promoted to the CCP CC!

Interesting are the affiliations of the new leaders appointed to the PBSC, whose number remains at seven. The composition of the new PBSC shows that while Xi Jinping has followed the Party's informal rules and conventions regarding the retirement age of senior echelon cadres, he has avoided inducting younger cadres who could be potential successors in the PBSC. The field for advancement to the next PBSC and as successors to Xi Jinping and Li

Keqiang have, therefore, been left wide open for the younger cadres now in the PB. The field is open too for Xi Jinping to continue in office as, which some of his acolytes have been saying since 2013, China enters a new thirty-year era like those of Mao Zedong and Deng Xiaoping earlier!

Apart from the seven PBSC members, among the remaining 17 PB members also, Xi Jinping has a clear majority. At least 12 of them are his long-time loyalists not including the two Vice Chairmen of the Central Military Commission (CMC) who are also his very close and long-time associates. Some of the PB members are poised to take over as heads of Central Party organisations. They all owe their rise to him. Equally important is the CCP CC Secretariat, which has in the past five years under Xi Jinping become a powerful body. It reports directly to Xi Jinping. Xi Jinping has packed the important new 7- member CCP CC Secretariat with loyalists and Wang Huning is its seniormost member. The previous 18th CCP CC Secretariat was headed by Liu Yunshan who also, like Wang Huning is now, was in charge of ideology, the propaganda apparatus and Party organisation. Three of the Secretariat's members are persons with a background in security or the military, namely, Yang Xiaodu, Guo Shengkun and Huang Kunming. The indication is that Party controls on these sectors will continue to become progressively tougher.

At least two members of the new CCP CC Secretariat have a background in Tibet affairs. In addition to Wang Huning, who has in the past been a member of Tibet Autonomous Region (TAR) delegations to the National People's Congress (NPC), these are Yang Xiaodu, a 'sent down youth in the Cultural Revolution' and till recently Minister of Supervision who served in the TAR from 1976-2001, and Guo Shengkun who as the Minister of Public Security (MPS) attended meetings of the Leading Small Work Group on Tibet. Huang Kunming, another member of the Secretariat has served in the People's Liberation Army (PLA).

As anticipated, TAR Party Secretary Wu Yingjie has been promoted to the new 19th CC as a full member. In addition, this time there are two ethnic Tibetans, Qi Zhala and Luosang Jiangcun, as full members of the CC, or one more than in the previous CC. Sun Chunlan who was head of the CCP CC United Front Work Department and handling Tibet affairs, continues as the solitary woman in the PB despite being 67 years old, which actually puts her in the retirement zone. Interestingly, Zhang Qingli, who was born in 1951 and earned a reputation as a hardline TAR Party Secretary for his derogatory comments about the Dalai Lama, continues as a full member of the 19th CC. Zhang Yijiong, present Executive Deputy Head of the United Front Work Department (UFWD) of the CCP, and Vice Minister who on the sidelines of the 19th Party Congress, outlined China's new strong policy towards the Dalai Lama, has been promoted from alternate member of the 18th CC to full member of the 19th CC. Both of them will have a strong say in the Tibet policy.

The new CMC consists of military officials who are all solid supporters of Xi Jinping. The composition and size of the new Central Military Commission (CMC) has also changed. For the present, it comprises only four members and does not include the heads of the different services like the PLA Air Force (PLAAF), PLA Navy (PLAN), etc. The two CMC Vice Chairmen, former PLAAF Commander Xu Qiliang and PLA Gen Zhang Youxia, are both 'princelings' with a long-time association with Xi Jinping. The new CMC Vice Chairman, Zhang Youxia's father Zhang Zongxun fought alongside Xi Jinping's father and they were called 'partners in blood'. Zhang Youxia had fought in the Sino-Vietnam War in 1979.

The presence of Xu Qiliang, Zhang Youxia and PLA Rocket Force Commander Wei Fenghe in the CMC point to an emphasis on the development and acquisition of modern, advanced defence technology. The induction of Gen Li Zuocheng, head of the Joint Staff Department under the CMC, and Lt. Gen Zhang Shengmin, Secretary of the PLA Discipline Inspection Commission, indicate that Xi Jinping will maintain the stress on 'clean' and corruption free armed forces. Zhang Shengmin, incidentally, previously served in the 52th, 55th and 56th Bases of the Second Artillery in the Lanzhou Military Region and was Political Commissar of the Second Artillery Command College between 2012 and 2013. Gen Miao Hua as head of the Political Work Department under the CMC will further Xi Jinping's agenda of expanding Party control and supervision over China's armed forces, ensuring that the personnel are 'red and expert'.

The new appointments in the CCP's top bodies will allow Xi Jinping to pursue his ambitious agenda with little restraint.

*(This article was published by the Centre for China Analysis and Strategy, New Delhi, on October 25, 2017.)*

# 9. Initial Assessment of Xi Jinping's Work Report at 19th Party Congress

The crucial 19th Congress of the Chinese Communist Party (CCP) opened in Beijing on October 18, 2017, amidst stringent security restrictions in Beijing and other major cities in China. Nearly 1,000 foreign reporters from 130 countries were reported to be covering the Congress. The Congress was preceded by other important meetings, namely the 7th and last Plenum of the 18th CCP Central Committee (CC), and of the Party's powerful anti-corruption body, the Central Discipline Inspection Commission (CDIC) chaired by Xi Jinping's close associate and Politburo Standing Committee (PBSC) member, Wang Qishan.

CCP CC General Secretary Xi Jinping, who holds 14 formal positions—more than any other CCP leader so far—is poised to emerge stronger from this Congress. His sustained anti-corruption campaign has eliminated opposition in the Party and military, and drastically reduced the influence wielded by his predecessor once removed, Jiang Zemin. In September 2017, China's official media publicised that more than 176 CCP cadres equivalent to the rank of central Vice Minister and above had been dismissed and arrested for corruption and that more than 14,000 officers of the People's Liberation Army (PLA) had been similarly dismissed, including more than 86 officers of and above the rank of Major General.

Just weeks before the Congress, Xi Jinping publicly demonstrated his authority by arresting two top Generals, appointing 20 Generals to command thirteen new Group Armies and promoting close associates to head the PLA Army (ground forces) and PLA Air Force. In a rare move, the names of thirteen delegates selected by Chongqing municipality were deleted, reducing the total number of delegates to 2,287. Politburo member and Chongqing Party Secretary Sun Zhengcai, viewed as a likely candidate for the PBSC, was also suddenly dismissed on charges of graft. He had been admonished in February for not doing enough to eliminate the influence of the imprisoned former Politburo (PB) member Bo Xilai.

Xi Jinping has also been projecting himself since November 2012. The *People's Daily*, for example, during Jiang Zemin's tenure, used to publish approximately 3,000 stories per year mentioning him, and during Hu Jintao's term, it published 2,000 each year mentioning Hu Jintao. In stark contrast, the *People's Daily* already publishes 5,000 stories each year mentioning Xi Jinping.

An estimated 34 PLA officers, from the 41 who are members of the CCP CC, and nearly 200 of the 376 members of the CC will be replaced, making it the highest turnover since the 9th Party Congress in 1969 and providing Xi Jinping an unprecedented opportunity to induct persons of his choice. Xi Jinping has paved the way for the induction of many loyalists or individuals who would owe their allegiance to him by promoting, or positioning, them in key slots in the PLA and Party apparatus. Important will be how many people of his choice he is able to bring into the PB and PBSC. If Xi Jinping does acquire full control of the PB and PBSC, he will be free of any restraints in pursuing realisation of the "Two Hundreds" namely, the 'China Dream' (by 2021 which marks the CCP's centenary) and the Belt and Road Initiative (BRI), and making China an advanced developed nation [by 2049, or the hundredth year of the founding of the People's Republic of China (PRC)]. It could additionally leave open the possibility of him extending his term till nearly 2049.

CCP CC General Secretary Xi Jinping took three and a half hours—twice the time taken by Hu Jintao at the 18th Party Congress in November 2012—to read the 32,000-character, 10-section Work Report to the 2,280 delegates representing 89 million CCP members. The emphasis on Party building, the Party's role, and the notion that "ideology determines culture" were predominant. Terms like "four cardinal principles" and "let a hundred flowers bloom and let a hundred schools of thought contend" prevailed. There was specific reference to the "evolution of principle contradiction" which was subsequently explained in a separate Xinhua despatch. There was a new special section devoted to ecology and the environment.

The delegates included 253 from the PLA and 50 from the People's Armed Police Force (PAPF), with 186 from central government agencies, 109 from departments directly under the CCP CC, 53 from central State owned Enterprises (SoEs), and 44 from the financial sector. There were 551 women and 264 ethnic minorities delegates. All the delegates were elected through a competitive process except in the Xinjiang and Tibet Autonomous Regions.

Xi Jinping was watched by 74 senior veteran Party cadres who attended. These veteran cadres remain very influential but do not have voting rights. Included among them were 102-year-old Song Ping, who was the most senior, and Xi Jinping's immediate predecessors Hu Jintao and Jiang Zemin who are 75 and 91 years old respectively. Also attending were former Premiers Wen Jiabao and Zhu Rongji; former Chinese Vice President Zeng Qinghong; and former Politburo Standing Committee members Li Ruihuan and Jia Qinglin.

The 32,000-character Work Report outlined a confident, bold two-stage plan for goals to be achieved by China by 2050. Xi Jinping, for the first time set timelines and declared that by the end of the first phase (2020-35) China will be an innovative, technologically advanced, large, middle-income country ranking among the top nations in the world. By completion of the second stage (2035-50), China should be a nation with "pioneering global influence". Implicit in this is that China will rival or surpass the US in strength and be proactive in international affairs to promote its interests. The Work Report outlined the leadership's plans for China over the next five years and though essentially its focus is on domestic issues, it did, as per past practice, touch on international affairs. The Party, China and Army were mentioned often, along with a specific reference to the Belt and Road Initiative (BRI). Less mentioned were the economy, reform and development.

Xi Jinping described the situation at home and abroad as "undergoing profound and complex changes", but added that "China's development is still an important strategic opportunity, the prospects are bright" though "the challenge is also very serious". He advised all Party members to take a long-term perspective and be vigilant.

There was emphasis on the PLA with the term 'Army' mentioned more than double the number of times than in the Work Reports presented at the 17th and 18th Congresses. It was mentioned 86 times in Xi Jinping's Work Report to the 19th Party Congress and 49 and 54 times in the Work Reports presented at the 18th and 17th Party Congresses respectively. Xi Jinping announced that the Army's focus will be on realisation of the 'Chinese Dream' for which it must develop "a new military strategy under the new situation". National defence and military modernisation will be promoted. Clarifying that by 2020, mechanisation will be basically achieved and that the modernisation of national defence and armed forces should be basically completed by 2035, Xi Jinping said that "IT has come a long way and strategic capabilities have seen a big improvement." He underscored technology as the PLA's "core combat capability". Xi Jinping asserted that the goal is to make the PLA a "world class force" that "can fight and win" by 2050. This timeline coincides with the realisation of the BRI and China becoming a nation with "pioneering global influence". Xi Jinping pointedly described the PLA as a "People's Army".

The section on foreign policy did not name any country. It contained a reference to the 'Five Principles of Peaceful Coexistence'. Xi Jinping called "on all peoples to work together to build a human destiny, build lasting peace, universal security, common prosperity, open tolerance, a clean and beautiful world". He asked countries to "respect each other, have mutual consultation, and resolutely abandon the Cold War mentality and power politics" and said it is necessary to "follow a new road of state-to-state engagement without forming any alliances". He said, "We must insist on resolving disputes through dialogue, resolving differences through consultation, coping with traditional and non-traditional security threats, and opposing all forms of terrorism". He stressed that "China firmly pursues an independent foreign policy of peace, respects the rights of all peoples to choose their own path of development, upholds international fairness and justice, opposes the imposition of their will on others, opposes interference in the internal affairs of other countries and opposes strong bullying".

Appearing to take note of the criticism prompted by the huge debt burden on Sri Lanka because of the BRI and criticism in Pakistan, he said, "China will never sacrifice the interests of other countries at the expense of the development of their own, and never give up their legitimate rights and interests... no one wants to let China damage their own interests and have a bitter fruit". He assured that "China pursues a defensive national defense policy. China's development does not pose a threat to any country. China, no matter what degree of development it follows, will never seek hegemony, never engage in expansion".

The references to Hong Kong, Macau and Taiwan were uncompromising with a strong suggestion of limits imposed on the three. With regard to Taiwan, Xi Jinping said, "We have the resolve, the confidence and the ability to defeat separatist attempts for 'Taiwan independence' in any form. We will never allow anyone, any organisation or any political party, at any time or in any form, to separate any part of Chinese territory from China". He asserted that the CCP "stands firm in safeguarding China's sovereignty and territorial integrity, and will never allow the historical tragedy of national division to repeat itself". Referring to Hong Kong and Macau, he said the policy of "one country, two systems" has proved to be the best institutional guarantee for the long-term prosperity and stability of Hong Kong and Macao after their return.

Xi Jinping's imprimatur on the Work Report was clearly visible. It gave a prominent and leading role to the Party in every sphere. Xi Jinping unambiguously declared that China would not have made the progress it had without the leadership of the CCP. He claimed that "historic shifts" had been made in the cause of the Communist Party of China and the country in the past five years. There was pronounced emphasis in the Work Report on "the Party exercising leadership over all areas of endeavour in every part of the country", clearly indicating that Party controls will be expanded and ideology will remain predominant. Xi Jinping emphasised that "sweeping efforts" had been made to "strengthen Party leadership and Party building" while dismissing any notion of copying "Western style democracy". There were 331 references to the 'Party' in this Work Report, many more than in the Work Reports at the past eight Congresses. The word 'Party' figured 235 and 234 times in the Work Reports presented at the 18th and 17th Party Congresses.

A significant achievement for Xi Jinping was inclusion of the "Thought on Socialism with Chinese Characteristics for a New Era", already being headlined throughout the Chinese media as "Xi Jinping's Thought" and which will be incorporated by an amendment in the Party Constitution. An entire section of the Work Report defined this 'thought'. This includes: "The Party's goal of building a strong military in the new era is to build the people's forces into world class forces that obey the Party's command, can fight and win, and maintain excellent conduct"; "major country diplomacy aims to foster a new type of international relations and build a community with a shared future"; and the "defining feature of socialism with Chinese characteristics is the leadership of the Chinese Communist Party". These imply a global role for the CCP.

Reading the report, Xi Jinping said the CCP "has given shape to the Thought on Socialism with Chinese Characteristics for a New Era" which "builds on and further enriches Marxism-Leninism, Mao Zedong Thought, Deng Xiaoping Theory, the Theory of Three Represents, and the Scientific Outlook on Development." Saying, "It represents the latest achievement in adapting Marxism to the Chinese context", Xi Jinping called it a long-term "guide to action" which the Party must adhere to and develop. It is uncertain whether Xi Jinping's name will be attached to the "thought". In any case, by having his contribution to China's guiding ideological principles designated as "thought", Xi Jinping has succeeded in elevating his stature next only to that of Mao Zedong and Deng Xiaoping.

While Xi Jinping's ambition to be included in the pantheon of Chinese Communist revolutionary thinkers was glimpsed early in June 2014 when the Party theoretical fortnightly *Qiu Shi* (*Seeking Truth*) described him as "one of China's greatest Communist leaders" who had put forward "new thinking, new views and new conclusions", the public campaign to promote inclusion of Xi Jinping's thinking in the Party Constitution seriously kicked off in June 2017. The social media account of the overseas edition of the CCP's official mouthpiece *People's Daily* had then revealed that the Director of the CCP CC General Office Li Zhanshu had announced in an internal speech in February that President Xi Jinping's political philosophy was "basically complete." This was followed by a series of speeches eulogising Xi Jinping's political wisdom. In the weeks leading to the 19th Party Congress and between August 7 and September 18, 2017, Party Secretaries of 31 provinces and autonomous regions wrote signed articles in the official CCP newspaper *People's Daily* (see Appendix). Interestingly, in apparent indication of support to Xi Jinping, PBSC members Zhang Dejiang, Liu Yunshan and Yu Zhengsheng separately praised the "Thought on Socialism with Chinese Characteristics for a New Era" to delegates from the provinces during their group discussions on the sidelines of the ongoing Congress.

Over the next couple of days, they were joined by others publicly displaying their loyalty to General Secretary Xi Jinping. Among them were: Beijing Party Secretary Cai Qi, who called it "the third historic leap forward in China's application of Marxist-Leninism, after Mao Zedong Thought and Deng Xiaoping Theory"; Shanghai Mayor Ying Yong; Gen Xu Qiliang, Vice Chairman of the Central Military Commission; Jiangsu Party Secretary Li Qiang who said he felt "warmth and affection" for Xi Jinping's report; Shanghai Party Secretary Han Zheng, who called it a "thrilling" report; Tianjin Party Secretary Li Hongzhong who said the report was "magnificent, visionary and a pioneer of the era"; Chongqing Party Secretary Chen Min'er who praised Xi Jinping by name several times in his seven-minute speech at the municipality's panel; Liu Shiyu, Chairman of the China Securities Regulatory Commission who said Xi Jinping had saved socialism by bringing down high-ranking officials who intended to "usurp the Party leadership and seize state power" and described Xi Jinping as a saviour of the Communist Party; and Guangdong Party Secretary Hu Chunhua, though reports claimed he was more restrained. Earlier, China's Foreign Minister Wang Yi wrote in the *Study Times*, the official newspaper of the Central Party School (September 1, 2017) that Xi Jinping's "diplomatic thought" "innovates upon and transcends the past 300 years of traditional Western international relations theory." Much earlier, on July 19, State Councillor Yang Jiechi praised Xi Jinping Thought in a signed article in Xinhua. PLA units across China have been formed into 'group study sessions' since October 18, 2017, to study Xi Jinping's Work Report.

Declaring that corruption is "the greatest threat" the Party faces, Xi Jinping promised in the report that the anti-corruption campaign will continue. He announced that the intra-Party disciplinary practice of *Shanggui*, that requires a CPC member under investigation to cooperate with questioning at a designated place and a designated time, will be replaced with detention. Suggesting that the anti-corruption campaign will be elevated to a higher pitch, Xi Jinping disclosed that a National Supervision Law—under discussion for passing at the National People's Congress (NPC) session in March 2018—will be enacted and supervisory commissions at the national, provincial, city, and county levels will be established. There has, incidentally, been speculation in Beijing that Wang Qishan, who, in the normal course is expected to retire at this Congress, could be nominated Chairman of the new National Supervision Commission which could oversee even the Central Discipline Inspection Commission (CDIC).

Highlighting that economic growth had picked up in the last five years since 2012, Xi Jinping mentioned a 6.8 per cent growth rate target. He said China's Gross Domestic Product (GDP) rose from Yuan 54 trillion to Yuan 80 trillion (US$ 8.2-US$ 12.1 trillion) over the past five years. He also said 1,500 reform measures had been introduced in the past five years and a lot of pending plans had been implemented. However, while he said, "We will further reform of SoEs, develop mixed-ownership economic entities, and turn Chinese enterprises into world-class, globally competitive firms", there was a hint of resistance to the streamlining of SoEs when he added that there will be further reform of these to make them "stronger, better and bigger".

Regional and individual income inequalities and poverty were emphasised repeatedly in the Work Report as requiring close attention. Barely a month earlier, on September 14, the Hurun Rich List revealed that at least 74 individuals had joined this year's list with fortunes of at least US$ 300 million, adding to the 2,056 who made last year's list. Rupert Hoogewerf, Hurun Report Chairman and Chief Researcher, said, "Overall, the Hurun Rich List has grown faster than any year since 2007, with the possible exception of 2015." Poverty alleviation had been a key theme this year and merited its own paragraph in the Report. Xi Jinping also opted to represent the poverty-stricken Guizhou province as its delegate to the 19th Congress. He said that more than 60 million people have been lifted out of poverty over the past five years, but much remains to be done.

While there was no direct reference to the Dalai Lama or India in the Work Report, or for that matter to any other country, Xi Jinping did state: "We will fully implement the Party's policy on religious affairs, uphold the principle that religions in China must be Chinese in orientation and adapt to socialist society". The section on national security indicated Xi Jinping's policy when he said, "We must rigorously protest against, and take resolute measures to combat, all acts of infiltration, subversion, and sabotage, as well as violent and terrorist activities, ethnic separatist activities and religious extremist activities".

At a press conference on the sidelines of the ongoing Party Congress on October 21, the Executive Deputy Head and Vice Minister of the CCP CC United Front Work Department, Zhang Yijiong was more direct. In a remark with implications for India, he asserted that the Dalai Lama had "established a so-called government-in- exile, whose goal and core agenda is the independence of Tibet and to separate (from) China. For decades, the group headed by the 14th Dalai Lama has never stopped such attempts. As head of the group, the 14th Dalai Lama has never stopped his activities in this regard over the past decades". Zhang Yijiong warned foreign officials that they cannot get away by saying they were meeting the exiled Tibetan leader in a personal capacity as they still represent their governments. He added, "Any country, or any organisation of any one, accepting to meet with the Dalai Lama, in our view, is a major offence to the sentiment of the Chinese people. The Chinese government opposes governments and organizations in any country in the world to receive the Dalai Lama in any name. We consider such visits as a severe insult to the feelings of the Chinese people…". Zhang Yijiong added that Tibetan Buddhism was a special religion "born in our ancient China". It's a Chinese religion. It didn't come in from the outside.

The Work Report made it clear that the anti-corruption campaign will continue unabated. Party ideology will become more dominant with increased curbs to stall tendencies towards 'liberal' or 'Westernised' thinking. Instructions cautioning Party members to be atheists, avoid any religious practice and abide by Party regulations were reissued just days prior to the Congress, indicating that there will be no relaxation in religious policy or towards Tibetans and Uyghurs. The trend towards expanding the security apparatus will continue, with Xi Jinping probably exercising greater direct control over it.

It is apparent that China will continue to pursue its objectives in the South China Sea. Suspicion of the ruling Democratic Progressive Party (DPP) in Taiwan will ensure continued pressure on it, possibly with efforts to further squeeze its diplomatic space. The comments regarding India made at the press briefing on the sidelines of the Congress give little room for comfort.

# Appendix

## List of Op-Eds by Party Secretaries

1. Cai Qi (蔡　奇), Beijing Party Secretary, 7/8/2017, *People's Daily*
2. Li Hongzhong (李鸿忠), Tianjin Party Secretary, 8/8/2017, *People's Daily*
3. Zhao Kezhi (赵克志), Hebei Party Secretary, 9/8/2017, *People's Daily*
4. Luo Huining (骆惠宁),Shanxi Party Secretary, 10/8/2017, *People's Daily*
5. Li Xi (李希), Liaoning Party Secretary, 11/8/2017, *People's Daily*
6. Bayin Chaolu (巴音朝鲁), Jilin Party Secretary, 14/8/2017, *People's Daily*
7. Zhang Qingwei (张庆伟), Heilongjiang Party Secretary, 15/8/2017, *People's Daily*
8. Han Zheng (韩正), Shanghai Party Secretary, 16/8/2017, *People's Daily* (also member of CCP Politburo)
9. Li Qiang (李强), Jiangsu Party Secretary, 17/8/2017, *People's Daily*
10. Che Jun (车俊), Zhejiang Party Secretary, 18/8/2017, *People's Daily*
11. Li Jinbin (李锦斌), Anhui Party Secretary, 21/8/2017, *People's Daily*
12. You Quan (尤权), Fujian Party Secretary, 22/8/2017, *People's Daily*
13. Lu Xinshe (鹿心社), Jiangxi Party Secretary, 23/8/2017, *People's Daily*
14. Liu Jiayi (刘家义), Shandong Party Secretary, 24/8/2017, *People's Daily*
15. Xie Fuzhan (谢伏瞻), Henan Party Secretary, 25/8/2017, *People's Daily*
16. Jiang Chaoliang (蒋超良), Hubei Party Secretary, 28/8/2017, *People's Daily*
17. Du Jiahao (杜家毫), Hunan Party Secretary, 29/8/2017, *People's Daily*
18. Hu Chunhua (胡春华), Guangdong Party Secretary (also member of CCP Politburo), 30/8/2017, *People's Daily*
19. Peng Qinghua (彭清华), Guangxi Autonomous Region Party Secretary, 31/8/2017, *People's Daily*
20. Liu Cigui (刘赐贵), Hainan Party Secretary, 1/9/2017, *People's Daily*
21. Chen Miner (陈敏尔), Chongqing Party Secretary, 4/9/2017, *People's Daily*
22. Wang Dongming (王东明), Sichuan Party Secretary, 5/9/2017, *People's Daily*
23. Chen Hao (陈　豪), Yunnan Party Secretary, 6/9/2017, *People's Daily*
24. Sun Zhigang (孙志刚), Guizhou Party Secretary, 7/9/2017, *People's Daily*
25 Li Jiheng (李纪恒), Inner Mongolia Autonomous Region Party Secretary, 8/9/2017, *People's Daily*
26. Wu Yingjie (吴英杰), Tibet Autonomous Region Party Secretary, 11/9/2017, *People's Daily*

27. Lou Qinjian (娄勤俭), Shanxi Party Secretary, 12/9/2017, *People's Daily*
28. Lin Duo (林 铎), Gansu Party Secretary, 13/9/2017, *People's Daily*
29. Wang Guosheng (王国生), Qinghai Party Secretary, 14/9/2017, *People's Daily*
30. Shi Taifeng (石泰峰), Ningxia Autonomous Region Party Secretary, 15/9/2017, *People's Daily*
31. Chen Quanguo (陈全国), Xinjiang Autonomous Region Party Secretary, 18/9/2017, *People's Daily*

## Comparison of References to 'Party' and 'Army' in Work Reports to Party Congresses

| Party Congress | 19th | 18th | 17th | 16th | 15th | 14th | 13th | 12th |
|---|---|---|---|---|---|---|---|---|
| Party (党) | 331 | 235 | 234 | 284 | 222 | 230 | 295 | 60 |
| Army (军) | 86 | 49 | 54 | 46 | 33 | 27 | 13 | 8 |

*(This article was published by the Centre for China Analysis and Strategy, New Delhi, on October 21, 2017.)*

# 10. Analysis of China's 19th Party Congress

Already holding over 14 formal positions—more than any other Chinese Communist Party (CCP) leader so far—CCP Central Committee (CC) General Secretary Xi Jinping has, as anticipated, emerged considerably stronger from this Congress. By skilful use of the sustained anti-corruption campaign, he has eliminated opposition in the Party and military and drastically reduced the influence wielded by his predecessor once removed, Jiang Zemin. In September 2017, China's official media publicised that more than 176 CCP cadres equivalent to the rank of central Vice Minister and above had been dismissed and arrested for corruption and that more than 14,000 officers of the People's Liberation Army (PLA) had been similarly dismissed. At least 120 officers of the PLA of and above the rank of Major General have been dismissed and retired.

Just weeks before the Congress, Xi Jinping publicly demonstrated his authority by arresting two top Generals (Fang Fengui and Zhang Yang), appointing 20 General Officers to command 13 new Group Armies and promoting close associates to head the PLA Army (ground forces) and PLA Air Force (PLAAF). In a rare move, the names of 13 delegates selected by Chongqing municipality were deleted, reducing the total number of delegates to 2,287. A couple of days before the commencement of the Congress, another seven were 'disqualified'. Politburo (PB) member and Chongqing Party Secretary Sun Zhengcai, viewed as a likely candidate for the Politburo Standing Committee (PBSC), was also suddenly dismissed on charges of graft. He had been admonished in February for not doing enough to eliminate the influence of imprisoned former PB member Bo Xilai.

Xi Jinping had also been projecting himself since November 2012. The *People's Daily*, for example, during Jiang Zemin's tenure used to publish approximately 3,000 stories per year mentioning him and during Hu Jintao's term it published 2,000 each year mentioning Hu Jintao. In stark contrast, the *People's Daily* already publishes 5,000 stories each year mentioning Xi Jinping.

A major highlight of the week-long (October 18-24, 2017) 19th Congress of the CCP, which was held in Beijing, was its recognition of Xi Jinping's contribution to Chinese Communist ideology. The Congress unanimously approved its incorporation into the Party Constitution as "Xi Jinping Thought on Socialism with Chinese Characteristics for a New Era". He is the first CCP leader to have his contribution, attached to his name, enshrined in the Party Constitution while still alive. This places it next in heft to those of Mao Zedong and Deng Xiaoping, especially with the Chinese media already having begun to headline it as "Xi Jinping Thought"!

Xi Jinping's ambition to be included in the pantheon of Chinese Communist revolutionary thinkers was glimpsed early in June 2014 when the Party theoretical fortnightly *Qiu Shi* (*Seeking Truth*) described him as "one of China's greatest Communist leaders" who had put forward "new thinking, new views and new conclusions". The public campaign to promote inclusion of Xi Jinping's thinking in the Party Constitution seriously kicked off in June 2017. The social media account of the overseas edition of the CCP's official mouthpiece *People's Daily* had then revealed that the Director of the CCP CC General Office Li Zhanshu had announced in an internal speech in February that President Xi Jinping's political philosophy was "basically complete." This was followed by a series of speeches eulogising Xi Jinping's political wisdom. In the weeks leading to the 19th Party Congress and between August 7 and September 18, 2017, Party Secretaries of 31 provinces and autonomous regions wrote signed articles in the official CCP newspaper *People's Daily*.

The approval by the 19th Party Congress to the appointment of many Xi Jinping loyalists, who now constitute the majority of the membership of the Politburo Standing Committee (PBSC), Politburo (PB), CCP Central Committee's (CC's) Secretariat and Central Military Commission (CMC), underscores the unmistakable—and anticipated—enhancement of Xi Jinping's authority and influence. Pertinent in this context are the revelations by China's official media in the weeks before the 19th Party Congress of the successes achieved by the campaign against corruption and, on the sidelines of the Congress on October 20, by Liu Shiyu, Chairman of the China Securities Regulatory Commission, who said, "Xi Jinping had saved socialism by bringing down high-ranking officials who intended to usurp the Party leadership and seize state power" and described "Xi Jinping as a saviour of the Communist Party". Liu Shiyu has since been promoted to the CCP CC!

Interesting are the affiliations of the new leaders appointed to the PBSC, whose number remains at seven. The composition of the new PBSC shows that while Xi Jinping has followed the Party's informal rules and conventions regarding the retirement age of senior echelon cadres, he has avoided inducting younger cadres who could be potential successors in the PBSC. The field for advancement to the next PBSC and as successors to Xi Jinping and Li Keqiang has, therefore, been left wide open for the younger cadres now in the PB. The field is open too for Xi Jinping to continue in office as, which some of his acolytes have been saying since 2013, China enters a new thirty-year era like those of Mao Zedong and Deng Xiaoping earlier!

The new Politburo, like the previous one, has 25 members. Apart from the seven PBSC members, among the remaining 17 PB members also, Xi Jinping has a clear majority. At least 12 of them are long-time Xi Jinping loyalists, not including the two Vice Chairmen of the Central Military Commission (CMC) who are also his close and long time associates. Some of the PB members are poised to take over as heads of Central Party organisations. They all owe their rise to him.

Equally important is the CCP CC Secretariat, which has in the past five years under Xi Jinping become a powerful body. It reports directly to Xi Jinping. Xi Jinping has packed the important new 7-member CCP CC Secretariat with loyalists and Wang Huning is its seniormost member. The previous 18th CCP CC Secretariat was headed by Liu Yunshan who also, like Wang Huning is now, was in charge of ideology, the propaganda apparatus and Party organisation. Three of the Secretariat's members are persons with a background in security or the military, namely, Yang Xiaodu, Guo Shengkun and Huang Kunming. The indication is that Party controls on these sectors will continue to become progressively tougher.

At least two members of the new CCP CC Secretariat have a background in Tibet affairs. In addition to Wang Huning, who has in the past been a member of Tibet Autonomous Region (TAR) delegations to the National People's Congress (NPC), these are Yang Xiaodu, a 'sent down youth in the Cultural Revolution' and till recently Minister of Supervision who served in the TAR from 1976-2001, and Guo Shengkun who as the Minister of Public Security (MPS) attended meetings of the Leading Small Work Group on Tibet. Huang Kunming, another member of the Secretariat, has served in the PLA. As anticipated, TAR Party Secretary Wu Yingjie has been promoted to the new 19th CC as a full member. In addition, this time there are two ethnic Tibetans, Qi Zhala (Choedak) and Luosang Jiangcun (Lobsang Gyaltsen), as full members of the CC, or one more than in the previous CC and one, Norbu Dhondup, as an alternate member of the CC. Sun Chunlan who heads the CCP CC United Front Work Department (UFWD) and handles Tibet affairs, continues as the solitary woman in the PB despite being 67 years old, which actually puts her in the retirement zone. Interestingly, Zhang Qingli, who was born in 1951 and earned a reputation as a hardline TAR Party Secretary for his derogatory comments about the Dalai Lama, continues as a full member of the 19th CC. Zhang Yijiong, present Executive Deputy Head of the United Front Work Department (UFWD) and Vice Minister, who on the sidelines of the 19th Party Congress, outlined China's new strong policy towards the Dalai Lama, has been promoted from alternate member of the 18th CC to full member of the 19th CC. All of them will have a strong voice in the formulation of the Tibet policy.

The new CMC consists of military officials who are all solid supporters of Xi Jinping. The composition and size of the new Central Military Commission (CMC) has also changed. For the present, it comprises only four members and does not include the heads of the different Services like the PLA Air Force (PLAAF), PLA Navy (PLAN), etc. The two CMC Vice Chairmen, former PLAAF Commander Xu Qiliang and PLA Gen Zhang Youxia, are both 'princelings' with a long-time association with Xi Jinping. The new CMC Vice Chairman, Zhang Youxia's father Zhang Zongxun fought alongside Xi Jinping's father and they were called 'partners in blood'. Zhang Youxia had fought in the Sino-Vietnam War in 1979. The presence of Xu Qiliang, Zhang Youxia and PLA Rocket Force Commander Wei Fenghe in the CMC point to an emphasis on the development and acquisition of modern, advanced defence technology. The induction of Gen Li Zuocheng, head of the Joint Staff Department under the CMC, and Lt. Gen Zhang Shengmin, Secretary of the PLA Discipline Inspection Commission, indicate that Xi Jinping will maintain the stress on 'clean' and corruption free armed forces. Zhang Shengmin, incidentally, previously served in the 52th, 55th and 56th Bases of the Second Artillery in the Lanzhou Military Region and was Political Commissar of the Second Artillery Command College between 2012 and 2013. Gen Miao Hua as head of the Political Work Department under the CMC will further Xi Jinping's agenda of expanding Party control and supervision over China's armed forces, ensuring that the personnel are 'red and expert'.

The new appointments in the CCP's top bodies will allow Xi Jinping to pursue his ambitious agenda with few constraints. He will be free of any restraints in pursuing the realisation of the "Two Hundreds" namely, the 'China Dream' (by 2021 which marks the CCP's centenary) and the Belt and Road Initiative (BRI), and making China an advanced developed nation by 2049, or the hundredth year of the founding of the People's Republic of China (PRC). It additionally leaves open the possibility of him extending his term till nearly 2049.

There were some important additional highlights of the 19th Party Congress. The Party, China and Army were mentioned often in Xi Jinping's Work Report along with a specific reference to the Belt and Road Initiative (BRI). Less mentioned were the economy, reform and development. Xi Jinping for the first time made a direct linkage between the completion of China's second and final stage of development in 2035 and the PLA becoming a world class fighting force.

There was emphasis on the PLA, with the term 'Army' mentioned more than double the number of times than in the Work Reports presented at the 17th and 18th Congresses. It was mentioned 86 times in Xi Jinping's Work Report to the 19th Party Congress and 49 and 54 times in the Work Reports presented at the 18th and 17th Party Congresses respectively. Xi Jinping announced that the Army's focus will be on realisation of the 'Chinese Dream' for which it must develop "a new military strategy under the new situation". National defence and military modernisation will be promoted. Clarifying that by 2020, mechanisation will be basically achieved and that the modernisation of national defence and the armed forces should be basically completed by 2035, Xi Jinping said that "IT has come a long way and strategic capabilities have seen a big improvement." He underscored technology as the PLA's "core combat capability". Xi Jinping asserted that the goal is to make the PLA a "world class force" that "can fight and win" by 2050. This timeline coincides with realisation of the BRI and China becoming a nation with the "pioneering global influence". Xi Jinping also pointedly described the PLA as a "People's Army".

The references to Hong Kong, Macau and Taiwan were uncompromising with a strong suggestion of limits imposed on the three. With regard to Taiwan, Xi Jinping said, "We have the resolve, the confidence and the ability to defeat separatist attempts for 'Taiwan independence' in any form. We will never allow anyone, any organisation or any political party, at any time or in any form, to separate any part of Chinese territory from China". He asserted that the CCP "stands firm in safeguarding China's sovereignty and territorial integrity, and will never allow the historical tragedy of national division to repeat itself".

There was pronounced emphasis in the Work Report on "the Party exercising leadership over all areas of endeavour in every part of the country", clearly indicating that Party controls will be expanded and ideology will remain predominant. Xi Jinping emphasised that "sweeping efforts" had been made to "strengthen Party leadership and Party building" while dismissing any notion of copying "Western style democracy". There were 331 references to the 'Party' in this Work Report, many more than in the Work Reports at the past eight Congresses.

Finally, Xi Jinping has lost no time in further consolidating his position and concentrating more power in his person. The first meeting of the new Politburo (PB) on October 27, in its notification, formally recognised Xi Jinping as the ruling Communist Party's *lingxiu*—a reverential term for "leader" instead of the usual *lingdao* or *lingji*. It also stated that henceforth, all PB members will not only inspect all organisations and cadres under them and submit annual reports to the concerned central Party organisations and the PB, but also to Party General Secretary Xi Jinping. He has already announced that the anti-corruption campaign will continue to be pursued with vigour, and appointed his long-time loyalist and PBSC member Zhao Leji as head of the Central Discipline Inspection Commission (CDIC).

A clear indication of China's confidence in founding a modern socialist country by 2050 was articulated by the state-owned *Global Times* on October 25, 2017. Stating that some Westerners find this level of confidence challenging, it said that they should actually see this as an opportunity and that "it is time for these people to open their hearts to China". Emphasising that

China will not only be a strong nation with a first-class Army, but will focus on its continued pursuit of harmony, balancing an ecological environment, and democracy, it said, "This modernized country will serve its people, rather than seek revenge upon the world in efforts to establish global hegemony". At the same time, it warned that "China will not tolerate disruptions of any kind during this new phase of socialist modernization" adding that "if, for whatever reason, the nation's peaceful development is thwarted by external influence, China will not hesitate to strike back with sharp strategic force, or if necessary, prepare for a full-scale showdown. Of course, a situation of this nature will lead to consumption, and have a negative impact on the realization of the nation's goal for 2050". It said also that when "China's peaceful ascension is realized, it will be a watershed moment for humanity, a form of development completely removed from the laws of the jungle. The determination to grow into a powerful and peaceful nation will remain intact". Pertinent to recall in this context is the resolution adopted at the Conference on Peripheral Diplomacy in October 2013, that countries which oppose China will face periods of sustained opposition and pressure!

In conclusion, the 19th Party Congress has sent out the following clear messages:

- The Party will pervade and dominate all sectors in China i.e. government, military, economy and society.
- China is confident it will achieve the developmental goals set out for the first time by Xi Jinping i.e. 2020-35—to make China a technologically advanced and moderately developed country in the top ranks of the world—and 2035-50 to make China a strong developed nation having "pioneering global influence".
- "Xi Jinping Thought on Socialism with Chinese Characteristics for a New Era" is an alternative to Western-style democracy.
- Incorporation of the BRI in the Party Constitution now elevates it to a national development goal with the warning against its obstruction issued on October 25 taking on added significance.

*(This article was published by the Centre for China Analysis and Strategy, New Delhi, on November 18, 2017.)*

# 11. Distancing the PLA From Politics: Representatives in CCP Standing Committees

Chinese President Xi Jinping has maintained a firm focus on the People's Liberation Army (PLA) ever since he was appointed General Secretary of the Chinese Communist Party (CCP) and Chairman of the Central Military Commission (CMC) at the 18th Party Congress in November 2012. Since then, he has initiated the most extensive reform ever of the PLA, including the demobilisation of 300,000 personnel. He has additionally brought the PLA within the purview of the Central Discipline Inspection Commission (CDIC), the Party's anti-corruption watchdog body. Xi Jinping has simultaneously taken steps to divest it of its business enterprises, quietly push the PLA back into the barracks and insulate it from local politics. The latter probably motivated by the need to obviate recurrence of incidents like when ousted Politburo member Bo Xilai created "cliques" within the PLA. From 2015, PLA officers began being removed from the Provincial Party Standing Committees. Indications are now surfacing that this policy is under review and possibly being reversed.

High on Xi Jinping's list of priorities has been the tightening of the Party's control over the PLA, professionalisation of the PLA and keeping it focussed on military training. At an 'enlarged' meeting of the CMC the day after taking over as its Chairman, he declared that political reliability will be the determining criterion for promoting PLA officers. This has been bolstered by Xi Jinping's conviction that that by designating the Army as the "Army of the state", the Soviet leadership had actually "disarmed" the Communist Party of the Soviet Union (CPSU). Consecutive campaigns in the PLA "educate" its personnel that it is an "Army of the Party" and that its officers must "absolutely obey" the Party. An important reason for the campaigns is the worry that has dogged the CCP leadership, particularly since 2011-12, that new college graduates joining the PLA who might have been exposed to 'Western' and 'liberal' ideas advocating that the PLA should be an 'Army of the state' could carry these into their Army careers.

In the meantime, since 2015, apparently as part of the military reform, Xi Jinping began quietly dismantling the military-political coordination mechanism set up since before the Great Proletarian Cultural Revolution (GPCR) and which proved effective to an extent in reining in the excesses of the Red Guards. There was, consequently, since that date, a gradual effort to drop PLA representatives from the Party's provincial-level Standing Committees. Till December 2017, 17 provinces and autonomous regions out of a total of 31 had no PLA representative in their Party Standing Committees. These were: Xinjiang, Anhui, Henan, Shanxi, Jiangxi, Tibet, Hunan, Jiangsu, Guangxi, Hebei, Inner Mongolia, Fujian, Liaoning, Yunnan, Shanghai, Tianjin and Gansu.

Interestingly, the two troubled Autonomous Regions of Tibet and Xinjiang were among those where there was no PLA representative on the Party Standing Committees. The official *Beijing Daily* observed that this was part of the military reform and that the Xinjiang Military Region, Tibet Military Region and Beijing garrison had been transferred directly to the PLA's control, implying that they would report to the CMC. It added that the other 28 provincial military commands would come under the National Defence Mobilisation Department (NDMD) under the State Council and CMC.

Lt. Gen. Sheng Bin, former Deputy Commander of Shenyang Military Region who is now the Director of the CMC's NDMD that was established on January 11, 2016, under Xi Jinping's military reforms, said in an interview with the *China National Defence News* in March 2016, that as per existing laws and regulations, the provincial military command is at par with the Party's military, local government military service agencies and local garrison coordinating agencies. He clarified that with the new changes, the NDMD's functions would include: the Emergency Response Command, local Party military affairs, Reserve Force of the Ministry of Construction, military service department of the same level and coordination of military and civilian affairs. The Military District system is now managed by the NDMD, relieving Theatre Commands of many administrative burdens, including the supervision of militia work in the provinces. The exact role of Theatre Commands in the development of national defence mobilisation capabilities is, however, not yet clear.

Well-informed Beijing-based Chinese analysts and some state-owned Chinese papers have observed that the major concerns behind the move were to prevent PLA officers from exercising influence for personal profit; curb corruption in the PLA; prevent senior military officers from getting involved in politics in the provinces; and prevent senior PLA officers from building lobbies in the CCP. A major factor cited by them was Xi Jinping's emphasis on professionalisation of the PLA, which implies elevated levels of training and keeping PLA personnel focussed on military training tasks. Another important factor would be that as the PLA downsizes and its resources get stretched, the administrative burden on PLA officers needs to be reduced.

Prof. Xu Yaotong of the Chinese Academy of Governance said that the withdrawal of military officers from the Standing Committees would have a positive impact on the development of a modern military force. In an interview to *China News Weekly,* Prof Xu Yaotong said not choosing military officers as Provincial Party Standing Committee members would help to create well-equipped military forces in the future.

A major reversal in this policy has, however, become evident from December 2017, since when PLA officers have begun to be brought back into the Provincial Party Standing Committees. PLA Maj Gen Han Xiaodong, Political Commissar of the Hebei Military District was inducted on December 30, 2017 to the Hebei Provincial Party Standing Committee and PLA Maj Gen Wang Bianjiang, Political Commissar of the Liaoning Military District was inducted on December 30, 2017, to the Liaoning Provincial Party Standing Committee. Clearly confirming the reversal of the earlier policy, Lt Gen Xu Yong, Commander of the Tibet Military Region, has also been reinducted into the Tibet Autonomous Region (TAR) Party Standing Committee. Till now, however, there is no PLA representative in the Party Standing Committee of the Xinjiang-Uyghur Autonomous Region.

A total of 15 provinces and autonomous regions have till January 28, 2018, now got PLA representatives in their respective Party Standing Committees. These are: Hubei, Anhui, Hebei, Hainan, Liaoning, Hunan, Guangdong,

Gansu, Jiangsu, Jiangxi, TAR, Shandong, Sichuan, Beijing and Guangxi-Zhuang AR. Seven of the 15 are PLA Commanders while the remaining are Political Commissars.

A list of the PLA officers appointed to the Provincial Party Standing Committees is appended.

## Appendix

1. Maj Gen Ma Tao (马涛), member of Hubei Provincial Standing Committee (Date of announcement: January 2, 2018), Commander of Hubei Military District (appointed in August, 2017)
2. Maj Gen Yang Zheng (杨征), member of Anhui Provincial Standing Committee (Date of announcement: January 2, 2018), Commander of Anhui Military District (appointed in August, 2017).
3. Maj Gen Han Xiaodong ( 韩 晓 东 ), member of Hebei Provincial Standing Committee (Date of announcement: December 30, 2017), Political Commissar of Hebei Military District (appointed in August 2017).
4. Maj Gen Chen Shoumin (陈守民), member of Hainan Provincial Committee and Standing Committee (Date of announcement: January 2, 2018), Commander of Hainan Military District (appointed in May 2016).
5. Maj Gen Wang Bianjiang (王边疆), member of Liaoning Provincial Standing Committee (Date of announcement: December 30, 2017), Political Commissar of Liaoning Military District (appointed in December 2016).
6. Maj Genl Feng Yi (冯毅), member of Hunan Provincial Committee and Standing Committee (Date of announcement: January 3, 2018), Political Commissar of Hunan Military District (appointed in April 2017).
7. Maj Gen Zhang Liming (张利明), member of Guangdong Provincial Committee and Standing Committee (Date of announcement: January 3, 2018), Commander of Guangdong Military District (appointed in January 2015).
8. Maj Gen Pu Yongneng (蒲永能), member of Gansu Provincial Committee and Standing Committee (Date of announcement: January 3, 2018), Political Commissar of Gansu Military District (appointed in July 2017).
9. Maj Gen Meng Zhongkang (孟中康), member of Jiangsu Provincial Committee and Standing Committee (Date of announcement: January 3, 2018), Political Commissar of Jiangsu Military District (appointed in May 2017).

10. Maj Gen Yang Xiaoxiang (杨笑祥), member of Jiangxi Provincial Committee and Standing Committee (Date of announcement: January 3, 2018), Political Commissar of Jiangxi Military District (appointed in March 2015).
11. Lt Gen Xu Yong (许勇), member of TAR Standing Committee (Date of announcement: January 6, 2018), Commander of TAR Military Region.
12. Maj Gen Zhao Jilu (赵冀鲁), member of Shandong Provincial Committee and Standing Committee (Date of announcement: January 4, 2018), Commander of Shandong Military District (appointed in May 2017).
13. Maj Gen Jiang Yongshen (姜永申), member of Sichuan Provincial Committee and Standing Committee (Date of announcement: January 5, 2018), Commander of Sichuan Military District (appointed in July 2015).
14. Lt Gen Jiang Yong (姜勇), member of Beijing Standing Committee (Date of announcement: January 4, 2018), Political Commissar of Beijing Garrison (appointed in January 2015)
15. Maj Gen Jiang Yingyu (姜 英 宇), member of Guangxi Autonomous Region Committee and Standing Committee (Date of announcement: January 3, 2018), Political Commissar of Guangxi Military District (appointed in July 2016).

*(This article was published by the Centre for China Analysis and Strategy, New Delhi, on January 27, 2018.)*

# 12. Initial Assessment of China's CPPCC Plenary Session, 2019

Earlier in March this year, China successfully concluded plenary meetings of the Party's top two bodies, which set the agenda for the year ahead. Some 2,158 delegates of China's top political advisory body, the Chinese People's Political Consultative Conference (CPPCC) gathered in the Great Hall of the People in Beijing from March 9-11, 2019. The CPPCC's responsibilities include supervising the United Front Work Department (UFWD) and overseeing work relating to China's ethnic minorities, enacting regulations and policies for China's ethnic minorities, interacting with non-Communist entities and forging relations with foreign political parties, creating pro-Beijing lobbies abroad, etc. The plenary sessions are intended to formalise the approval of the 89 million-strong Chinese Communist Party (CCP) to its leadership's policies, programmes and the budget for the coming year.

This year, the plenums of the CPPCC and China's version of a Parliament, the National People's Congress (NPC), had as their backdrop the noticeably widening popular dissatisfaction with Xi Jinping and his policies among China's populace. The unabated restiveness in the Tibet and Xinjiang Autonomous Regions have been causes of serious concern to the Chinese authorities, especially as this year marks the sixtieth anniversary of the 14th Dalai Lama's flight from Tibet and of the failed 1959 Tibetan uprising against Chinese occupation. A consequence is the imposition of more stringent security controls in both these autonomous regions. China's approximately 10,000-word White Paper released on March 18, 2019, noted that "some of the most notorious terrorist attacks" that have taken place in the world and, in a bid to justify the internment camps that have been set up in Xinjiang where 1.5 million Uyghurs are incarcerated, claimed that it has arrested nearly 13,000 people it describes as terrorists and has broken up hundreds of "terrorist gangs" in Xinjiang since 2014. While neither Tibet nor Xinjiang were reported by the official Chinese official media to have been prominent in the deliberations, they certainly hung over the plenary sessions.

The Tibet Autonomous Region (TAR) witnessed a series of security conferences in Lhasa and the other administrative districts in the months leading up to the CPPCC plenary session. These were reinforced with the imposition of sterner measures in Tibetan Buddhist monasteries and on Tibetans. At least one 'reeducation' camp, akin to those established in the Xinjiang Uyghur Autonomous Region (XUAR), is reported to have been established in the TAR's second largest town of Shigatse and is managed by the People's Armed Police Force (PAPF), now under the People's Liberation Army (PLA). Tibet was declared off-limits to journalists and foreigners for an extended period till April 30 and TAR leaders inspected Tibetan Buddhist monasteries and convened a series of conferences of security cadres to "uncover" and "eliminate" the "double-faced cadres" owing loyalty to the Dalai Lama. Chinese armed police personnel and armoured police cars staged a show of force in Lhasa on March 7. The issue of a White Paper on Tibet on March 27, within days of conclusion of the CPPCC session, suggests it would have been discussed by that body. Politburo Standing Committee (PBSC) member and CPPCC Chairman Wang Yang also visited Xinjiang immediately after the CPPCC plenary.

Despite these signs of discontent, the reports presented to the plenary sessions by Chinese Premier Li Keqiang and CPPCC Chairman Wang Yang bore the firm imprimatur of Chinese President Xi Jinping and affirmed his authority. Li Keqiang and Wang Yang opened their reports with acknowledgments of Xi Jinping's position as the "core of the Party". Li Keqiang's report contained 15 references to Xi Jinping and not one to Mao Zedong, Deng Xiaoping, or his predecessors. Only Xi Jinping's political ideology found mention in the reports. Of the 15 and 19 tasks mentioned in the reports to the NPC and CPPCC plenary sessions respectively, the first two listed following "the strong leadership of the Party Central Committee with Xi Jinping at the core" and "Xi Jinping Thought on Socialism with Chinese Characteristics in the New Era".

As per tradition, the CPPCC met first. CPPCC Chairman and Politburo Standing Committee (PBSC) member Wang Yang delivered the CPPCC's annual work report to the 2,158 assembled CPPCC delegates on March 4, 2019. Unlike on previous occasions, interestingly, on this occasion, the

CPPCC Chairman's report acknowledged Chinese President Xi Jinping's preeminent position and said that in 2019, "top priority will be given to studying and implementing Xi Jinping Thought on Socialism with Chinese Characteristics for a New Era." He clarified, "The second task is offering high-quality suggestions on the central tasks of the Party and the country." The body's four other major tasks for the year are: (i) "making greater efforts for unity and friendly ties [between the Party and non-Party elements]"; (ii) "contributing wisdom and strength to major country diplomacy with Chinese characteristics"; (iii) "making solid progress in the self-improvement of the CPPCC"; and (iv) "holding celebrations for the 70th anniversary of the CPPCC's founding".

China's authoritative official Xinhua News Agency (March 8) said that during the sessions of the NPC and the CPPCC, Chinese President Xi Jinping told the delegates to the two conferences that social science and the works of art and culture relate to the theoretical foundation and propaganda vehicles of the Chinese Communist Party's ideology. He said that social science and art should focus on socialism with "Chinese characteristics." Xinhua added that Xi Jinping said that without a soul, a country and a nation cannot stand. Works of culture and the arts, philosophy, and social science belong to "the work of casting for souls". They play an important role in the new era of developing socialism. Xi Jinping advised that "philosophy and social science research should be based on the great practice of socialism with Chinese characteristics" and should put forward creative and original theories. He emphasised that the year is "the 70th anniversary of the founding of the New China. It is necessary to present China's historical achievements and the theoretical and cultural advantages of socialism with "Chinese characteristics".

The CPPCC also, quite unusually, held its second, third, and fourth plenary meetings in quick succession between March 9 to 11, 2019. Briefly, in the second plenary session on March 9, 14 CPPCC National Committee members spoke about building an economic and ecological civilisation. They stressed on the importance of "realizing high-quality development," "stimulating the innovative vitality of enterprises", resolving "zombie company" issues, enhancing the quality of poverty alleviation, pushing forward rural vitalisation, and protecting the ecological environment of the

Tibetan plateau. At the third plenary meeting, 15 members spoke on cultural and social construction. Their speeches focussed on "telling the China Story well" through works of art and literature, improving child care and elder care services, promoting the healthy development of the Artificial Intelligence (AI) industry, continuing "the discovery of space with Chinese characteristics" and strengthening employment support. The fourth plenary meeting discussed political construction and the work of the United Front and CPPCC. They highlighted the importance of "deepening civil exchanges between the two sides of the Taiwan Strait," utilizing the "unique advantage of overseas Chinese" for the Belt and Road Initiative (BRI), "establishing a robust and new type of supervision management mechanism," and "adhering to the direction of the Sinicization of our country's Christianity."

Speaking at the session Yang Jie, a CPPCC member and researcher from an agriculture academy in Suzhou city of East China's Anhui province, stressed that "Chinese Muslims are Chinese citizens first" and that "[religious people] must unite and lead the religious masses well... must study and use the common spoken and written Chinese language well... must lead the fight against separatism, extreme terrorism, and religious extremism... [and] must lead the masses to be grateful for the Party, listen to the Party, and follow the Party."

Also, at the fourth plenary meeting, the head of the National Committee of the "Three-Self Patriotic Movement", Xu Xiaohong stressed the need for Chinese Christians to "adhere to China's Sinicization of Christianity orientation and actively adapt to socialist society." Stating that "many outstanding problems exist in Christianity, including outside infiltration, a lack of high-quality pastors who love their country and religion", etc., he warned that "without further attention, [these problems] could produce serious political consequences." Xu Xiaohong emphasised that attempts by "Western anti-China forces to continue influencing China's social stability and even subverting its regime through Christianity are doomed to failure."

CPPCC National Committee President Wang Yang and Vice Premier Hu Chunhua attended all the meetings.

An important disclosure was made by Wang Jiangping, Vice Minister of Industry and Information Technology, while speaking to CPPCC delegates on March 7. He disclosed that China has a secret programme to support the microchip and software industries. His comments were leaked to reporters. Wang Jiangping said, "Last year, the Ministry of Industry and Information Technology planned the 'Zhengxin Zhuhun' project under the leadership of the Party Central Committee and the State Council." He added, "The state will give strong policy and funding support, because industries such as microchips and software need to be iteratively developed." Wang Jiangping also said, "[We] spoke very little to the outside world [about the program]." However, Wang Jiangping's remarks were soon removed from the Chinese internet.

Another interesting disclosure was by biophysicist Rao Zihe, a CPPCC delegate. He said (March 10) that Research and Development (R&D) spending would hit 2.5 per cent of Gross Domestic Product (GDP) in 2019, citing Beijing's medium and long-term plans for science and technology development for 2006 to 2020.

To mark the end of the CPPCC meeting, the Party's official *People's Daily* published an editorial on March 14, congratulating the CPPCC on a successful meeting. The editorial affirmed that "we will be able to surmount all difficulties and obstacles in our path moving forward as long as [we] congregate Chinese people of different party affiliations, religions, ethnicities, and [social] statuses at home and abroad, and form the broadest patriotic united front that is devoted to realizing the reunification of the motherland and the China Dream of the great rejuvenation of the Chinese nation."

The CPPCC plenum clearly indicated that China would continue with its current policies of the CCP 'Sinicising' Buddhism, Christianity and Islam in China. It affirmed that Beijing would appoint the high-ranking Tibetan Buddhist religious personages, with the White Paper on Tibet (March 27, 2019) emphasising that Beijing had appointed the 17th Karmapa as one example. There was no suggestion of 'negotiations' or 'contacts' with the Dalai Lama and noticeable too, was the absence of direct personal criticism of the 84-year-old Dalai Lama. It is apparent that Beijing has decided to 'appoint' its 'own' Dalai Lama and is waiting out the present Dalai Lama.

*(This article was published by the Centre for China Analysis and Strategy, New Delhi, on March 30, 2019.)*

# 13. A Brief Assessment of China's 3rd Session of the 13th CPPCC, May 2020

As usual China's top political advisory body, the Chinese People's Political Consultative Conference (CPPCC), held its annual plenary session in Beijing along with the National People's Congress (NPC). The plenum was delayed this year and held two months later from May 21 to May 27, 2020, because of the coronavirus pandemic. The pandemic cast a shadow over the plenary meetings, which were shortened to a week instead of the usual ten days and restrictions curtailed the number of press conferences and correspondents allowed to attend. For the first time, provision for video conferencing was made for those not physically attending the CPPCC and NPC Plenums.

Han Fangming, Vice Chairman of the Foreign Affairs Committee of the CPPCC National Committee, said prior to start of the sessions, that "due to the COVID-19 epidemic and the shortened session, the accommodation and meeting venues for CPPCC members and NPC delegates are simpler, stricter and more efficient." Hotels and meeting rooms for the sessions accordingly provided reduced services, with fewer newspapers and no banners, red carpets, flowers, bars or cafes. CPPCC members and NPC delegates were asked to bring their own pens or notepads and at the venue, they were provided only a single bottle of water, a tea cup, and a pack of antiseptic wipes. Full-page reminders on how to avoid catching the virus and block its spreading were handed out to each invitee. 'Social distancing' was enforced and attendees were encouraged not to shake hands, congregate outside the meeting rooms or linger in confined places, as well as not leave their hotels or the convention areas without permission from the organisers.

To burnish the credibility of the Chinese Communist Party (CCP), which was dented by unprecedented public criticism, particularly during the coronavirus pandemic, the state-owned China Central Television (CCTV) on the eve of the 'Big Two' sessions reported (May 21), that CCP members had donated RMB 8.36 billion (US$ 1.18 billion) for the fight against the coronavirus in the past three months. It said all the money was sent to the 'Party Central Committee' for redistribution. Chinese President Xi Jinping also sought to further tighten his grip over the Party and People's Liberation Army (PLA) and shore up his position, with the sudden announcement on May 21 that 17 Deputies to the NPC had been asked to resign. Four of them were senior PLA officers, with a Lieutenant General and one Major General having outstanding records.

Some developments timed to coincide with the opening of the 'Big Two' on May 21, did, however, occur to embarrass China's leadership. At least three critics of Chinese President Xi Jinping and the CCP succeeded in publicising their criticism. These included: Shanghai-based Chinese constitutional lawyer, 43-year old Zhang Xuezhong, posting an 'open' letter on WeChat on May 9, addressed to all NPC Deputies; retired senior Central Party School Professor Cai Xia whose scathing criticism of Xi Jinping and the CCP on a 20-minute recording circulated for almost a month on the Chinese web; and the publication on May 21, in Hong Kong's *Mainland China* of an over 2,000-character essay penned by Xu Zhangrun, former Professor of Law at Beijing's prestigious Tsinghua University who has near iconic status among China's academics and intellectuals. Separately, the White House released a toughly worded 16-page document titled "The United States Strategic Approach to China" on May 20, which put the spotlight on the strained US-China relationship that has adversely impacted China's economy and realisation of its 'Two Centenary' goals. Quite interestingly, the document comments: "Our approach is not premised on determining a particular end state for China", possibly to assure the CCP that the American objective is not to destroy it!

Preparatory to the CPPCC and NPC plenums, Xinhua (May 15) reported that the Politburo met on May 15 to discuss the draft of the State Council's Government Work Report that Chinese Premier Li Keqiang would present to the third meeting of the 13th NPC. Xinhua said the meeting believed that in the past year "China's development has faced many difficult challenges", but "the Party Central Committee, with Comrade Xi Jinping at the core" united all the people to overcome difficulties and complete the main goals and tasks of the year. It said the Party Central Committee has made epidemic prevention and control a top priority. The meeting, it said, "emphasised that the current global epidemic situation and the world economic situation are still grim and complex, and the challenges facing China's development are unprecedented". It claimed "to do a good job in the government this year", the "strong leadership of the Party Central Committee with Comrade Xi Jinping at the core, and under the guidance of Xi Jinping's socialist ideology with Chinese characteristics in the new era" was necessary. It emphasised the importance of expanding domestic demand, achieving the goal of tackling poverty, promoting the agricultural harvest and increasing the farmers' incomes.

Some 2,158 CPPCC delegates and 2,878 Deputies to the NPC, who included the 290 Deputies representing the People's Liberation Army (PLA) and People's Armed Police (PAP), assembled in Beijing's Great Hall of the People from May 21 for the week-long plenary sessions. As per practice, CPPCC delegates were permitted to sit-in on NPC meetings though not vote.

On May 21, the opening day of the third session of the 13th National Committee of the Chinese People's Political Consultative Conference (CPPCC), Wang Yang, CPPCC Chairman and PBSC member, in his report announced: "We will ensure the long-term stability of 'one country, two systems. "We will continue to support the improvement of the implementation of the systems and mechanisms of the Constitution and Basic Law." *The Global Times* (May 21) said the CPPCC would also organise people from minority ethnic groups and religious fields to hold coordination meetings; strengthen members from Hong Kong and Macao on their political responsibilities in carrying out their missions centred on the "one China, two systems" principle; firmly support the implementations of the Constitution and the Basic Law in the Special Administrative Regions (SARs); and deepen exchanges between the Chinese Mainland and people from Taiwan island. The CPPCC would deepen work on building consensus. Guided by patriotism and socialism, it would seek common ground while shelving differences and building consensus among all domestic and overseas Chinese in realising the Chinese people's rejuvenation.

Later, on May 21, representatives from Beijing's Hong Kong and Macao Affairs Office (HKMAO) met the Hong Kong Deputies to the NPC to explain the details of the National Security Law. Xia Baolong, a close, old associate of Chinese President Xi Jinping and Vice Chairman of the CPPCC National

Committee, who was recently appointed Director of the HKMAO, was present. According to *Ta Kung Pao* (May 28), meeting 200 CPPCC delegates on the final day of the plenary sessions on May 28 in Beijing, Xia Baolong said it is "Hong Kong independence", tyranny and external hostile forces that cause harm to Hong Kong. These forces, especially the United States, attempt to turn Hong Kong into an independent or semi-independent region. They want to undermine the central government's overall governance of Hong Kong or even seize Hong Kong's governance and turn Hong Kong into their colony. He warned, "We must not underestimate the determination of the central authorities ... to implement the 'one country, two systems' policy". Xia Baolong also quoted President Xi Jinping's three "unchanging" positions on the central government's stance on Hong Kong last year, including his unwavering determination to safeguard national sovereignty, security and development interests, his unwavering determination to implement the "one country, two systems" policy, and his opposition to naysayers. He asserted that the determination of external forces to interfere in Hong Kong affairs is unwavering.

A Tibet Autonomous Region (TAR) delegation led by TAR Party Secretary Wu Yingjie and which included China's Minister of Public Security Zhao Kezhi, participated in the deliberations. State Councillor and Minister of Public Security Zhao Kezhi said, "We must do our best on the anti-separatism campaign and the implementation of various measures to maintain stability, strengthen infrastructure construction of stability, make preparations for long-term struggle."

There were some CPPCC delegates whose suggestions attracted the notice of China's official media. Mutanlip Khasem, a member of the CPPCC and Deputy Head of the Xinjiang Uyghur Autonomous Region People's Congress Standing Committee, said on the sidelines of the 'Big Two' meetings that the Xinjiang Uyghur Autonomous Region has recorded no terror related incidents in the past three and half years. He said after the 18th Party Congress, the region struck hard and maintained high pressure on the three forces of separatism, extremism and terrorism, and effectively contained the spread of terrorism in Xinjiang. Criticising the so-called Uyghur Human Rights Policy Act of 2019 passed by the US House of Representatives, he said its purpose is to sow dissension among various ethnic groups in China and that the anti-China forces deliberately smear, vilify and demonise China.

Gonjo Chozin, a CPPCC member from Zhari township in Tibet said, "The poverty alleviation work in Tibet has achieved a decisive victory. Our poverty alleviation measures are systematic. At the grassroots level, actions speaks louder than words. Our work matters for the last mile of ending extreme poverty in Tibet. Only by doing all the poverty reduction work wholeheartedly can we really help the ones who are in need." She added, "During the poverty eradication process, we met a lot of challenges, as we focused on meeting such demands as a proper arrangement to help them settle down. We encouraged them to join in our efforts to get off from poverty." The state-owned China Global Television Network (CGTN) added that by the end of 2019, all 19 counties and county-level prefectures in the Tibet Autonomous Region, which was known as one of the regions with the highest poverty rates in China, were lifted out of poverty.

Zhao Xiaojin, Party Chief of the China Academy of Space Technology (CAST) and a member of the 13th CPPCC National Committee, said (May 23) that the Chinese space industry insiders are considering using the country's upcoming space station as a facility for large-scale space-borne biology experiments in order to constantly increase China's ability to safeguard its biosecurity. He disclosed that China plans to send two more advanced Earth observation satellites from the Gaofen satellite family in 2020 and will conduct a Mars sample return mission by around 2030, as well as a Jovian system probe mission.

Wu Changde, CPPCC member and former Deputy Director of the CMC Political Work Department suggested arrangements for the employment of veterans. He said job security for veterans is critical for maintaining social stability and keeping employment stable. It is also important for stabilising and boosting the military's will and morale and strengthening national defence and military development. Wu Changde suggested: (i) education and guidance should be strengthened, and former ideological concepts should be changed. As veterans are valuable for economic and social development, the Chinese military and localities should make joint efforts to ensure their employment. At the same time, veterans should also take the initiative to adapt to the needs of local economic and social development and take bold steps to start their careers at the forefront of the market economy after demobilisation or retirement. (ii) The key to achieving high-quality and full employment for veterans is to rely on secondary vocational institutions to conduct employment skills training, formulate qualification certification standards, step up support and strengthen supervision and management to ensure the quality of training. Vocational and technical colleges and enterprises could cooperate so that veterans can sign work contracts upon entering the school and accept targeted training in correspondence with their respective positions. They could get relevant training on grassroots organisation work and leadership management and be assigned to the municipal or county Party committee schools, or relevant colleges and universities, for special short-term training courses.

Wang Lianying, CPPCC member and Deputy Director of the Military Sports Training Centre under the CMC Training and Administration Department, made three proposals: (a) scientific research on military sports shall be intensified to better guide military training and the Military Sports Training Centre shall provide good services for the troops in that area; (b) training of military sports talents in grassroot military units shall be improved to make them more capable in organising training; (c) new ways and methods shall be explored to better serve the service members, such as inviting military sports experts and stars to answer their questions online.

President Xi Jinping met CPPCC delegates from the economic sector attending a joint group meeting on May 23. He joined them in the discussion and heard their comments and suggestions.

Chinese Premier Li Keqiang, speaking to the CPPCC, dropped the word 'peaceful' whilst talking about the unification of Taiwan. Meanwhile, the People's Liberation Army (PLA) Sichuan Academy of Fine Arts, published some images simulating the takeover of Taiwan by the PLA. This was corrected in the final Government Work Report approved by the NPC.

All seven Politburo Standing Committee members, including Vice President Wang Qishan and the Vice Chairmen of the CPPCC, attended the opening session of the CPPCC. None of them was wearing a mask while everyone else was!

*(This article was published by the Centre for China Analysis and Strategy, New Delhi, on June 15, 2020.)*

# 14. An Assessment of the Second Plenum of China's 13th National People's Congress

As per tradition, China convened the plenary sessions of its top political advisory body, the Chinese People's Political Consultative Conference (CPPCC) and China's version of a Parliament, the National People's Congress (NPC), in the Great Hall of the People in Beijing in the first fortnight of March. Popularly referred to as the '*Lianghui*', or 'Big Two', the plenary sessions set the agenda for the year ahead. Some 2,158 delegates of the CPPCC and 2,948 Deputies of the NPC, gathered in Beijing from March 9-11, 2019 and March 5-15, 2019 respectively to formally accord the approval of the entire 89 million-strong Chinese Communist Party (CCP) to the policies, programmes and budget of the CCP leadership for the coming year.

The backdrop to the plenary sessions was the dissatisfaction with Xi Jinping and his policies that has been spreading throughout China since the latter half of last year. Senior Party cadres and reputed Chinese academics like the former editor of the Communist Youth League's (CYL's) official newspaper Li Datong, Peking University alumnus Fan Liqun and Tsinghua University's Xu Zhangrun, have publicly articulated their discontent, including against the abolition of age and term-limits for the posts of Chinese President and Vice President and the CCP Politburo. They specifically warned against any return after thirty years to the 'one-man' rule of Mao Zedong. Worker discontent has also been on the rise, with 1,795 strikes—higher than in the previous year—reported across China. They occurred in every province of China except the Tibet Autonomous Region (TAR). Protests by veteran and demobilised soldiers added to the CCP leadership's anxieties and their concern is reflected in the series of measures adopted since mid-2018 to ameliorate the unhappiness of veterans and demobilised personnel. Chinese Premier Li Keqiang specifically referred to the need for promoting their welfare in his "Report on the Work of the Government" presented to the NPC on March 5.

Economists and owners of private enterprises too were unusually candid in their criticism of government policies. Renmin University Prof. Xiang Songzuo highlighted serious doubts about the economy at a public function, which was promptly censored on the Chinese internet, declaring that a "research group of an important institution" released an internal report stating China's Gross Domestic Product (GDP) growth this year was about 1.67 per cent! Chen Hongtian, Chairman of the Cheung Kei Group and member of the CPPCC, warned China's private business entrepreneurs to prepare for a "winter colder and longer than expected". Others were critical, for example, of the restrictions in the Party's Constitution on private property, and failure to reform the State owned Enterprises (SoEs) which, they said, had, on the contrary, expanded to enter every area of economic activity. There is disaffection among students and PLA personnel too.

To prevent disruptive incidents and avoid embarrassment to China's leadership, elevated levels of security were enforced in the period around the meetings. Beijing, Tianjin and other cities initiated "stability maintenance" measures and Chinese State Councillor and Minister of Public Security, Zhao Kezhi was in Tianjin from February 22 to 23, to supervise the safety measures. Li Chunsheng, head of the Guangdong Provincial Public Security Department, told public security officials in Guangzhou that there were sensitive anniversaries this year and warned that "hostile forces inside China have long marked this year as an important time to implement their plan—which is a vain attempt—to overthrow our system."

Enhanced security measures were similarly evident in Tibet because of the 60th anniversary this year of the abortive 1959 uprising against Chinese rule in Tibet and the 14th Dalai Lama's flight to India. Tibet was declared off-limits to journalists and foreigners for an extended period till April 30 and TAR leaders inspected Tibetan Buddhist monasteries and convened a series of conferences of security cadres to 'uncover' and 'eliminate' the 'double-faced cadres' owing loyalty to the Dalai Lama. Chinese armed police personnel and armoured police cars staged a show of force in Lhasa on March 7.

Despite these signs of discontent, the reports presented to the plenary sessions by Chinese Premier Li Keqiang and CPPCC Chairman Wang Yang bore the firm imprimatur of Chinese President Xi Jinping and affirmed his authority.

Reports presented to the NPC by Chinese Premier Li Keqiang, the Ministry of Finance and National Development and Reform Commission (NDRC) all opened with acknowledgments of Xi Jinping's position as the "core of the Party". Chinese Premier Li Keqiang's report contained 15 references to Xi Jinping and not even one to Mao Zedong, Deng Xiaoping or his predecessors. Only Xi Jinping's political ideology found mention in the reports. Of the 15 tasks mentioned in his report, the first two listed following "the strong leadership of the Party Central Committee with Xi Jinping at the core" and "Xi Jinping Thought on Socialism with Chinese Characteristics in the New Era". The final day too closed with the exhortation, "The Chinese nation is in a crucial period of great rejuvenation. We must be more closely united around the Party Central Committee with Comrade Xi Jinping as the core."

Chinese Premier Li Keqiang took over 100 minutes to read the Report on the Work of the Government to the 2,948 NPC Deputies. The 16,160-word, 44-page report attributed China's achievements of the past year to the leadership of the Chinese Communist Party (CCP) "with Xi Jinping at its core". Li Keqiang said, "We owe our achievements of the past year to the strong leadership of the Party Central Committee with Comrade Xi Jinping at its core, to the sound guidance of 'Xi Jinping Thought on Socialism with Chinese Characteristics for a New Era', and to the concerted efforts of the Party, the military, and the people of all ethnic groups in China." Specifically endorsing Xi Jinping's "core position" in the Party, he declared, "We should resolutely uphold General Secretary Xi Jinping's core position on the Party Central Committee and in the Party as a whole, and resolutely uphold the Party Central Committee's authority and its centralized, unified leadership. And we should maintain a high degree of unity in thought, stance, and action with the Party Central Committee, with Comrade Xi Jinping at its core, and exercise full and rigorous self-discipline in the Party".

Li Keqiang's report acknowledged the pressures that China had faced the previous year mainly because of the US-initiated 'tariff war' and strain in Sino-US relations and candidly admitted, "Setbacks in economic globalization, challenges to multilateralism, shocks in the international financial market, and especially the China-US economic and trade frictions, had an adverse effect on the production and business operations of some companies and on market expectations". Nevertheless, reviewing the previous year's performance, he claimed that the "joint efforts to pursue the Belt and Road Initiative are producing a pace-setting effect, cooperation mechanisms for countries along its routes are steadily improving, and economic cooperation, trade, and cultural and people-to-people exchanges under the Initiative have gathered momentum". He also said growth in hi-tech industries and equipment manufacturing had outstripped that of other industries and there had been a number of technology innovations with an average of 18,000 new businesses opening daily.

Chinese Premier Li Keqiang's report, however, anticipated a tougher year ahead. He said, "In pursuing development this year, we will face a graver and more complicated environment as well as risks and challenges... that are greater in number and size." He added, "We must be fully prepared for a tough struggle." Indicating that China will nevertheless press ahead with its goals, he underscored that "China is still in an important period of strategic opportunity".

In a bid to stimulate the economy, Li Keqiang told NPC delegates that China would aim to deliver nearly Yuan 2 trillion ($ 298 billion) of cuts in taxes and other company fees. A Value-Added Tax (VAT) for the transportation and construction sectors will be sliced from 10 per cent to 9 per cent, and VAT for manufacturers will fall from 16 per cent to 13 per cent. On the concluding day of the session on March 15, the National People's Congress (NPC) passed the Foreign Investment Law (FIL). The law was fast-tracked as part of efforts to appease the US in the ongoing trade negotiations. To ensure its quick passage, legislators scrapped some of the thornier issues raised in a previous draft, and instead passed a relatively vague piece of legislation. The practical implications of the law are, therefore, still unknown. However addressing the concerns of foreign businesses, Chinese Premier Li Keqiang said at his press conference (March 15), "The government will introduce a series of matching regulations and directives to protect the rights and interests of foreign investors." He reiterated, "These will be the important things for the government to do in the following weeks and months to see that this law will be truly operable."

The Report on the Work of the Government took note of the popular discontent. Li Keqiang said, "There is still public dissatisfaction in many areas such as education, health care, elderly care, housing, food and drug safety and income distribution". He noted that there are 250 million people over 60 years of age. He also acknowledged that the difficulties faced by private firms and small and micro businesses in accessing affordable financing have not been effectively solved.

Highlights of this NPC session included the lowered GDP growth rate of 6—6.5 per cent for 2019; commitment to provide 11 million new jobs; reduce rural poverty by 10 million; increasing the national defence budget by 7.5 per cent to approximately US$ 177.6 billion; and approval of a 5 per cent increase in national security expenditure. Pensions were raised by 5 per cent. There was emphasis on innovation, Research and Development (R&D), agriculture and food grain production and rural development. An interesting disclosure was that there are 80 million taxpayers in China. Li Keqiang stated that the rate of increase of the defence budget was a "little faster" than the GDP growth and emphasised the need to "realise the dream of national rejuvenation"!

He also dwelt on military-civil integration and military modernisation. Unprecedentedly, the Premier's report admitted that "China faced a complicated and challenging domestic and international environment of a kind rarely seen in many years, and its economy came under new downward pressure". In an obvious attempt to ease US pressure, his report omitted all reference to the hi-technology 'Made in China-2025'. Similarly, mention of the Belt and Road Initiative (BRI) was buried in a single line in a sub-paragraph on domestic connectivity.

The Finance Ministry report mentioned that an Individual Tax Law is being considered. It reiterated the curbs on ostentation, prohibited the purchase of official vehicles and imposed cuts on travel, hospitality, etc. The budget for poverty alleviation, a programme personally driven by Chinese President Xi Jinping, was increased by 8 per cent to Yuan 126.095 billion with particular mention of the TAR and Xinjiang, while Yuan 577.6 billion was set aside for infrastructure investment, with Yuan 200 billion for railways including the Sichuan-Tibet Railway. Other highlights were the 7.4 per cent increase for the Ministry of Foreign Affairs raising its budget to 62.71 billion Yuan and enhancement by 13.4 per cent of the investment in Science and Technology (S&T), which now totals Yuan 354.312 billion.

But there was an attempt at dismissing reports on debts incurred by nations participating in the BRI. China's Vice Minister of Commerce, Qian Keming, said at a press conference (March 9) in Beijing that trade and infrastructure strategy was not a "one-way street". He said, "Historically, the international debt problem is an old problem. While some countries' debts have risen, this is the result of long-term accumulation." Giving the example of Pakistan and the China-Pakistan Economic Corridor, he said 42 per cent of the country's debt was from multilateral institutions, while "only around 10 per cent" could be attributed to China. Referring to criticism of the BRI, he said, "Only those who need money are willing to borrow. From the perspective of lenders, as long as your relationship is good and the funds are safe, then you will be willing to lend. I don't think third parties should worry about the borrowers and lenders." He added that across Asia, US$1.7 trillion in infrastructure investment was needed every year up to 2030, but only half of that amount was being met. Qian Keming added that the Commerce Ministry would step up economic and trade cooperation zones and investment activities overseas to facilitate development of the belt and road programme.

NPC Chairman Li Zhanshu delivered the NPC's annual work report, which laid out the priorities for the coming year. He said they will continue to deliberate on the civil code and listed the eight laws presently before the legislature namely: (i) Amendment No. 11 to the Criminal Law; (ii) Basic Healthcare and Health Promotion Law; (iii) Property Tax Law; (iv) Export Control Law; (v) Community Corrections Law (vi) Civil-Military Integration Development Law; (vii) Veterans Protection Law; and (viii) Governmental Sanctions Law. The NPC will also revise six laws: Securities Law; Officers in Active Service Law; Military Service Law; People's Armed Police Law; Organic Law of the National People's Congress; and Rules of procedure of the National People's Congress. The NPC will additionally begin studying and drafting the Biological Safety Law and Yangtze River Protection Law.

Of these, the most talked about is the Property Tax Law. Observers say if the government ever introduces a property tax, it will have major ramifications for the property market and the larger economy. More importantly, it could change the relationship between the citizens and the state.

On the sidelines of the NPC sessions and probably to make it easier for enterprises to access funds, the People's Bank of China (PBoC) Governor Yi Gang said (March 7), China has cut the ratio of cash that banks must hold as reserves five times in the past year, in the face of the weakest economic growth in 28 years amid slowing consumption and the trade conflict with Washington. He revealed that the yuan-dollar exchange rate has been a subject of discussion in trade talks with Washington. While Yi Gang claimed, "There has been an obvious increase in support from financial institutions to small and private business recently," PBoC Vice Governor Pan Gongsheng said the central bank has a goal of increasing loans by large commercial banks to small companies by 30 per cent from 2018—a target Premier Li Keqiang mentioned in his government work report. The central bank also appeared to be managing investor expectations on the traditionally risk-free bond market, with the Deputy Governor saying it's good to have some defaults. He noted there was an increase in bond defaults last year, but the level is still lower than in most other countries. [Comment: Chinese officials use the term "56789" to refer to the importance of private enterprise. These companies, many of them small, are said to account for 50 per cent of tax revenue, 60 per cent of Gross Domestic Product (GDP), 70 per cent of innovation, 80 per cent of urban labor, and 90 per cent of the total number of companies in the country.]

Interesting were the comments of Yin Zhongqing, Deputy Director of the NPC Financial and Economic Affairs Committee, wherein he cast doubts on the accuracy of the economic data furnished by the government. *Beijing News* quoted him as saying, at a press conference on March 10, during the NPC, that the total amount of all local GDP added together is greater than the national GDP due to data fraud. He said, "There is a discrepancy between regional and national GDP figures and it has negatively affected the credibility of the government. Some local governments tend to cook their books, inflate some statistics, or conceal some data to stand out from the competition." Yin Zhongqing added that a number or factors contribute to data fraud. First, people do not comply with the law and data fraud persists despite repeated crackdowns. Second, local governments, businesses, and residents are overburdened with data calls from different government agencies. Third, many government agencies apply different standards, resulting in inconsistencies in the data collected. Fourth, punishment over data fraud is "too light." Fifth, a lot of statistical indicators are still defined according to the planned economy and do not reflect actual development.

The Tibet Autonomous Region (TAR) figured at the NPC. TAR Party Secretary Wu Yingjie addressed a press conference of 127 foreign and Chinese journalists. Speaking at the NPC meetings on March 6, in Beijing, the Mayor of Lhasa and Deputy Party Secretary of TAR, Go Khok, stated that the TAR government had restricted religious activities in Tibet and that the number of days spent observing religious events, and the number of people attending them, both had been reduced to less than 10 per cent. He told Tibetan Deputies and journalists in the Great Hall of the People, "In 2018, Lhasa … took a clear-cut stand in eliminating the negative influence the Dalai Lama exerted via religion and took great effort in ridding the passive religious influence."

The *People's Daily* (March 9) reported that Politburo Standing Committee (PBSC) members Xi Jinping, Li Zhanshu, Wang Yang, Wang Huning, and Zhao Leji participated in the deliberation sessions for Fujian, Jiangsu, Tibet, Xinjiang, and Hainan, respectively. Xi Jinping focussed on fighting poverty, promoting innovation and entrepreneurship, and strengthening cross-Strait integration. There were specific references during the NPC session and in Li Keqiang's report to Taiwan and the '1992 consensus'. Li Zhanshu said that the Foreign Investment Law shows China's "clear stance" on pursuing win-win strategies and building an "open world economy." Zhao Leji spoke about accelerating plans for Hainan's experimental free trade zone, as well as the importance of strengthening supervision. Wang Yang and Wang Huning participated in Tibet's and Xinjiang's deliberation sessions, respectively, and emphasised promoting national unity and stability in each region.

Xi Jinping also attended a plenary meeting of representatives from the People's Liberation Army (PLA) and People's Armed Police (PAP). He said it is essential to complete the final tasks of the 13th Five-Year Plan for 'military construction' by the deadline in 2020. He emphasised that it is necessary to strengthen inspection and oversight, including with regard to finance and corruption. Speaking about the 14th Five-Year Plan for 'military construction', Xi Jinping said the plan must be adapted to the "strategic requirements" of national development, security, and the military. Outlining some of the military's duties, he said they were wide-ranging and included protecting China's sovereignty, maintaining social stability, supporting local economic and social development, responding to disasters, and helping "impoverished villages and people." CMC Vice Chairman Xu Qiliang chaired the session where all members of the CMC, namely, Zhang Youxia, Wei Fenghe, Li Zuocheng, Miao Hua and Zhang Shengmin were in attendance.

While relations with foreign countries do not receive much attention at these meetings, reflecting the tension in the China-India and India-Pakistan relationships this year, India came in for lengthy mention. On March 13, *Global Times* reported that An Ran, a Deputy to the NPC and Professor at South China University of Technology in Guangzhou (Guangdong province), had proposed that the country allow residents in the border area with India to trade to improve China-India relations, reduce military confrontations and benefit the local inhabitants. He said this could also showcase the achievements of China's Tibet Autonomous Region to India and other countries. He said that the proposal was based on field work conducted by a group of researchers from Yunnan University in Southwest China. Yunnan province borders the Tibet region, Vietnam, Laos and Myanmar. Professor Guo Jianbin, the group's team leader, told the *Global Times* that his team went to some counties, including Lhozhag, Lhunze in Shannan prefecture and Medog and Zayu in the city of Nyingchi, "South Tibet" in July and August 2018, and found that because the restrictions of the militaries of China and India in the illegal "McMahon Line" are "tight, residents in the border areas are not allowed to cross the line freely". However, in some areas, some residents, mainly those from the Lhoba ethnic minority group, have crossed the "line" to trade. He added, "We found that the villages in the border areas have wide roads and a clean environment. If China allows residents living on the other side to trade, all these achievements and developments will help better unite the residents in border areas." Separately, Hu Zhiyong, a Research Fellow at the Shanghai Academy of Social Sciences' Institute of International Relations, told the *Global Times* (March 13) that the move could help deepen understanding between China and India. He added, "Indian Prime Minister Narendra Modi may welcome it to gain support in the elections", however, China should watch India's moves as India has been suspicious and hostile toward China.

There were some other interesting, though tangential, references to the India-China relationship. On the sidelines of the NPC on March 8, Chinese Foreign Minister Wang Yi claimed that Beijing had played a "constructive role" in defusing tensions between India and Pakistan over Pulwama and, referring to the "historic" Wuhan meeting asserted that "the strategic understandings of our leaders trickle down to our people and become a common view". He said that New Delhi and Islamabad should "meet each other halfway" to deescalate the crisis. Describing Pakistan as "China's iron brother", Wang Yi said, "China has stressed from the beginning the need to exercise calm and restraint, prevent an escalation, find out what has happened, and resolve the matter through dialogue." He added, "China hopes that Pakistan and India will transform the crisis into an opportunity and meet each other halfway. We advise both parties to quickly turn this page and seek fundamental, long-term improvement in their relations."

Apparently to balance the comments, Xinhua reported that at the same press conference, Chinese Foreign Minister Wang Yi spoke in positive terms about the India-China relationship. He said China and India should be each other's partner in pursuing their respective dreams and each other's important opportunity for advancing their respective economies. He said the two countries should collectively make due contribution to Asia's revitalisation and prosperity. Wang Yi added that the historic meeting between President Xi Jinping and Prime Minister Narendra Modi last year has created a new model of high-level interactions between the two countries, enhanced the mutual trust and friendship of leaders of the two countries, and set the direction for future relations. Government departments on both sides have done a lot and made considerable progress in following through on many of the understandings reached by the leaders. Wang Yi said, "The priority now is to see that the strategic understandings of our leaders trickle down to our people and become a common view and conscious efforts." He added that China will work with India to comprehensively strengthen pragmatic cooperation and people-to-people exchanges, so that "our friendship and cooperation will surge ahead like the Yangtze and the Ganges, giving strong and sustained impetus to our relationship."

The stand-off at Doklam, which seems to still rankle the Chinese, also figured obliquely. Discussing China's military modernisation with two Chinese military experts on the state-owned China Global Television Network (CGTN), well known Chinese TV anchor Yang Rui referred to Doklam during his programme on March 16. Earlier on February 15, the state-owned *PLA Daily* reported that 37 NPC Deputies had proposed amendments to China's Criminal Law to curb military-related rumours online to protect the image of the People's Liberation Army (PLA). Jiang Yong, Political Commissar of the PLA Beijing Garrison Command and one of the NPC Deputies, specifically cited, "China offering soft loans of 20 billion yuan ($2.95 billion) to India in exchange for their retreat" as a "major false rumour." This rumour which spread rapidly across China (and was reported in my article in the *Sunday Guardian* on September 2, 2017) had caused serious concern to China's leadership. It was, very unusually, denied at the time by China's Ministry of National Defence, its Ministry of Foreign Affairs (MFA) and the CCP's official mouthpiece, *People's Daily.*

*(This article was published by the Centre for China Analysis and Strategy, New Delhi, on April 7, 2020.)*

# 15. An Assessment of the 13th Session of China's 13th NPC, May 2020

China held its 'Big Two'—as the plenary sessions of its top advisory body, the Chinese People's Political Consultative Conference (CPPCC) and its version of a Parliament, the National People's Congress (NPC) are called—from May 21 to May 28, 2020. Annually held in March, the plenary sessions were delayed this year because of the coronavirus pandemic. The pandemic's shadow was evident in the caution that the plenum would be shortened to a week instead of the usual ten days with restrictions on the number of press conferences and correspondents allowed to attend. Provision for video conferencing was, for the first time, made for those not physically attending the CPPCC and NPC Plenums.

Reflecting the adverse impact of the coronavirus on China's economy, Han Fangming, Vice Chairman of the Foreign Affairs Committee of the CPPCC National Committee, set the tone for frugality. He said, "Due to the COVID-19 epidemic and the shortened session, the accommodation and meeting venues for CPPCC members and NPC delegates are simpler, stricter and more efficient." Hotels and meeting rooms for the sessions provided curtailed services, with fewer newspapers, and no banners, red carpets, flowers, bars or cafes. CPPCC members and NPC delegates were asked to bring their own pens or notepads, and just a single bottle of water, a tea cup, and a pack of antiseptic wipes were provided at the venue. Each member and delegate was given a full-page reminder about how to avoid catching the virus or block its spreading. 'Social distancing' was enforced and attendees were encouraged not to shake hands, congregate outside the meeting rooms or linger in confined places, as well as not to leave their hotels or the convention areas without permission from the organisers.

To burnish the credibility of the CCP which got dented particularly during the coronavirus pandemic, the state-owned China Central Television (CCTV) on the day of the 'Big Two' sessions, reported (May 21), that CCP members had donated RMB 8.36 billion (US$ 1.18 billion) for the fight against the coronavirus in the past three months. It said all the money was sent to the 'Party Central Committee' for redistribution.

A surprise development intended to shore Chinese President Xi Jinping's position after the spate of personal criticism he was subjected to in the past few months, including calls for him to step down, was the announcement on May 21 that 17 Deputies to the NPC had been asked to resign. Four among them were senior People's Liberation Army (PLA) officers who were charged with "serious violations of discipline and law". The list of PLA Deputies to the NPC, which was finalised on May 10, 2020, did not mention their names. Corruption, which is often listed as one of the charges, was not mentioned suggesting that doubts about their political reliability or factionalism could have been factors for their dismissal. Two of the officers, Lt Gen Rao Kaixun, the former Deputy Commander and Chief of Staff of the PLA Strategic Support Force (SSF) and Maj Gen Meng Zhongkang, former Political Commissar of the Jiangsu Military District, had outstanding career records. The unexpected dismissal of the NPC Deputies confirms that Xi Jinping continues to closely monitor the PLA and the Party for any signs of factionalism or wavering in political reliability. More importantly, their dismissal would have sent a chill through PLA and Party cadres, enabling Xi Jinping to further tighten his grip.

There were some developments, however, that were timed to coincide with the opening of the 'Big Two' on May 21 and embarrass China's leadership. Following the 'open' letter posted on WeChat on May 1, listing 15 demands, 43-year old Zhang Xuezhong, a Shanghai-based Chinese constitutional lawyer who was subsequently detained, posted an 'open' letter addressed to all NPC Deputies on WeChat on May 9, calling for reforms and freedom of speech. Describing China's governance as very backward, he asked the NPC Deputies to create a representative committee to draft a Constitution conforming to "modern political principles". He urged the NPC to pass resolutions, which enshrine that no political party should enjoy the "status of a national public service institution". Meanwhile, a 20-minute audio recording of retired senior Central Party School Professor Cai Xia's scathing criticism of Xi Jinping and the CCP circulated widely over the Chinese web for almost a month! This was followed by the over 2,000-character essay penned by Xu Zhangrun, former

Professor of Law at Beijing's prestigious Tsinghua University and who has near iconic status among China's academics and intellectuals, advising NPC Deputies on twelve things they should do. A strident critic of Xi Jinping since 2018, banned from writing and using the social media, Xu Zhangrun had the essay published in the Hong Kong magazine *Mainland China* on May 21.

Xu Zhangrun blamed "the Axlerod [that is, Xi Jinping] and the cabal" for the rapid spread of the coronavirus across the world and China's isolation globally. In addition to demanding a State Council White Paper investigating actions taken during the initial stages of the outbreak and especially between January 3 and 7, Xu Zhangrun demanded that all officials be required to publicly disclose their assets; remove Communist Party cells from all academic and educational institutions; enshrine the protection of private property in the Constitution and return the right of ownership to the people themselves; and "eliminate the state-sanctioned monopoly exercised by the Communist Party as China's sole landlord". It is interesting that critics of Xi Jinping and the CCP continue to be able to post their criticisms on Chinese social media platforms.

Separately, putting the spotlight on the strained US-China relationship, which is adversely impacting China's economy and its 'Two Centenary' goals, was the toughly worded 16-page document titled "The United States Strategic Approach to China" released by the White House on May 20. The document effectively restricts engagement with China as US policy. It announced, "Our goal is to protect the United States' vital national interests, as articulated in the four pillars of the 2017 National Security Strategy (NSS) of the United States of America". With this document, the US government essentially shed all pretence of cooperation and engagement with the People's Republic of China (PRC) and opted for a competitive approach. It could be the prelude to tougher actions against China. Rather interesting is the comment, "Our approach is not premised on determining a particular end state for China", possibly to assure the Chinese Communist Party (CCP) that the American objective is not to destroy it.

Preparatory to the CPPCC and NPC Plenums, Xinhua (May 15) reported that the Politburo met on May 15 to discuss the draft of the State Council's Government Work Report that Chinese Premier Li Keqiang would present to the third meeting of the 13th NPC. Xinhua said the meeting believed that in the past year "China's development has faced many difficult challenges", but "the Party Central Committee with Comrade Xi Jinping at the core" united all the people to overcome difficulties and complete the main goals and tasks of the year. It said the Party Central Committee has made epidemic prevention and control a top priority. The meeting "emphasised that the current global epidemic situation and the world economic situation are still grim and complex, and the challenges facing China's development are unprecedented". It claimed that "to do a good job in the government this year" the "strong leadership of the Party Central Committee with Comrade Xi Jinping at the core, and under the guidance of Xi Jinping's socialist ideology with Chinese characteristics in the new era" was necessary. It emphasised the importance of expanding domestic demand, achieving the goal of tackling poverty, and promoting the agricultural harvest and increasing farmers' incomes.

*The South China Morning Post* (May 20) said that PLA officers were pushing for a defence budget hike of 9 per cent, or higher than the 7.5 per cent increase of last year. Separately, China's economists were debating in the run-up to the plenum on whether, in view of the bleak and uncertain economic situation, the Government Work Report should at all mention a growth rate target. Items assessed as likely to figure in the Premier's report included measures to alleviate distress caused by the pandemic, Chinese President Xi Jinping's 'Poverty Alleviation' programme, the huge problem of unemployment, and jobs for China's almost nine million graduates. By March 2020, the number of unemployed in China had jumped to an estimated over 70-80 million from approximately 17-20 million in 2019.

Some 2,878 Deputies to the NPC, who included the 290 Deputies representing the PLA, assembled in Beijing's Great Hall of the People from May 21 for the week-long plenary sessions. As per practice, the 2,158 CPPCC delegates were permitted to sit in the NPC meetings though not vote.

A day before its inaugural session on May 22, the NPC elected a 174-member presidium, with Wang Chen as Secretary General of the NPC session. The meeting also adopted the agenda for the session: deliberate on the report on the work of the government; review the report on the implementation of the 2019 plan and on the draft plan for national economic and social development in 2020; review the report on the execution of the central and local budgets for 2019 and on the draft central and local budgets for 2020; deliberate on the bill put forward by the NPC Standing Committee on reviewing the draft civil code; deliberate on the bill put forward by the NPC Standing Committee on reviewing a draft decision of the NPC on establishing and improving the legal system and enforcement mechanisms for the Hong Kong Special Administrative Region to safeguard national security; deliberate on the work report of the NPC Standing Committee; deliberate on the work report of the Supreme People's Court; and deliberate on the work report of the Supreme People's Procuratorate.

The *China Daily* pointed out that the Draft Civil Code to be deliberated on by the CPPCC and NPC consists of seven volumes, and includes general provisions and sections on property, contracts, personality rights, marriage and family, inheritance and torts. Shi Jiayou, Professor at Renmin University of China and Executive Director of the National Research Centre of Civil and Commercial Law, told the state-owned China Global Television Network (CGTN) that compilation of personal rights in a separate volume is a major development and innovation in the democratic legislation and civil code. It will help strengthen legal protection of personal dignity and individual rights.

Chinese Premier Li Keqiang presented the draft of the Government Work Report for approval to the NPC on May 22. The report was only 9,500 (Chinese) characters in length, or half last year's 16,000-character report. Predictably, it praised Chinese President Xi Jinping with 13 mentions of him and his position as "the core" of the CCP. There was no reference to Deng Xiaoping or Mao Zedong. The report stressed Party discipline and emphasised that it was the Party's "strong and courageous" leadership that had enabled China to face difficulties. The report mentioned the Party 29 times! It was noticeably temperate in tenor, and subdued while recounting the achievements of the past year and listing the tasks for the coming year. Reflecting on the deleterious impact of the coronavirus pandemic and impending uncertainty, it stated that China had promptly shared information about the outbreak of the coronavirus. The Belt and Road Initiative received very brief mention, with no mention of 'great' progress. In his draft report, Li Keqiang omitted to mention the word "peaceful" while referring to Taiwan's reunification, thereby causing quite a stir. This was rectified in the final version on May 28.

For the first time in 26 years, the report did not set an annual economic growth target for Gross Domestic Product (GDP) as it has since 1994. China's economists had been debating for at least the past two months whether to specify a target growth rate. Because the economic damage is far higher than officially acknowledged by China, and factors like the economic uncertainty caused by the coronavirus and the growing anti-China sentiment that could affect China's exports, the leadership probably decided not to mention a target which it might not be able to reach. It emphasised the difficulties confronting China and extended concessions, tax and fee cuts totalling RMB 500 billion by a year to Micro, Small and Medium Enterprises (MSMEs) and industries to help them recover. It said the reduction in electricity prices by 5 per cent will be extended till the end of the year. Chinese Premier Li Keqiang's report instead prioritised the goals of stabilising employment, alleviating poverty and preventing risks in 2020, but again, without mentioning the target dates as it used to in the past. He said they would create 9 million jobs in the year, a drop from the previous years' 11 million despite the huge surge in unemployment. The budget deficit is slated to rise to Yuan 3.76 trillion (US$ 529 billion) this year, 36 per cent higher than in 2019, while the target for the deficit as a percentage of GDP will increase to "more than 3.6 per cent" from last year's 2.8 per cent, exceeding the 3 per cent threshold which has long been seen by China's policy-makers as a red line that must not be crossed.

At the press conference after the concluding session of the 13th NPC on May 28, the *People's Daily* (May 28) reported that Chinese Premier Li Keqiang said that the government would focus its stimulus measures on domestic economics, while admitting that China is a developing country with a large population and an average annual per capita disposable income of Yuan 30,000 (US$ 4,213.30). There are 600 million people—or two out of every five Chinese—who have low and middle incomes, whose average monthly income is barely Yuan 1,000 (US$ 140.40). He added, "It may be difficult even to rent an apartment with an income of 1,000 yuan in a medium-sized city." Li Keqiang promised to make people's livelihood a high priority. He said the task of poverty alleviation is a "sophisticated commitment" that the CCP General Secretary Xi Jinping has made to the entire society and it must be completed as scheduled this year. There were originally five million people living in poverty. Under the impact of the epidemic, some more people may have fallen back into poverty and the task of poverty alleviation has become even tougher.

Poverty alleviation is a top priority for Xi Jinping and he has been emphasising it during his tours outside Beijing since March 2020. The PLA too is publicising its efforts in poverty alleviation. China has 52 officially recognised 'impoverished counties' with 551,000 rural impoverished people concentrated in the central and western regions. The regions comprise to the Tibet Autonomous Region, four Tibetan-inhabited provinces and four prefectures in the southern Xinjiang Uyghur Autonomous Region, while the three prefectures are Liangshan Yi Autonomous Prefecture in Sichuan province, Nujiang Lisu Autonomous Prefecture in Yunnan province and Linxia Hui Autonomous Prefecture in Gansu province. The official poverty line in China is about US$ 47 per month or Yuan 4,000 per year and covers only about 550,000 people. The Chinese National Bureau of Statistics (NBS) later commented that most of these 600 million people are migrant workers.

The Finance Minister's report approved by the NPC revealed that budgetary cuts had been imposed on most government departments. Central government expenditures are down 0.2 per cent and projected at Yuan 3.5035 trillion. Highlights of a summary breakdown are: Yuan 172.176 billion on general public services, down 13.3 per cent; Yuan 54.305 billion on foreign affairs, a drop of 11.8 per cent; Yuan 1.268 trillion on national defence, up 6.6 per cent; Yuan 183.272 billion on public security, up 0.7 per cent; Yuan 169.909 billion on education, a drop of 7.5 per cent (national spending on education, which includes local outlays, will increase by 5.4 per cent); Yuan 319.651 billion on science and technology, down 9.1 per cent (national spending in this area, which includes local outlays, will rise by 3.1 per cent); Yuan 121.618 billion on stockpiling grain, edible oils, and other materials, up 1 per cent; Yuan 539.943 billion, on debt interest payments, up 18.2 per cent; Yuan 8.3915 trillion to be transferred to local governments, which amount has increased by 12.8 per cent, in a new one-time special payment of Yuan 605 billion for the year. This is to be used for supporting local governments to ensure security in the six areas, with a focus on guaranteeing basic living standards, ensuring normal functioning of primary-level governments, developing the public health system and emergency supply system, and responding to uncertainties in the second half of the year.

China's defence budget was hiked by 6.6 per cent to Yuan 1.268 trillion (US$ 178.2 billion) from last year's allocation of US$ 177.6 billion. The low increase is due to the serious disruption to China's economy by COVID-19. The state-run Xinhua news agency noted that it is the lowest growth rate in recent years. China's *Global Times* (May 22) observed that the 6.6 per cent rise in the defence budget was lower than the 7.5 per cent of 2019, when the defence budget was Yuan 1.19 trillion. It quoted Song Zhongping, a Hong Kong-based retired officer of the PLA Second Artillery and a Chinese military expert and TV commentator, as saying that this year's 6.6 per cent is not a significant slowdown in view of the pandemic. He added, however, that "China is facing national security threats, including those taking place very nearby to China and in non-traditional security fields. Compared to these threats, China's military expenditure was far from enough". Wei Dongxu, a Beijing-based military analyst, told the *Global Times* that the increased defence budget can ensure that the Chinese military's major programmes and key spending fields are not affected by the pandemic and will remain on schedule. Unnamed military experts quoted by the *Global Times* said, "China has huge national defence demands, which is a crucial factor in the military budget. In the post-pandemic period, China faces more military threats from other countries, mainly the US. With Taiwan secessionists becoming more and more rampant, reunification by force with the island of Taiwan is always on the table", adding that in this situation, "increasing the defence budget must not stop". Song Zhongping said, "People should ask first, which countries are threatening China's national security in the first place? They should ask the US, they should ask India, and some other neighbouring countries and regions."

Interesting was the comment of the spokesman of China's Ministry of National Defence, Senior Col Wu Qian. He said (May 26), "China's spending is still lower than what is needed to protect the nation's sovereignty, security and development interests, as well as to carry out its international duties and fulfil the nation's development needs. It is thus reasonable and necessary to keep growing China's military spending in a moderate and stable manner." He said that on the international level, there is the rise of hegemony and power politics, coupled with unilateralism, geopolitical risks and challenges to the current global security order and "the world is not that peaceful." Domestically, Wu Qian said, China is facing an ever more complex security situation as the fight against secessionist movements becomes more intensified. The pro-secession Democratic Progressive Party in Taiwan is "inviting foreign powers to serve its own goals and is going further in its pursuit of separating the country." Security on Chinese soil and of Chinese investments overseas is also facing real threats.

During the NPC session, Chinese President Xi Jinping met the Deputies representing the PLA/PAP (People's Armed Police) and from the Nei Mongol Autonomous Region. Xinhua (May 26) reported that speaking to the PLA/PAP delegations, Chinese President Xi Jinping appreciated the military's response to the coronavirus outbreak. He said the important contributions of the military "once again proved that the people's Army is a heroic force that the Party and people completely trust." He pointed out that efforts to continue national defence and Army construction should proceed in spite of the novel coronavirus pandemic, highlighting the need to "accelerate the preparation for battles, flexibly carry out actual-combat military training, and comprehensively raise the capabilities of our forces to carry out military missions." He said the battle against the novel coronavirus served as a barometer for the effectiveness of the military's reforms and placed new requirements for reform on the military. Xi Jinping exhorted the delegates to "complete the designated reform tasks on time" and, in response to new issues that surfaced because of the outbreak, he "emphasized resolution [of new issues] using thoughts and methods based on reform and innovation." Xi Jinping specifically stressed the need to improve military medical research, strengthen national defence technological innovation, and cultivate talent—particularly through the "three-in-one" (三位一体) training system. The military should "support local economic and social development and winning the tough battle against poverty and assist local [authorities] in doing well the work of maintaining overall social stability." Xi Jinping told the delegates to accelerate Research and Development (R&D) of COVID-19 drugs and vaccines. According to

Xinhua, Xi Jinping told them that "the world is an increasingly dangerous place" and "the epidemic has brought a profound impact on the global landscape and on China's security and development as well." He ordered the military to think about worst-case scenarios, scale up training and battle preparedness, promptly and effectively deal with all sorts of complex situations and resolutely safeguard national sovereignty, security and development interests. Conscious of the low rise in the national defence budget, Xi Jinping told PLA officers not to take the money for granted and that "every penny must be well spent to produce maximum results." In conclusion, Xi Jinping called upon various levels of the Party and government to support national defence and military construction. Among those who attended the meeting were Central Military Commission (CMC) Vice-Chairmen Xu Qiliang and Zhang Youxia, as well as CMC members Wei Fenghe, Li Zuocheng, Miao Hua, and Zhang Shengmin.

Deputies from the Tibet Autonomous Region (TAR) led by TAR Party Secretary Wu Yingjie and including China's Minister of Public Security Zhao Kezhi, participated in the NPC sessions. State Councillor and Minister of Public Security Zhao Kezhi, who was a Deputy to the NPC representing the TAR, said, "We must do our best on the anti-separatism campaign and the implementation of various measures to maintain stability, strengthen infrastructure construction of stability, make preparations for a long-term struggle." At the TAR NPC delegation's review meeting on May 23, TAR Party Secretary Wu Yingjie said that they should "strive to open up a new era of rapid development of Tibet and a new situation of long-term stability." He said they must "embody absolute loyalty to General Secretary Xi Jinping and the Party Central Committee with practical actions." TAR delegates to the NPC and CPPCC session submitted nine proposals focussed on socioeconomic infrastructure development and ecological environment protection. Three proposals were: "Suggestions on Supporting Operation and Maintenance of Heating Projects in Tibet," "Suggestions on Supporting the Construction, Operation and Maintenance of Oxygen Supply Projects in High Altitude Areas in Tibet"; and "Proposal on Increasing Investment to Support the Construction of the Tibet Desertification Control Project." There were six proposals from individual Deputies on: (i) "Supporting Lhasa to be

Built as the Frontier Central City"; (ii) "Accelerating the Implementation of the Ecological Restoration and Comprehensive Management of Nyangchu (Chinese: Niyang) River"; (iii) "Approving the Master Plan of the Yarlung (Chinese: Yalong) River Scenic Area for Boosting Cultural and Eco-tourism"; (iv) "Further Strengthening the Capacity Building of Primary Medical and Health Services in Tibet"; (v) "Leading the High-Quality Development of the Power Industry in the 14th Five-Year Plan,"; and (vi) "Further Strengthening the Capacity Building of Primary Medical and Health Services in Tibet."

A number of Deputies made suggestions at the NPC. A few are highlighted: (i) Cao Jingyi, a Deputy to the NPC and Research Director with the PLA Navy Academy, said that her team has extensively researched and offered strategic suggestions to the PLAN on its requirements for AI-based future naval warfare. She added that her team is also committed to tackling existing practical problems in upgrading corrosion prevention of naval equipment and the application of advanced materials and had undertaken more than 110 scientific research tasks and taken the lead in launching a special corrosion control project of the PLA naval equipment in 2019. It has done research on the application of new-generation materials to vessel structure and laid a solid foundation for the development and building of future naval vessels. She said, "The corrosion issue has become the number one killer that triggers equipment failures and accidents, the biggest headache that pulls down combat readiness and maintenance capabilities, and the number one enemy that affects the quick reaction and strategic deployment of equipment. This issue implies lasting combat on an invisible battlefield" . (ii) Zhang Chuanwei, a Deputy to the NPC who is also the chairman of Mingyang Smart Energy, a wind turbine manufacturer and clean energy integrated solution provider based in South China's Guangdong province, proposed on May 23 that China should accelerate the pace in the adjustment of its energy structure to shape a clean energy support belt around the sea by building multiple wind power projects on the sea. He recommended that China should build up and multiply the "Three Gorges projects on the sea", which focusses on wind power in the ocean-based Exclusive Economic Zones (EEZ) 12 to 200 nautical miles in the South China, East China, Yellow and Bohai Seas. (iii) Zhao Xiaojin, Party chief of the China Academy of Space Technology (CAST) and a member of the 13th CPPCC National Committee, said (May 23) that the Chinese space industry insiders are considering using the country's upcoming space station as a facility for large-scale space-borne biology experiments in order to constantly increase China's ability to safeguard its biosecurity. He also disclosed that China plans to send two more advanced Earth observation satellites from the Gaofen satellite family in 2020, and will conduct a Mars sample return mission by around 2030, as well as a Jovian system probe mission. And (iv) China's Minister of Agriculture and Rural Affairs Han Changfu commented, "I can definitely say that China will have no food crisis, with absolute grain security" which stirred a discussion on China's microblog platform Weibo on May 23 with some Chinese netizens saying that China's grain storage could sustain the country for more than one year. Han Chanfu's comments came at a time when many grain exporting countries around the world have stopped or reduced their exports amid the COVID-19 pandemic.

The *China Youth Daily* (May 28) reported that the final version of the Government Work Report contained 89 revisions to the version delivered by the Chinese Premier on May 22. It noted that an important addition to the Taiwan section of the report was made, namely: "Adhere to the one-China principle and promote the peaceful development of cross-strait relations on the basis of the '1992 Consensus'". It is curious that the word "peaceful" was omitted in the draft version of the Government Work Report, causing quite a stir among observers, despite the draft having been approved by the Politburo!

The plenary session of the 13th National People's Congress (NPC) officially closed in Beijing on May 28, 2020, and Li Zhanshu, PBSC member and Chairman of the NPC Standing Committee, delivered the closing speech. At the meeting, the NPC voted to pass the Government Work Report, the "Civil Code", and the "Hong Kong Version of the National Security Law". The "Hong Kong Version of the National Security Law", was passed with 2,878 votes, with one vote against and six abstentions. Li Zhanshu said at the meeting that the adoption of the "Hong Kong Version of the National Security Law" is a major measure to implement the spirit of the Fourth Plenary Session of the 19th Central Committee of the Communist Party of China and adhere to, and improve, the "one country, two systems" system. It is in compliance with the Constitution and the Basic Law of the Hong

Kong Special Administrative Region (HKSAR) and includes Hong Kong compatriots and the fundamental interests of all the Chinese people. The meeting also voted to approve the implementation of the 2019 central and local budgets and the 2020 central and local budgets, and approve the 2020 central budget. The meeting adopted a resolution on the work report of the Standing Committee of the 13th National People's Congress, a resolution on the work report of the Supreme People's Court, and a resolution on the work report of the Supreme People's Procuratorate.

Efforts by the authorities prior to the NPC to promote the images of the CCP and Chinese President Xi Jinping pointed to popular dissatisfaction not having abated. Fairly strident criticism of Xi Jinping and the CCP, together with demands for reform still appeared on the Chinese web, probably to the discomfiture of the leadership. Interesting is that criticism of the CCP and Xi Jinping managed to get posted on China's social media platforms like WeChat and Weibo despite the intensive cyber security measures. Chinese Premier Li Keqiang's report to the NPC frankly projected that uncertain and tough times lie ahead. It was temperate in tenor and devoid of the usual hype regarding progress on the Belt and Road Initiative, other international initiatives or China's economic successes. It hinted at the leadership's inability to provide jobs for the huge numbers of unemployed or achieve poverty alleviation targets. Li Keqiang's report praised Xi Jinping and his leadership, but at the same time, hinted that China's leadership is aware that extant popular dissatisfaction could grow.

*(This article was published by the Centre for China Analysis and Strategy, New Delhi, on June 16, 2020.)*

# 16. China's Military and the National People's Congress

The annual plenary meetings (May 21 -28), of China's top political advisors who comprise the Chinese People's Political Consultative Conference (CPPCC) and Deputies to the National People's Congress (NPC)—China's version of a Parliament—in Beijing, are important events that give an insight into China's economic situation, plans for the coming year and the thinking of China's leadership. Commonly called the 'Big Two', the list of People's Liberation Army (PLA) delegates attending the event yields clues as to the Chinese Communist Party (CCP) leadership's areas of emphasis in the military as do their discussions. The recently concluded 13th session of the 13th NPC and 3rd session of the 13th CPPCC have been no different.

As per practice, Chinese President Xi Jinping, who is also Chairman of the Central Military Commission (CMC) and Commander-in-Chief of the PLA, met the PLA Deputies. Xinhua (May 26) reported that he appreciated the military's response to the coronavirus outbreak and said the important contributions of the military "once again proved that the people's Army is a heroic force that the Party and people completely trust." He told them that "the world is an increasingly dangerous place" and that "the epidemic has brought a profound impact on the global landscape and on China's security and development as well." He ordered the military to "think about worst-case scenarios, scale up training and battle preparedness, promptly and effectively deal with all sorts of complex situations and resolutely safeguard national sovereignty, security and development interests." Xi Jinping also asked the military to "support local economic and social development and winning the tough battle against poverty, and assist local [authorities] in doing well the work of maintaining overall social stability."The hike in China's defence budget by the lowest increment in recent years of only 6.6 per cent to US$ 178.2 billion, elicited some negative comments. Hong Kong-based retired officer of the PLA Second Artillery, now renamed the PLA Rocket Force, and prolific commentator on China's state-owned TV and media, Song Zhongping, said, "China is facing national security threats, including those taking place very nearby to China and in non-traditional security fields. Compared to these threats, China's military expenditure was far from enough". The *Global Times* quoted unnamed military experts as saying, "In the post-pandemic period, China faces more military threats from other countries, mainly the US. With Taiwan secessionists becoming more and more rampant, reunification by force with the island of Taiwan is always on the table", adding that "in this situation, increasing the defence budget must not stop". With this as the backdrop, Xi Jinping told the PLA officers not to take the money for granted: "Every penny must be well spent to produce maximum results." Exhibiting apparent confidence in the PLA, he asked them to accelerate research and development of COVID-19 drugs and vaccines.

Interesting was that through the entire week's deliberations of the CPPCC and NPC, none of the delegates was reported by China's official media as having made any reference to the tensions along the Line of Actual Control (LAC) between India and China. Chinese President Xi Jinping made no reference to the tension on the LAC and neither did Chinese Foreign Minister Wang Yi at his press conference on the sidelines of the NPC meeting on May 24. The solitary comment mentioning India was by a Hong Kong-based retired officer of the PLA Second Artillery, now renamed the PLA Rocket Force, and a frequent commentator on China's state-owned TV and media like the *Global Times*. Commenting on China's defence budget, Song Zhongping was quoted by the *Global Times* (May 22) as saying, "People should ask first, which countries are threatening China's national security in the first place? They should ask the US, they should ask India, and some other neighbouring countries and regions."

The other surprise development was the announcement on May 21 that 17 Deputies to the NPC had been asked to resign. Among them were four senior PLA officers who were ordered to resign, including as NPC Deputies, due to "serious violations of discipline and law". Investigations of the four had started earlier between August and December last year but the list of PLA Deputies to the NPC, which was finalised on May 10, 2020, did not mention their names. Corruption, which is often listed as one of the charges, was not mentioned, suggesting that possibly doubts about their political reliability or factionalism could have been the factors for their dismissal.

The PLA officers are: Lt Gen Rao Kaixun, the former Deputy Commander and Chief of Staff of the PLA Strategic Support Force (SSF); Maj Gen Meng Zhongkang, former Political Commissar of the Jiangsu Military District; Maj Gen Xu Xianghua, the former Deputy Commander of the Army in the Western Theatre Command; and Maj Gen Ye Qing, the former Political Commissar of the Hainan Military Region.

At least two of them were decorated officers with good records. Lt Gen Rao Kuixun, born in April 1964, was an officer on the fast, upward mobile track and had received rapid promotions. He was appointed Commander of a Group Army at the age of 48, becoming the youngest Group Army Commander at that time. He was honoured as an "excellent commanding officer of the PLA Army" in 2008. Rao Kuixun was also the first Deputy Commander and Chief of Staff of the newly formed PLA Strategic Support Force (SSF). He was ordered to resign from his post by the SSF Party Committee on July 31.

The second officer was Maj Gen Meng Zhongkang. He was born in April 1961, in Zhuji, Zhejiang, and studied at the X'ian Politics College. He trained at the Shijiazhuang Army Command College, Nanjing Political College Shanghai Branch and graduated from the National Defence University. In 1998, he led a team to Liaohe to fight against the floods. In 2006, he travelled with a PLA delegation on a study tour to Britain and the Southeast Asian countries. At the time he resigned from service, he was Political Commissar of the Jiangsu Military Region. Maj Gen Meng Zhongkang was awarded the 'third-class merit' five times.

The remaining two officers were Maj Gen Xu Xianghua and Maj Gen Ye Qing. Born in Haian in Jiangsu province in May 1965, Xu Xianghua was promoted to the rank of Major General in December 2014. Maj Gen Ye Qing was born in August 1962, in Hebei. He served in the 65th Group Army and as Political Commissar of the Shanxi Jinzhong Army Division and Deputy Director of the Political Department of the Shanxi Provincial Military Region. When he was asked to resign he was the Political Commissar of the Hainan Military Region.

The unexpected dismissal of the four Generals further confirms that Xi Jinping continues to closely monitor the PLA and the Party for any signs of factionalism or wavering in political reliability. More importantly, announcing the dismissal of the two decorated senior officers on the eve of the NPC would have sent a chill through the PLA officer cadre, thereby enabling Xi Jinping to further tighten his grip on the PLA.

The PLA Deputies to the NPC were divided into nine panels on May 22, to discuss the Government Work Report presented to the NPC by Chinese Premier Li Keqiang. Central Military Commission (CMC) Vice Chairmen Gen Xu Qiliang and Gen Zhang Youxia led the discussions. Gen Xu Qiliang urged the PLA's NPC Deputies to actively make suggestions and respond to the concerns of all the service members by focussing on national defence and military modernisation, and highlighting important issues concerning reform, development and stability of the nation. Addressing ideological issues, he said that the CCP "Central Committee with Comrade Xi Jinping at the core, has won the heartfelt trust and support of the whole Party and the whole Army in successfully responding to a series of risk challenges, and the great rejuvenation of the Chinese nation is moving forward with perseverance". He urged the whole Army to further enhance the "four consciousnesses", strengthen the "four self-confidences", achieve the "two safeguards", implement the responsibility system of the Chairman of the Centre Military Commission, and always maintain a high degree of ideological and political action with the Party Central Committee, the Central Military Commission and Chairman Xi. Xu Qiliang emphasised the necessity of strengthening the fighting spirit, adhering to the "bottom line thinking", deepening military training and preparing for war, being ready to respond to various emergencies at any time, and resolutely completing the mission of the "new era" entrusted to it by the Party and the people.

Gen Zhang Youxia asserted that the "hard-won major achievements in Party, country, and Army building since last year are fundamentally led by Chairman Xi as the Party's central nucleus and the whole Party's nucleus". He said, "The whole Army should thoroughly implement Xi Jinping's thinking on strengthening the Army" and firmly implement the instructions of the Chairman of advancing the reform and development of Army building, maintaining the 'bottom line' for security and supporting economic development, the fight against poverty, and preventing and controlling the epidemic. He repeated the call for "thoroughly eliminating the effects of Guo Boxiong, Xu Caihou, Fang Fenghui, and Zhang Yang, so that the troops can feel the new effects of the change in style".

Based on its interviews with PLA Deputies to the NPC on the opening day (May 21) of the NPC Plenum, the *PLA Daily* highlighted that they had emphasised "the Party's absolute leadership over the Army" and said that "the soul of a strong Army is stronger, and the core maintenance is more firm". It said a constant theme in their comments was that the "PLA is loyal to the Party and is always ready to go to battle". Referring to CMC Chairman Xi Jinping, they "agreed that the ship is heavy and has one helm".

During the panel discussions, the PLA Deputies disclosed that military strategy guidelines of the new era were being implemented in-depth and that there had been major advancements in military training and preparations, and a "comprehensive strengthening of actual combat military training". They said the PLA is more cohesive and its morale is high. The mobilisation order for training issued by Xi Jinping for three years in a row had, they said, established a clear direction for military training and stimulated enthusiasm and creativity to intensify actual combat military training. The Deputies emphasised that 'joint training' and 'confrontation' drills were becoming the norm.

A sampling of the comments by the PLA Deputies to the NPC is given below:

- Zhang Xuefeng, Deputy Commander of the PLA Eastern Theatre Command Army, who often visits the grassroots units said that "achieving the Party's goal of strengthening the Army in the new era and building a world-class Army in an all-round way will also require the leadership core to lead the helm". He asserted that "this understanding has already been deeply rooted in people's hearts" .... And "the officers and soldiers of the Army are full of deep feelings for President Xi, and maintain the core".
- Lu Lingbao, NPC Deputy from the People's Armed Police (PAP), described the report as very distinctive because it "sticks to the people-centered development thinking throughout, and it reflects the Party's and government's love for the people".

- Miao Runqi, NPC Deputy representing the Air Force Command Academy, observed that the government work report had pointed out that important progress has been made in national defence and Army building and that the PLA "demonstrated the excellent style of listening to the Party's command, being eager to follow orders, and bravely shouldering heavy burdens during the epidemic situation". He said this was "basically the Party's absolute leadership over the PLA". Miao Runqi added, "It is fundamentally the strong leadership of the Party Central Committee, with Comrade Xi Jinping at the core, and it is fundamentally the scientific guidance of Xi Jinping's socialist ideology with Chinese characteristics in the new era". He called for applying the spiritual achievements in the fight against the epidemic to "build the spiritual power to educate people and prepare for war".
- Liu Shilei, NPC Deputy and Researcher at the Academy of Military Sciences, said she believes that a strong Army should be strong in science and technology, with strong scientific talent, as this would promote military reforms. Stating that reform and innovation systems are particularly conducive to the development of scientific research, she recommended building a network of laboratories across the country to systematise scientific and technological forces and contribute to national construction. Liu Shilei expressed satisfaction that despite the difficulties, the state will still increase its investment in scientific research, which will definitely greatly encourage the military, scientific research staff.
- Cao Jingyi, a Deputy to the NPC and Research Director with the PLA Navy Academy, in a recent interview, said that her team has extensively researched and offered strategic suggestions to the People's Liberation Army Navy (PLAN) on its requirements for Artificial Intelligence (AI)-based future naval warfare. She added that her team is also committed to tackling existing practical problems in upgrading corrosion prevention of naval equipment and the application of advanced materials. She said her team had undertaken more than 110 scientific research tasks and taken the lead in launching a special corrosion control project of the PLA naval equipment in 2019. It has achieved some progress on the corrosion prevention and control front, it has completed the comprehensive

demonstration of the research on the new-generation materials' application to vessel structure and laid a solid foundation for the development and building of future naval vessels. She said, "The corrosion issue has become the number one killer that triggers equipment failures and accidents, the biggest headache that pulls down combat readiness and maintenance capabilities, and the number one enemy that affects the quick reaction and strategic deployment of equipment. This issue implies lasting combat on an invisible battlefield".

- Wang Jianguo, NPC Deputy representing the Strategic Support Force, emphasised that promoting the development of national defence science and technology innovation is an urgent task. Xi Jinping, he recalled, "often said that core technology cannot be bought and must be developed on its own". He said this must be done quickly, including building adequate talent and construction of laboratories, software, new processes, and new materials.
- Yang Zheng, Commander of the Hainan Military Region, said improving the national defence mobilisation system includes leadership management, the national defence mobilisation organisation and the command system. He observed that for strengthening the provincial military region system, it is important to give the reserve force system for national defence mobilisation thorough practical training. Other representatives of the national defence mobilisation system stressed the importance of "always making the military, government, and civilians unite as a rock".
- Xiu Zhizhi, NPC Deputy and Political Commissar of the Chongqing Armed Police Corps, said, "I am particularly encouraged" by the National Security Law for Hong Kong. It is timely and of great significance. He stressed the importance of maintaining and implementing the "one country, two systems" concept.
- Jiang Jianyu, NPC Deputy and Political Commissar of the Hunan Armed Police Corps, said the changes occurring today have "not been seen in a hundred years" and that "the People's Army had comprehensively and thoroughly implemented the responsibility system of the Chairman of the Military Commission" He added, "The most important thing for Chairman Xi Jinping's command is to do a good job in training

and preparing for war, keep an eye on strong opponents, improve core military capabilities, and always maintain a high level of alertness on the string, ensuring that the Party Central Committee, the Central Military Commission, and Chairman Xi Jinping are able to win decisively and not insult the mission."

- Zhang Hongying, NPC Deputy representing the CMC Joint Staff Department, recalled the CMC work meetings in January 2019 and November 2019 when President Xi Jinping emphasised that it is necessary to focus on actual combat military training and improve the quality and level of military preparations. He had called for enhancing combat effectiveness and strengthening the thinking of combat teams. He said the conferences had prompted officers and soldiers to carry out military training and preparations throughout the year to strengthen the military, which is the key to be able to fight and win battles.
- Xie Zhengyi, NPC Deputy of the PLA Army said that training is now more practical, and since the last year, mass military and cross-regional training activities, chemical training, joint special training and actual military confrontation exercises had improved the Army's military preparations.
- Zang Jihui, NPC Deputy and Political Commissar of the PLA Northern Theatre Command commented that equipment upgrade and transformation is at a critical stage and that mechanisation will be basically achieved by 2020. He said that significant progress will be made in building 'informationisation' and strategic capabilities.
- Wu Changde, member of the CPPCC and former Deputy Director of the CMC Political Work Department, emphasised that job security for veterans is critical to maintain social stability and is also important for stabilising and boosting the military's will and morale and strengthening national defence and military development. He called for education and guidance on a variety of subjects for the veterans so that there could be high-quality and full employment for them.
- Narbakzhu, a Tibetan NPC Deputy representing lower-level troops of the Army, said, "We Tibetan people will not forget the kindness of the Communist Party from generation to generation. Witnesses of the people's

happy life, we resolutely listen to the Party 's command and sincerely support Chairman Xi Jinping." He added, "Listening to President Xi's command, being responsible to President Xi, and letting President Xi rest assured have become the loudest vows and firmest determination of the Generals of the whole Army!"

- A representative from the CMC Training and Management Department told reporters that many troops have formed different types of commando teams to push forward the annual major military tasks.

*(This article was published by the Centre for China Analysis and Strategy, New Delhi, on June 5, 2020.)*

# 17. No Change in Chinese President Xi Jinping's Assertive Policies Despite Pressure

Since more than the past 18 months Chinese President Xi Jinping and the Chinese Communist Party (CCP) have been under increasing pressure because of the US-China tariff war. Washington has also been trying to create an adverse international environment for China. The recent troubles in Hong Kong, blamed by the official Chinese media as the handiwork of hostile foreign forces, are additionally problematic. Domestically too, the cost of living is rising and China's economy has been slowing down, thereby contributing to increased unemployment and sparking worker unrest. There is dissatisfaction among academics and students who, since the National People's Congress (NPC) session in March 2019, have, at assured personal risk, spoken out publicly against Xi Jinping's policies. So have, quite unusually, former senior Party cadres, a couple of members of the Chinese People's Political Consultative Conference (CPPCC) and a few 'princelings', suggesting that cohesiveness in the upper echelons of the Party leadership is fragile. Despite this, Xi Jinping has not modulated either the increasingly stringent domestic policies or his assertive and, at times aggressive, foreign policy.

Recent events illustrate that China will continue to follow its assertive policies. The South China Sea, of which China claims over 3 million sq km, remains at the centre of China's efforts. Since Xi Jinping took over as President, China has been aggressively moving to militarise islands and islets in the South China Sea—portions of which are also claimed by six other countries—and establish its claim. In the process, China has deployed its military and missiles on seven of them. Notwithstanding Xi Jinping's commitment in 2015 to not militarise these features, China has persisted in its actions. Revealing in this context are the disclosures recently in two official Chinese publications.

*Qiu Shi*, the Party's leading fortnightly theoretical journal, in its April 16 issue, published an article authored jointly by the People's Liberation Army Navy (PLAN) Commander Vice Admiral Liu Shijong and the PLAN

Political Commissar Vice Admiral Qin Shengxiang to mark the 70th founding anniversary of the PLAN. Reviewing the PLAN's achievements over the years, the article revealed that President Xi Jinping has been promoting the construction projects on certain islands and reefs in the South China Sea "with a firm will", which has "changed the strategic situation of military struggle at sea and demonstrated the steadfast determination to fight for every inch of territorial land and waters within China's sovereignty". Observing that on April 23, 2018, China unveiled a monument to mark its construction work on Yongshu Reef, Nansha Islands, the article said President Xi Jinping had announced the decision to establish China's first overseas military base in Djibouti.

The present stand-off between China and Vietnam similarly shows that despite being under pressure, China is unwilling to suspend its quest for domination of the South China Sea. While the respective Communist Parties exchange visits and talk of fraternal ties, tension is high in the waters of the South China Sea where China has questioned Vietnam's claim. Reports confirm that the Chinese survey ship *Haiyang Dizhi* conducted seismic surveys of Vietnam's exclusive economic zone for ten days from July 12. It was escorted by at least three escort ships including a 12,000- ton China Coast Guard cutter, with a helicopter and another 2,200-ton Coast Guard ship. While neither country has officially confirmed the stand-off, in the last few days, people on Vietnam's social media have criticised Vietnamese leaders for being submissive to China.

China has also not stopped pressing its territorial claims with Japan. There have been repeated violations of air space by People's Liberation Army Air Force (PLAAF) aircraft over the Miyako Strait and Bashi Channel. Recently, on July 23, two PLAAF Xian H-6K long-range bombers and two Russian Air Force Tupolev Tu-95MS strategic bombers for the first time ever, flew together over the Dokdo Islet, violating South Korea's Air Defence Identification Zone (ADIZ). Interestingly, the Dokdo Islet, called Takeshima by Japan, is also claimed by Russia.

China has, at the same time been steadily increasing diplomatic, political and military pressure on Taiwan to accept the '1992 consensus'. The PLAAF aircraft have overflown the Taiwan Strait and circled around Taiwan while

PLAN warships including China's aircraft carrier have, in a show of strength, sailed through the Taiwan Strait. Between June 29 and July 3, China test-fired a series of DF-21 anti-ship, medium-range ballistic missiles into a 22,000 sq km bloc of the South China Sea, between the disputed Paracel and Spratly Island groups. Beijing seems to have assessed that it has adequate military capability to deter the US from coming to Taiwan's aid. This calculation has led to instances of brinkmanship by the PLAN against US Navy vessels sailing in the area.

Separately and more recently, China's Defence White Paper entitled "China's National Defence in the New Era", released in the midst of the US-China tension on July 24, 2019, included a candid assertion of future intent. Describing itself as "the only major country yet to be completely reunified, and one of the countries with the most complex peripheral security environment", it said that "China faces serious challenges in safeguarding national sovereignty, territorial integrity, and maritime rights and interests". The observation that China is "the only major country yet to be completely reunified" clearly hints at the 'China Dream' and points to China's long-term future plans and likely policy on settlement of outstanding border and territorial disputes. This is of direct relevance to India with which China has territorial disputes as well as China's other neighbours like Taiwan, Japan and Vietnam.

Intrusions by Chinese armed forces across the Line of Actual Control (LAC) between India and China need to be viewed in this backdrop and, as candidly stated in the White Paper, as part of China's ambition to 'completely' reunify the country. The lengthy confrontation at Doklam, is suggested in this White Paper on Defence, as yet unfinished business. The recent 'demonstration' by Chinese personnel at Demchok in Ladakh, coinciding with the Dalai Lama's birthday on July 6, is similarly deliberate. On this occasion, the Chinese action combined the issue of the Dalai Lama with that of the India-China border for the first time, indicating a shift in Beijing's policy. It presages potentially increased pressure on India on the issue of the Dalai Lama and the Central Tibetan Administration in the days to come and certainly after the 14th Dalai Lama is no longer on the scene.

These actions, as well as the rejection of the US-proposed draft agreement carried back to Beijing by Vice Premier Liu He in mid-May, show that

Chinese President Xi Jinping and the CCP Central Committee are unwilling to compromise with Washington on issues they consider as affecting national interest. Additionally, Xi Jinping has apparently calculated that he will press ahead with his ambition of the 'reunification' of China, especially as he perceives that some of the countries that have problems with China are close to the US. China under Xi Jinping has obviously decided to last out the Trump Administration -- though this may entail managing his administration through another term.

*(This article was published by the Centre for China Analysis and Strategy, New Delhi, on July 26, 2020.)*

# 18. CCP CC's 4th Plenum Could Suggest a Dilution in Xi Jinping's Authority

The Chinese Communist Party (CCP) held the long overdue 4th plenary session of its 19th Central Committee (CC) from October 28–31, 2019. Held after a delay of nearly 20 months, the 4th Plenum took place at a time of some uncertainty in China, indicated also by speculative reports suggesting that the Politburo Standing Committee (PBSC) could be expanded with the addition of a couple of new members. This speculation, which claimed that the induction of new members would signal a political setback for Xi Jinping, proved erroneous. However, while the plenum communique unequivocally emphasised the Party's importance in all spheres it, along with the Plenum Resolution issued on November 5 evening, did contain a hint that possibly Xi Jinping's power has been slightly diluted.

The 6,153-character communique issued promptly after the plenum concluded on October 31, mentioned that 202 full members and 169 alternate members attended. Also attending the plenum were members of the Standing Committee of the Central Discipline Inspection Commission (CDIC), senior officials of relevant departments, a number of delegates to the 19th Party Congress who work at the grassroots level, as well as experts and scholars. The state-owned China Central Television (CCTV) showed Chinese Vice President Wang Qishan arriving for the plenum meeting at the Great Hall of the People along with the members of the PBSC. The 271 full and alternate members of the CCP CC were accommodated, as usual, in the Jingxi Hotel managed by the People's Liberation Army (PLA), for greater security.

Some Chinese commentators have observed that the prompt issue of the plenum communique by the official Chinese media on the day that the plenary session ended, showed that it had been finalised prior to the start of the plenum. This showed also that differences had been ironed out before the start of the plenary meeting. Noticeable too is that after publication of the communique, no local officials have yet made statements in their local media.

The plenum filled the two vacancies occasioned by the dismissal in January of Liu Shiyu from the post of Chairman of the China Securities Regulatory Commission and the death of Zheng Xiaosong, China's former top official in Macau who fell to his death in 2018, from among the alternate members of the CC. Those elevated were Ma Zhengwu, Chairman of state-owned investment conglomerate Chengtong Group, and PLA Navy engineer Rear Admiral Ma Weiming, who received the PLA's highest award last year.

An unfortunate incident on the last day of the plenary session was the suicide of 54-year-old alternate CC member Ren Xuefeng, Deputy Party Secretary of the centrally controlled Chongqing municipality, on October 31. Rumours circulating in China claimed that he was being investigated and preferred to commit suicide by jumping from the Jingxi Hotel in Beijing instead of serving jail time. Adding to these rumours was the fact that his remains were cremated at the Changping District Crematorium in Beijing instead of Beijing's Babaoshan Revolutionary Cemetery. Coincidentally, the now disgraced former PBSC member Bo Xilai was also formerly Party Secretary of Chongqing.

The 4th Plenum normally concerns itself with Party issues and, at times, personnel appointments. This plenum followed past practice. The plenum communique was devoted mainly to the subject of the Party's control as was the work report delivered at the plenum by CCP CC General Secretary Xi Jinping. According to the communique, the plenum approved the "Decisions on Some Major Issues Concerning Upholding and Improving the System of Socialism with Chinese Characteristics and Advancing the National Governance System and Modernization of Governance Capacity." It discussed 13 "outstanding strengths" of Chinese governance of which five were devoted entirely to maintaining the Party's leadership and socialism. Pertinent among the others were: (i) "upholding equality of all ethnic groups, creating a strong sense of community for the Chinese nation, realizing a common united struggle and common prosperity and development"; (ii) "selecting officials based on integrity and ability and on the basis of merit to cultivate more talented individuals"; (iii) "keeping the armed forces under the Party's command and ensuring that the people's armed forces are completely loyal to the Party and the people so as to safeguard China's sovereignty, security and development interests"; (iv) "upholding the principle of 'one country, two systems,' maintaining lasting prosperity and stability in Hong Kong and Macao, and promoting the peaceful reunification of the motherland"; and (v) "adhering to the unity of independence and self-reliance and opening up to the rest of the world, actively participating in global governance, and continuing to contribute to the building of a community with a shared future for humanity".

Emphasis on the need to ensure that the Party keeps the PLA under its command and that they "are completely loyal to the Party and the people" suggests that the armed forces will continue to be subjected to strict ideological controls and education. Political reliability will remain the main criterion for promoting PLA officers.

The 18,441-character 4th Plenum Resolution issued on November 5 evening clearly revealed that Hong Kong was discussed at some length at the plenary session. The annual summer meeting of senior CCP leaders and veteran cadres at the seaside resort of Beidaihe had earlier this year also discussed the troubles in Hong Kong and, according to reports, unanimously described it as a 'colour revolution'. Special mention of this in the Plenum Resolution could suggest oblique criticism of Xi Jinping for the inaction in sorting out the Hong Kong issue. Soon after the 4th Plenum meeting, it was disclosed that Chinese President Xi Jinping had a one-on-one meeting with Hong Kong Special Administrative Region (HKSAR) Chief Executive Carrie Lam in Shanghai. China's Minister of Public Security Zhao Kezhi, who was recently added to the Party's Central Leading Small Group on Hong Kong, was also present. This was Xi Jinping's first meeting with Carrie Lam since the trouble in Hong Kong began five months ago. Xinhua reported Xi Jinping as assuring her, *"The central government has high trust in you and fully affirms the work of you and the governance team of Hong Kong."* Carrie Lam was also scheduled to meet PBSC member Han Zheng, who is in charge of Hong Kong affairs, on November 6 in Beijing.

Indications that Beijing will introduce tougher policies to govern Hong Kong and Macau were evident in the 371-character paragraph in the 4th Plenum Resolution dealing specially with the two Special Administrative Regions (SARs). This resolved to "improve the central system for appointing mechanisms of the Special Administrative Region Chief Executive and principal officials", thus, signalling that Hong Kong will be brought more directly under Beijing's control. Promising a more robust and immediate response in the future, it resolved to "establish a sound legal system and enforcement mechanisms in the Special Administrative Region to safeguard national security", and "strengthen the law enforcement forces". More importantly, the resolution asserted that Beijing will make "efforts to solve deep-seated contradictions and problems that affect social stability and long-term development" in Hong Kong, "enhance the national consciousness and patriotism of the young people" and "resolutely prevent and curb the external force to interfere in Hong Kong and Macao affairs and divide, subversion, infiltration, sabotage, ensure that Hong Kong and Macao have long-term stability". It is apparent that as the Hong Kong Special Administrative Region (HKSAR) is brought back to normalcy, Beijing will impose severe ideological and political education controls on its education system, its youth and civil servants.

References in Xi Jinping's speeches and documents issued by the CCP over the past many months to Deng Xiaoping, Jiang Zemin, Hu Jintao, etc have decreased. More recently, the document jointly issued by the Party Central Committee and the People's Republic of China (PRC) State Council on October 27, mentioned only "Xi Jinping Thought" as the "guiding principle" with no reference at all to Mao Zedong, Deng Xiaoping, Jiang Zemin or Hu Jintao! The 4th Plenum communique, however, included two separate references asserting that "the Political Bureau of the Central Committee holds high the great banner of socialism with Chinese characteristics and adheres to Marxism-Leninism, Mao Zedong Thought, Deng Xiaoping Theory, the important thinking of the 'Three Represents', and the scientific development concept. Guided by Xi Jinping's new era of socialism with Chinese characteristics".

The just concluded 4th Plenum of the 19th CC of the CCP has endorsed the political education campaigns launched by Xi Jinping and his endeavour to enhance the Party's authority and ensure it is present in virtually every sphere of government and military activity. It has also not overtly weakened Xi Jinping's position by inducting potential successors to the PBSC. However, its communique and the resolution issued subsequently do suggest that the troubles in Hong Kong were extensively discussed, with some criticism for the delay in acting to resolve them probably directed towards Xi Jinping and possibly PBSC member Han Zheng. The reference in the communique to "Marxism-Leninism, Mao Zedong Thought, Deng Xiaoping Theory", etc appear to reinforce this.

*(This article was published by the Centre for China Analysis and Strategy, New Delhi, on November 6, 2019.)*

# 19. Chinese President Xi Jinping Faces Difficult Times Ahead

There are clear indications that popular dissatisfaction and discontent with Chinese President Xi Jinping inside China continue to simmer just below the surface. The economic slowdown, unemployment and rising cost of living have contributed to the discontent. In fact, accentuated by the US-China trade war, the economic slowdown has begun to impact other areas including the strategic geoeconomic Belt and Road Initiative (BRI) which has seen a drop in investments, and possibly China's defence build-up, with discussions underway in China's military establishment as to whether, for example, the rapid pace of ship-building should be slowed down. The negative sentiments could get sharpened as huge numbers of people travel to their hometowns and villages to meet relatives during the annual Chinese New Year holidays in end January. The situation in Hong Kong too shows no signs of abating. Chinese President Xi Jinping is likely to face troubled times ahead in the upcoming Year of the Rat.

Aware of the spreading negative sentiment inside China, Xi Jinping, who has concentrated unprecedented power and continues to build his personality cult, is strengthening the country's public security apparatus and reinforcing surveillance with Artificial Intelligence (AI). He is, additionally, imposing increasingly restrictive ideological controls combined with strict political 'guidance'. 'Patriotic education' and ideology have become the dominant themes over the past few months, with citizens constantly exhorted to live by the "Twelve Socialist Core Values". Party cadres are assembled across the country for regular training and study sessions under the slogan: "Never forget the original ideal and ambition, keep in mind the mission". This heightened Party supervision includes academia. From October 2019, 'student spies' have been mobilised to monitor and report on 'radical' political views, including of their teachers. They reinforce the Party and Public Security Personnel (PSP) deployed in schools and university campuses since 2018.

Several professors and schoolteachers have been dismissed or disciplined for voicing opinions not in conformity with the Party line. Liang Xin, a teacher at a top secondary school in eastern China was last year demoted to school janitor following a report by a student. In April 2019, the Mathematics teacher at the Beijing University of Civil Engineering and Architecture, Xu Chuanqing, was penalised after her students accused her on social media of comparing them unfavourably to hard-working Japanese students and two months later in June, a teacher at a Beijing secondary school was dismissed for discussing the Tiananmen Square crackdown. More recently, in December, Professor Zhao Siyuan, Deputy Dean of the Arts School at Communication University of Zhejiang, was given a "severe warning" for "using inappropriate terms" while addressing new students. Chu Zhaohui, a senior researcher at China's National Institute of Education, told the *South China Morning Post* (October 20), "The number of students reporting their teachers has increased recently but official statistics are not available. … in some cases, high school and university students have been asked by relevant [government] departments to report inappropriate classroom comment."

Guo Shengkun, former Minister of Public Security who as head of the Chinese Communist Party's (CCP's) Political and Legal Affairs Commission now oversees the country's entire security apparatus, recently ratcheted up the security environment. The troubles in Hong Kong would have been a contributory factor. In an article in the *People's Daily* on November 28, 2019, he called for the firm defence of "national political security," described as "the lifeline of the Party's and the nation's security, and an unshakable bottom line." Guo Shengkun vowed "resolutely and severely to prevent and crack down on" the infiltration of hostile forces and said that construction of the "people's defense line for national security" should be strengthened. The whole country and the entire population should enhance their awareness of the sense of national security and enhance the nation's ability to prevent, and defend against, national security risks. He said that everyone ought to be "on high vigilance, take resolute precautions, and severely punish" infiltration by hostile forces and their destructive and subversive activities to promote secession, thus, "building a solid copper and iron wall for national security." Guo Shengkun advocated concerted efforts to advance national security work and walk the "path of national security with Chinese characteristics." Regarding issues causing potential social unrest, Guo Shengkun demanded that "small matters stay in the village, big issues go no further than the township, and conflicts are not passed on to higher level authorities."

Notwithstanding the growing restrictions and personal risk, resentment has occasionally spilt over into the public domain. China has always been sensitive to criticism by its leading academics. On October 31, 2019, Tsinghua University Professor Lao Dongyan (劳东燕) emulated another reputed academic and, risking certain punishment, posted a sharply worded approximately 2,900-character article on her public Wechat account, expressing her worries about facial recognition technology. Professor Lao Dongyan was, incidentally, one of nearly 300 faculty and students at Tsinghua who signed a letter in support of Tsinghua Professor Xu Zhangrun, suspended in July 2019 for warning against the return to totalitarianism and for criticism of the Communist Party. Arguing against the use of facial recognition in the Beijing Subway, Professor Lao Dongyan wrote: "I can only say: forgive me, but I cannot accept this type of kindness…We must know that in our society, any personal data, as long as it is controlled by enterprises or other institutions, is also controlled by the government. Because this huge organization is run by specific people, this is equivalent to saying that all personal data, including highly recognizable biometric data, are controlled by a few people in that group…The people who control our data are obviously not God. They have their own selfish desires and weak points. Therefore, it is unknown how they will use our personal data and how they will manipulate our lives. Not to mention, such data may be leaked or hacked due to improper storage, leading to harmful results that may be exploited by criminals." Stating that she also objected to forcing people to undergo face recognition inspections in airports and hotels, she asked whether in a few years genes or fingerprint recognition would be implemented. She recommended that the National People's Congress (NPC) Standing Committee conduct a basic legitimacy review of the Beijing Metro 's use of face recognition for classified security checks; at the same time, it should consider initiating corresponding legislative procedures for the arbitrary use of faces.

In an unrelated but similar case of academia objecting to Party regulations, students at the prestigious Fudan University in Shanghai were outraged after "freedom of thought" was removed as a core value from its charter. Instead, references strengthening the CCP's leadership were added to the charters of Fudan and two other universities. On December 18, students of Fudan University gathered at the Danyuan cafeteria in Guanghua Building at Fudan University to sing the school's anthem, which specifically mentions "independent thinking." By December 18 afternoon, a hashtag discussing the Fudan University's charter changes had been viewed more than 1.7 million times on Weibo, before being censored later that evening. Lu Xiaoping, Vice President of the Literature School at Nanjing University, whose charter was also rewritten, posted a comment on Weibo on December 18—which was later deleted—saying, "If we do not speak out today about such a blatant challenge to the bottom line of education and academic ethics, I am afraid we will never have the chance!" In addition to Fudan and Nanjing, the Shaanxi Normal University, in northwestern China was the third university to have its charter altered.

A BBC Chinese report (December 6, 2019) reflected the popular dissatisfaction with state surveillance. Stating that the Chinese people now had to undergo facial scanning while registering their new mobile phone numbers, it reported the findings of a recent Chinese survey. It disclosed that a research centre affiliated with the Guangzhou-based *Southern Metropolis Daily* had conducted a survey on facial recognition during October and November 2019. It said that among the respondents to the centre's online questionnaire, 57 per cent were worried that their personal whereabouts were recorded, while nearly 50 per cent were worried that criminals may use fake information to perpetrate fraud or theft. Nearly 84 per cent of the respondents wanted operators of the facial recognition system to provide them with a channel to view or delete facial data; 74 per cent of respondents wanted to choose whether to use facial recognition or traditional methods. The survey, however, also showed that about 60 to 70 per cent of respondents believed that facial recognition made public places safer. According to the Chinese media, the Metro system in Zhengzhou city of Henan province started "riding with face" (using facial recognition in the Metro system) in early December.

The *China Daily* reported that riders can use facial recognition to authorise payment automatically instead of scanning the QR code on their mobile phones. Currently, passengers can voluntarily choose whether to use facial recognition or not.

Other indicators of internal discontent are the 'leaks' to the foreign press about the wealth allegedly illegally accumulated by the Chinese leaders, and to the *New York Times* of more than 400 pages of 'internal' Chinese documents relating to the detention of the Uyghur minority in heavily guarded camps in the Xinjiang-Uyghur Autonomous Region.

While there are presently no signs of any threat to Chinese President Xi Jinping's authority or position, these challenges to the authority of the state have the potential to escalate or be exploited by Xi Jinping's opponents.

*(This article was published by the Centre for China Analysis and Strategy, New Delhi, on January 1, 2020.)*

# 20. Popular Protests Undermine Chinese President Xi Jinping's Credibility

Popular discontent and dissatisfaction with Chinese President Xi Jinping and the Chinese Communist Party (CCP) simmering since March 2018, erupted into overt public criticism from the end of January 2020, prompted by news of the Wuhan virus epidemic becoming public. There is presently little indication of it abating till at least the epidemic begins to peter out. By then, it would have palpably dented, if not damaged, the credibility and image of Chinese President Xi Jinping and the CCP.

The immediate provocation for this outburst has been the mishandling of the 'Wuhan virus', or '2019-COVID', by the Chinese authorities. China's social media has been awash with angry posts criticising the excessive secrecy of the system and the tardy response of the authorities, the reluctance to admit to the epidemic and its spread, and the absence of transparency. Interesting was a report in the authoritative, official news agency Xinhua on February 10, which revealed that Beijing's Ditan Hospital was treating coronavirus patients as early as January 12, more than 10 days before the city's first cases were publicly announced at another hospital in the Daxing district, and Chinese epidemiologist Zhong Nanshan confirmed that the disease was being transmitted from person-to-person! Video clips being posted on China's social media showed that preparations to tackle the epidemic were inadequate, with overcrowded hospitals and medical personnel pleading for medicines and medical supplies. The death of the 34-year-old doctor and 'whistle-blower' on February 7, gave a fillip to the criticism and sharp condemnation. Xi Jinping's disappearance from the official media and public functions from January 29 till February 10 were commented upon. The spate of public criticism has questioned the system of governance, the CCP's legitimacy and undermined Xi Jinping's credibility.

Criticism has been unusually blunt. People posted criticisms on their personal accounts despite the certain personal risk. Critics include at least two prominent Chinese intellectuals and academics and a judge of the Supreme

People's Procuratorate. A prominent Chinese civil rights activist and former Lecturer at the Beijing University of Post and Telecommunications, 46-year-old Xu Zhiyong, posted an article on social media on February 3, urging Xi Jinping to step down for his "inability to handle major crises". He cited several examples, including the China-US trade war, the anti-government protests in Hong Kong and the coronavirus outbreak. He called Xi Jinping's political ideology "confusing", his governance model "outdated" and said he had ruined China with "exhaustive social stability maintenance measures". Xu Zhiyong said, "Seven years ago, I appealed to you to lead China to become a nation that respects democracy and the Constitution, but in return, I was thrown into jail for four years. And now, your men are still looking for me trying to throw me back in jail again. I don't think you are a villain, just someone who is not very smart. For the public's sake, I'm asking you again: Step down, Mr Xi Jinping."

Reputed Tsinghua University Professor Xu Zhangrun, on February 5, posted a scathing 6,246- character criticism of Xi Jinping and the Chinese authorities captioned "Angry People No Longer Fear", which went viral on China's social media. The article accused the authorities in Zhongnanhai and specifically Xi Jinping of being out of touch with the people's needs and perpetuating an elite with so-called 'Red Genes'. It accused Xi Jinping and a "small circle of leaders" of creating a "state within a state and engaging in "big data terrorism". He charged, "The political system has collapsed under the tyranny, and a governance system [made up] of bureaucrats, which has taken [the Party] more than 30 years to build, has floundered". He accused the authorities of spending the "taxpayers' hard-earned money for feeding the massive internet police to monitor every word and deed of nationals". Xu Zhangrun said they have not only "stifled public discussion of all ideas of life, but also stifled social communication and early warning mechanisms that existed originally" and blamed this for the failure of the authorities in Hubei to take precautions to control the epidemic. The article, which called Xi Jinping a "political tyrant", declared "the people no longer fear" and "the Sun will eventually come to this land of freedom!" Another major 10,000-character article published by Xu Zhangrun on July 24, 2018, had ricocheted across China, creating a stir among Chinese academics and students. He was suspended from his post, banned from leaving China and not allowed to publish his writings freely in China.

Pertinent is that though both Xu Zhiyong and Xu Zhangrun have been penalised and prohibited from writing, they have been able to post their articles on China's social media.

Unprecedented is the lengthy article posted on February 13 on the public social media account of Duan Zhanjiang, a judge of China's Supreme People's Procuratorate. The article on the account criticised the shortcomings in governance, not allowing civil society to have a larger role, suppression of free speech, etc and predicted a far, serious fallout for the Chinese economy. It referred also to Tsinghua University Professor Xu Zhangrun's recent lengthy article. The article is a clear indictment of Chinese President Xi Jinping. The article did, though, end with the curious disclaimer that these are not the personal views of the judge.

Surprising was the instigation via a Twitter account calling on the people of Wuhan to protest aganist "the Communist government's suppression of freedom of speech and its hiding of information". It urged the people to protest from their homes from 8 pm to 8:30 pm on February 14, 2020 by turning off the lights for one minute at 8 pm; simultaneously knocking on pans and shouting "Protest"; the slogans "Cheers, Wuhan People!"; "Wuhan People, Save Ourselves!"; "Release Chen Qiushi!" and "Release Fang Bin!" (both arrested for revealing the truth about the epidemic situation in Wuhan); singing China's national anthem; throwing flyers and other pieces of paper from their homes; and doing a live broadcast or recording short videos to disseminate on the internet.

Dissatisfaction with Xi Jinping and the regime has been simmering since at least 2018. The economic slowdown, unemployment, rising cost of living and consumer inflation at a near six-year high have all contributed to the discontent. Accentuated by the US-China trade war, the economic slowdown resulted in the closure of factories and restaurants, and lay-offs of millions of workers. The relentless campaign against corruption, which has felled hundreds of senior Party, military and government cadres along with millions of Party members, added to the pools of popular discontent. The negative sentiments would have got accentuated as people met relatives in their hometowns and villages during the annual Chinese New Year holidays in end January. The onset of the epidemic and quarantine regulations would have compelled many to extend their stay.

Clear indications of discontent were the sharp reactions to the proposal mooted at the National People's Congress (NPC) in March 2018 to abolish term limits on the posts of China's President and Vice President. Senior prominent academics, students and others reacted negatively to the proposal saying they did not want a return to Mao's 'one-man rule' and asked Deputies to the National People's Congress (NPC) to reject it. Many Party members, including in the CCP Central Committee, still retain unpleasant memories of the Cultural Revolution. Popular resentment has mounted since then.

Popular discontent was further heightened by the imposition of controls and Party ideology on academia. Party cadres have been posted in classrooms since 2018 to monitor the content of lectures, libraries have been inspected and books deemed to contain 'liberal' Western thought have been weeded out. 'Student spies' have been recruited to monitor the utterances of university Professors within and outside the classrooms. The effort to strengthen the Communist Party's leadership in universities included, for example, the removal of "freedom of thought" as a core value from the charter of the prestigious Fudan University in Shanghai and its replacement by references strengthening the Communist Party's leadership. Students at Fudan protested with sit-ins and demonstrations on December 18, 2019, and sang Fudan University's anthem, which specifically mentions "independent thinking." Lu Xiaoping, Vice President of the literature school at Nanjing University, whose charter was similarly rewritten, posted a comment on Weibo on December 18—which was later deleted—saying, "If we do not speak out today about such a blatant challenge to the bottom line of education and academic ethics, I am afraid we will never have the chance!"

The increasingly intrusive and strict security and 'social stability' measures being enforced over the past few years have upset the people. Numerous reports in the official Chinese media refer to implementation of the 'social credit management' programme in a growing number of cities across China. Often they indirectly point to the inconvenience caused. This was brought out by Tsinghua University Professor Lao Dongyan on October 31, 2019, who expressed her worries about facial recognition technology. In a 2,900-word post on her public Wechat account, she wrote: "I cannot accept this type of kindness…We must know that in our society, any personal data, as long as it is controlled by enterprises or other institutions, is also controlled by the government. Because this huge organization is run by specific people, this is equivalent to saying that all personal data, including highly recognizable biometric data, are controlled by a few people in that group…The people who control our data are obviously not God. They have their own selfish desires and weak points. Therefore, it is unknown how they will use our personal data and how they will manipulate our lives. Not to mention, such data may be leaked or hacked due to improper storage, leading to harmful results that may be exploited by criminals." Interestingly, Professor Lao Dongyan was one of nearly 300 faculty and students at Tsinghua who signed a letter in support of Tsinghua Professor Xu Zhangrun, suspended for criticism of the Communist Party.

A BBC report (in Chinese) on December 6, 2019, reflected the public sentiment about the usage of security controls and facial recognition software. Commenting on a new Chinese government initiative requiring Chinese people to undergo facial scanning while registering their new mobile phone numbers, it referred to an online survey on facial recognition done by a research centre affiliated with the Guangzhou-based official *Southern Metropolis Daily*. Among the respondents, 57 per cent were worried that their personal whereabouts were recorded while nearly 50 per cent were worried that criminals may use fake information to perpetrate fraud or theft. Nearly 84 per cent of the respondents wanted operators of the facial recognition system to provide them with a channel to view or delete facial data; 74 per cent of respondents wanted to choose whether to use facial recognition or traditional methods. However, the survey also showed that about 60 to 70 per cent of respondents believe that facial recognition makes public places safer.

In addition to the poor economy and imposition of security and ideological controls, Chinese President Xi Jinping is viewed as responsible for the setbacks in China's foreign policy, namely the US-China trade war, the situation in Hong Kong and the recent victory of the pro-independence Democratic Progressive Party (DPP) in Taiwan. Some Chinese strategists and academics have said that the China-US relationship was mishandled due to arrogance and over-confidence. According to them, China is not powerful enough to challenge the US and Xi Jinping's declaration at the 19th Party Congress in October 2017 of the 'China Dream'-2021, 'Made in China-2025' and China reaching the level of the world's advanced global powers by 2049, challenged US primacy. They assess that the US-China trade war has placed China in a difficult situation, is isolating it, and could delay realisation of its ambitions. Chinese academics have suggested that Beijing revert to its earlier policy of 'biding one's time'.

The situation in Hong Kong is directly linked to Xi Jinping's 'China Dream', which includes reunification of China. By not acting swiftly, Xi Jinping has allowed the situation in Hong Kong—which reverted to China's rule 23 years ago—to slip into the control of the protestors for almost 10 months and provide an example to others, like Taiwan, of a successful challenge to Beijing's rule. While Chinese analysts say that Xi Jinping did not want a repeat of the Tiananmen 'event' or to shed Chinese blood, the indecision points also to differences within the Politburo that possibly hamper a consensus. The inaction despite concerns about a 'colour revolution', being voiced by Xi Jinping at a Politburo Standing Committee meeting and other Directors of the Provincial Public Security Bureaus, is inexplicable. It was only on January 4, that Xi Jinping took steps to apparently demonstrate he was in charge and replaced the head of the Liaison Office in Hong Kong with 65-year-old former Shanxi Province Party Secretary Luo Huining. But till the Hong Kong issue is resolved, the matter of Taiwan's reunification with Mainland China will stay in limbo and Xi Jinping's 'China Dream' will not be achieved.

A lot is at stake for Xi Jinping and the CCP. Unless the economy picks up, unemployment is checked and gains made in foreign policy and the 'China Dream', the CCP and Xi Jinping risk their legitimacy being seriously dented. In the event of there being no substantive visible improvement, Chinese President Xi Jinping, who has consistently pushed ideology and nationalism since coming to office in 2012, might be coerced by the Party and its veterans to share power in the run-up to the upcoming 20th Party Congress and not continue thereafter.

*(This article was published by the Centre for China Analysis and Strategy, New Delhi, on February 17, 2020.)*

# 21. The COVID-19 Epidemic and China's Economy

The coronavirus epidemic struck China when it was in the midst of serious economic problems and high unemployment, and Chinese economists were already candidly warning of a one per cent drop in growth this year. The attempted cover-up by Chinese authorities of the coronavirus epidemic for nearly two months—unimaginable in democracies—exacerbated economic losses and disruption in addition to causing the loss of numerous lives and delaying an international medical response to the virus. Reports say at least two international pharmaceutical companies are to start human trials of vaccines against the coronavirus by next month and could have the vaccines ready by early next year. Chinese economists had warned in January that if the epidemic was not contained by mid-February, China's growth rate could drop by two per cent. The absence of transparency in efforts to, initially, inform the people and, later, combat the coronavirus, led subsequently to the imposition of unavoidable drastic measures and sharply accentuated the already high level of distrust between the people and China's Communist regime.

The US-based Rhodium Group assessed (March 11) that while the pace of new COVID-19 transmissions is coming down in China, the "pathway to economic recovery remains deeply uncertain". It asserted that China has endured a severe economic downturn in the first quarter of 2020. The report pointed to the transportation sector which registered 82 per cent fewer trips in the 25 days following the Lunar New Year in 2020 relative to 2019, signalling that workers were not returning from the countryside. It recorded that coal consumption by China's six largest power plants fell over 40 per cent; property sales in major cities were near-zero in February; manufacturing and services recorded major contractions; and the shutdown of China's economy is even visible from space, with satellite readings showing almost non-existent nitrogen oxide and dioxide emissions from swaths of the industrial heartland.

Despite the economic losses and disruption caused by the coronavirus epidemic, Chinese President Xi Jinping sought to keep the focus on China's economic targets and the 'Two Centenary' goals. In a teleconference directly with over 170,000 officials across the country on February 23 on "Coordinating and Promoting New Crown Pneumonia Epidemic Prevention and Control and Economic and Social Development Work", Chinese President Xi Jinping focussed on reviving the economy. He said that over 46 per cent of China's counties and districts are classified as 'low risk' and should be getting back to normal soon. Those facing 'moderate risk' need to be more cautious—resuming work only gradually. Xi Jinping also assured that top leaders are ready to employ fiscal and monetary policies if needed and "macro policies… should prevent the economy from slipping out of a reasonable range." He urged local governments to address supply chain congestion in and between provinces. Xi Jinping expressed concern about China's role in global trade saying: "[We] need to secure the smooth operation of foreign trade supply chains and stabilize [China's] share in the international market."

At the Politburo Standing Committee (PBSC) meeting on March 4 to "study the current epidemic prevention and control work and economic and social stability", Xi Jinping claimed there was overall improvement in the epidemic situation across China and resumption of economic activities had accelerated. He had earlier issued instructions to speed up resumption of work in factories, etc. He reminded PBSC members of the "complexity" of the current epidemic prevention and control and the economic and social developments. He urged deepening international cooperation and giving full play to China's role as a "responsible great power." The meeting specifically stated that prevention and control efforts must persist in Wuhan, Hubei, and the Beijing region and emphasised the importance of enhancing scientific efforts to develop treatments and vaccines. It stressed the imperative to minimise economic losses and also that China must assist companies, stabilise employment, and facilitate the hiring of key groups such as college graduates and migrant workers. The adoption of various "point-to-point" transportation methods should continue to allow employees to return to work as soon as possible. Additionally, China will push for the construction of major projects including 5G and increase investments in public health services and production of emergency supplies. The meeting urged for stabilising foreign trade and investment and facilitating foreign-invested companies in China to resume work. In conclusion, the meeting emphasised the importance of the spring agricultural production, stabilising prices of agricultural products, and increasing poverty alleviation efforts.

In step with Chinese President Xi Jinping's exhortation and despite the severe disruption caused by the COVID-19 epidemic, China has continued trying to further the objectives of the 'China Dream'. The Economics and Technology Research Institute (CNPC-ETRI) of the state-owned China National Petroleum Corporation (CNPC), for instance, disclosed that it was exploring the possibility of a Beijing-led global health organisation that would rival the World Health Organisation (WHO). Carice Witte, founder and Executive Director of the Israeli company SIGNAL, confirmed the idea and described it as "very interesting in the context of China's aim to reshape global governance, including setting up parallel institutions." Chinese Foreign Minister Wang Yi, while highlighting (March 2) the Chinese government's strengths in combatting the coronavirus epidemic, referred to China's 'Two Centenary Goals' and vision of building "a community with a shared future for mankind"! On March 8, the Chinese government announced its decision to donate US$ 20 million to the WHO to support it in carrying out international cooperation in fighting the outbreak of novel coronavirus disease (COVID-19).

The impact of the coronavirus epidemic on China has been severe. With over 80,000 persons infected by the coronavirus; millions of persons under quarantine; schools, colleges, restaurants and public places closed resulting in laying-off millions of workers to join the millions of those already unemployed; stringent transport restrictions imposed throughout China; and 18 cities placed under strict isolation, the economic losses are enormous. Additionally, the Chinese government's delayed response to the epidemic and lack of transparency further raised the existing serious trust deficit between the authorities and the public of which there were frequent public demonstrations.

A number of China's factories, Research and Development (R&D) centres and companies, many headquartered in Wuhan, were shut down, with efforts to reopen them beginning in late February with patchy results. Navy shipyards, aircraft factories and weapons production plants were closed. Regulations were issued to restrict the activities and training of China's

People's Liberation Army (PLA). Recruitment to the PLA, which had been planned in two phases, was postponed. China's major internet companies, including Tencent, ByteDance, Baidu and Didi, deferred the date for their employees to return to offices.

After January though, the government made huge efforts, including severe isolation measures for entire cities and populations. It constructed three hospitals within weeks, using China's Air Force to transport medical equipment, supplies and personnel, and deploy military doctors and medical staff to Wuhan.

Restaurants, food stalls, etc closed due to the coronavirus epidemic, rendering millions of workers unemployed. A China Cuisine Association survey reported that around 95 per cent of caterers experienced major losses over the Lunar New Year. The report said the impact of the coronavirus outbreak on China's restaurants, fast-food joints and snack stands will be several times greater than that caused by the Severe Acute Respiratory Syndrome (SARS) outbreak of 2003. Besides losses over the holiday, businesses are likely to face serious cash flow issues and difficulty obtaining financing in the coming months. More than 300 Chinese companies including smartphone-maker Xiaomi and China's ride-hailing giant Didi Chuxing are seeking bank loans totalling at least US$ 8.2 billion to ease the impact of the coronavirus epidemic. China has decided to provide medium-term funding to banks and cut the interest rate it charges as officials seek to cushion the economy from the epidemic.

The well-known Chinese news site Sina reported on January 27, that China's Ministry of Human Resources and Social Security issued new regulations to relax certain labour laws for the period when the nation is combating the coronavirus. The new regulations prohibit laying off workers or stopping their pay if the workers are not able to work due to government bans. Companies have been instructed to provide a minimum living payment to those not able to work. For those involved in the rescue activities of the epidemic who temporarily lose their income and are not able to pay off credit card debts or a mortgage, this will not be recognised as a breach of contract. Delayed payments should be allowed. The State Grid for electricity also announced that customers would be allowed to continue to use electricity even if their date for payment of dues is past. The State Grid will also arrange for customers to do business remotely online without visiting local offices.

Soon after the coronavirus struck and its magnitude was gauged, Chinese economists said in early January that China's services sector alone was suffering a loss of US$ 144 billion a week! Some of China's major internet companies, including Tencent, ByteDance, Baidu and Didi, deferred the date for their employees to return to offices. Apple iPhone maker Foxconn, which employs more than 400,000 on the Chinese Mainland, delayed complete reopening until March. A broad survey of American companies in China released on February 18, showed that more than three quarters had insufficient staff to run a full production line. Data released by the Chinese software company Gaode on March 10, showed that while Wuhan's work resumption rate stood at just 12.54 per cent, most companies planned to ramp up work to 80 per cent by end March. Meanwhile, to encourage companies to resume work amid the coronavirus outbreak, China's Ministry of Transport said (February 15) that China's roads will be toll-free starting February 17. The policy would be in force until the epidemic is deemed to be over.

China's official *The Paper* observed (March 5) that while businesses are reopening, the "economy remains severely depressed". It cited Baidu's Big Data as showing that over 50 per cent of offline [businesses] had resumed work nationally. It said, "The percentage of offline [businesses] that have resumed work exceeds 63 per cent in Xining, Dalian, and Changchun, which lead the country in this respect." Separately Xinhua reported that less than half of small and medium enterprises were back at work: "Around 45 per cent of China's Small and Medium Enterprises (SMEs) had resumed work" by March 2, up from 32.8 per cent as of February 26, according to the Ministry of Industry and Information Technology (MIIT). *MySteel*, a magazine reporting on the coal industry, said, "The capacity utilization rate as of March 3 [of coal mines was] 83.4 per cent, according to official data from China's National Energy Administration." In a rare and major step, China National Offshore Oil Corp., China's biggest Liquefied Natural Gas (LNG) buyer, invoked *force majeure* and told some suppliers it would not take delivery of cargo because of constraints caused by the coronavirus. French oil and gas giant Total SA have rejected the declaration. Soon thereafter, the Chinese copper smelter Guangxi

Nanguo also declared it would refuse to take delivery of raw materials. China's biggest oil refiner, Sinopec Group, is similarly likely to ask Saudi Arabia to reduce crude supplies next month.

Xinhua reported on February 13 that according to data for January released by the China Association of Automobile Manufacturers (CAAM), Chinese national automobile manufacturing volume declined 33.5 per cent, month-over-month, and 24.6 per cent, year-over-year. The sales volume declined 27 per cent, month-over-month and 18 per cent, year-over-year. Passenger car sales declined 27.1 per cent month-over month and 20.2 per cent, year-over-year. New energy source automobile sales declined 54.4 per cent year-over-year. According to CAAM officials, the coronavirus impact started later in January so February numbers are expected to be much worse, as they will start to show the impact on market activities, manufacturing capacity, export limitations, financial bottlenecks and tougher government regulations. They anticipate that the Chinese automobile market may slump further.

The coronavirus epidemic also has hidden costs. For example the Deputy Governor of the People's Bank of China (PBoC), Fan Yifei disclosed (February 15) that the bank was 'sanitising' bank notes as well as blocking their movement between cities in regions most affected by the outbreak to limit transmission of the virus. Other banks could be expected to do the same. There was indication too of capital flight. China's central bank in February announced increased punishment for financial institutions that failed to adequately guard against money laundering and imposed fines of more than Yuan 10 million (US$ 1.4 million) for the first time. The China Minsheng Banking Corp. was fined Yuan 23.7 million and China Everbright Bank Co. Ltd. Yuan 18.2 million. They were penalised for failing to properly perform the required customer identification checks, failing to keep customer data and transaction records and failing to report large or suspicious transactions. The PBoC fined the brokerage Huatai Securities Co. Ltd. Yuan 10.1 million for similar violations.

The severe blow to the Chinese economy caused by the coronavirus, however, has come atop an already deteriorating economy. Singapore's primary Chinese-language newspaper *Lianhe Zaobao* reported (December 31) that China saw its lowest level of overseas acquisitions in 2019, with a total value of US$ 41 billion, or half the 2018 volume. Acquisitions in the US declined by 80 per cent in 2019. Analysts in the global banking industry believe that the sharp decline in overseas acquisition is directly attributable to the US-China trade war and significantly tightened government regulatory measures imposed in many countries against Chinese buyers. It observed that with the economic slowdown in China, the Chinese government began strictly controlling the volume of capital flowing out of China, making it especially difficult for Chinese investors to pay back the debts acquired overseas. It is expected that more domestic investments will be seen in China than overseas.

Reuters reported (January 22) that about two-thirds of China's provinces, regions and municipalities had cut their 2020 growth targets from last year, despite easing trade tensions with the US. It added: "Of China's provincial-level regions, 22, including Beijing, Guangdong, Zhejiang, Henan, Hainan, and Fujian, set lower growth targets this year compared to last year. Beijing, Shanghai, and the southern export hub of Guangdong all dropped their targets from 6-6.5 per cent growth to 'around 6 per cent' in 2020, in line with the expected change to the national target ... At least 11 provincial-level regions missed their 2019 GDP targets, according to preliminary statistics released by local governments. Targets for 2020 ranged from around 5 per cent growth—for the north-eastern province of Heilongjiang and the northern city of Tianjin—to around 9 per cent growth for the Tibet Autonomous Region."

There have been other earlier warnings of the downturn in China's economy. In mid-December 2018, Renmin University Prof. Xiang Songzuo highlighted serious doubts about the economy at a public function, which was promptly censored on the Chinese internet. He questioned China's real rate of growth—declaring that a "research group of an important institution" had released an internal report stating China's GDP growth this year was about 1.67 per cent—the poor state of private businesses in China, and a lack of confidence. Within days, 59-year old Chen Hongtian, Chairman of the Cheung Kei Group and member of the Chinese People's Political Consultative Conference (CPPCC), warned nearly 150 tycoons based mainly in Shenzhen and Hong Kong, that China's private business entrepreneurs should prepare for a "winter colder and longer than expected". The group included Tencent Chairman Pony Ma, the Chairman of car-maker BYD, Wang Chuanfu, and the Chairman of courier service SF Express, Wang Wei. Meanwhile, State owned Enterprises (SoEs) expanded to enter virtually every sector of economic activity.

More recently on November 27, Gao Shanwen, a well-known economist in China, in a speech at an internal annual strategy meeting predicted that China's economic slowdown would last several years and that the average annual economic growth between 2020 and 2030 will stay below 5 per cent. Gao Shanwen was even concerned about whether GDP would grow above 4 per cent. He identified two contributing factors: first, the impact of the trade war; and second, the stagnation of China's economic reform as seen in the "advancement of the state enterprises and the retreat of the private sector." Gao Shanwen said that the government has used strong counter-cyclical measures to prevent the economic downturn, but these have barely supported the growth rate at about 6 per cent. The stimulus policies are less and less effective and, with a weak domestic market, the economy of 2020 doesn't look good. Gao Shanwen's speech was widely circulated on the internet, but deleted within a day.

On December 8, Sina.com published economic data posted on the internet by an unnamed author which explained that China's economy is at its most difficult time. It was widely disseminated across the internet in China. Its main points are: (i) the number of people using Baidu to search for jobs in 2019 jumped to 28.54 million from the under 7.5 million people job seekers in 2018; (ii) all four Chinese companies ranked in the top ten companies with the highest profits in the world are banks, suggesting that China's banking sector is squeezing profits out of other industries. China's banking sector claims 40 per cent net income return; (iii) China's SoEs are growing and the private companies and foreign companies are shrinking; (iv) people are short of money. The fund industry (both mutual funds and hedge funds) raised Yuan 500 billion (US $72 billion) in the third quarter of 2017 alone. However, for the whole year of 2019, it only raised Yuan 180 billion; (v) 1,884 movie or TV related companies closed in 2019; (vi) new car sales dropped 2.76 per cent in 2018 compared to 2017. From January to October 2019, the number of new cars manufactured and sold dropped 10.4 per cent and 9.7 per cent respectively, compared to a year ago; (vii) China is departing from real (manufacturing) businesses. Among the total assets of companies in China, the financial and real estate industries claim 47.9 per cent of the assets, whereas the manufacturing sector accounts for only 11.7 per cent; (viii) in the first six months of 2019, all provinces in China, except Shanghai, ran into a fiscal deficit.

The coronavirus had an important political impact too. The attempts by the government to cover up news of the epidemic, the delayed response and the lack of transparency in the initial weeks generated an angry public reaction. It provoked seldom seen public criticism of Chinese President Xi Jinping and the Chinese Communist Party (CCP). Xi Jinping's till now unexplained absence between January 29 and February 10 from public view and the official media and state-owned national TV at a time when China was facing a national medical crisis, drew added critical comment. Reputed Chinese intellectuals and scholars at certain personal risk posted criticism of Xi Jinping and the CCP on their public social media accounts. Well known Chinese Professor Xu Zhangrun of Beijing's Tsinghua University, on February 5, posted scathing criticism of Xi Jinping and the Chinese authorities captioned "Angry People No Longer Fear", that went viral on China's social media. He was arrested shortly thereafter. There were similar displays of anger by other Chinese intellectuals and even one Supreme Court judge!

Videos surfaced of Wuhan residents shouting "fake, fake" and "this is not real" during an inspection by Politburo member Sun Chunlan. A call by Wuhan Party Secretary Wang Zhonglin, a close associate of Xi Jinping, to "carry out gratitude education among the citizens of the whole city, so that they thank the General Secretary [Xi Jinping], thank the Chinese Communist Party, heed the Party, walk with the Party, and create strong positive energy" evoked sharp rebukes and widespread anger. Chu Zhaoxin, a local journalist posted (March 7) an article on his public WeChat account entitled "Have a Bit of Conscience: It's Not Time to Ask the People of Wuhan for their Thanks", adding that Wang Zhonglin's timing was "insensitive". He said, "If this is Wang Zhonglin's idea, I think he needs to educate himself. You are a public servant, and your job is to serve the people. Now the people you serve are broken, the dead are still cold, and the tears of the living have not yet dried. The sick have not yet recovered, and much of their dissatisfaction is completely reasonable. Rather than blaming the people in Wuhan you serve for not being grateful, you should reflect and be ashamed because you and your team are not working properly." Predictably, the post was removed by March 7 night. The *South China Morning Post* reported (February 18) that He Weifang, Professor of Law at Peking University, shared a 2-page handwritten article with friends on WeChat on February 17, calling for press freedom. Xu Zhiyong, a former law lecturer and founder of the social campaign New Citizens Movement, was arrested on February 15 for his article of February 3, wherein he urged Xi Jinping to step down for his "inability to handle major crises".

With their image substantively dented, if not damaged, Chinese President Xi Jinping and the CCP have a long and arduous road ahead to revive economic growth and create jobs. A top priority will be to rebuild and restore public trust which is crucial to the CCP's legitimacy as the sole ruling party. For Xi Jinping, it is imperative that he demonstrates that the 'China Dream' and China's goal of becoming "a major world power with pioneering global influence" remain intact. China will need to try and reestablish international supply chains, but more important will be whether global markets will be willing and in a position to procure and absorb Chinese products as they themselves struggle to recover from the after effects of the coronavirus epidemic.

*(This article was published by the Centre for China Analysis and Strategy, New Delhi, on March 15, 2020.)*

# 22. China's Economic Revival will Face Serious Headwinds

Quite apart from the huge tragic cost to human life caused by the coronavirus (COVID-19) pandemic, mishandling of which by China's leadership has angered and frustrated the country's citizens as evidenced by the riots at the border check-post between Hubei and Jiangxi provinces on March 28, the pandemic has severely impacted China's economy. The epidemic virtually stopped China's economic growth for nearly three months and rendered millions jobless. Unemployment has risen to over 6 per cent. China's services sector alone suffered an estimated loss of US$ 144 billion each week. Financial services assess a 30 per cent contraction of the Chinese economy and Chinese economists estimated that, if the epidemic was not contained by mid-February, China's growth rate could drop by 2 per cent. Recovery has been slow, prompting, according to a Hong Kong-based Chinese magazine, leading Chinese businessmen like Ma Yun ('Jack' Ma) and Liu Chuanzhi, founder of Lenovo, to sign a 9-point letter addressed to Chinese President Xi Jinping reviving demands for comprehensive reforms, including of the economy.

Economic losses have been widespread and have adversely affected almost all sectors. Bloomberg financial services reported a contraction of 9.9 per cent in incomes of central and local governments in the first two months of the year compared to the previous year and called it the "deepest fall since February 2009". It said, "Tax revenue declined more than 11 per cent, with drops in value-added taxes, corporate income taxes and car purchase taxes". It noted, "Spending also dropped, but a surge in outlays on health-care and social security kept the decline to 2.9 per cent from a year ago."

Already, because of the economic slowdown and US-China trade war, Reuters had reported on January 22, that about two-thirds of China's provinces, regions and municipalities had cut their 2020 growth targets from the previous year. These included Beijing, Guangdong, Zhejiang, Henan, Hainan, and Fujian. Beijing, Shanghai, and the southern export hub of

Guangdong—all economic high performers that dropped their targets from 6-6.5 per cent growth to "around 6 per cent" in 2020, in line with the expected change in the national target. According to preliminary statistics released by local governments, at least 11 provincial-level regions missed their 2019 Gross Domestic Product (GDP) targets.

Detailing the extent of damage, Lu Hai, Professor at Peking University, on March 25, said that a joint survey by Peking University's Guanghua School of Management and China's largest hiring platform Zhaopin, revealed that job openings in China for the first two months of 2020 dropped more than 30 per cent as the coronavirus epidemic severely disrupted economic activity. Hardest hit were the media, entertainment, sports and services sectors, all of which saw recruitments fall more than 40 per cent over the past year in the first two months of 2020. The Information Technology (IT), telecom, and internet sectors followed with advertisements for new jobs dropping by over 30 per cent. The survey revealed that smaller firms suffered more. Companies with staff strengths of more than 10,000 advertised 15 per cent fewer new jobs, companies with between 20 and 99 employees advertised 30 per cent fewer recruitments and firms with less than 20 personnel advertised 40 per cent fewer job openings.

China's leaders, and particularly Chinese President Xi Jinping, have been straining to revive the economy because they consider it domestically and geopolitically important to achieve the 'China Dream' by the hundredth year of the founding of the Chinese Communist Party (CCP) in 2021 and keep China on track to become "a major world power with pioneering global influence" by 2049—the centenary year of the establishment of the People's Republic of China (PRC). The former includes doubling of incomes by 2020 and the latter implies acquiring the capability to rival the US and be able to influence and create world organisations. Failure to achieve these goals and bring growth back to a reasonable level would impact adversely on their authority and legitimacy. However, despite their efforts, economic recovery has been slow.

As early as February 3, when there was still no easing of the coronavirus epidemic in China, Xi Jinping told local officials during a meeting of the Politburo Standing Committee—the Chinese Communist Party's (CCP's) apex body—that some of the actions taken to contain the virus were harming the economy and urged them to refrain from "more restrictive measures". He said some of the steps had sown fear among the public. Separately, China's provincial-level governments were permitted to issue a further Yuan 290 billion (US $41.6 billion) of Special-Purpose Bonds (SPBs) adding to the Yuan 1 trillion of such debt approved in November to boost infrastructure spending amid an already slowing economy now hit also by the epidemic.

On February 23, Chinese President Xi Jinping directly exhorted over 170,000 officials across the country to "prevent the economy from slipping out of a reasonable range". He expressed concern about China's role in global trade and said: "[We] need to secure the smooth operation of foreign trade supply chains and stabilize [China's] share in the international market." In a bid to push these efforts, Xi Jinping claimed at a meeting of the Politburo Standing Committee (PBSC) on March 4, that there had been overall improvement in the epidemic situation across China and in the resumption of economic activities. He stressed the need to promote international cooperation and maximise China's role as a "responsible great power".

Chinese Premier Li Keqiang convened a State Council Executive Meeting on March 10, to call for more efforts to stabilise foreign investment. The meeting decided to: (i) shorten the negative list of sectors restricting foreign investment and expand the list encouraging foreign investment; (ii) refund all export tax rebates in full and on time, except for those for energy intensive, polluting, and natural resource-related products; and (iii) encourage financial institutions to increase foreign trade loans by deferring principal and interest payments. On March 11, the National Development and Reform Commission (NDRC) published a policy focussing on stabilising foreign investment. Stating that it wants to boost foreign investment, the NDRC said big investments will get some benefits and it will coordinate with other ministries to iron out problems for investments of over US$ 1 billion in the manufacturing and high-tech sectors.

China has kept its strategic interests in mind. Chinese companies have stepped up production of medical equipment and supplies like respirators, masks and gloves, to take advantage of the urgent global demand and simultaneously expand their markets. China also took benefit of the drop in oil prices to an 18-year low and OilChem China purchased almost 1.5 million tonnes of commercial crude oil to add to its strategic oil stockpiles on March 7, the day after talks between the Organisation of Petroleum Exporting Countries (OPEC) and Russia collapsed and prices began to plummet. A manager at a Chinese oil storage company said, "All of China's coastal storage tanks and those near rivers are all booked, wherever they are in the country". The total quantum of oil in OilChem China's "strategic storage" is now 29.45 million tonnes.

To ameliorate distress, China decided to provide medium-term funding to banks and cut the interest rate. More than 300 Chinese companies, including Xiaomi, China's ride hailing company Didi Chuxing, facial recognition company Megvii Technologies and internet security company Qihoo 360 are seeking bank loans totalling at least US $8.2 billion to ease the impact of the coronavirus epidemic. This has been accompanied by efforts to revive economic activity and resume production. Transport authorities waived toll taxes and village cadres encouraged workers to return to their work place. *Xinhua Daily,* reported on March 14, that to encourage the service industry's recovery, the Nanjing government has begun handing out coupons worth Yuan 318 million (US $45million) each with a monetary value of Yuan 50 Yuan or 100. These include a dining coupon, book coupon, village tour coupon, living subsidy, labour union coupon, etc. Among the cities resorting to such monetary encouragement it listed: Macao issuing electronic coupons worth M$ 3000 (US $375) to each resident; Hong Kong announcing financial support totalling HK $120 billion (US $15.4 billion), including giving HK $10,000 to each person over 18 years old; Ji'nan city, Shandong Province issuing Yuan 20 million worth cultural consumption coupons; De city, Zhejiang province issuing Yuan 10 million in travel coupons; Zhejiang Provincial Culture and Tourism Department providing Yuan 1 billion to stimulate cultural and tourism consumption and Yuan 100 million in gifts directly to people; and Ningbo city, Zhejiang province issuing Yuan 100 million in coupons. In Jiangsu province, several senior leaders went to restaurants or stores to encourage people to go out and spend money.

Despite these efforts, China's Ministry of Industry and Information Technology (MIIT) disclosed that by March 24, only 71.7 per cent of small and medium-sized enterprises had resumed operations. Another National Business Activity Index said the next day that the economy was operating at 73.9 per cent, or less than three-fourths of normal levels. Identifying transportation and energy as two pertinent indicators, the New York-based Rhodium Group observed there were 82 per cent fewer trips in the 25 days following the Lunar New Year in 2020 compared to 2019, signalling that workers were not returning from the countryside. It observed that coal consumption by the six largest power plants in China fell over 40 per cent, property sales in major cities were near zero till March, and that government and private surveys had recorded major contractions in manufacturing and services. Economists have observed that if the economy doesn't get rebooted quickly, the damage will be intense and long-lasting.

A gradual improvement was reported by end March 2020. The official *The Paper* stated that businesses are reopening and observed, "Big data from Baidu searches shows that, at present, over 50 per cent of offline [businesses] have resumed work nationally." It said, "The percentage of offline [businesses] that have resumed work exceeds 63 per cent in Xining, Dalian, and Changchun, which lead the country in this respect." Separately, Xinhua reported that less than half of small and medium enterprises are back at work. It cited Ministry of Industry and Information Technology (MIIT) figures to say, "Around 45 per cent of China's Small and Medium sized-Enterprises (SMEs) had resumed work" by March 6, up from the 32.8 per cent of February 26. A magazine reporting on the coal industry, however, said, "The capacity utilization rate as of March 3 [of coal mines was] 83.4 per cent, according to official data from China's National Energy Administration", which marked a two-fold increase on that recorded on February 1. *The Paper* observed, however, that the economy remains "severely depressed".

The economic damage to the economy caused by the coronavirus epidemic has adversely affected private businessmen and entrepreneurs who have been complaining since mid-December 2018 that private businesses are being denied opportunities and expressed a lack of confidence in the system. Their dissatisfaction could well hamper China's efforts to rebuild and revive its economy.

In mid-December 2018, Renmin University Prof. Xiang Songzuo at a public function questioned China's real rate of growth—declaring that a "research group of an important institution" had released an "internal" report stating China's GDP growth in 2018 was about 1.67 per cent—the poor state of private businesses in China, and a lack of confidence. Within days, Chen Hongtian, Chairman of the Cheung Kei Group and member of the Chinese People's Political Consultative Conference (CPPCC), warned nearly 150 tycoons based mainly in Shenzhen and Hong Kong that China's private business entrepreneurs should prepare for a "winter colder and longer than expected". The group included Tencent Chairman Pony Ma, the Chairman of carmaker BYD, Wang Chuanfu, and the Chairman of courier service SF Express, Wang Wei. They asserted that contrary to assurances, the State owned Enterprises (SoEs) have expanded to enter virtually every sector of economic activity. Supermarket tycoon and founder of Wumart Stores, Zhang Wenzhong, on November 1, told entrepreneurs at a forum that the courts had released him and returned his property after five years of imprisonment and cautioned that this could happen to any of them. He said this is because "our basic economic system has been written into the country's and the Party's Constitution. It won't change." These complaints continue to be occasionally voiced.

As China tries to revive growth, the Chinese businessmen have now again taken up their demand for reforms. Coincidentally, they have increased pressure on Chinese President Xi Jinping and the CCP. On March 26, 2020, the Hong Kong magazine *China in Perspective* claimed that prominent Chinese businessmen had signed and handed over to Chinese Premier Li Keqiang a letter addressed to Xi Jinping stipulating nine comprehensive demands, including discarding of China's aggressive foreign policy. These are: (i) adhere to the Deng Xiaoping line; (ii) negate the Cultural Revolution; (iii) start the political reform; (iv) do not discriminate against private enterprises; (v) protect entrepreneurs; (vi) establish the national discovery fund; (vii) accountability for the coronavirus (COVID-19) epidemic; (viii) release Ren Zhiqiang; and (ix) reinvestigate the Li Wenliang incident. The magazine mentioned that five senior veteran Chinese Communist leaders, namely Li Ruihuan, Wen Jiabao, Li Lanqing, Tian Jiyun, and Hu Qili had also signed the letter. Interesting was the magazine's disclosure that Chinese billionaire tycoon and 'princeling' Ren Zhiqiang has been detained at the Changping Mangshan Base of the Beijing Municipal Commission for Discipline Inspection. The timing of this news comes at a difficult time for Xi Jinping and appears to confirm that, at the least, a group of powerful 'princelings' is opposed to him.

As China strives to energise growth and rebuild economic growth, a lot will depend on the global economy and the attitudes of other countries. US-China rivalry will probably escalate. As the US, Europe and other countries grapple with the coronavirus pandemic, trade will be limited and low on their list of priorities. China may hope to capitalise on distractions and plummeting stock markets to acquire hi-technology, pharmaceutical and other technologies and companies, but suspicions and its negative image could be major impediments. Current reports of Chinese companies stepping up production to meet global demand for respirators, masks, gloves and other urgently needed medical equipment, many of poor quality, will add to reservations about China. There is likely to be resistance to China's efforts to enlarge its global market share.

Countries will introspect and reexamine current trade policies, as should India, with priority on eliminating dependence on a single source of supply, especially in vital sectors of national importance like pharmaceuticals, precision engineering, communications, etc. With the possibility of biological warfare now a reality, serious complications for China will be its image, suspicions of its role in the pandemic and whether it shared pertinent information on the coronavirus epidemic fully and in time. China is likely to face a tough economic and political climate in the time ahead and blocking discussion on the pandemic at the UN Security Council only heightens suspicions.

*(This article was published by the Centre for China Analysis and Strategy, New Delhi, on March 31, 2020.)*

# 23. Dissatisfaction with Chinese President Xi Jinping Mounts

Expressions of popular discontent in China have increased and are mounting pressure on Chinese President Xi Jinping and the Chinese Communist Party (CCP). The widespread anger among Chinese citizens at the lack of transparency and attempt to withhold information about the outbreak of the coronavirus epidemic was the spark that fanned the latent discontent which, provoked by the abolition of term-limits on appointments to China's apex posts of President, Vice President and cadres to the Politburo and its Standing Committee, has been simmering since the 19th Party Congress in October 2017. The death of Wuhan hospital doctor Li Wenliang further spiked discontent. A number of reputed Chinese citizens, including many Party cadres, or at the least Party members, and at least one former member of the CCP's 350-odd-member powerful Central Committee (CC) and a Judge of China's Supreme Court, have been blunt and direct in their criticism of Xi Jinping and his policies.

Criticism has been aimed at the imposition of the progressively increasing security controls backed by expanding Party surveillance and centralisation of authority. Party presence and surveillance in college and school classrooms as well as campuses to monitor the lecturers and teachers has irked academia. There has been a steady hardening of China's security establishment reflected in the annual enhancements of the national security budget from 2013—which coincided with Xi Jinping taking over as CCP CC General Secretary, Chairman of China's Central Military Commission (CMC) and China's President. This has been accompanied by a progressive tightening of surveillance over the population and introduction of security technologies like closed circuit cameras, facial recognition and Artificial Intelligence (AI). Till now unexplained absence of Chinese President Xi Jinping—whose activities otherwise feature daily on the front pages of Chinese newspapers and as the lead news-item on state-owned TV—from January 29 till February 10, attracted adverse notice with a number of messages on Chinese social media criticising the handling of the crisis by the Chinese central and provincial governments and many critical of Xi Jinping. At least two reputed academics clearly suggested in late January that the poor handling of the crisis would have an impact on Xi Jinping's position!

On March 2 and February 23, 2020, Zhao Shilin, a retired Professor of China's Minzu University, Deputy Director of the Culture and Arts Commission and former member of the CCP CC, posted two open letters to President Xi Jinping. They were scathing in their criticism. In his letter of February 23, Zhao Shilin said China had "missed the golden window of time" around the time of the Chinese New Year, resulting in the "epidemic spreading with great ferocity". He described the costs of this mistake as "enormous" and "unspeakably painful". Referring to Xi Jinping's remark that the battle against the coronavirus "is a grand test of the capacity of our nation's system of governance", Zhao Shilin bluntly declared, "Regrettably, I must say, you're scoring zero so far!" He identified five factors as responsible, with stringent security, ensuring the Party and Xi Jinping's image and pre-eminence, and centralisation of authority, topping the list. The five factors are: (i) the habitual use of extreme social stability measures; (ii) the institutional practice of only reporting good news, not reporting the bad; (iii) rigid institutional supremacy; (iv) loss of a functioning civil society; and (v) lack of information transparency. Elaborating on each of them, he said these inhibited cadres and officials from doing their job or taking initiatives. He stressed that "people from within and without the system are calling for systemic political reform" and that these must include implementing the "socialist core values of freedom, democracy, equality, and rule of law" and guaranteeing the political rights of citizens, such as freedom of speech. In the letter of March 2, he reiterated that "there should be more than one voice in a 'healthy society' to demand free speech".

Guo Yuhua, a prominent Professor in the Sociology Department of Beijing's prestigious Tsinghua University, indirectly criticised Xi Jinping and the Chinese leadership in her interview with Radio Free Asia, published on March 3, 2020. While addressing the coronavirus epidemic and China's systemic limitations, Guo Yuhua alleged that the CCP's view of human worth remains narrowly utilitarian and inhumane and restricted particularly to its usefulness in achieving and maintaining political power. She was one of the first people to speak out in protest against the overt official persecution of her colleague Xu Zhangrun, a Professor of Law at Tsinghua.

He Weifang, Professor of Law at Peking University, shared a two-page handwritten article with friends on WeChat on February 17, 2020 calling for press freedom. Though handwritten in an effort to bypass the censors, the posts were deleted about an hour after he forwarded the two-page article to several chat groups. In his letter, He Weifang said, "I hope the heavy price [of the outbreak] will make Chinese authorities come to realise that without press freedom, people will live in distress and the government in mendacity." He said the absence of press freedom limited the country's ability to develop good governance.

A lengthy article criticising the shortcomings in governance, not allowing civil society to have a larger role, suppression of free speech, prediction of a far more serious fallout for the Chinese economy, and referring to Tsinghua University Professor Xu Zhangrun's recent lengthy article, was posted on February 13, on the public social media account of Duan Zhanjiang, Judge of the Supreme People's Procuratorate, China's version of a Supreme Court. The post carried the curious disclaimer that these were not the personal views of the judge.

Others also posted articles on their public social media accounts, similarly risking almost certain punitive action. Reputed Tsinghua University Professor Xu Zhangrun authored a 6,246-word essay on February 5, captioned "Angry People No Longer Fear", which went viral on China's social media. It accused China's leaders and specifically Xi Jinping of being out of touch with the people's needs and perpetuating an elite with so-called "Red Genes". It accused Xi Jinping and a "small circle of leaders" of creating a "state within a state" and engaging in "big data terrorism". He charged, "The political system has collapsed under the tyranny, and a governance system [made up] of bureaucrats, which has taken [the Party] more than 30 years to build has floundered". He accused the authorities of spending the "taxpayers' hard-earned money for feeding the massive internet police to monitor every word and deed of nationals". Xu Zhangrun said the authorities have not only "stifled public discussion of all ideas of life, but also stifled social communication and early warning mechanisms that existed originally" and blamed this for the failure of the authorities in Hubei to take precautions to control the epidemic. He called Xi Jinping a "political tyrant", declared "the people no longer fear" and "the Sun will eventually come to this land of freedom!" Xu Zhangrun's earlier article published on July 24, 2018, had ricocheted across China creating a stir among Chinese academics and students. He was then suspended from his post, banned from leaving China and not allowed to publish his writings freely in China. He has since been placed under house arrest, barred from social media and cut off from the internet.

Forty-six-year old Xu Zhiyong, a former Lecturer at the Beijing University of Post and Telecommunications, posted an article on February 3, urging Xi Jinping to step down for his "inability to handle major crises". He called Xi Jinping's political ideology "confusing", his governance model "outdated" and said that he had ruined China with "exhaustive social stability maintenance measures". Xu Zhiyong said, "Seven years ago, I appealed to you to lead China to become a nation that respects democracy and the Constitution, but in return, I was thrown into jail for four years. And now, your men are still looking for me trying to throw me back in jail again. I don't think you are a villain, just someone who is not very smart. For the public's sake, I'm asking you again: step down, Mr Xi Jinping."

Acts of apparent subtle protest by official and Party organisations have also been noticed. *People Magazine*, a publication under China's People's Publishing House, in its March 2020 edition, published an article captioned "The Person Who Handed out Whistles" about Ai Fen, Director of the Intensive Care Unit (ICU) at Wuhan Central Hospital, which treated several coronavirus patients in December, 2019 and who forwarded the SARS-Coronavirus Diagnostic Report to Dr. Li Wenliang who then blew the whistle. The Hubei Province Communist Party authorities removed all posted versions of the article within three hours. *Southern Weekly*, a newspaper owned by the Guangdong Communist Party Committee and based in Guangzhou city, also published a detailed report on March 11 about Ai Fen and how the hospital authorities hid the information and forced medical staff not to talk about the outbreak.

Similarly, the *Wall Street Journal* reported (March 19) that people were 'outraged' as Chinese propaganda authorities glorified a veteran Xinhua News Agency reporter Liao Jun at a news conference in March, for her "heroic" coverage of the coronavirus epidemic in Hubei province. Gu Wanming, a retired Xinhua reporter, reacted with an essay widely circulated on a public social-media account stating: "If you have a little conscience, then you should refuse the accolade and decline to speak, otherwise people will say that you 'trod on the blood of others to ascend the podium.'" The essay was soon removed. Shao Yiming, a prominent virologist who is chief HIV/AIDS expert at the Chinese Centre for Disease Control and Prevention (CDC) was reported by Caixin as saying (March 20) that Chinese health authorities initially failed to identify and control the threats posed by Covid-19 because of "faulty assumptions and weaknesses in a carefully constructed direct reporting system".

Resentment was evident among the populace of Wuhan city, capital of Hubei province and epicentre of the coronavirus outbreak. On February 14, they protested against "the Communist government's suppression of freedom of speech and its hiding of information". When Politburo member and Vice Premier Sun Chunlan inspected Wuhan on February 14, after the epidemic had been brought under control, the residents shouted from their apartments "Don't believe them", "They are telling lies", "Cheers, Wuhan People!" "Wuhan people, save ourselves!", etc. That resentment persists was evident in the sharp and angry reaction when on March 6, when Wuhan Party Secretary and close associate of Chinese President Xi Jinping, Wang Zhonglin called for carrying out "gratitude education among the citizens of the whole city, so that they thank the General Secretary [Xi Jinping], thank the Chinese Communist Party, heed the Party, walk with the Party, and create strong positive energy." The story was reported in the *Changjiang Daily*, official newspaper under Wuhan's Party Committee and shared widely across social media. In a WeChat post on March 7, captioned "Have a Bit of Conscience: It's Not Time to Ask the People of Wuhan for their Thanks", journalist Chu Zhaoxin described Wang Zhonglin's timing as "insensitive". Chu Zhaoxin said, "This is public opinion, this is reality. People who are not blind or deaf can see and hear, and those who are not blind can feel it. If this is Wang Zhonglin's idea, I think he needs to educate himself. You are a public servant, and your job is to serve the people. Now the people you serve are broken, the dead are still cold, and the tears of the living have not yet dried. The sick have not yet recovered, and much of their dissatisfaction is completely reasonable. Rather than blaming the people in Wuhan you serve for not being grateful, you should reflect and be ashamed because you and your team are not working properly. " The post was removed by late night on March 7.

China's leadership has taken note of this outburst of criticism. More than a month after the National Supervisory Commission (NSC) launched an investigation into the handling of the case of Dr. Li Wenliang, a whistleblower doctor in Wuhan who was punished by local authorities, it reported on March 19 that the local police and Wuhan Public Security Bureau had revoked the reprimand issued to him, apologised to Dr. Li Wenliang's family and disciplined two police officers who oversaw the case. The NSC also acknowledged the good that Li Wenliang had done which "helped to push for the strengthening of virus prevention and control." In an attempt to deflect and blunt criticism of the regime, the NSC asserted that Li Wenliang was a Party member and not a so-called "opposition figure".

Further indication of the extent of discontent surfaced last week with the report that children of high-level veteran Party cadres, also called 'princelings', posted on WeChat a call for an "Emergency Enlarged Meeting of the Chinese Communist Party's (CCP's) Politburo" to discuss Xi Jinping's replacement. Radio France International (March 22) and Voice of America (March 23) also reported this. Chen Ping, son of a former high ranking People's Liberation Army (PLA) scientist and himself a 'princeling' and owner of the Hong Kong-headquartered Sun TV,said the meeting had a 13-point agenda and was to "discuss whether Xi Jinping is suitable to continue to be the President of the country, the CCP's General Secretary, and Chairman of the Central Military Commission." He said the 'princelings' had suggested constitution of a three-person group with Li Keqiang, Wang Yang, and Wang Qishan to organise the meeting. Stating that the post reflected many people's thoughts, Chen Ping added, "Now eventually it needs a (solution to fix the current policy) and it cannot always be this way. It is not good for China if the current policies continue." Sun TV has offices in Shanghai and Beijing and focusses on China's elite and the Chinese diaspora.

Opposition has been mobilised not only by mishandling of the outbreak of the coronavirus epidemic. Pools of anger already existed among the over 4,500 officers of the PLA dismissed on charges of corruption and their extended families; the almost one million Party members and cadres, including 175 at the level of Vice Minister expelled for corruption and violations of Party law; and academics and students stifled by the presence in college and school classrooms, campuses and libraries of Party cadres and 'student spies'. These resentments coalesced with the anger of the millions of jobless and unemployed.

The appearance of the WeChat post by some 'princelings', further publicised out of Hong Kong, hints at serious inner-Party conflict. While the CCP will emerge bruised, it will remain intact, but Xi Jinping faces a potentially troubled period of uncertainty ahead.

*(This article was published by the Centre for China Analysis and Strategy, New Delhi, on March 26, 2020.)*

# 24. Chinese President Xi Jinping Reacts to Inner Party Opposition

After an extended hiatus when Covid-19 and the economy appeared to preoccupy the Chinese leadership, Chinese President Xi Jinping fired a warning shot across the bow of opponents and potential opponents in the middle and higher echelons of the Chinese Communist Party (CCP). A meeting of the Politburo on April 17, 2020, chaired by Chinese President Xi Jinping approved the establishment of a new 'Small Group' on Security. It also approved its membership.

Designated the "Safe China Construction Coordinating Small Group", China's official news agency Xinhua said (April 21) the new organisation's declared task is to: "Prevent and crack down on activities that endanger the political security of the country"! Reflecting the Party's anxieties about domestic social unrest, it quickly held its first meeting on April 21. This small group is headed by Guo Shengkun, Politburo (PB) member and Secretary of the Political and Legal Affairs Commission (PLAC), which is at the apex of China's security apparatus. All the nine members of the "Safe China Construction Coordinating Small Group" are Xi Jinping loyalists, with some continuing in office beyond what was the age for retirement as per the CCP's convention till 2017. Shaken by the failed grab for power in 2012 by Zhou Yongkang, who was then Politburo Standing Committee (PBSC) member and Chairman of the Political and Legal Affairs Commission and informally referred to as China's 'Security Czar', Xi Jinping has ensured since coming to power at the 18th Party Congress in 2012 that his, and the CCP's, grip over the country's security apparatus and Chinese society is firm and unyielding. Xi Jinping has since then headed the PLAC with a handpicked Politburo member as Secretary.

Xi Jinping has paid a lot of attention to security and maintenance of public order, or "social stability" as it is euphemistically called, including at the micro level. At the Central Political and Legal Work Conference in January 2019, he announced that China's leadership has accorded higher priority to political-legal work since the 18th Party Congress. Chinese President Xi Jinping has also made major changes in China's security structure. The National Security Commission (NSC) (中央国家安全委员会) was set up in November 2013; the National Supervisory Commission (国家监察委员会) was established in 2018; and the People's Armed Police (PAP) (中国人民武装警察部队) was restructured in 2017-18. Since their establishment, the NSC and National Supervisory Commission have extended the Party's and central government's authority throughout the country and set up subordinate offices in provinces and counties.

The new "Safe China Construction Coordinating Small Group" is an organisation with an apparent different focus. It has a very wide ambit and the task of preventing "activities that endanger the political security of the country", gives it sanction to monitor the political and other activities of Party members. This encompasses not only sabotage and subversion, but all other activities that could be deemed to threaten the 'Party Centre' or weaken the CCP. It can be anticipated to reinforce the Party's anti-corruption body, the Central Discipline Inspection Commission. The organisation has been set up at this time when, provoked by mishandling of the coronavirus pandemic at Wuhan, there is increasing criticism from various sections of Chinese society directed at the CCP and Xi Jinping personally. Reflecting the public mood, some Party members and cadres too joined academics, intellectuals, students, economists, 'private' entrepreneurs and others, and posted their criticism on personal or official public social media accounts, risking certain punishment. Some even called for Xi Jinping to step down. There is discontent also among the millions of unemployed workers and demobilised soldiers and veterans who have not been rehabilitated or feel they have not got their due. The coronavirus, or COVID-19, pandemic, which has adversely impacted the economy and rendered millions more jobless, has added to China's economic difficulties. Worrying Xi Jinping in particular would be the two letters purported to have been written by 'princelings', China's influential and powerful elite consisting of the children and relatives of veteran Party leaders.

The brief bio-profiles of the nine members of the "Safe China Construction Coordinating Small Group" are given below: (i) Guo Shengkun: He is 65 years old. He is from Jiangxi province and was Minister of Public Security from 2012 till October 2017. He entered politics in 2004 in the Guangxi Zhuang region after working in State-owned Enterprises (SoEs) and the non-ferrous metals industry for over 20 years. He became Party Secretary of the Guangxi-Zhuang Autonomous Region in 2007. (ii) Zhao Kezhi: He visited India in October 2018. In addition to being Minister for Public Security, Zhao Kezhi has worked closely with two of Xi Jinping's long time confidants, namely, Li Zhanshu and Guo Shengkun. Zhao Kezhi was again appointed Minister of Public Security at the 19th Party Congress in October 2017. (iii) Zhao Qiang: Born on April 25, 1960, Zhou Qiang was appointed Party Secretary of Hunan in April 2010 making him one of the youngest provincial Party Secretaries in the country. He has headed the Communist Youth League and in March 2013, was appointed President of the Supreme People's Court. He is considered to be aligned with Xi Jinping and speaking at a Supreme People's Court meeting on January 14, 2017, asserted: "[China's courts] must firmly resist the Western idea of 'constitutional democracy' and 'judicial independence'. Describing them as erroneous Western notions that threaten the leadership of the ruling Communist Party and defame the Chinese socialist path on the rule of law, he said, "We must stay firm on the Chinese socialist path on the rule of law". (iv) Zhang Jun: He has had a steady, uninterrupted rise in China's law enforcement system. In February 2017 he was appointed Minister of Justice and in March 2018 took over as Procurator General. (v) Chen Yixin: A "Cultural Revolution Rusticated Youth", Chen Yixin joined the CCP in 1982. He spent his entire career in Zhejiang where he proved himself in the Wenzhou City Party Committee. He was brought to Beijing by Xi Jinping as Deputy Director in the CCP CC's Central Small Leading Group on Comprehensively Deepening Reform in the General Office. He is now Secretary General of the Political and Legal Affairs Commission (PLAC). (vi) Chen Wenqing: Born in 1960, he is a graduate of the Department of Law, Southwest University of Political Science and Law and joined work in 1984. He served for 12 years in the public security apparatus of Sichuan and later from 2006 in Fujian, where he subsequently served as Secretary of the Provincial Discipline Inspection Commission. He was brought to Beijing in 2012 by Xi Jinping as Deputy Secretary of the Central Discipline Inspection Commission till his appointment in November 2016 as

Minister of State Security. (vii) Tang Yijun: A former Governor of Liaoning, Tang Yijun was formally appointed as China's new Minister of Justice by the Standing Committee of the National People's Congress on April 29, 2020. It is significant that he was invited to attend the first meeting of the "Safe China Construction Coordinating Small Group" on April 21, though he was at that time only Acting Minister of Justice. Tang Yijun spent the first 40 years of his career in Zhejiang, eventually becoming its Deputy Party Secretary and later Governor of Liaoning since October 2017. Zhejiang is one Xi Jinping's key power bases and this, along with Tang Yijun being promoted twice in two and a half years, strongly suggests that he is Xi Jinping's ally. (viii) Wang Ning: A highly decorated military officer, 1955-born Gen Wang Ning was brought to the People's Armed Police (PAP) from the People's Liberation Army (PLA) in December 2013 when Xi Jinping undertook a major reshuffle of the PAP. PAP Commander Wang Ning, who has worked with Xi Jinping in Fujian, participated in the Sino-Vietnam War on the Yunnan border. (ix) Wang Renhua: His appointment to this sensitive position indicates he is trusted by Xi Jinping and the Central Military Commission (CMC) leadership. Little else is yet known about him.

Armed with wide ranging powers, the "Safe China Construction Coordinating Small Group" certainly reports directly and only to Xi Jinping. It appears similar to a Central Small Leading Group, but is chaired by a Politburo member. While little is presently known of its functions, it will probably investigate cases and decide on punishments in secrecy while reporting to, and obtaining approvals directly from, Xi Jinping.

*(This article was published by the Centre for China Analysis and Strategy, New Delhi, on April 29, 2020.)*

# 25. Xi Jinping Shores up Position to Fend off Opponents

Chinese Communist Party (CCP) General Secretary and Chinese President Xi Jinping and the CCP have been badly bruised by public criticism, which was accentuated by the initial mishandling of the coronavirus epidemic in Wuhan. After an extended hiatus, which included Xi Jinping's unexplained disappearance from public view at the peak of the crisis between January 29 and February 10, Xi Jinping is now demonstrating his political authority and influence to shore up his position and fend off opponents.

Reviving the economy is important for the CCP to retain legitimacy. It is domestically and geopolitically important for it to achieve the 'China Dream' by the hundredth year of the founding of the CCP in 2021, and keep China on track to become "a major world power with pioneering global influence" by 2049—the centenary year of the establishment of the People's Republic of China (PRC). By announcing these goals at the 18th and 19th Party Congresses respectively, Xi Jinping staked his prestige and personal reputation on these. The former includes doubling of incomes by 2020 and the latter envisages acquiring the capability to rival the US and influence and create world organisations. Failure to achieve these 'Two Centenary' goals and bring growth back to a reasonable level would impact adversely on the CCP and Xi Jinping's personal authority and legitimacy.

Resentment has been brewing, especially since the 19th Party Congress in October 2017 and the National People's Congress (NPC) Plenum that followed in March 2018, when Xi Jinping abolished term limits on China's top posts of President and Vice President. These were instituted by Deng Xiaoping as safeguards against a single leader becoming too powerful. Many serving as well as retired and veteran Party cadres and members, a number who had suffered during the Cultural Revolution decade, publicly declared they did not want a return to the 'one man rule of Mao'! Rising prices, growing inflation and the unemployed, whose number burgeoned from 25 million to an estimated 70 to 80 million by March 2020, added to the discontent. Ex-servicemen and PLA veterans also had complaints. Academics, students and intellectuals had grievances provoked by enhanced ideological and political education in colleges and schools, increased Party surveillance of Professors and Lecturers, and deployment of Party members in classrooms even of primary schools. The 'social credit management system' to be implemented across China by the end of this year is a source of constant worry for the Chinese.

The economic slowdown because of the US-China trade war and now COVID-19 has aggravated the widespread discontent. China's 'private' businessmen and entrepreneurs have since mid-December 2018, complained that private businesses are being denied opportunities, and have expressed a lack of confidence in the system. They have asserted that contrary to assurances, State owned Enterprises (SoEs) have expanded to enter virtually every sector of economic activity. These businessmen include tycoons like Chen Hongtian, Chairman of the Cheung Kei Group and member of the Chinese People's Political Consultative Conference (CPPCC), Zhang Wenzhong, founder of Wumart Stores, Pony Ma, Chairman of Tencent, Wang Chuanfu, Chairman of carmaker BYD and Wang Wei, Chairman of courier service SF Express. In mid-December 2018, Renmin University Professor Xiang Songzuo questioned China's real rate of growth, its poor state of private businesses, and the lack of confidence. He revealed that an "internal" report had stated that China's Gross Domestic Product (GDP) growth in 2018 was about 1.67 per cent!

With bleak prospects for an early economic recovery, Chinese economists have been debating on whether China should at all mention a growth target in the report to be presented at the NPC on May 22, 2020. Ma Jun, an academic member of the People's Bank of China's (PBoC's) monetary policy committee, recommended it be dropped "because growth will largely depend on how the pandemic develops in Europe and the United States." Yu Yongding, a former PBoC adviser, urged the government to mention a target even if it is low.

Xu Xiaonian, a Professor of Economics and Finance at the China Europe International Business School, was blunt and cautioned that "as long as the pandemic in Europe and America is not over, Chinese export companies will have no orders, workers will have no wages and there will be no consumption and a recession is inevitable". He said, "We are not only short of food and oil, but we are also short of markets; we are short of orders. Our per capita GDP is one-fifth of that of the United States and one-fourth that of Europe. The domestic purchasing power cannot support our enormous manufacturing capacity." He added, "We still lack raw materials, especially the technology-intensive basic raw materials, which must be imported from South Korea, Japan and Germany. We lack technology, and technology cannot be developed rapidly when we close the door."

The seriousness of the bleak economic situation was reflected by the *People's Liberation Army (PLA) Daily*, which on May 5 published an essay titled: "We Should Guard against the 'High Explosive Point' of the Strategic Financial 'Chess Game' and Earnestly Safeguard the National Financial Security". The slow pace of economic recovery additionally prompted prominent Chinese businessmen like Jack Ma, founder of the Alibaba Group, and Liu Chuanzhi, founder of Lenovo, to sign and personally hand over to Chinese Premier Li Keqiang on March 26, 2020, a nine-point letter addressed to President Xi Jinping reviving demands for comprehensive reforms.

Criticism increased with the onset of the coronavirus pandemic. Among the critics were ordinary Chinese, academics, students, senior Party cadres and officials. Criticism centered mainly on the Party controlling everything; progressively increasing and stringent security controls; expanding Party surveillance; undue centralisation of authority; and discarding of Deng Xiaoping's policy of "lie low, bide your time". A number of Party cadres and officials in Chinese think-tanks have in private conversations blamed Xi Jinping's aggressive foreign policy for China's growing international isolation, rapidly deteriorating relations with the US and poor international image. Rare for China, Xi Jinping has been criticised by name, with calls for him to step down.

Noticed were acts of apparent subtle protest by official and Party organisations. *People Magazine*, a publication under China's People's Publishing House and *Southern Weekly*, a newspaper owned by the Guangdong Communist Party Committee and based in Guangzhou city, published reports praising Dr Ai Fen of Wuhan Hospital in the March 2020 edition and on March 11 respectively.

Public indication of the seriousness of discontent surfaced on March 22, with reports that children of high-level veteran Party cadres, called 'princelings', had posted a call on WeChat for an "Emergency Enlarged Meeting of the Chinese Communist Party's (CCP's) Politburo" with a 13-point agenda to discuss Xi Jinping's replacement.

Probably provoked by this, Chinese President Xi Jinping began taking steps to contain criticism and fend off opponents from February/March. From February 3, he began exhorting cadres to resume production and revive the economy. To assuage public anger, the reprimand issued to the deceased Dr. Li Wenliang was revoked, an apology conveyed to his family and two police officers disciplined. Domestic controls were, however, not eased and the authorities detained many who had criticised Xi Jinping. Censorship of social media was enlarged and on April 25, the Publicity Department of the Party Committee of the Beijing International Studies University notified that the CCP will impose large-scale censorship and monitoring of Twitter, YouTube and Facebook accounts overseas.

Hong Kong, where Beijing's inaction, despite the continuous protests since May 2019, prompted speculation that Beijing was losing its grip, witnessed action to retrieve the situation. Reports claimed that nearly 4,000 officers from China's People's Armed Police (PAP) had joined the Hong Kong police to monitor protesters and their tactics to deepen the PAP's understanding of the situation. In January and February 2020, two Xi Jinping loyalists with tough reputations, namely, Luo Huining, former Shaanxi Party Secretary and Xia Baolong, Xi Jinping's former deputy in Zhejiang who had retired, were appointed Director of the Liaison Office of the Hong Kong Special Administrative Region (HKSAR) and Head of the Hongkong Macao Affairs Office (HKMAO) respectively. On April 13, the Liaison Office of HKSAR stated that it was not subject to the Basic Law. In a surprise move on April 19, the Hong Kong authorities arrested 15 pro-democracy leaders, including former Legco member Martin Lee and the owner of Apple Daily Lai Chee-Ying (Jimmy Lai). The HKMAO, on May 6, warned, "The scorched-earth action of the black-clad violent protesters is a political virus in Hong Kong society and a big enemy to 'one-country-two-systems'", adding, "As long as the protesters are not removed, Hong

Kong will never be calm." It said China's central government will not sit idly and has the greatest responsibility in maintaining order and safeguarding national security.

China maintained its tough stance towards Taiwan President Tsai Ing-wen and the Democratic Progressive Party (DPP) to wear them down. The *PLA Daily* claimed that sentiments favouring forceful reunification of Taiwan are rising in China—recently indirectly confirmed by retired PLA Maj Gen Qiao Liang a reputed 'hawk'—and Beijing stepped up military pressure with increased sailings of PLA Navy (PLAN) warships and its aircraft carrier. People's Liberation Army Air Force (PLAAF) aircraft began overflying Taiwan and on April 1, they conducted a 36-hour-long-endurance exercise. Beijing blocked calls for interaction between the World Health Organisation (WHO) and Taiwan over the coronavirus pandemic. On April 24, the *Nanfang Daily* disclosed that Guangzhou city's National Security Bureau had finished investigations into Lee Henley Hu Xiang, a Belizean national and Taiwan resident. It said that the investigations "confirmed that the suspect provided a large amount of funds to hostile elements in the United States, colluded with foreign anti-China forces to intervene in Hong Kong affairs, and funded the implementation of criminal activities that endangered our national security." He is the first foreigner to be identified for involvement in Hong Kong.

Xi Jinping's aggressive foreign policy style has not changed. There has been no easing of propaganda or military pressure as evidenced by the Xinhua article of March 4, threatening the US with stoppage of medical supplies. China continues to flex its military muscle in the East Sea and substantively advance its claims over the South China Sea. Despite seeking entry to the Indian market, China's official media continue negatively portraying India's economy and health infrastructure. China raised the Kashmir issue for the fifth time at the United Nations Security Council (UNSC) on April 8. It underlined its comprehensive ties with Pakistan with the first "Sea Guardians 2020" naval exercises featuring anti-submarine and submarine rescue training in the Arabian Sea. The People's Liberation Army (PLA) has held at least six military exercises in Tibet since February/March including a 'combat' exercise by several helicopters in the Lhasa area on April 21. On April 27, between 300-500 PLA vehicles were observed in the Tashigong area opposite Demchok.

There are other indicators suggesting that Chinese President Xi Jinping has become active in domestic politics to shore up his position and fend off opponents. On April 8, three Xi Jinping 'loyalists' were appointed as new Party Secretaries. The same day, the Beijing Western District Supervisory Commission announced the arrest of 'princeling' tycoon Ren Zhiqing, a trenchant critic of Xi Jinping, notwithstanding the 'princelings' publicising their support for Ren Zhiqing and urging Xi Jinping for his release. On April 14, Politburo Standing Committee (PBSC) member and CPPCC Chairman Wang Yang chaired a meeting of the Committee on Poverty Alleviation, apparently replacing PBSC member Han Zheng. Poverty alleviation is a priority for Xi Jinping who promised eradication of poverty by 2020 in the 'China Dream'. Han Zheng's inaction on Hong Kong affairs had prompted Xi Jinping to say in late January that "those responsible should resolve it".

Significant, however, are two developments which suggest that discontent within the Party and inner-Party factionalism are causing Xi Jinping considerable anxiety. On April 17, Xi Jinping chaired a Politburo meeting which approved the creation and membership of a new "Safe China Construction Coordinating Small Group". Headed by Guo Shengkun, Politburo member and Secretary of the powerful Political and Legal Affairs Commission (PLAC), each of its nine members have been handpicked Xi Jinping 'loyalists'. Xinhua (April 21) mentioned its task as to "prevent and crack down on activities that endanger the political security of the country", indicating that the "Safe China Construction Coordinating Small Group"has a wide, ambiguous ambit. The National Security Commission, National Supervisory Commission and Central Discipline Inspection Commission (CDIC) all have separate defined functions. The 'Small Group' will report to Xi Jinping.

The other is the Radio Free Asia (April 27) report that Xi Jinping's followers held 'emergency' meetings at the Ministry of Public Security (April 20), the Secret Service Bureau of the Ministry of Public Security (April 21), and the CCP Political and Legal Affairs Commission (April 22). Radio Free Asia disclosed that at the Secret Service Bureau's meeting, Wang Xiaohong, Executive Deputy Minister of Public Security and Director of the Secret Service Bureau stated, "(We) must increase the monitoring of the 'top leaders' decision-making power, staff appointment power, and financial approval power, to let the 'top leaders' get used to working and living under monitoring."

The last two developments clearly indicate that in addition to the widening public dissatisfaction, it is the inner-Party discontent, accompanied by calls for him to step down that is causing Xi Jinping a lot of anxiety. However, as demonstrated by the creation of the new 'Small Group' and by Xi Jinping's personality, he is unlikely to quietly back-off in the face of inner-Party opposition. The new 'Small Group', on the other hand, is a clear warning to senior Party echelons, 'princelings' and Party veterans to fall in line, but whether they will depends on the extent of opposition to Xi Jinping at the middle and higher echelons of the Party and among Party veterans.

*(This article was published by the Centre for China Analysis and Strategy, New Delhi, on May 17, 2020.)*

# 26. Qiu Shi Calls for Protecting Xi Jinping as "Core" of the Whole Chinese Communist Party

There have been important developments in China's domestic politics in recent weeks. These have built on the Party's assessment of Chinese President Xi Jinping's Communist credentials. Coming as these do at a time when Xi Jinping and the Chinese Communist Party (CCP) are under considerable pressure due to domestic criticism and the economic situation, in addition to the all-round pressure exerted by the United States which has severely accentuated China's difficulties, they assume significance. The CCP's flagship theoretical magazine *Qiu Shi (Seeking Truth)* had in June 2014—within nineteen months of Xi Jinping's assumption to power—described Xi Jinping as "one of China's greatest Communist leaders" who had put forward "new thinking, new views and new conclusions"! That article signalled Xi Jinping's capture of the CCP.

More recently, *Qiu Shi* (2020/14 dated July 15, 2020) published two important articles. One was authored by Xi Jinping and was a selection of 18 phrases culled from his speeches spread over seven years between December 2013 and October 2019. Not quite like Mao's Red Book, it is an attempt to more readily publicise and disseminate his thoughts to a national audience. More important, however, was the accompanying *Qiu Shi* editorial, which definitively seeks to elevate Xi Jinping's standing in the pantheon of Chinese Communist leaders. While Mao obviously stands on a different pedestal as the leader who steered the CCP to victory through the arduous Long March and as founder of the People's Republic of China (PRC), this editorial describes Xi Jinping alone as the "core of the CCP Central Committee" which, in turn, is the "core" of the Party. Neither Deng Xiaoping nor Mao Zedong enjoyed such preeminence within the CCP as both had powerful veteran and stalwart Chinese Communist leaders to contend with.

Nonetheless, the emphasis on the "two maintenances" and the "two safeguards" hints at inner-Party differences and suggests that *Qiu Shi* is trying to rally the Party around Xi Jinping. It highlights his contributions, but also categorically states that he "personally" commanded the effort to fight the coronavirus epidemic—a sensitive topic inside China and the subject of much of the criticism. Particularly revealing is the direction that "Party organisations at all levels, all Party members, especially senior cadres, must follow the Party Central Committee", the Party's line, etc. The *Qiu Shi* editorial appeared weeks before two important events, the annual "informal" gathering of veteran leaders at the Beidaihe seaside resort and the Fifth Plenum of the 19th Party Central Committee recently announced for October 2020.

The lengthy 6,359-word, 6-section editorial contained over 60 references to Xi Jinping, making clear his leading position. It credited him and the CCP with guiding China to its present stage and asserted that the Chinese people are "lucky" to have Xi Jinping as their leader. The editorial especially called on Party institutions, Party cadres and Party members to "protect" Xi Jinping who is the "core" of the CCP and the whole Party. This call is distilled into the phrase the "two safeguards", also translated as the "two defends". Salient highlights of the editorial are given below.

The first few paragraphs of the *Qiu Shi* editorial stress on Chinese President Xi Jinping's personal leadership and involvement in tackling the coronavirus epidemic. It said that under his "personal command" the Party, government, Army and civil and the East, West, South, North and Centre all launched an all-out war against the pandemic. Describing Xi Jinping as the "core of the Party Central Committee" and the "core of the whole Party", it credited him with working to achieve "the great rejuvenation of the Chinese nation".

The section captioned "Leadership of the Chinese Communist Party (CCP)" described Xi Jinping's selection of the 18 phrases. Calling it "the most essential feature of socialism with Chinese characteristics", it averred that this "important" article will "further strengthen the 'four consciousnesses', 'four self-confidences' and achieve the 'two safeguards' for the entire Party".

Elaborating on the role of the Party, the section entitled "Party Leads Everything" underscored that this "is the fundamental point of China's stability, economic development, national unity and social stability". It listed some important points namely: "upholding and strengthening the overall leadership of the Party is related to the future and destiny of the Party and the country". In this, it said, "There must be no ambiguity and vacillation". It added that "without the leadership of the CCP, our country and nation would not be able to achieve the achievements it has today, nor can it have the international status it has today, with the CCP in power, it is China and the Chinese people". The section highlighted Xi Jinping's role and emphasised that he has "strengthened the overall leadership of the Party in all fields". It added, "The core position of General Secretary Xi Jinping and the core position of the whole Party have been established". "A big country like ours with a population of 1.4 billion must have a leader that everyone counts.... a big Party like ours with more than 90 million party members must have a strong core". It stated that the "sixth plenary session of the 18th Central Committee of the CCP formally established General Secretary Xi Jinping's core position of the Party Central Committee and the core position of the whole Party. The 19th National Congress of the Party included General Secretary Xi Jinping's core position of the Party Central Committee and the core position of the whole Party into the Party Constitution". It called this "the luck of the Party, the country, the people and the Chinese nation".

Discussing the "two maintenances", the article said, "Adhering to the leadership of the Party is to first uphold the authority of the Party Central Committee and centralised and unified leadership. This is the highest principle of the Party's leadership. Under the circumstances, it must not be vague or shaken". "Maintenance of authority has always been a major issue in the building of the Marxist parties. It is vital to ensure the unity and centralisation of the Party". It elaborated that "after the Zunyi (Tsunyi) conference established Comrade Mao Zedong's leadership position in the party Central Committee, our Party began to form a strong leadership core". It warned that without the Party's central authority and centralised unified leadership, "the Party leadership will inevitably weaken and the Party's cause will inevitably suffer frustration".

Reiterating Xi Jinping's position, it recalled that the "Sixth Plenum of the 18th Central Committee of the Party officially established General Secretary Xi Jinping as the core of the Party Central Committee and the entire Party". It was a "major event related to the authority of the Party

Central Committee and the vitality and centralisation of the entire Party". Implicitly praising Xi Jinping and justifying his position as the "core" of the Party, the editorial said, "The political leadership is skilful and superb, the people's feelings are sincere and broad, and the historical role is strong and firm, which fully proves that it is worthy of being the core of the Party Central Committee and the core of the entire Party". The editorial said China has overcome difficulties and "the fundamental reason lies in maintaining the core position of General Secretary Xi Jinping, the Party Central Committee and the core position of the entire Party, and resolutely maintaining the authority and concentration of the Party Central Committee". It again emphasised that "unified leadership will unite the entire Party, people of all ethnic groups across the country".

Important was the explicit explanation of the "two maintenances", which are essentially one, and is: "maintaining the core position of General Secretary Xi Jinping means maintaining the authority of the Party Central Committee and centralised and unified leadership; maintaining the authority of the Party Central Committee and centralised and unified leadership must first maintain the core position of General Secretary Xi Jinping".

An important feature of the editorial was the introduction of the "two safeguards", also translated as the "two defences", with its clear connotations and requirements. The *Qiu Shi* editorial declared: "To safeguard the core position of General Secretary Xi Jinping, the target is General Secretary Xi Jinping rather than anyone else; to maintain the authority and centralised unified leadership of the Party Central Committee, the target is the Party Central Committee and not any other organisation. The authority of the Party Central Committee determines the authority of Party organisations at all levels. The authority of Party organisation at all levels comes from the authority of the Party Central Committee. The 'two safeguards' can neither be applied layer by layer nor extended at will".

These were further reinforced with the exhortation that it is necessary to strengthen the "four consciousnesses" and "four confidences" and maintain "a high degree of consistency with the Party Central Committee, with Xi Jinping as the core in ideological and political actions". Importantly, it emphasised, "Party organisations at all levels, all Party members, especially senior cadres, must follow the Party Central Committee, follow the Party's theory, line, principles and policies, follow the Party Central Committee's decision-making and deployment, and unswervingly maintain the core and all aspects of General Secretary Xi Jinping's Party Central Committee".

The editorial stressed that these attributes strengthen the Party's overall leadership. Elaborating this, it pointed out that Xi Jinping has "pioneered the proposal that the most essential feature of socialism with Chinese characteristics and the greatest advantage of the socialist system with Chinese characteristics is the leadership of the Party...". It underscored that the "Party Central Committee and Xi Jinping have comprehensively strengthened and continuously perfected the Party leadership".

The timing of the *Qiu Shi* editorial's publication as well as its message are important. There are indications that Xi Jinping and the CCP are both under pressure, with greater pressure on Xi Jinping. Criticism levelled against him includes adopting an assertive foreign policy and prematurely challenging the United States, which is much more powerful than China and has left China friendless during the confrontation. There is additionally considerable apprehension in the mid to higher echelons of the CCP as to what the US, which has taken punitive actions against China each week, plans to do next.

A Chinese official writing under the pseudonym Liang Jing wrote on July 22, 2020, that the US Administration knows "that due to his major mistakes in the epidemic and the Hong Kong issues, Xi is in his most dangerous predicament since taking office. The US has a chance that it dared not imagine: to force Xi to step down, completely changing the confrontation between the US and China".

*(This article was published by the Centre for China Analysis and Strategy, New Delhi, on August 13, 2020.)*

# 27. Xi Jinping Launches 'Yan'an Style' Campaign to Cleanse China's Security Apparatus

The national security apparatus is the crown jewel of any country. Authoritarian regimes pay particular attention to these as they help preserve the regime and keep the population compliant and in check. China's Communist leaders have, for obvious reasons, been conscious of the importance of the security apparatus. In the backdrop of the increasing criticism since 2017—including by senior Communist cadres and 'princelings'—of him personally and his policies, Xi Jinping too has turned his attention to ensuring the loyalty of the security apparatus. He has just this month unleashed a severe year-long 'rectification' campaign throughout China's security system.

Acutely conscious that in the previous couple of years a potentially alternate centre of power led by China's security czar and Politburo Standing Committee (PBSC) member Zhou Yongkang had sought to emerge, Chinese President Xi Jinping—ever since he was appointed to China's top jobs in November 2012—retained direct supervision over China's security apparatus by allotting this portfolio to a Politburo (PB), instead of a PBSC, member. He also introduced a system whereby each Politburo member submits a report each week directly to Chinese Communist Party (CCP) Central Committee (CC) General Secretary Xi Jinping. All key positions in the security apparatus are held by Xi Jinping loyalists. The security budgets have also risen each year during his regime. A couple of years ago the Public Security Bureau (PSB) budget was higher than China's national defence budget and continues to at least rival that. While nearly half of all departments, including the Ministry of Foreign Affairs had their budgets cut in 2020, China's central public security budget alone rose by 0.7 per cent and in the current year, is Yuan 183.272 billion (US$ 26.2 billion). This PSB budget, incidentally, does not include other security-related expenditure such as on stability maintenance, electronic and technical surveillance, Ministry of State Security (MoSS), etc., or of the provinces.

Given the importance of the country's security apparatus—referred to as the "knife handle" by Party cadres—China's leaders have tried to ensure that the security system remains loyal to the CCP, and them personally, by appointing loyalists to head it and in key positions. After Mao Zedong's death and the ouster of CCP CC General Secretary Hua Guofeng and the Gang of Four in 1979, Deng Xiaoping carried out a clean-up of the security system. Again, after PBSC member Zhou Yongkang was discredited and subsequently arrested in 2012, Xi Jinping's predecessor CCP CC General Secretary Hu Jintao sent 3,000 security cadres for 'reeducation'. This was barely enough in an organisation with more than 1.97 million personnel. In view of the still continuing campaign to weed out "two-faced" Party and military cadres on charges of violation of Party discipline and corruption, it is apparent that the 'loyalty' of many including in the security set-up continues to be doubted.

Xi Jinping has undoubtedly been unnerved by the persistent criticism aimed at him since late 2017 when he abolished term limits for senior posts—including by senior Communist cadres and 'princelings'—which intensified with the outbreak of the coronavirus epidemic. He effected important personnel changes in the Ministry of Public Security (MPS) over the past two years, replacing a total of nine 'leaders' and additionally established a new security body.

On April 21, Xinhua announced that the Politburo had constituted a new security body called the "Safe China Construction Coordinating Small Group" headed by Guo Shengkun, Politburo member and Secretary of the Political and Legal Affairs Commission (PLAC), which is at the apex of China's security system. All nine members of the Small Group are trusted loyalists of Xi Jinping. Interesting is that this Small Group has a wide ambit and its task of "preventing activities that endanger the political security of the country" would give it sanction to monitor the political and other activities of Party members. The latter is substantive indication that some of the criticism would be known to have originated from senior Party cadres and 'princelings'.

Nonetheless, criticism continues to be voiced. A number of 'open letters' criticising Xi Jinping have stayed for days and even months after being posted on the internet and before being deleted by the authorities, suggesting the complicity of elements within the system. Pointing to the importance that

Xi Jinping gives to 'cleaning up' China's cyber space was the participation in the first meeting of the "Safe China Construction Coordinating Small Group Task Force" on June 8 of Lin Rui, Vice Minister of Public Security in charge of cyber security. One of Xi Jinping's trusted allies, having worked for many years in Fujian province where Xi Jinping spent 17 years in the earlier stages of his political career, Lin Rui has a degree in applied computing and is a specialist in cyber security and cyber crime prevention. This becomes even more relevant consequent to the important article and accompanying commentary published in the latest issue (2020/14; July 15, 2020) of the flagship Party theoretical fortnightly *Qiu Shi* (*Seeking Truth*).

*Qiu Shi* announced the publication of a new book of 18 phrases drawn from seven years of Xi Jinping's speeches, crediting him with its authorship. The quotations highlight the "absolute" and "leading" position of the CCP in all matters and declare that had it not been for the CCP's leadership, China would not have achieved the successes it has. It includes the warning that one cannot afford to falter even a little bit on the issue of "adherence to the Party's leadership." The accompanying and especially significant *Qiu Shi* commentary hinted at the elevation of Xi Jinping's position in the Chinese Communist pantheon, with implied comparison with Karl Marx! The commentary refers to "two safeguards", which unequivocally call for "protecting" the Central Committee which is the "core" of the CCP, with Xi Jinping at its "core" and "protecting" Xi Jinping's position as the "core" of the Central Committee.

On July 8, 2020, Chen Yixin, a trusted associate of Xi Jinping and alternate member of the 19th CCP CC and Secretary General of the Political and Legal Affairs Committee (PLAC), launched a 3-month (July to October) pilot programme to prepare for what will be a penetrating nationwide education and rectification of China's entire security apparatus next year. The campaign will encompass all political-legal institutions, including the supervision commissions, courts, procuratorates, police and prisons. Chen Yixin called it "a self-revolution with the blade inward and bone scraping to cure poison". Chen Yixin said, "We must drain away the filth and bring in fresh water." He called for a "turbulent and clear-cut Yangqing style 'Yan'an Rectification Movement' and 'soul-stirring Yangwei-style themed education' to "strive to build a political and legal iron Army that the Party and people can trust, trust, and can rest assured". He explained that the political and legal team is an important force to defend the leadership of the Party and the state power of the people's democratic dictatorship. He said while the system has been increasing its efforts each year to eliminate black sheep, "the situation remains grim". He said because of this, "a self-revolution in the form of scraping the bones and drugs should be carried out. The knife should be inward, the malignant tumour should be completely cut, the black sheep should be eliminated, and the political and legal teams should be absolutely loyal, absolutely pure, and absolutely reliable". He gave particular stress on adherence to "Xi Jinping Thought on Socialism with Chinese Characteristics for the New Era", earnestly implementing the important instructions of General Secretary Jinping and achieving the "two safeguards". The campaign will commence at the beginning of 2021 and end in the first quarter of 2022.

Taking the cue from Chen Yixin's exhortation, the following day (July 9) China's Ministry of Public Security convened a meeting on mobilisation for the new "Persist in Political Construction of Police, Comprehensively and Strictly, Govern Police" education and rectification campaign. Speaking at the meeting State Councilor and Minister of Public Security Zhao Kezhi emphasised implementation of the 'spirit' of Xi Jinping's guidance, the Central Committee's opinions on political construction, and the ministry's work meeting, strengthening the "four consciousnesses," "four confidences," and "two safeguards" and "closely centering on loyalty to the Party", service to the people, fair law enforcement, and strict requirements for discipline. He said that in its campaign, the ministry must focus on leadership at all levels and use "the courage of self-revolution and spirit of rectification (整风 的精神)," work to further solidify loyalty, strengthen Party leadership, improve its "political ecology," and make its goals for disciplined work style even stricter. Zhao Kezhi called on the ministry to address "impurity" of ideology, politics, organisation, and work style, "get rid of bad apples", purify its ranks, and ensure that the ministry's ranks "provide a staunch political guarantee for earnestly carrying out the New Era mission and tasks entrusted by the Party and people well."

The rectification campaigns in the PSB and the Procuratorate have been publicised by the *People's Daily* (July 9 & 10), which also noted the "two safeguards". As indicated in Chen Yixin's speech, the campaign can be anticipated to be thorough and result in the dismissal and arrests of numerous PLAC cadres. It will include ideological indoctrination, criticism and self-criticism, which implies persuading people to report on the wrong doings of others. The campaign appears intended to secure for Xi Jinping full control over the law enforcement system, which is the one pillar of the Party-state where Xi Jinping has never fully consolidated control. The PLAC oversees China's judiciary and law enforcement bodies.

Underlying the campaign's objectives will be the identification and weeding out of those suspected of loyalty to other leaders, thus, securing for Xi Jinping full control over the law enforcement system. Xi Jinping's objectives in launching such a tough campaign at this time when he is under domestic and international pressure, would be to stem the criticism of himself and the CCP, which could undermine his authority. It will also be to try and more effectively blunt US efforts to undercut the CCP, as indicated by the reported proposal to deny visas to CCP members.

*(This article was published by the Centre for China Analysis and Strategy, New Delhi, on July 27, 2020.)*

# 28. Xi Jinping's Efforts to Consolidate Marxist Ideology among CCP Members to Counter US

Confronted with growing tensions as US-China relations rapidly deteriorate, Chinese President Xi Jinping has asked Chinese Communist Party (CCP) members to prepare for a "protracted war" on multiple fronts. In addition to anticipated difficulties on the technology, economy and potentially military fronts, China's Communist leadership has taken special note of repeated American statements—particularly by US Secretary of State Mike Pompeo—about the threat from Chinese Communism. For example, on August 25, the official CCP mouthpiece the *People's Daily* published a lengthy 3-page, 34,000-character response to Pompeo's speech of July 23, at the Richard Nixon Presidential Library in California.

Fears of a 'peaceful evolution' have been a serious concern to the CCP leadership since the time of Mao Zedong and, more so after the collapse of the Soviet Union. 'Peaceful evolution' is interpreted as the US effort to introduce multi-party democracy; replace the socialist command economy with a free-wheeling capitalist system; and eliminate the CCP's monopoly as China's sole ruling political party, in other words, dismantling of the CCP.

CCP Central Committee (CC) General Secretary Xi Jinping has consequently visibly redoubled efforts to further consolidate Marxist ideology and 'socialism with Chinese characteristics'. Xi Jinping has consistently maintained that only "socialism with Chinese characteristics is socialism, and not some other doctrine," and it is a significant ideological issue that "concerns the future fate of the Party, the long-lasting peace and stability of the country, and the cohesion and solidarity of the nation." Since the time he took over as Party General Secretary at the 18th Party Congress in November 2012, Xi Jinping has launched numerous campaigns in the Party, military and government to stress the importance of Marxism and the CCP. Writing in a recent (2020/16; August 16,2020) issue of the Party's flagship theoretical magazine *Qiu Shi* (*Seeking Truth*), Xi Jinping emphasised that "the Marxist political economy is an important part of Marxism" and that the foundation of China's "political economy can only be Marxist political economy, not other theories".

In the wake of steadily increasing US pressure on China in recent months, escalated by the imposition of sanctions against CCP cadres and proposal to ban US visas to members of the CCP, a number of new ideological campaigns have been launched to strengthen adherence by the Party's 92 million members to the CCP's policies and principles. An earlier editorial in *Qiu Shi* (July 15) exhorted cadres to "protect" Xi Jinping's position as the "core" and warned Party members that "upholding and strengthening the overall leadership of the party is related to the future and destiny of the Party and the country".

It emphasised, "There must be no ambiguity and vacillation". It also cited Xi Jinping's speech to the Politburo on June 29, where he listed five goals as the Party's organisational line in the new era. *Qiu Shi* explained these as to: (i) uphold and improve the Party's leadership and develop socialism with Chinese characteristics. Xi Jinping stated this was important because political and organisational lines are linked. Xi Jinping also highlighted the importance of ensuring ideological and political consistency at all levels of the government with the Central Committee; (ii) arm the entire Party with the Party's scientific theory. Xi Jinping stated that Marxism should be used as a guide to strengthen and centralise party thought; (iii) build the Party's organisational system to unify and strengthen grassroots and local governance. Most important was to ensure their resolute obedience to the Central Committee; (iv) build the backbone of the ruling ranks and talent team, focussing on recruiting talented and virtuous people. Essential to this goal, Xi Jinping said, is to strengthen the education and training of cadres and deepen cadre system reform efforts; and (v) build the Party's organisational system. He focussed on democratic centralism as the key to the leadership system of the party, and expressed the need to "continuously improve the institutionalisation, standardisation, and the scientific level of the Party's organisational construction."

On July 8 2020, Xinhua reported the start of a new, comprehensive ideological campaign with the CCP CC General Office issuing a "Notice of the Central Propaganda Department and the Central Organisation Department on Earnestly Organising and Studying the Third Volume of Xi

Jinping: The Governance of China". Published by the Central Propaganda Department, the third volume of "Xi Jinping: The Governance of China" is a selection of 92 reports, talks, comments and speeches of Xi Jinping covering 19 topics and spanning the period October 18, 2017, to January 13, 2020. The notice declared that the volume is instrumental in promoting understanding of "Xi Jinping Thought on Socialism with Chinese Characteristics for a New Era", strengthening the "four consciousnesses" (四个意识), consolidating the "four confidences" (四个自信), and achieving the "two defends" (两个维护), and advancing global understanding of the appeal of the Chinese system. It stated that "studying the volume is an important political task" , and "theoretical study groups of Party committees and Party organizations" at all levels "should incorporate the volume in their study plans. The same applies for Party and cadre schools, as well as universities, Party committee lecture groups, new era civilisation practice centres, county-level media convergence centres, and the 'Xuexi Qianguo' learning platform app, so as to innovatively advance the "[flying] into the homes of ordinary people of the Party's scientific theories". Lastly, the notice highlighted the need to connect theory with practice in order to overcome the negative impact of the novel coronavirus, ensure economic stability and well-being, achieve a prosperous society, combat poverty, and "seize the opportunity to begin a new national journey" in constructing socialist modernisation.

Independently, 60-year-old Chen Yixin, Secretary-General of the Party's Political and Legal Affairs Commission (PLAC) and a protege of Chinese President Xi Jinping, convened a meeting in Beijing on July 8 to launch another new nationwide "education and rectification" campaign, this time targeting the country security apparatus. In a hard-hitting speech to officials attending the meeting, Chen Yixin said, "We must scrape the bone to remove the poison"; and "We must drain away from the filth and bring in freshwater." He called for a "turbulent Yangqing style 'Yan'an rectification', and soul-stirring Yangwei-style themed education which strives to build a political and legal iron Army that the Party and people can trust, trust, and can rest assured". The campaign is initially planned to be conducted in only five cities and four counties, but will go nationwide from early 2021. The campaign will come to an end in 2022. It is anticipated that the campaign will be thorough and result in the dismissal and arrest of numerous PLAC cadres.

The following day (July 9) China's Ministry of Public Security convened a meeting to mobilise personnel for the new "Persist in Political Construction of Police, Comprehensively and Strictly Govern Police" education and rectification campaign. Delivering a speech to start the campaign, the Minister of Public Security (MPS) Zhao Kezhi emphasised implementing the spirit of Xi Jinping's guidance, the Central Committee's opinions on political construction, and the Ministry's work meeting. He called for strengthening the "four consciousnesses," "four confidences," and "two defends," and "closely centering on loyalty to the Party", service to the people, fair law enforcement, and strict requirements for discipline. He said that in its campaign, the Ministry must focus on leadership at all levels and use "the courage of self-revolution and spirit of rectification (整风的精神)," further solidify loyalty, strengthen Party leadership, improve its "political ecology," and specify stricter goals for a disciplined work style. Zhao Kezhi instructed the ministry to address "impurity" of ideology, politics, organisation, and work style, "get rid of bad apples," purify its ranks, and ensure that its ranks "provide a staunch political guarantee for earnestly carrying out the New Era mission and tasks entrusted by the Party and people well." The two campaigns appear designed to allow Xi Jinping full control over the law enforcement system, which is the one pillar of the Party state where he has not fully consolidated control.

Weeks later, the *People's Daily* reported the commencement of a new campaign aimed at primarily the legal establishment. It said that on July 14, the CCP CC's Propaganda Department, Organisation Department, Political and Legal Affairs Commission, Cyberspace Administration of China, General Office of the National People's Congress Standing Committee, Ministry of Education, Ministry of Justice, and National Legal Awareness Office had jointly issued a notice launching a programme of study and education about the National Civil Code. The notice called for "thorough study and propaganda of General Secretary Xi Jinping's important treatises on governing the country fully according to the law, especially the spirit of important directives on the civil code," and study and propaganda on the significance of the code's implementation, its basic principles, and its content.

The notice urged departments to create multimedia news propaganda on Party and media-affiliated websites, detailed "new media" plans, focussed reports, authoritative interviews, various commentary series, and propaganda and activities for "modern platforms of dissemination" like the social media. It also mandated that study of the civil code should be incorporated into compulsory legal classes for leading cadres and that it should be made a more substantial component of education on rule of law in elementary, secondary, and higher education.

Another more extensive nationwide campaign encompassing students, the academic community and Party members was launched in mid-July. This new campaign requires CCP members, school students and academics to study the "Four Histories." The "Four Histories" are: "the history of the CCP, the history of new China, the history of the reform and opening up, and the history of socialist development." Parents have been told that there will be exams when the new semester begins and students will be tested. China's official media described the "Four Histories" as a new political drive and "key task" to promote the contents in classrooms at colleges and universities. The East China Normal University in Shanghai has incorporated the campaign material in its seminar series so that students will learn, and also "preach" its contents to people outside the campus.

Writing in the *China Education Daily* (August 13) Lu Yanqin, Deputy Secretary of the Party Committee of Zhejiang Jiaxing University, reiterated the importance of studying the "Four Histories" and said it will "help young people understand why the leadership of the Communist Party of China is the people's choice and history's choice". He said carrying out the "Four Histories" education among young people and integrating the "Four Histories" education into the teaching of ideological and political courses and related professional courses, will "help young people have a deep understanding of the hard-won New China's 'red regime' and the hard-won socialism with Chinese characteristics".

Liu Yanqin also explained the 'Red Gene' campaign and its significance. He cited CCP CC General Secretary Xi Jinping's recent congratulatory letter to the Eighth National Congress of the Chinese Young Pioneers when he pointed out that it is necessary to "inherit the Red Gene, cultivate new generations, unite, educate, and lead the young pioneers to be the successors of the cause of Communism". He described the "Red Gene" as the "life code of the Chinese Communists. It records the path of the Communists' descent into the past. It contains the nature and purpose of a Marxist Party. It is embedded with the ideals and beliefs of the Communists to fight for. It gathers the great revolutionary spirit of the Communist Party of China—the original intention and mission of the Communist Party of China". He further said, "To strengthen ideological and political education for young people, it is necessary to carry on the Red Gene well, and strive to cultivate socialist builders and successors who develop comprehensively in the new era of morality, intelligence, sports, and art".

The Red Gene campaign was first started in the People's Liberation Army (PLA) in 2018. In June 2018, the Central Military Commission (CMC) promulgated the "Outline for the Implementation of Inheriting Red Genes from Generation to Generation". Its objective is to develop the Red Culture so that the officers and men will always accept the influence of the Red Culture, so that the Red Gene will remain viable and show its power.

These campaigns are intended to strengthen the commitment of Party members and cadres to Marxist ideology and ensure they don't waver as US pressure intensifies. Xi Jinping is aware that US intentions include putting the CCP under enormous pressure and moving him out of office, which is why the stress in recent months on the "two defends", or "protecting" Xi Jinping as the "core" of the CCP CC. However, together with the imposition of increasingly restrictive security controls, the strain on the Chinese people could be considerable.

*(This article was published by the Centre for China Analysis and Strategy, New Delhi, on August 29, 2020.)*

# 29. China and the Post COVID-19 World

In the midst of the black clouds of the coronavirus, or COVID-19, spreading uncertainty around the globe and governments grappling to stop the immense loss to human life and damage to their economies, world leaders have begun assessing the possible contours of the post COVID-19 world. The US and the West particularly are trying to keep their economies strong and retain the advantage in advanced technologies to ensure that the global balance of power does not change, as that could mean a new China dominated world order with potential consequences for forms of government, individual freedoms and social values. US-China rivalry is anticipatedly escalating.

US President Trump has declared on record that he will not allow America to lose its advantage, implying it will strive to retain global primacy. On April 8, he questioned the role of the World Health Organisation (WHO) and bluntly observed that it appeared to be acting on China's orders and was responsible for delaying the warning to the rest of the world. There have been doubts about the WHO's role since it's Tweet of January 14 denying human-to-human transmission of the coronavirus, though by that time, China was already reporting such cases and Taiwan subsequently publicly announced it had informed WHO of this in late December. In a review of its earlier decision and a blow to China's hi-tech sector, the UK is likely to ban Huawei's fifth generation (5G) in British telecommunications networks. Chinese President Xi Jinping too, in early February well before China made gains in tackling the coronavirus epidemic, instructed the Chinese Communist Party's (CCP's) apex Politburo Standing Committee (PBSC) and his officials that China must not allow its economy to slip, must resume manufacturing and economic activity, try to reestablish global supply chains and expand its market share. Alluding to China's global ambitions, he said it must behave like a "responsible global power", while Chinese Foreign Minister Wang Yi spoke of creating a "community of shared future for mankind". An interesting coincidence was the disclosure by a Chinese government think-tank of its proposal for a Beijing-led rival to the World Health Organisation!

While the rest of the world is combatting the COVID-19, recent Chinese actions signal that Beijing's ambition to dominate the Indo-Pacific region has not changed. On April 3, Chinese Navy warships attacked and sank a Vietnamese fishing boat engaged in normal fishing activities near Fulin Island. China's People's Liberation Army Air Force (PLAAF), on April 1, undertook a 36-hour combat oriented exercise near Taiwan. The aircraft engaged in tactical acrobatics, reconnaissance, early-warning and surveillance work, airborne strikes and other unspecified tasks. The same day, two PLA Navy Air Force Xian H-6G maritime strike bombers and one Shaanxi Y-9JB (GX-8) electronic warfare and surveillance aircraft flew through international air space between the Japanese islands of Okinawa and Miyako in the East China Sea, triggering an immediate response by the fighter jets of the Japan Air Self-Defence Force (JASDF). Again, on April 15, the PLAAF conducted a long-range military drill when Xian H-6K bombers, a Shaanxi KJ-500 Airborne Early Warning and Control (AWAC) aircraft, a Shaanxi Y-9JB (GX-8) electronic warfare and surveillance plane, as well as Su-30 and J-11 fighter jets passed through the Bashi Channel, a strategically pivotal waterway between the Philippines and the Taiwanese island of Orchid connecting the South China Sea with the western Pacific Ocean. Some flew through the Miyako Strait. Earlier in March 2020, an Artillery Brigade of the 76th Group Army in the Western Theatre Command carried out 'live fire' exercises in the Tibet Military Region, and a week earlier, the PLA Rocket Force carried out high-altitude 'live fire' exercises at 4,500 metres in Tibet. These were clearly intended to convey to Japan, Vietnam, Taiwan and India, as well as the US, that China retains the capability and intent of becoming the dominant power of the Indo-Pacific.

Perceiving this time as opportune, China launched a worldwide diplomatic and media offensive to propagate that its model of government had been efficient and successful in controlling the coronavirus epidemic—implying that it could replace democracies—and that it stood ready to assist other countries in the spirit of the "community of shared future for mankind". Extensive publicity was, accordingly, given to the arrival of Chinese doctors and medical equipment in Italy. This diplomatic effort, also dubbed 'mask diplomacy', has, however, been undermined by the publicised admissions of the deceased Dr Li Wenliang and Dr Ai Fen, Director of the Intensive Care Unit (ICU) at Wuhan Central Hospital. Numerous reports, including videos, that filtered out from inside China also contest the official Chinese figure of approximately 3,335 dead due to the coronavirus and estimate the actual number at between 46,000 and 48,000! They point to the 5-hour long queues outside Wuhan's seven mortuaries, each of which are to receive 300 urns a day till end April, to collect the ashes of their relatives. China additionally sought to aggressively counter reports about the coronavirus 'escaping' from one of two Biolabs in Wuhan, or that China had delayed providing full information thereby facilitating spread of the virus. It objected to US President Trump and US Secretary of State describing it as the "Wuhan virus", threatened to sue reporters using that term, and countered that the virus had, in fact, been spread by US servicemen visiting Wuhan in October. The aggressive tone used by some of China's younger diplomats triggered a debate within China, with veteran diplomats, including former Vice Foreign Minister Fu Ying, pointing out that it could be counter-productive. Meanwhile, Chinese officials and the official media sought to convey that the medical equipment and supplies shipped to various countries were 'donations'. But these claims were stoutly rebuffed with the UK, Italy, the Netherlands, France and Spain declaring that the supplies were paid for and, furthermore, that they were of poor quality and unusable. This has tarnished China's reputation and image. China is widely viewed as a country intent on benefiting from other people's miseries.

Public opinion and popular sentiment are powerful factors that influence government policy in democracies. Strong suspicions about China's role in the coronavirus pandemic persist. These have been substantiated by the report in the independent Chinese media outlet 'Caixin Global', which revealed that Chinese laboratories had identified a mystery virus — later identified as COVID-19 — to be a highly infectious new pathogen by late December 2019, but were ordered to stop further testing, destroy samples, and suppress the news. Reports additionally revealed that while the first case of a coronavirus patient occurred on November 19, the Chinese authorities chose to disclose and share the information that there was human-to-human transmission with the world only towards the end of January. This denied the world community a crucial two-months of warning and preparation time, and medical scientists, researchers and pharmaceutical companies lost a vital two months in the race to develop life-saving vaccines.

Popular suspicions about China's role have been fuelled by reports of the research done by Dr Shi Zhengli, a leading scientist of the Key Laboratory of Special Pathogens and Biosafety, Wuhan Institute of Virology, Chinese Academy of Sciences, who published her finding that the Severe Acute Respiratory Syndrome (SARS) virus originated in bats in *Science* in 2005 and another on "Bat Coronavirus in China" published in March 2019, and reports of similar research by other Chinese scientists. They have been further heightened by the publication at regular intervals of books like *Unrestricted Warfare* (February 1999) authored by two serving PLA Colonels; the *War for Biological Dominance* (2010) by Guo Jiwei, Professor and Chief Physician at the Third Military Medical University, Army University; an essay in 2015 by He Fuchu, later Vice President of the PLA Academy of Military Sciences, which asserts that biotechnology—ranging from biomaterials to "brain control" weapons—would become "a new strategic commanding height" in national defence; the *New Highland of War* (2017) authored by Zhang Shibo, retired General and former President of the PLA National Defense University; and the inclusion for the first time in the 2017 edition of *Science of Military Strategy* — an authoritative textbook published by the PLA National Defense University — of a new section on "biology as a domain of military struggle", which includes discussion of "specific ethnic genetic attacks."

The COVID-19 pandemic has severely damaged world economies with international financial organisations anticipating a worldwide recession. The repercussions of China's failure to disclose information in time will be felt even after the world has dealt with, and overcome, the coronavirus as it is likely to affect human behaviour and social interaction for many months. In the post COVID-19 world, many countries will review trade policies. The US and many others, for example, are unlikely to ignore a Xinhua commentary of March 4, 2020, stating that it can send the US to "the hell of the novel coronavirus pandemic" by banning the export of medical supplies. It warned that it can announce "the strategic control of medical products and a ban on exports to the US" which imports most of the masks from China. It added that most of the drugs in the US are imported with production bases of almost 90 per cent in China. There will be an effort, certainly by the major powers which must include India, to eliminate dependence on a single source of supply in areas critical or vital to the nation. The developed Western countries, with active encouragement from the US, will probably seek alternate sources of supplies and set up alternate global supply chains. The US and the West remain the world's most developed and wealthy regions, which give them a degree of resilience and will cushion the economic fallout. Nevertheless, till they are able to revive their economies and create jobs for their populations, global trade will be low. China's effort to position itself as a world power rivalling the US will continue to be, possibly more aggressively, resisted.

China's own prospects for an early economic recovery presently do not appear promising. Chinese economists are debating whether China should at all mention a growth target, with Ma Jun, an academic member of the People's Bank of China's monetary policy committee, recommending it be dropped "because growth will largely depend on how the pandemic develops in Europe and the United States" , and Yu Yongding, a former Central Bank adviser, urging the government to mention a numerical goal for expansion in Gross Domestic Product (GDP), even if it is low. Separately, Xu Xiaonian, a Professor of Economics and Finance at the China Europe International Business School, said that till the pandemic in Europe and America gets over, Chinese export companies will have no orders, workers will have no wages and there will be no consumption, and a recession is inevitable. He said, "We are not only short of food and oil, but we are also short of markets; we are short of orders. Our per capita GDP is one-fifth that of the United States and one-fourth that of Europe. The domestic purchasing power cannot support our enormous manufacturing capacity." He added, "We still lack raw materials, especially the technology-intensive basic raw materials, which must be imported from South Korea, Japan and Germany. We lack technology, and technology cannot be developed rapidly when we close the door." In addition to the projected drop in China's growth rate, the unemployment rate could exceed 10 per cent, half of the small and medium enterprises have closed, and manufacturing and economic activity have been slow to resume. The Beijing-led alternative to the World Health Organisation (WHO) will be opposed. Note will have been taken too of the UN awarding a contract to the Chinese telecom company Huawei for its 70th anniversary celebrations, which will be seen as an instance of China's growing influence in international organisation. The resentments that are building up against China will be an important factor that China will have to contend with. China's decision to reject Estonia's request for a discussion on the coronavirus in the United Nations Security Council (UNSC) has served only to heighten suspicions.

*(This article was published by the Centre for China Analysis and Strategy, New Delhi, on April 9, 2020.)*

## 30. The US-China Trade War: A Strategic Move

Major changes in the international geopolitical landscape, anticipated since the global economic downturn in 2008, are now beginning to occur. The Sino-US relationship, one of the world's most important in the past nearly four decades, is undergoing fundamental change, with US President Donald Trump translating into action the apprehensions of the US establishment about China's rise and potential challenge to US primacy. He is the first US President since Nixon to begin altering the nature of the US' relations with China.

By initiating the so-called 'trade war' with China this April, Trump has effectively put China on notice. Chinese analysts and strategic experts have been quick to assess—quite correctly—that the trade war is actually a bid to 'contain' China's rise. Many Chinese analysts have harboured suspicions about Trump's true attitude towards China ever since his precedent-breaking telephone conversation with Taiwan President Tsai Ing-wen in December 2017. Shi Yinhong, Professor of International Relations at Renmin University in Beijing, at that time promptly asserted, "The US President-elect hates China and will encourage Tsai to resist pressure from the mainland."

On September 17, 2018, President Trump announced that the would impose tariffs on an additional $ 200 billion of imports from China. The new round of tariffs took effect from September 24 at a 10 per cent rate. The rate jumps to 25 per cent on January 1, 2019. The announcement surprised observers who had thought Trump would wait till Chinese Vice Minister of Commerce Wang Shouwen and the US Treasury Department's Under Secretary for International Affairs, David Malpass concluded negotiations in Washington. Chinese Vice Premier Liu He had also been invited for talks which were scheduled for September 27 or 28. Punitive tariffs contemplated by US President Trump so far total nearly $ 500 billion.

This so-called 'trade war' between the US and China initiated by US President Donald Trump coincides with the perceptible slowing down of China's economy—the Shanghai market is down roughly 23 per cent in dollar terms so far this year—and puts Chinese President Xi Jinping under increasing pressure as it shows no signs of easing since it began in April 2018. There are, additionally, indications of inflation, but despite that Beijing has been printing money thereby possibly aggravating the problem. In the first two weeks of September, the People's Bank of China injected approximately Renminbi (RMB) 90 billion into the economy. The slowing down of China's economy would be particularly troubling for the CCP leadership as it could trigger an eruption of demonstrations and protests by a disgruntled populace and spell difficult times ahead for Xi Jinping.

Adding to this pressure is the definitive pushback on Xi Jinping's signature Belt and Road Initiative (BRI) by a growing number of countries. Germany, France, Britain, the European Union, Australia, Japan and Canada have also intervened to stop Chinese companies from purchasing technology and hi-tech companies. On August 1, the US Congress increased pressure on China, and the US Senate passed a defence policy bill to make national-security reviews of Chinese deals in the US, by the interagency Committee on Foreign Investment, more stringent. Export controls governing which US technologies can be sent abroad have been revamped. One provision of the bill requires an annual report on China to include information on efforts by the Chinese government to influence US media and cultural institutions. China's official news agency Xinhua and state-owned television China Global Television Network (CGTN) have been asked to register themselves as 'foreign agents'. The bill additionally limits Chinese funding of language programmes at US universities, restricts Chinese involvement in joint military exercises and calls for bolstering US ties with India and Taiwan.

Chinese intellectuals and academics, including from the Chinese Communist Party's (CCP's) prestigious Central Party School in Beijing, have, since last year, been warning that China should tone down its aggressive rhetoric and not have an exaggerated sense of its economic or military strength. In September 2017, Luo Jianbo, Head of the China Foreign Policy Centre at the Central Party School, cautioned against overestimating China's strength and said the people need to guard against "arrogance" and "conceit". He made particular mention in this context of the nationalist fervour generated by the Belt and Road Initiative and the BRI Forum in April 2017, and recommended that Beijing revise its assertive foreign policy and avoid the risk of over-reach.

Earlier, after the US announced tariffs on an additional $16 billion worth of Chinese goods in late August, China's Ministry of Commerce announced that China has filed a complaint with the World Trade Organisation (WTO) against the US levies. Bai Ming, Deputy Director of the Ministry of Commerce's International Market Research Institute said, "Launching the complaint against the US at the WTO can help China gain legitimacy for its retaliation and win sympathy from other countries." Trump's recent announcement that the US could quit the WTO, however, has the potential to deprive China of a possible neutral interlocutor in the dispute. The Chinese government on September 18, announced it would impose tariffs on US goods worth $60 billion following the Trump Administration's announcement that it was hitting $200 billion worth of Chinese goods with new tariffs. It said China's new tariffs will be levied at rates of 5 per cent or 10 per cent, depending on the product and affect more than 5,000 US goods including meat, nuts, alcoholic drinks, chemicals, clothes, machinery, furniture and auto parts.

China's reaction to the US actions was initially unusually temperate, but became sharper later. Since the US first decided to impose tariffs on US$ 34 billion worth of Chinese exports on July 6, the CCP's official newspaper the *People's Daily* published seven commentaries on the 'trade war'. In keeping with the CCP Central Committee (CC) directive of early June, none of these was belligerent and sought instead to portray China as the 'wronged' party. The first commentary cautioned the US that "bullying, rude and unreasonable acts" will have "disastrous consequences that harm the interests of Chinese and American companies and people, seriously threaten global free trade and the multilateral system, and impede the advancement of the world economy's recovery". The second said, "Some people openly ignore the overwhelmingly obvious truth that a trade war is a double-edged sword." Another commentary argued that "America's 'zero-sum theory of trade,' violation of rules, and going against trends not only attacks China-US trade cooperation but also brings great uncertainty to the entire world economy." It said, "The history of international trade has repeatedly proven unilateral protectionism is a zero-sum game and whoever plays it will have bad luck". The fourth asserted that the only aim of America's talk about "so-called 'fair trade' is to have every country of the world pay the bill for

US global hegemony". The fifth commentary warned of the "danger of making the normal world trade structure slip into the 'Cold War trap' of trade protectionism and unilateralism". The sixth commentary was published after Trump threatened on July 10, to impose tariffs on an additional $200 billion worth of Chinese exports. It vowed to work with the international community to "jointly defend the rules of free trade and the multilateral trade system and fight back against US trade bullying". The final commentary said that US actions had hurt the world economy, the American people, and China's poor. It stressed that "the US does not have the right to make a 'recessionary trap' for the world."

By August, though, the Chinese official media had begun to escalate the level of rhetoric. On August 6, 2018, the *People's Daily* Foreign Edition launched an attack against US President Trump's trade policy using the Wang Hailou column, an important column directed at members of the Chinese diaspora. Written by a senior editor for the newspaper, Hu Jihong, the article criticised the logic of Trump's foreign policy. Hu Jihong summarised it as based on the belief that "the US has taken on too many responsibilities and all countries across the world are taking advantage of the US." He explained that Trump has chosen the most "simple and crude" way to revitalise the US economy and had bypassed the WTO. Stating that Trump's aim is to "force China to make major concessions at the negotiating table," Hu Jihong said, "If Mr. Trump is familiar with modern and contemporary Chinese history, then he cannot be unaware that in matters of national interest and national dignity, China will absolutely not accept blackmail. It will stand upright and respond." He described Trump's effort as "wishful thinking.

Separately, the official *Global Times* said, after Trump threatened an additional $ 267 billion in tariffs, "We are looking forward to a more beautiful counter-attack and will keep increasing the pain felt by the US". Beijing's Ministry of Commerce on August 18, warned of "synchronized countermeasures." A day earlier, the US White House cautioned, "If China takes retaliatory action against our farmers or other industries, we will immediately pursue phase three, which is tariffs on approximately $267 billion of additional imports." US President Trump had said days earlier that the $ 267 billion of tariffs is ready to be announced.

Consensus in China has simultaneously coalesced around the view that the trade war camouflages the real US agenda of severely retarding China's rise. There are indications that China's leadership is preparing to contend with an altered, more competitive if not confrontational, relationship with the US. The latest issue of *Qiushi* (*Seeking Truth*), the CCP CC authoritative theoretical journal, carried a lengthy commentary defending China's economic system and asserted that America's real goal in launching the trade war is to thwart China's rise. In another commentary in the *People's Daily* on August 26,Long Guoqiang, Vice President of the PRC State Council's in-house think-tank, Development Research Centre, said that he expects "deep structural change" in the relationship between the US and China after the trade war, with the US treating China as a key rival. He added, "The trade war is not just a measure for the US to gain more economic benefits, it is also an important strategy to contain China." He advocated that China should not engage in angry rhetoric, but should continue to match the US action for action while being ready to resume negotiations any time. Long Guoqiang recommended that in the short-term, the government should offer assistance to companies hit by the tariffs and help find new markets for exporters and substitute sources for imports. He said China should not make the same mistakes as the Soviet Union and must not abandon the domestic agenda.

Important is the article written in April 2018 by Yuan Peng, Vice President of the China Institutes of Contemporary International Relations (CICIR), which stated that a fundamental structural change in the Sino-US relationship is taking place. The CICIR, incidentally, is the think-tank of China's Ministry of State Security which is responsible for foreign intelligence. Yuan Peng described the ongoing trade war as the first serious clash between China and the US. He noted that unlike on previous occasions, this time the political, commercial, academic and military sectors—in other words, the entire American society—are involved, with the US government taking the lead. Again, unlike in the past, this time there is no voice supporting China. He attributed this to the view in the US today that China is a competitor in all respects and that China and the US are competing not only in the Asia-Pacific region but also globally. He pinpointed the launch of "One Belt and One Road" and the Djibouti Safeguard Base project as the triggers that convinced the US that China is a global opponent. Observing that today the US and China have no common enemies like the Soviet Union or Osama bin Laden, Yuan Peng cautioned that the Sino-US bilateral relationship will be impacted by third parties and be constrained by the issues in North Korea, Japan, India, Ukraine, and Iran. Conflicts between China and US and these countries, he assessed, will, without exception, ultimately become conflicts between China and the US.

Crucial to the trade war is the 'Made in China-2025' programme representing the CCP leadership's declared effort to make China a hi-technology power, at par with the world's most advanced nations by 2025. The technology sector is critical to China's emergence as a major world power. The prohibition on the fast-growing Chinese telecom company ZTE, which has substantive investments from China's defence State-owned Enterprises (SoEs) and is closely tied to China's security apparatus, from doing business in the US, was a clear indication that China's technology sector would be targeted. The ban and punitive fines crippled ZTE, which is dependent on purchase of micro-chips and semi-conductors from the US, and brought home to Chinese leaders their vulnerabilities, especially dependence on foreign semi-conductors. Dong Yunting, Director of the Expert Committee at the China Information Technology Industry Federation, reacted quickly saying that the semi-conductor industry cannot be restricted to national boundaries. Arguing that "there are hundreds of semi-conductor components, and ... no country can do them all", he recommended that the "industry must be globalized." The US action has brought home to Beijing that other countries too can use trade and exports as weapons!

This was soon followed by the US decision in August to levy punitive tariffs on 44 Chinese military companies and entities, which will hit China's ambitions hard because these conglomerates are the leaders in development of new military products. In fact, 4,038 patents were declassified to aid military-civilian integration as soon as the trade war started in April. Among the military entities are eight companies and dozens of their subsidiaries, including the China Aerospace Science and Industry Corporation Second Academy (a research unit of the largest missile systems developer in China); the communications system manufacturer Hebei Far East Communication

System Engineering; the state-owned China Electronics Technology Group Corporation (CETC) which develops semi-conductors, radar technology and micro-electronic devices; China Volant Industry, which exports and imports aerospace technologies; and China Hi-Tech Industry Import and Export Corporation. The 'entity list' clarifies that it "identifies entities reasonably believed to be involved, or to pose a significant risk of being or becoming involved, in activities contrary to the national security or foreign policy interests of the United States." There was an immediate reaction in the markets with share prices for businesses related to those on the export control list plummeting downwards. GCI Science & Technology, the parent company of Hebei Far East Communications and Glarun Technology, a subsidiary of CETC, dropped over 7 per cent on the Shenzhen exchange and 6 per cent on the Shanghai markets respectively.

On September 20, the US sanctioned Russia's Rosoboron export and the Chinese military's Equipment Development Department. Though US officials clarified that Russia was the target, it would not have been lost on the Chinese, who are dependent on Russia for military technology and hardware, that they are dangerously close to US 'red lines'. China's response was swift. It recalled People's Liberation Army Navy (PLAN) Commander Vice Admiral Shen Jinlong who was visiting the US, deferred a meeting on joint staff communications scheduled for September and gave a demarche to the US Ambassador.

Meanwhile, US Administration officials are expressing confidence that they have the stronger hand because the US economy is picking up while China's is slowing down and China is more dependent on trade than the US. The trade war between the US and China is unlikely to ease any time soon unless Beijing, in what would be a very surprising move, decides to capitulate. Such a decision will greatly diminish Xi Jinping's personal standing.

*(This article was published by the Centre for China Analysis and Strategy, New Delhi, on September 24, 2018.)*

# 31. The US-China Trade War: Fall-Out in China

The mood in the Chinese Communist Party (CCP) hierarchy is sombre.

The US-China trade war, as it is called, marks a substantive change in the US-China relationship. Mutual suspicion now taints what Beijing has for decades described as its most important relationship. The bipartisan support that Trump's new policy towards China enjoys points to strains in the relationship lasting for quite some time and, in any case, fundamentally altering it.

Throughout his election campaign Trump consistently highlighted terrorism and China as two issues that he would attack. Even prior to Trump, there was recognition in the US strategic establishment that China's rise did not portend well for the US, but US President George Bush got distracted by the war in Afghanistan and Obama was unable to fashion a strategy. Trump is the first US President after Nixon—i.e. after 30 years—to begin to reshape US strategy and policy towards China.

Chinese Party cadres assess that the trigger for the US initiating the trade war was Chinese President Xi Jinping's decision to abolish fixed tenures for top Party positions and the ambitious goal posts enunciated by him at the 19th Party Congress in October 2017. These are the 'China Dream', the target date for achieving which was set to coincide with the centenary of the founding of the CCP in 2021; 'Made in China-2025' designed to propel China into the ranks of the world's most advanced hi-tech nations; and the declared ambition to make China a "major world power with pioneering global influence" by 2049, the 100th year of the founding of the People's Republic of China (PRC). If at all a warning was required that China intends to surpass US power, this was it!

The US was precise in its targeting to prevent China's rise and singled out 'Made in China-2025' as well as its adjunct agenda of 'Civil-Military Integration', seen as the militarising of technology. The US picked on China's rapidly rising Shenzhen-based telecommunications company ZTE in April 2018. US sanctions on ZTE, including the conditions imposed following a reprieve granted on the personal intervention of Chinese President Xi Jinping, have virtually destroyed it. Next was China's fastest expanding hi-tech telecommunications company Huawei. Like ZTE, this too has clear ongoing links to China's People's Liberation Army (PLA). The US charged Meng Wanzhou, Chief Financial Officer (CFO) of Huawei and daughter of Huawei's founder Ren Zhengfei, with illegally selling prohibited components to Iran in violation of US sanctions. The US has approached the Canadian courts to extradite Meng Wanzhou, under detention in Canada since December 2018, to the US. Meanwhile, the US imposed sanctions against six Chinese technical entities of which four are headquartered in Hong Kong. The latter move implies that Hong Kong might no longer benefit from the more relaxed application of trade restrictions by the US government. There are currently 68 Chinese companies on the banned list in the US. In addition, 144 Chinese companies linked to the Chinese military are also on the banned list.

The sanctions have hit China hard. The Chinese leadership was severely jolted by their impact on China's hi-tech sector, which had been claiming to be self-reliant and a world leader. According to indications the leaderships of ZTE and Huawei were also surprised at the dependence of their companies on a few foreign companies—primarily four US companies—for vital hi-tech components crucial for their products. Huawei's Ren Zhengfei, a former PLA engineer, after initially asserting that Huawei will not be impacted, recently admitted that Huawei would take a long time to develop key components like laser imaging chips, etc., required to stay in the business.

With trade talks making no progress and purchase of US-made hi-tech components and parts banned, Chinese companies are in dire financial trouble as their production capacities have been severely hit. Shares have fallen sharply. Huawei's mobile phone handsets which are their major consumer product, for example, have lost 48 per cent market share, severely impacting the company's revenues. After brave initial comments that Huawei can weather this temporary storm, Huawei founder and Chief Executive Officer (CEO) Ren Zhengfei recently conceded that Huawei is in serious trouble. In addition, Trump is applying further pressure and urging countries and US allies not to purchase Huawei's 5G on grounds of national security. There is no indication yet that the US will ease the pressure on China and the latest round of trade talks that began in Shanghai on July 30, ended with US President Trump tweeting another 10 per cent hike on tariffs.

These new tariffs are in addition to those already imposed by the US on $250 billion in imports from China. Beijing, which retaliated with tariffs on $110 billion in US products, has only about $10 billion in US goods left to hit in response against the threatened US tariffs on $300 billion in Chinese products. The latest new tariffs of 10 per cent starting September 1 on an additional $300 billion a year of Chinese imports sent a shock wave through Chinese tech stocks on August 2. In Hong Kong, Tencent slumped by 2.6 per cent that day, while Meituan Dianping was down 3.6 per cent. Struggling smartphone maker Xiaomi went down 1.7 per cent. Similarly, on Wall Street, shares of Alibaba and JD.com both fell more than 4 per cent, while search giant Baidu finished down 2.2 per cent.

China's initial reaction to the US actions was to try and "buy off" Trump. After the US hit China with 25 per cent tariffs on $50 billions of exports in July and August 2018 and added 10 per cent tariffs on another $200 billion in September 2018, and with Trump threatening later that year to boost that tariff to 25 per cent, China began serious negotiations with US Trade Representative Lighthizer and other US officials. China simultaneously activated pro-China lobbies and individuals to propagate that China would not be affected but that the US itself would be hurt by this action. The CCP began drumming up nationalism and xenophobia. China's official media gradually shifted to portraying the US as unfair and a bully, and asserting that China can withstand US pressure. The official Party mouthpiece *People's Daily*, for instance, published 13 commentaries in May and June, accusing the US of hegemonistic behaviour. An example of the effectiveness of China's campaign are the numerous articles in the US and international media detailing how American consumers and businesses will suffer because of the trade war, how it will adversely impact international trade, and how China is dominant in global supply chains which will get disrupted. An example is the 'open letter' to the US President addressed by the US foreign affairs and China scholar community. Beijing played on these apprehensions, adding that it is reviewing its policy on the export of rare earths. But the US has stayed firmly on course. The draft amendments it gave Chinese Vice Premier Liu He to carry back to Beijing in mid-May were not accepted by the CCP Central Committee (CC) Politburo which felt they impacted China's sovereignty. The meeting failed. Chinese Foreign Ministry spokeswoman Hua Chunying declared: "The Chinese side will not give in to any extreme pressure, intimidation or blackmail and we will never concede an inch on major issues of principle."

But the suspicion that is beginning to run deep in China and the US is exhibiting itself in other areas. US business travellers in China are being harassed and questioned. By late July, companies issued advisories to US citizens to postpone avoidable trips to China. Canadians are specially being singled out for harassment and two, of whom one is a serving diplomat, have been arrested and sentenced to death. While this is connected to the detention of Huawei CFO Meng Wanzhou, the threat to them is serious. In the US there are increasing reports of Chinese students being questioned on arrival and often deported. The services of Chinese scientists and researchers including in the National Institutes of Health (NIH) have been terminated. The Federal Bureau of Investigation (FBI) has begun investigating espionage cases in all its field offices in 51 states of the US with each linking back to Beijing.

The US-China trade war has come at an inopportune time for Xi Jinping. It coincides with the slowing down of China's economy and the spreading discontent among students, workers and ex-PLA personnel. The instances of criticism of Xi Jinping's policies by prominent academics, members of the Party's top advisory body the Chinese People's Political Consultative Conference (CPP CC), 'princelings' and former senior officials, including at least two Commerce Ministers, have been increasing. Reports suggest some prominent academics approached veteran retired leaders to pressure Xi Jinping to amend his policies or quit. Academics who, at a meeting in Beijing, expressed the view that China should modify its policies and not antagonise the US were 'disciplined'. Party cadres have been critical of Xi Jinping's policies saying that he has "over-reached" himself. Others have questioned the hyper-nationalism that surrounded the first Belt and Road Initiative (BRI) Forum and advised lowering of rhetoric. That was visibly toned down at the second BRI Forum in Beijing this April. In private conversations, many senior Chinese cadres express the sentiment that "China is alone" and "everyone is against us". Other countries are also beginning to reassess China's economic might and realise that China is not invincible.

In the face of growing pressure, the CCP CC has decided on a tough stance. Chinese President Xi Jinping has begun preparing the Party and the people for difficult times ahead. Visiting Jiangxi in late June, he asked the assembled cadres to prepare for the "second Long March". Five hundred journalists were tasked to write eulogies of the Long March. China's official media reflected this decision. A *People's Daily* commentary said it was "laughable" to say the Chinese economy was being adversely impacted by the US tariffs, adding, "These irrefutable facts are not negated by anyone raising a hubbub." The CCP's leading theoretical fortnightly journal *Qiu Shi* asserted, "China will not be afraid of any threats or pressure the United States is making that may escalate economic and trade frictions. China has no choice, nor escape route, and will just have to fight it out till the end. No one, no force should underestimate and belittle the steel will of the Chinese people and its strength and tenacity to fight a war."

The trouble that erupted in Hong Kong on June 9 and shows no signs of abating, is an additional serious complication for Xi Jinping. The protestors are becoming progressively more articulate and have escalated their demands to scrapping of the Extradition Bill and resignation of the Beijing-appointed Hong Kong Chief Executive Carrie Lam. Beijing has chosen not to interfere yet, but that it will at a time of its choice is certain. Meanwhile, an interesting divergence in tenor of the officially owned Chinese news outlets is visible. It suggests differences within the top leadership and the factions in the CCP. This could be an indicator of the vulnerability of Xi Jinping's position.

Xi Jinping's personal background shows his unwavering commitment to the CCP and realising the ambition of his forbears to see China as a major global power. His instinct will be to resist pressure and push ahead with achieving the goals set at the 19th Party Congress. Whether this will mean China becoming more aggressive in its foreign policy, with possible military encounters with neighbours like Taiwan, Vietnam, Japan and India, is uncertain. China's recent posture indicates that its People's Liberation Army (PLA) is confident of deterring the US from intervening on behalf of its allies in the region. The annual informal meetings at Beidaihe over the next few days could yield clues about whether Xi Jinping will come under fire from senior veterans who will also be attending the informal conclave.

*(This article was published by the Centre for China Analysis and Strategy, New Delhi, on August 8, 2019.)*

# 32. China's View of Ties with the US: Hints of Concessions?

High anxiety is apparent in the upper echelons of the Chinese Communist Party (CCP) leadership in Beijing at the present state of China-US relations. There is concern that the escalating China-US tensions could further deteriorate relations, leading to conflict. Tension in the relationship has been sharply accentuated by the coronavirus pandemic and consequent worldwide rise in anti-China sentiment. This is explicit in the comments on May 5, of Shi Yinhong, an International Relations Professor at China's Renmin University and an adviser to China's State Council—China's version of a Cabinet. He said, "The United States and China are actually in the era of a new Cold War. Different from the Cold War between the US and the Soviet Union, the new Cold War between the US and China features full competition and a rapid decoupling. The US-China relationship is no longer the same as that of a few years ago, not even the same as that of a few months ago."

A sampling of a few comments made in April/May by informed Chinese and the Chinese Communist Party's (CCP's) authoritative official mouthpiece *People's Daily* give an idea of how Beijing presently views China-US relations. Zhou Xiaoming, former Deputy Head of China's mission in Geneva, wrote that the West's efforts to blame China for the global outbreak is "a carefully coordinated PR campaign initiated by the American government to contain China. It is a new battle ground carved out by the US in its war to contain China's rise. We must not underestimate it." The CCP's official mouthpiece *People's Daily* wrote, "Facing the epidemic, cooperation is the only correct choice for China and the US. This mentality is unhealthy, unethical and lunatic," adding that China has been transparent all along and has been aiding others including the Americans. It said that China has been restrained at the smear campaign of the US, but "on the major issues related to our principles we dare to draw the sword, and we will never concede." Hu Xijin, Editor-in-Chief of the *Global Times* wrote on his public Weibo account: "Honestly,

America today won't back off before crippling China. Many people keep saying the situation today is a result of China's actions. They argue that China should show some goodwill to the US, and make major concessions, so to win back the Americans' trust so that relations can get back to normal. But I have to say ... they are too naïve ... the biggest drive behind the US shift in attitude toward China is the change of power balance between the two countries. The US won't accept the possibility that China may become an equal power. That's the most fundamental."

In April alone, at least two major Chinese government think-tanks and one ostensibly private, but well connected to the Party hierarchy, issued reports examining different aspects of China-US relations and recommending ways to arrest the slide in the relationship. It is clear that the US continues to be recognised as crucial to China's rise and the revival of its economy. Interestingly, none recommended yielding concessions to the US, but neither did any of them suggest actions that would provoke the US. Instead, they recommended ways of blunting US propaganda attacks on China and tapping pro-China lobbies in the US and other countries to turn the tide in the relationship and the anti-China sentiment. Two other prominent Chinese who voiced their views in the Hong Kong media similarly sought to play down tensions, raising doubts as to whether they represent the views of Chinese President Xi Jinping or another faction in the leadership.

On May 4, Reuters reported that the China Institutes of Contemporary International Relations (CICIR), a think-tank affiliated with the Ministry of State Security (MoSS), presented an 'internal' report to President Xi Jinping and top Chinese leaders in early April. The report warned that Beijing faces a rising wave of hostility in the wake of the coronavirus outbreak that could tip relations with the United States into confrontation. It concluded that global anti-China sentiment is at its highest since the 1989 Tiananmen Square crackdown and could fuel resistance to China's Belt and Road infrastructure investment projects. Washington could also step up financial and military support for regional allies, making the security situation in Asia more volatile. The report said Beijing consequently faces a wave of anti-China sentiment led by the United States in the aftermath of the pandemic and needs to be prepared for a worst-case scenario of armed confrontation between the two global powers. The paper stated that Washington views China's rise as an economic and national security threat and a challenge to Western democracies. The United States, it added, was aiming to undercut the Chinese Communist Party by undermining public confidence.

Separately, an article in the *People's Liberation Army (PLA) Daily* on May 5, 2020, alluding to the major powers utilising the difficult global economic situation for gaining overall strategic advantage, cautioned they could use the economic crisis to cause a recession in China and provoke social unrest. Advocating that financial and military preparedness would have to be commensurate, it warned that an economic crisis could, in turn, cause a political crisis.

China's biggest government think-tank, the Chinese Academy of Social Sciences (CASS), on April 24, 2020, published a lengthy 3,152-character report in its *China Social Science Journal* analysing US media attacks against China during the Covid-19 pandemic. Published only in Chinese, the report said this had made it difficult for China to cooperate with other countries and fight the pandemic globally. It identified six main characteristics of US media attacks "slandering and denigrating China" and said China not only needed to clamp down on this propaganda, but prepare itself for future propaganda wars during major emergencies. The CASS report recommended six basic focus areas for winning "public opinion battles" in other countries. These are: (i) Prepare for "attacks" from the US and other media by understanding how foreign media works. (ii) Establish a coordination mechanism for 24-hour monitoring and responding to US media and foreign public opinion. Involve government media, private media, diplomats, enterprises and think-tanks to coordinate quick and effective counter-attacks. (iii) Use supervision of public opinion to increase trust and reduce doubt. ("Don't cover up, scapegoat, or show partiality in proven shortcomings. some deficiencies in the process of foreign aid and epidemic prevention should be reported to government developments for improvement".) (iv) Diversify external communications. Strengthen non-mainstream media, support WeChat, Weibo and Tiktok to counterbalance Twitter, FB and YouTube. Mobilise companies, think tanks, foreign scholars and experts who are "China-friendly" to speak and write articles on foreign platforms. (v) Improve empathic communication to create an image of objective, fair media. Use statistics e.g. Pew survey showing 65 per cent of Americans think Trump's coronavirus response is slow. "Use foreign audiences' favourite expressions and narrative forms to affect them," especially on social media. (vi) Strengthen and train human talent for foreign communications. Hire and train people to write op-eds in foreign languages. Hire or "borrow" think-tank experts and foreign journalists for China's use, e.g. to edit Chinese state media abroad and help it reach native standards.

The third think-tank is the 'private' Beijing-based 'Minzhi International Research Institute' headed by Prof. Zhang Weiwei, a former Chinese Foreign Ministry official who has successively worked as a translator for Li Peng, Wan Li , and Deng Xiaoping. He is best known as an advocate of the 'China Model'. It published an article on US-China relations on April 24 authored by Meng Weizhan, Assistant Researcher at the China Research Institute at Fudan University. Asserting that "there is no doubt that we can achieve a great renaissance and may even surpass the United States", the article highlighted that US-China relations are at a "dangerous" juncture and claimed that "senior Chinese officials are also very clear-headed that they must improve Sino-US relations". The article discussed ways of reducing the anti-China influence in the US.

Some of its main points are: (i) "today's China-US relations are rather dangerous"; (ii) "it is an indisputable fact that no country, including the United States, can stop the development of China today"; (iii) "there is no doubt that we can achieve a great renaissance and may even surpass the United States. However, there is a problem of faster and slower development, and there is a problem of higher and lower living standards of the people"; (iii) "in the view of Americans, in the whole non-Western world, China is most likely to be transformed into a Christian country"; (iv) it is necessary to 'win over' America's leftists to improve Sino-US relations; (v) "in another 20 years, we will have no dependence on the United States. But today, we are dependent on the United States. Many people may not understand how serious the consequences will be for China once the United States immediately makes up its mind to "decouple" from China; (vi) "if we want to improve Sino-US relations, we are unlikely to rely on the American rightists. The rightists are mostly strategists, militarists and realists. Most of the leftists are propagandists, thinkers, liberals and literati. Today, the gap of interests between China and the United States is too large, there is no overlap, there are no common strategic interests. If we want to improve relations between the two countries through the American right, it means that we must make concessions on the political system and economic model. This will cost us dearly, discount the interests of the country and put the nation in jeopardy. This is impossible for us to accept. However, it is possible to improve relations between the two countries through the American left; (vii) Now some people in the United States are warning, "China must be contained immediately, or it will be too late!" (viii) senior Chinese officials are very clear-headed that they must improve Sino-US relations. "There is no reason to damage Sino-US relations"; (ix) "Sino-US relations are an overall project, and the essence of bilateral relations does not lie simply in foreign policy. The establishment of an exquisite ideological and strategic system plays a more critical role in safeguarding national interests"; (x) regardless of who becomes the US President, the important thing is to ensure that there is a relatively strong force of "China expertise" in the United States. We can win over the leftists, who do less harm to our national interests; (ix) we must improve our ideological strategy and deal with our opponents more flexibly and cleverly in order to safeguard our own fundamental political system and fundamental economic interests; (ix) unnecessarily magnifying the panic of Americans about China, will lead to further difficulties for China's development and rise and "is very likely to harm our own fundamental interests."

Curious was the interview given by retired PLA Maj Gen Qiao Liang, a known 'hawk' and co-author of the best seller *Unrestricted Warfare*, to Hong Kong's *Zijing Magazine* of the Bahunia Group around this same time. His comments suggested there should be no deadline for achieving Taiwan's reunification with the Mainland, or the 'China Dream', and appeared intended to lower temperatures. It is not known whether his comments were authorised and, if so, by whom. Expressing concern at the growing nationalist sentiment in China urging military action for the forcible reunification of Taiwan with the Mainland, he said in a social media post (May 4) that "nationalism appeared to be driving some proposals being raised in China, and that they would harm the country". He cautioned that while an attempt by the PLA to take Taiwan by force may not prompt Washington to declare war, the US could join forces with allies in the region to use their sea and air advantages to cut off Beijing's maritime lifeline in the South China Sea. Other Western countries may also be convinced to impose sanctions on Beijing that would curb China's economic development. He warned that in the event of a war over Taiwan, capital will flood out of China forcing many companies to close down and said, "This would just be a huge price to pay and it would jeopardise China's goal of national rejuvenation." He advised Beijing to clarify that its top priority was not to take Taiwan back but achieve its long-term goal of "national rejuvenation". He explained, "The Taiwan issue is actually a key problem between China and the US, even though we have insisted it is China's domestic issue. In other words, the Taiwan issue cannot be completely resolved unless the rivalry between Beijing and Washington is resolved." Qiao Liang noted in conclusion that the Chinese economy was "still heavily reliant on the US dollar".

Similarly curious is the article, also published in the Hong Kong media around this time, by Wu Shicun, President of China's state-backed National Institute for South China Sea Studies and Chairman of the Board of Directors of the China-Southeast Asia Research Centre on the South China Sea. Not widely known is that Wu Shicun has been a member of the CCP since 1983 and presently heads the Hainan Provincial Overseas Chinese Affairs Office and the Hainan Provincial People's Association for Friendship with Foreign Countries (PAFFC). Wu Shicun could possibly have come to the notice of former Chinese President Jiang Zemin in June 1989, when he was deputy head of the Party branch within the foreign languages department at Nanjing University and the huge student-led protests were suppressed.

Emphasising China's sovereignty and security in the South China Sea, Wu Shicun in his article appeared to hint that China would not precipitate matters in this maritime region. In his article published in the *South China Morning Post* (May 9), Wu Shicun said that though COVID-19 has dealt a "body blow to the United States, including its military combat capabilities and deployment" and "the virus has been found in at least 150 US military bases and on four aircraft carriers", the US military has nevertheless continued its "relentless pursuit of hegemony in the Western Pacific". It has increased the number and frequency of its flight missions in this region and this year itself conducted four types of military activities in the South China Sea. He observed: "From the US perspective, the South China Sea is indispensable to its hegemony in the Western Pacific. It is a vital artery for US-style sea power, and a handy issue to be manipulated amid China's rise and growing maritime power. From China's perspective, its sovereignty, security and development are all at stake in the South China Sea. The sea not only serves as a natural shield for its national security, but also hosts strategic sea lines of communication. Therefore, the US-China competition in the South China Sea is both strategic and structural. The Chinese are not so naive as to believe the US will ease off its competition with China in the South China Sea amid the pandemic. That is why China has calmly dealt with US operations, both in the air and at sea, amid the viral outbreak." He recommended that, "in the face of growing US military provocation during and after the COVID-19 pandemic, China needs to focus on enhancing its capacity to safeguard its territorial sovereignty and maritime rights in the South China Sea" and expand the civilian functions over the South China Sea islands. Suggesting that Beijing's maritime forces adapt to the changing mode of military operations at sea, he said they should pursue maritime cooperation with other littoral states in the South China Sea, build more consensus and speed up negotiations on a code of conduct.

Pertinent in the context of retired PLA Maj Gen Qiao Liang's and Wu Shicun's observations, is that a number of senior Party cadres and officials in Chinese think-tanks have, since mid-2018, in private conversations, blamed Chinese President Xi Jinping's aggressive foreign policy for China's growing international isolation, rapidly deteriorating relations with the US and poor international image. They said that China continues to be heavily dependent on the US, its technology and market.

The reports do indicate China's heightened concern at the rapid deterioration in US-China relations and Beijing's desire not to further annoy Washington. The interviews in the Hong Kong media could, however, suggest the existence of serious differences within the top echelons of China's leadership on ways to deescalate tension with the US and the reorientation of China's foreign policy.

*(This article was published by the Centre for China Analysis and Strategy, New Delhi, on May 11, 2020.)*

# 33. China's 'Big Two' have Domestic Discontent and US-China Tension as Backdrop: India Finds Mention in US-China Exchange

Domestic discontent and US-China relations are among the Chinese leadership's two top concerns. To the discomfiture of China's leadership both issues surfaced on May 21, 2020, the opening day in Beijing of the 'Big Two', as the plenary sessions of the Chinese People's Political Consultative Conference (CPPCC)—China's top advisory body—and the 13th National People's Congress (NPC) plenum—China's version of a Parliament—are known. Xu Zhangrun, former Professor of Law at Beijing's prestigious Tsinghua University and who has near iconic status among China's academics and intellectuals, penned an over 2,000- character essay advising NPC Deputies on twelve things they should do. The essay was published in the Hong Kong magazine *Mainland China* on May 21. Xu Zhangrun has, incidentally, been banned from writing and using the social media! The White House also, apparently coincidentally timed for release with China's NPC Plenum, issued a 16-page document titled "The United States Strategic Approach to China", which effectively restricts engagement with China as US policy.

In his 'advice' to the NPC, Xu Zhangrun stated that the outbreak of the coronavirus and its rapid spread across the world had isolated China globally and for this, blamed "the Axlerod [that is, Xi Jinping] and the cabal"! His first advice to the NPC Deputies was to comply with the people's demand for a State Council White Paper which should include a timeline detailing the actions taken by the central and local governments during the initial stages of the outbreak and especially between January 3 and 7. It was in this period that China's National Health Commission had issued a notice about biological samples and hazard reduction, and ordered the destruction of samples held by unregistered bodies. He insisted too that those held responsible must be punished regardless of seniority in the hierarchy. Second was the release of all citizen journalists, such as Chen Qiushi and Fang Binbin in Wuhan, rights lawyers, the leaders of faith communities, dissidents, and all innocent Chinese citizens. He demanded an end to the "persecution" of university Professors who dare to speak out and recalled that ten Wuhan University Professors had spoken out in February alone.

Xu Zhangrun made other far-reaching recommendations. These included: immediately banning the "abhorrent" practice of internet policing used to shut down the WeChat and WeiBo accounts of individuals and stopping the intimidation of teachers, medical personnel and writers accused of 'thought crimes'. He demanded that the government institute a "Sunshine Policy" requiring officials to publicly disclose their assets; remove Communist Party cells from all academic and educational institutions, particularly tertiary, secondary and primary schools; enshrine the protection of private property in the Constitution and return the right of ownership to the people themselves; and eliminate the state-sanctioned monopoly exercised by the Communist Party as China's sole landlord.

In addition, he listed symbolic measures such as a "Wailing Wall" listing the names of all who died in the national disaster and a sculpture in memory of the men and women who warned others and acted as whistle-blowers, like Dr Ai Fen, known as the 'Eight Righteous People'. He called for gazetting a 'Dr Li Wenliang Day' as "an annual reminder of the importance of free speech as guaranteed by the Chinese Constitution".

Earlier on May 1, after dates for the 'Big Two' had been announced, an open letter written in Chinese and addressed to the representatives of the CPPCC and NPC circulated widely on the internet. Unlike Xu Zhangrun's essay, this letter posed 15 specific questions, which, while targeting Chinese President Xi Jinping, did not name him. Some of the issues overlapped with those raised by Xu Zhangrun, but this May 1 letter appeared to have been authored by someone with 'inside' information. Among the more interesting questions it raised were: responsibility should be fixed for the deterioration in China-US relations; responsibility should be fixed to ascertain who allowed the turmoil in Hong Kong for so long which has "destroyed the 'one country, two systems'"; how the Belt and Road Initiative was authorised without the approval of the NPC and "now this program is about to be aborted. Who should bear the responsibility?"; and who authorised sending military police to provide "special protection" to retired senior comrades and current high-ranking officials of the Party, government, and military to actually restrict their communications, freedom of movement, and visitors, and prevent the retired senior comrades from proposing a collective motion to call for an expanded Chinese Communist Party (CCP) Politburo meeting.

Issued in the midst of rapidly escalating US-China tensions on a number of fronts, 'The United States Strategic Approach to China', outlined the Trump Administration's assessment of China's objectives and policies. Declaring that the US sees "no value in engaging with Beijing for symbolism and pageantry; we instead demand tangible results and constructive outcomes", it said the "US responds to the PRC's actions rather than its stated commercial threats". The document seemed to be careful to distinguish between the Chinese Communist Party (CCP) and the People's Republic of China (PRC) and left ways open for discussions where necessary.

Among its highlights is the assertion that "Beijing openly acknowledges that it seeks to transform this international order to align with the Chinese Communist Party's (CCP's) interests and ideology." It said that the CCP's expanding use of economic, political and military power are "harming vital American interests." Probably to assuage the concerns of the larger Chinese population, the document emphasised that the "approach is not premised on determining a particular end state for China". The document explained that the US' "competitive" approach to the People's Republic of China (PRC) has two objectives: to improve the resilience of US institutions, alliances and partnerships and "prevail against the challenges the PRC presents"; and "to compel Beijing to cease or reduce actions harmful to the US' vital, national interests and that of our allies and partners". In this context, it said, "The United States is working in concert with mutually aligned visions and approaches such as the Association of Southeast Asian Nations' Outlook on the Indo-Pacific, Japan's Free and Open Indo-Pacific vision, India's Security and Growth for All in the Region policy, Australia's Indo-Pacific concept, the Republic of Korea's New Southern policy, and Taiwan's New Southbound policy".

It detailed the challenges under the subheads 'Economic', 'Challenges to Our Values' and 'Security'. Listing the 'One Belt, One Road' (OBOR) under economic challenges, it said that it is "designed to reshape international norms and standards and networks to advance Beijing's global interests and vision, while also serving China's domestic economic requirements". It averred that Beijing will convert OBOR projects "into undue political influence and military access". Discussing 'Challenges to Our Values', the document focussed on the CCP and its "compellance of ideological conformity at home". It listed the persecution of ethnic minorities like Tibetans, Uyghurs, etc. Referring to security challenges, the document stated: "Beijing contradicts its rhetoric and flouts its commitments to its neighbours by engaging in provocative and coercive military and paramilitary activities in the Yellow Sea, the East and South China Seas, the Taiwan Strait, and Sino-Indian border areas".

Appearing to give the rationale, it said the document rethinks the policies of the last two decades and is guided by "principled realism". It said the US is responding to the "CCP's direct challenge by acknowledging that we are in a strategic competition and protecting our interests appropriately". The "US does not and will not accommodate Beijing's actions that weaken a free, open and rules-based international order." It asserted, "We will continue to refute the CCP's narrative that the US is in strategic retreat or will shirk our international security commitments." The US' new 'Strategic Approach to China' also warned that "the negative trend lines of Beijing's policies and practices threaten the legacy of the Chinese people and their future position in the world".

China's reaction to the release of the 'The United States Strategic Approach to China' was measured and not strident. Chinese Foreign Minister Wang Yi avoided sharp criticism of the US at his press conference on the sidelines of the NPC on May 24. He said, "China has no intention to change, still less replace, the United States", and, "It's time for the United States to give up its wishful thinking of changing China and stopping 1.4 billion people in their historic march toward modernization." Pointing to US President Trump and Secretary of State Mike Pompeo, Wang Yi said American politicians "are taking China-U.S. relations hostage and pushing our two countries to the brink of a new Cold War."

The CCP-owned *Global Times* (May 23) noted that the document claimed that previous hopes for a "fundamental economic and political opening" in

China have failed and called for the continuation of a whole-of-government approach toward China. The *Global Times* article was captioned "China Needs Flexible Approach as Relations with US Come to Cross-roads". It interviewed Wei Zongyou, a Professor at the Centre for American Studies, Fudan University and Zhang Tengjun, an Assistant Research Fellow at the China Institute of International Studies.

Wei Zongyou described the document as "filled with a sheer hegemonic mentality and every single sentence aims to protect US national interests". He added, "The US always hoped to change the world in accordance with its own will" and this "is the same approach with which it deals with China". Stating, "We can sense the US' toughness and even menace", he said "China must hold its strategic resolve and vision and adopt flexible approaches". Wei Zongyou said that if the "US abandons its stereotypical mindset regarding China" then "there is room for cooperation on regional and world matters". He observed, "The future trajectory of China-US relations depends on how the two interact… . China can still seek strategic initiatives". Zhang Tengjun took a more conciliatory stance. Assessing that "China-US relations have entered their darkest phase since the normalization of ties", he said that when the gap is widening and the Thucydides Trap is becoming a reality, China must have a clear understanding of how China-US ties serve its own development. Stating that "a stable China-US relationship is an important goal of China's major power diplomacy", he asserted that "this is not to cater to the US, but to create a favourable external environment for China's peaceful development".

The day after Chinese Foreign Minister Wang Yi's press conference, the *Global Times* (May 25) listed six basic facts as an "objective view' of China-US relations. These were: (i) China is a rising developing country. So far, it has not achieved the strength to pose a substantial challenge to the US, nor does China have such a will. (ii) The core of China's foreign relations is development. Chinese actions that can be described as "overseas military expansion" are negligible. China has been somewhat active in areas in which it has territorial disputes with neighbouring countries, but it has maintained restraint in general. One proof is that China has not engaged in any military conflicts with its neighbouring countries for over 30 years. (iii) China expands influence through its economic activities to the mutual benefit of the parties involved and does so under the US-led multilateral trading system. (iv) China has a different political system than the US and other Western countries, which has caused ideological disputes. "But China is generally not a country that exports ideology". China's "so-called overseas publicity" is only to increase the external world's understanding of China and not to subvert the Western system. The West is aggressive while China is defensive in ideological disputes. (v) The US elites want to "shape" China and are annoyed that China has firmly stayed on its own political path. They worry that the successful Chinese path may affect Western society's confidence. (vi) The Trump Administration's trade war against China "is indeed bullying". The "America First" doctrine has "caused widespread resentment worldwide and China is not the only victim. Since the COVID-19 outbreak, Washington has been passing the buck to Beijing. This is the odious move of the White House and the Republican Party for the sake of the 2020 election. This is typical international hooliganism".

China and the US have both been increasingly critical of each other as the trade war has escalated. A Central News Agency report (May 18) claimed that since 2019, data collected by a WeChat account shows that 70 per cent of the front-page editorials of the *Global Times* have been targeting the US. It said that among the recent 40 daily front page editorials in the *Global Times*, titles of 29 articles carry the words "the United States." The proportion is as high as 72.5 per cent. The figure was, however, only 18, or 45 per cent, out of 40 editorials over the same time period last year. In addition, the *People's Daily* virtually each day published a special commentary criticising the US.

Directly relevant for India is the statement in 'The United States Strategic Approach to China' that "Beijing contradicts its rhetoric and flouts its commitments to its neighbours by engaging in provocative and coercive military and paramilitary activities in the Yellow Sea, the East and South China Seas, the Taiwan Strait, and Sino-Indian border areas". US Assistant Secretary of State Alice Wells echoed this thought in her statement: "Flare-ups at the border are a reminder that Chinese aggressions aren't always rhetorical. The border dispute shows the threat China that poses to its neighbour". Pertinent is China's reaction. The reaction of the spokesman for the Chinese Embassy in Delhi was tough and sharper than the Chinese Foreign Ministry spokesman's comment at the weekly press conference in Beijing. Chinese Embassy

Counsellor Ji Rong said on May 20 evening: "We are firm in determination to oppose separatist activities and safeguard China's national sovereignty and territorial integrity. We are firm in determination to oppose foreign meddling in China's internal affairs. We are firm in determination to realise final reunification." The assertive last sentence is particularly relevant in the current context of the multiple intrusions along the Line of Actual Control (LAC).

*(This article was published by the Centre for China Analysis and Strategy, New Delhi, on May 28, 2020.)*

# 34. Chinese Researchers Suggest Modulation of China's Policy Towards United States

The growing strain in the US-China relationship continues to cause concern in the higher echelons of China's leadership. Chinese think-tanks have cautioned that the situation could worsen considerably more and some, like the Chinese Academy of Social Sciences, have recommended ways to bring about a change in public opinion in the US.

In a 3,000-word article published on July 6, 2020, on the popular portal Aisixiang.com managed by China's Ministry of Industry and Information Technology, three researchers of prestigious Chinese think-tanks and the Renmin University identified stable relations with the US as essential for China's development and said that Beijing should "actively manage" its differences with Washington. The article focussed on the West Pacific Ocean and the South China Sea. It equally noted the importance of managing "third-party factors" and, quite interestingly, said, "China and the United States should refrain from the urge to gather third party forces to block and counterbalance each other, nor should they force third parties to choose a side station between China and the United States". This suggests a major modification of the assertive policy being followed by Xi Jinping.

The article has been co-authored by An Gang of the Chinese Academy of Social Sciences (CASS) and the Tsinghua University Research Centre for Strategy and Security; Wang Yiming, a doctoral student at the School of International Relations, Renmin University of China; and Hu Xin, a National Defence Technology Associate Professor, Institute of Strategy and Security, University of International Relations. The 5-part article said that Beijing should seek to stabilise its relations with Washington and actively manage their differences and competition. It said, "In order to effectively prevent the 'new situation' from evolving toward full confrontation and conflict, China and the United States urgently need to reposition, deal with, and control the 'new paradigm' of mutual relations". The report added that the Trump

Administration, which views China as a "strategic and economic opponent" of the United States, "will stick to the end in terms of competition with China". It added that following the tone and direction established by the White House, various US government departments, powerful institutions, and strategic think-tanks have gradually formed a "whole government" strategic competition situation.

The report said "China's policy toward the US has placed greater emphasis on struggle, and the competitiveness of China and the United States has increased significantly". It assessed that the United States "believes that the essence of Sino-US competition on the international stage is the competition between the Western democratic political circle and the 'authoritarian camp' led by China and Russia". It added that the conflict of value systems and differences in political systems comprises the source of long-term mistrust between the two countries. It asserted, "China adheres to the socialist road, firmly maintains the basic system, and mobilizes the country to achieve the 'Two hundred years' strategic goal". It averred that it "is impossible to trade core interests". It acknowledged that "the development of structural contradictions on the ideological level between China and the United States will follow the rise of China. The deepening is more sharp and complicated".

The article stressed the importance of maritime power and said "maritime strategic competition will determine the overall strategic relationship to a large extent, and the narrowing of the contrast between China and the United States will increase the strategic competition at sea". Interestingly, the report observed, "The tendency of American pressure on China to concentrate on political systems and national sovereignty and security issues is to a certain extent, inspiring China's awareness of victimization and sorrow, boosting nationalist sentiment, and aggravating the atmosphere of public opinion that is not conducive to the long-term development of Sino-US relations and will impact the rational framework for diplomatic decision-making between the two countries from time to time". Assessing that the US "is a major opponent that China has to deal with strategically and an important target for cooperation in many practical fields", it candidly stated that China is "the weaker side of the strategic competition of major powers" and "should fully understand the strategic considerations of the United States, form a reasonable response strategy, and make the right choice of the times...China needs to carefully assess the risk of these confrontations dragging the two countries into conflict".

Stating that "communication and dialogue are important traditions in Sino-US relations even in the sharpest rivalry during the Cold War", the report listed a number of steps to keep dialogue open. These are: (i) "Improve the high-level dialogue and communication mechanism and establish an interactive channel that matches the importance of global power relations". (ii) "Reactivate the strategic dialogue mechanism whose efficacy is at a standstill and build a strategic stability framework". (iii) "Strengthen the institutional dialogue and professional exchanges between the Chinese and American armed forces". (iv) "Resist the trend of 'decoupling' and protect the mutually beneficial and harmonious relations between the two countries". The article noted, in an apparent hint to exploit the opportunity, "Generally speaking, a large number of people in the domestic business, education, and academic circles in the United States do not consider 'decoupling' to be desirable and feasible. They also dislike the monitoring and restriction measures by the Trump Administration against Chinese people". (v) Rationally and effectively cooperate at the global security level when "China is growing into a global power, and the interests of the United States are increasingly extending to the regional and global levels". (vi) Properly manage maritime strategic competition as "the West Pacific Ocean, especially the South China Sea, is becoming the home of Sino-US face-to-face strategic games. It is also the practice for the two countries to conduct strategic trials and explore new dynamic balances. As far as the megatrends are concerned, the two countries can neither ignore nor avoid conflicts in their strategic interests, nor can they completely exclude each other by strong means. Long-term strategic stalemate will become a normalized trend."(vii) "Clarify common interests and maintain normal cooperation" especially since "China and the United States still share common interests in a wide range of fields". (viii) Manage third-party factors, namely, China and the United States have close ties with other countries in the global arena, which has a profound impact on the interests of these countries. "China and the United States should refrain from the urge to gather third-party forces to block and counterbalance each other, nor should they force third parties to choose a side station between China and the United States" as the effect will be counter-productive. "The role of third-party countries should be defined as a common friend rather than an enemy of China and the United States". The more the United States retreats in the face of global responsibilities, the more China should join hands with third-party countries such as the European Union (EU) and Association of Southeast Asian Nations (ASEAN). "By strengthening the role of third parties, it can help promote the formation of a benign situation in which China and the United States actively strive for the support of the international community, and enhance the power and flexibility of the big country game". And, in conclusion, it said, (ix) "China must adjust its strategy toward the United States" and "focus on the long-term, focus on strategic thinking, maintain strategic determination, and work hard at the bilateral, regional, and global levels while striving to coordinate and interact with the US in a competitive game to create a new reasonable relationship paradigm and avoid falling into the guilt of the 'Thucydides Trap' advocated by the US". It stated that building a "Community of Human Destiny" is the general trend. The article emphasised that "whether it is China or the United States, or a third-party force whose behaviour is greatly affected by the trend of Sino-US relations, it is necessary to look at a broader time and space and have a more human perspective".

China's academics and strategic experts are increasingly concerned at the worsening trend in Sino-US relations. They are conscious of the huge differences in the respective economic, military and scientific strengths. Suggestions for changes in policy towards the United States, though now being more often articulated openly, are noticeably careful to avoid appearing contradictory to Chinese President Xi Jinping's assertive foreign policy.

*(This article was published by the Centre for China Analysis and Strategy, New Delhi, on July 10, 2020.)*

# 35. Tension is High Within China's Leadership Echelons as United States Maintains Unrelenting Pressure

As China-US relations deteriorate rapidly and tensions mount, concern is growing in the Chinese Communist Party's (CCP's) leadership echelons about the next punitive steps that the Trump Administration might take. Barely a week has gone by in recent months without at least one punitive sanction being slapped on China by the US. These sanctions are beginning to increasingly impact on the CCP and its members. Contributing to the concerns are worries in Beijing that US President Trump has a tough contest in the upcoming Presidential elections in November and could be tempted to take some military action against China to boost his ratings.

There are recent indications of heightened concern. On July 25, posters on how to handle air raids, which had not been posted for nearly 50 years, appeared in Beijing's Haidian district. A video circulating on the internet and reproduced on Twitter shows posters in Beijing and Shanghai instructing people how to go to underground bunkers if an alarm signals a military attack and air-raid billboards reminding residents "how to enter an air-raid shelter quickly after hearing the alarm ...". Coinciding with the US-led naval exercises and the presence of the US aircraft carriers *Nimitz* and *Reagan* in the South China Sea, public announcements have been posted (July 26) in some places along China's southeast coast notifying retired People's Liberation Army (PLA) Navy and PLA Air Force (PLAAF) personnel, including their families, that they must register with the community neighbourhood committee. This is being interpreted as preparations for possibly calling these persons to return to military service at short notice.

A notice issued by the Shuiyun Street Community Neighbourhood Committee in Chongqing city, Sichuan province, on July 24, informed families of active-duty border/island officers and soldiers living in its jurisdiction, especially those stationed in Xinjiang, Tibet, Yunnan, Guangxi, Hainan, and at other borders and islands, to register with the community neighbourhood committee. On July 27 evening, the state-run China Central Television (CCTV) Headline News telecast an old clip of January this year of Chinese President Xi Jinping's instruction to the PLA's Top Gun Sixth Company emphasising that the military must follow the CCP command to prepare for war. Using the 75th anniversary of its victory in the Sino-Japanese War this year, China's National Radio and Television Administration (NRTA) which controls state-owned TV and radio broadcasters, held a nationwide video conference with its subsidiary entities on July 17, to arrange programmes on the theme of the Sino-Japanese War during World War II and the Korean War. The programming will hype nationalism and simultaneously potentially promote anti American nationalist sentiments.

Around the same time the CCP-owned *Global Times* (July 29) quoted Chinese strategists and experts warning of the possibility of a military conflict between the two nuclear-armed powers caused by the "dangerous US attempts". It quoted Chinese experts as saying that while China could be restrained in retaliating to new US provocations on politics, diplomacy or economy, because China's policy-makers will not let the Trump Administration use them for his reelection, if Washington launches military provocations to challenge "the bottom line of China's national security and sovereignty" then China will immediately and effectively retaliate.

Expressing concern at possible developments over the next three months Jin Canrong, Associate Dean of Renmin University of China's School of International Studies in Beijing, said that "the collective hostility against China among US elites and policy-makers, which we didn't expect, will also make the US more aggressive." He noted that "direct China-US military conflicts, or even the severance of diplomatic ties, which used to be unimaginable, are being discussed more frequently by the mainstream media outlets and scholars, so the danger of military conflicts exists and is growing." The Beijing-based think-tank South China Sea Strategic Situation Probing Initiative (SCSPI) noted (July 29) that there is the possibility of small and medium-sized clashes, which could involve ship collisions and occasional firing incidents.

On July 27, China's Minister of Public Security Zhao Kezhi spoke at the video conference of the National Public Security Agency. He emphasised that "in the face of a profoundly changing external environment and severe and complex situations, public security organs at all levels must resolutely implement the decisions and deployment of the Chinese Communist Party's Central Committee with Comrade Xi Jinping at the core. We must ... carry forward the fighting spirit, make preparations, be on guard against different risks and challenges, and strive to achieve the 'two safeguards' in the actions of maintaining the nation's political security and social stability." The "two safeguards" is a new slogan meaning to safeguard the position of Xi Jinping as the core of the CCP Central Committee (CC) and the core of the whole Party, and to safeguard the authoritative and centralised leadership of the CCP CC. Zhao Kezhi also asked the personnel "to guard against and crack down on the disruptive sabotage activities of hostile forces at home and abroad, carry out anti-infiltration, anti-subversion, anti-separatism and anti-evil religion struggles, and resolutely safeguard national political security."

China's leadership had started preparing some months earlier to minimise the deleterious impact of other possible punitive US actions. An indication was given by Zhou Li, a recently retired former Vice Minister of the CCP CC's International Department. Among the six precautionary steps he suggested was that China must take measures to minimise the effects of US control over the Global Interbank Financial Telecommunications Association (SWIFT).

In an apparent endorsement of this concern, Reuters said (July 29) that a report by the investment banking unit of the Bank of China (BoC) recommended that China should prepare for potential US sanctions by increasing use of its own financial messaging network for cross-border transactions in the mainland, Hong Kong and Macau. The report said greater use of the Cross Border Interbank Payment System (CIPS) instead of the Belgium-based SWIFT system would reduce exposure of China's global payments data to the United States, BOC International (BOCI). The report looked at potential measures the United States could take against Chinese banks, including cutting off their access to the SWIFT financial messaging service. Saying, "We need to get prepared in advance, mentally and practically", it claimed that if the United States were to take the extreme action of cutting off access of some Chinese banks to dollar settlements, China should also consider stopping the use of the US dollar as the anchor currency for its foreign exchange controls.

Other articles and reports over the past few months have similarly reflected Beijing's concerns. The first was the briefing given to Chinese President Xi Jinping and the Politburo by the Ministry of State Security (MoSS) think-tank the Chinese Institutes of Contemporary International Research (CICIR). According to Reuters, this forecast a bleak outlook for the coming year, including, because of US pressure, the possibility of social upheaval and military conflict. This was echoed in an article in the *People's Liberation Army (PLA) Daily*. Confirming that China-US relations would deteriorate further as the current US Administration was hostile to China, a report by the Chinese Academy of Social Sciences (CASS) suggested ways to arrest the decline.

The CCP, however, appears to have got more worried as the US began applying sanctions against officials who it said were directly involved in suppressing the people and human rights in the Xinjiang-Uyghur Autonomous Region and the Hong Kong Special Administrative Region (HKSAR). Included among the officials was Xinjiang Party Secretary Chen Quanguo. This was followed by the *New York Times* citing US Secretary of State Pompeo as saying in late July that the US proposed to deny visas to members of the CCP, including members of the PLA and those already in the US and serving in State owned Enterprises (SoEs) and other Chinese government enterprises. Once implemented, this will directly and immediately affect approximately 300 million Chinese including 92 million CCP members and their family members. This quickly emerged as the most searched item on China's websites and generated lots of discussion and concern among CCP members who have been quoted as saying that 70 per cent of the children of CCP members at or above department level go to the US for studies. A Chinese official who wrote (July 22) under the pseudonym Liang Jing said that the US "decision-making elite has made an important breakthrough .... in its sanctions against the CCP. For example, the US has imposed restrictions on the entry of CCP members and their family members. I have heard the Party's voice of pain".

Indicative of the Chinese leadership's anger and inability to persuade the Trump Administration to change its policy, Beijing hit out at an ethnic

Chinese US citizen who it accused of being an "uber-hawk" and contributing to the proposed decision to ban visas for CCP members. The CCP-owned *Global Times* and Hong Kong's *South China Morning Post* both published (July 23) reports identifying Maochun Yu @ Miles Maochun Yu, a China-born Professor of Military History at the US Naval Academy in Annapolis, as one of the influential sources and a principal policy and planning adviser on China. It said, "He harbours some pretty dark visions about the world and Asia-Pacific in particular" and "is clearly an uber-hawk". The Chinese official Liang Jing separately pointed to "the involvement of Chinese immigrant scholars from Mainland China in this decision".

Chinese State Councillor and Foreign Minister Wang Yi's unusually unrestrained comments about the US during a telephone conversation with Russian Foreign Minister Lavrov on July 17, similarly indicated the tight corner that the Chinese leadership is in and the critical stage of the US-China bilateral relationship. According to the report posted on China's Foreign Ministry website on July 18, Wang Yi described the strategic leadership of the two heads of state as the biggest political advantage of Sino-Russian relations. It also said, "Wang Yi emphasized that the US nakedly pursues its own priority policies and promotes egoism, unilateralism, and bullying to the extreme, wherever there is a big country. The United States has passed on its own responsibilities and used the epidemic situation to discredit and dump pots in other countries. It has done everything possible. It has even created hot spots and confrontations in international relations, and has lost its reason, morality and credibility. Wang Yi said that the US has regained the infamous 'McCarthy Doctrine' and the outdated 'Cold War Thinking' in its China policy, deliberately provoking ideological confrontation and breaking through the bottom line of basic principles of international law and international relations. China will not be paced by a few American anti-China forces, but will firmly defend its legitimate interests and dignity".

Similar were Wang Yi's remarks to French Foreign Minister Jean-Yves Le Drian on July 28, when he spoke about the severe problem in US-China relations. He told Le Drian that "[A] certain political faction in the US, driven by the need to lift [presidential] campaign prospects and maintain unipolar hegemony, are going all out to negate the history of China-US relations, suppress China on every front, provoke China on its core interests, attack the social system chosen by the Chinese people, and vilify the ruling party." He said that China will deal with the US with like-for-like counter-measures, but is eager to see the situation stabilise. He said, "China will take firm counter-measures against the egregious behaviors that undermine China's legitimate rights and interests". He added, "China doesn't stir up troubles and always exercises maximum restraint", and, "We ... strive to maintain the stability of China-US relations through equal communication and exchanges with the US side." Wang Yi expressed the hope that other countries do not jump on the US-led anti-China bandwagon.

An indication of the thinking in Beijing are the comments of Mainland China's former official Liang Jing. He said that "due to his major mistakes in the epidemic and the Hong Kong issues, Xi is in his most dangerous predicament since taking office. The US has a chance that it dared not imagine: to force Xi to step down, completely changing the confrontation between the US and China". He added, "Even if Xi Jinping cannot be forced to step down before the election, even should Trump fail to win it, the hawks will have created a situation that the new government will have trouble reversing".

The US is unlikely to ease pressure on China and Xi Jinping is expected to come under increasing pressure. Xi Jinping is taking measures to counter the pressure and ensure his continuance and the CCP's legitimacy and monopoly as the sole ruling political party. Meanwhile, a couple of unconfirmed reports have filtered out of Beijing and Shanghai claiming that Xi Jinping's personal security has been increased and he changes the rooms he sleeps in within Zhongnanhai, the residential compound of China's top leadership.

*(This article was published by the Centre for China Analysis and Strategy, New Delhi, on August 14, 2020.)*

# 36. Chinese Assessments of the International Situation

China's largest and government-funded think-tank, the Chinese Academy of Social Sciences (CASS) and among the most influential, the Chinese Institutes of Contemporary International Relations (CICIR) of China's Ministry of State Security, or foreign intelligence establishment, published reports in May 2020 assessing the international situation. These presented the assessments of CASS President Xie Fuzhan and CICIR President Yuan Peng. Another assessment, which additionally listed precautionary steps that China should take, was published on June 29, 2020, by Zhou Li, former Deputy Minister of the Chinese Communist Party's (CCP's) Central Committee's (CC's) International Liaison Department (ILD) now called the International Department. Yuan Peng's and Zhou Li's assessments had higher political content, but Zhou Li's was particularly pointed.

Prior to his appointment in March 2018 as President of CASS, Xie Fuzhan was Party Secretary of Henan province. He has been a visiting scholar at the Economics Department of Princeton University and then completed executive programmes at the John F. Kennedy School of Government at Harvard University and another at the Judge Business School of the University of Cambridge. He is a full member of the Chinese Communist Party's (CCP's) 19th Central Committee and was also a member of the 18th Central Committee.

Observing that because of the global economic slowdown and intensified competition among major countries in 2019, the stability of international security strategies has declined, Xie Fuzhan focussed on the COVID-19 pandemic, describing it as now the most uncertain factor in analysing and judging the international situation. Fuelled by the pandemic, he said, various risks in the world economy have surfaced and continue to accumulate. The capital market is turbulent, crude oil prices have fallen sharply, and the world economy has contracted significantly.

Xie Fuzhan said new factors of instability have surfaced in relations among major countries in international politics. In a bid to deflect the blame, he said in order to escape responsibility for poor epidemic prevention and control and to safeguard the political interests of certain individuals or groups, politicians in some countries have politicised the fight against the COVID-19 pandemic. He accused them of making remarks that violate generally accepted moral standards and basic scientific common sense, "creating lies, panic, discrimination and prejudice" and casting a "new shadow on the stable development of international relations". Stating that the geopolitics has evolved and the international political system has been deeply transformed, he asserted that traditional and non-traditional security threats are intertwined, and national security faces unprecedented challenges.

Referring to China's Belt and Road Initiative (BRI), he acknowledged that it had been "greatly" impacted by COVID-19, but that despite this, BRI cooperation still shows strong resilience, and China's trade and investment with the countries and regions along the route is growing despite the pandemic. He claimed that the pandemic has brought opportunities for the high-quality advancement of the Health Silk Road and for the new Innovation Silk Road. He said that while the pandemic has had a major impact on traditional industries, it has simultaneously accelerated the application of new technologies, such as online technology, 5G, artificial intelligence and big data, thereby creating opportunities for innovative emerging industries to expand to countries and regions along the BRI.

A *Foreign Policy* (July 6, 2020) article elaborated on the impact of COVID-19 on the BRI with substantiating data. Citing a report by Gavekal Dragonomics, it said that the value of new projects spread across 61 countries involved in the BRI dropped 13 per cent to US$ 126 billion in 2018 compared to the previous year, with the figure falling a further 6.7 per cent in the period up to August 2019. Existing contracts also dropped 4.2 per cent over the first eight months of 2019. China, according to the report, committed to making only two Belt and Road Initiative related loans of over US$1 billion in the first half of 2019: US$1.2 billion to Egypt and US$2.5 billion to Pakistan. Overall, according to the China Global Investment Tracker from the American Enterprise Institute, China made 46 loans of over US$1 billion for overseas investment projects in 2016, with that figure dropping to 28 last year.

CICIR President Yuan Peng assessed that the international environment in 2020, which has seen "sudden" and "perplexing" changes, will be a worrisome year. He explained that in political rather than academic terms, he sees the world as "going through changes unseen in centuries, but also coinciding with the grand rejuvenation of the Chinese nation after 100 years of humiliation". Illustrating a few of the changes, he pointed out that "developing countries represented by China have achieved peaceful rise independently without benefitting from colonial expansion and waging foreign wars, which is epoch-making. In this manner, China has achieved its rise, while the West finds it rather hard to cope with." He added that regardless of whether the US takes recourse to a hot or cold war, it cannot stop China but, importantly, that "it is almost impossible for China to achieve national rejuvenation outside the US-dominant system".

He identified economic globalisation, political multi-polarisation, Information Technology (IT) application, cultural diversification and threat diversification, Science and Technology (S&T) revolution, impact of the digital age and social media as among the "great changes". Yuan Peng observed also that at a time the "established international system is collapsing and while the new world order is yet to emerge", China is approaching the political centre stage. Saying, "Great changes call for grand vision", Yuan Peng emphasised that China is in "presently the best period of its modern history". He justified anti-corruption, poverty alleviation, in-depth reform, the BRI and modernisation of governance as essential responses to the "great changes unseen in a century" although they will impose economic burdens. He called for the pursuit of the socialist system with Chinese characteristics and leadership of the Chinese Communist Party. He declared, "The East is rising and the West is falling, the South is ascending and the North is descending" while stressing that strategic confidence and will power are essential prerequisites for China achieving its 'Two Centenary' goals.

1955-born Zhou Li, a former career diplomat who is presently senior researcher at the Chongyang Institute of Financial Research of Renmin University and Director of the China Russia Humanities Exchange Research Center, observed that the Covid-19 pandemic had caused suffering and economic difficulties around the world and that unstable and uncertain factors have increased significantly. He asserted that "under the leadership of the

General Secretary, we have made arduous efforts throughout the country and made tremendous sacrifices", but there are new difficulties and challenges in resuming production and economic and social development. He said the Party Central Committee demands that leading cadres at all levels "should adhere to the bottom line thinking and make a long-term ideological preparation and work preparation for responding to changes in the external environment."

Zhou Li listed the following six measures that China could take to respond to the changes in the international environment: (i) China must prepare for the deterioration and "full escalation of the struggle" in Sino-US relations. Enumerating the string of punitive actions taken till now by the Trump Administration, he anticipated that many more would follow. He said it will be realistic to understand that "decoupling" is ultimately inevitable and that the "difficulties and challenges China will face will be unprecedentedly complex and unprecedentedly severe" as "the US ruling authorities continue to impose progressive and omni-directional, multi-disciplinary crackdowns" on China. At present, it is especially necessary to guard against the risk of the US pursuing claims against China. (ii) China must prepare to cope with shrinking external demand and disruption of the industrial and supply chains as, in the wake of the epidemic, most countries have had to adopt measures such as "closure of cities" and "shutdown", resulting in a sharp decline in the demand for various intermediate and consumer products. The orders of China's foreign trade export enterprises have been greatly reduced, production of upstream and downstream enterprises has been stalled and international transportation logistics have been blocked. The unavailability of raw materials and unsuccessful delivery of products has caused tremendous pressure on China's growth and employment. He said that China should actively adapt to the situation and adjust the global industrial chain and supply chain, and develop a fixed chain, supplementary chain, and strong chain. Domestic development should be accelerated and more infrastructure projects within China promoted. China will need to participate in international cooperation and competition under the "new situation". (iii) China should expect that it will take a long time to normalise post- the new coronavirus epidemic and must anticipate the long-term coexistence of the virus and humans. He observed there are still many uncertainties about whether the epidemic can be effectively controlled, as vaccine development is still underway. Therefore, China must remain fully mobilised at all levels with reserves of anti-epidemic materials, medical support, and clean up and reorganise food wholesale markets in large and medium-sized cities to eliminate possible sources of infection. He stressed the imperative of rationalising the medical and health system, reforming disease prevention and control systems, improving the capacity of epidemic monitoring and early warning and improving public health emergency laws and regulations and public health emergency management and treatment systems. (iv) China must make preparations for getting rid of the dollar hegemony and gradually decoupling the renminbi from the dollar. The US' international monopoly on the US dollar will threaten China's next steps and become increasingly more serious. He identified two problems, namely, the shrinking value of US dollar assets as the US Administration prints more dollar bills, diminishing their value, and the United States' control over the Global Interbank Financial Telecommunications Association ( SWIFT ), which makes international settlement and transactions more difficult as the United States continues to impose economic sanctions on Russia, Iran and countries having energy cooperation with China. He urged China to accelerate the pace of renminbi internationalisation, accelerate the promotion of larger-scale renminbi cross-border payments and renminbi clearing arrangements, establish local currency settlement mechanisms with more countries, and create conditions to maximise their use in the world. (v) Anticipating that global food production will be reduced by 30 per cent this year and further impacted by the pandemic and disruption in the supply, demand and circulation area of the grain market, he said China must prepare for the global food crisis. He assessed that major food-producing countries are faced with a large scale harvest failure due to various factors. Stating that the prices of major grains such as corn, soybeans and wheat have risen by 30 to 50 per cent and international speculative capital has exacerbated the rise in food prices, he said many countries have launched grain inventory plans, suspended exports or formulated grain export quotas, and strengthened control of the grain market. Food shortages and the food crisis will cause social unrest in more countries thereby accentuating the uncertainties of world economic development. China is the world's largest importer of soybeans and will be directly affected. It must take necessary measures to step up food production, increase policy support and subsidies for grain production, improve the grain reserve control system and emergency management mechanism, promote international cooperation in agriculture and the effective operation of the global agricultural and food supply chain, and jointly maintain international trade and market order. (vi) China must prepare for the resurgence of international terrorism. Because of the epidemic, many multilateral anti-terrorism mechanism meetings have been postponed or cancelled and the international anti-terrorism cooperation process has been interrupted. International terrorist extremist forces have, at the same time, turned more actively towards the internet to promote Islamic extreme religious ideas, anti-China speeches to incite anti-China hatred, instigate and plan terrorist attacks and even launch biochemical attacks. He claimed some forces actually cooperated with the United States to stigmatise China on the source of the virus, and attacked and discredited it on issues concerning Xinjiang. Asserting that terrorism is the common enemy of mankind, Zhou Li said China must continue to strengthen international counter-terrorism cooperation, especially in the Shanghai Cooperation Organisation (SCO), Brazil, Russia, India, China, and South Africa (BRICS) countries, Association of Southeast Asian Nations (ASEAN) Regional Forum, and the Global Counter-Terrorism Forum.

In addition to all the assessments underscoring the importance of good relations with the US for China, a couple of other threads also run through them. These assert that a very high degree of uncertainty and instability can be expected in the coming year and that the adverse impact of the COVID-19 pandemic will stay for a considerable length of time. CASS President Xie Fuzhan also referred to the difficulties confronting China's 'One Belt, One Road', or Belt and Road Initiative (BRI), while Zhou Li recommended focussing on infrastructure projects inside China, thereby implying reduction in expenditures on BRI. Interestingly, during his recent (July 6-7, 2020) visit to Guizhou province, Chinese Premier Li Keqiang advocated promoting domestic infrastructure construction. It is apparent that China's leadership is preparing for tough times ahead.

*(This article was published by the Centre for China Analysis and Strategy, New Delhi, on July 10, 2020.)*

# 37. CICIR's Assessment of China's Major Country Diplomacy

The Chinese Institutes of Contemporary International Research (CICIR), a think-tank of China's Ministry of State Security, published its analysis of 'Chinese Major Country Diplomacy' in May this year. The 9-page report, authored by Chen Xiangyang, Director of the Research Group at CICIR, was divided into 6 sections titled: (i) Relations with Major Countries; (ii) Neighbour Countries; (iii) Global Governance; (iv) Protect Sovereignty against Foreign Intervention; (v) National Day Celebrations; and (vi) A New Era.

Discussing "Relations with Major Countries", the report noted that despite being confronted by trade frictions with the US in 2019, which was also the 40th anniversary of the establishment of China-US relations, China held 13 rounds of negotiations between 2018 and October 2019 to try and settle differences and achieved positive progress in agricultural products and Intellectual Property Protection. The report observed that in Sino-US relations, head-of-state diplomacy plays a leading role and Chinese President Xi Jinping and US President Donald Trump have strengthened consultations and negotiations through phone calls. It stopped short of listing the developments in the US-China trade war after June 2019. It observed, however, that the US had since June 2019 "discouraged and banned bilateral normal people-to-people exchanges" and China had to protect the "lawful rights and interests of Chinese enterprises and people". It had also "warned the US that it is not a zero sum game now". The report said that "hundreds of US experts in academic, diplomatic, military and business circles have declared they want better Sino-US relations" and that "US scientific institutions and think-tanks have also called on the Trump Administration to stop bashing foreign scientists and researchers and deterring international scientific cooperation".

This section of the report stated that China has deepened strategic collaboration with Russia, and pointed to the June 2019 joint statement on strengthening global strategic stability as "one indication that bilateral relations are at an unprecedentedly high level". The third point under "Relations with Major Countries" noted China's stronger cooperation with "newly rising countries". It said that Chinese President Xi Jinping and Prime Minister Modi had "agreed measures should be taken to resolve the border dispute" and that during Brazilian President Bolsonaro's visit in October 2019, they decided to expand Belt and Road cooperation. At the 11th BRICS Summit, the leaders of Brazil, Russia, India, China and South Africa confirmed they would strengthen cooperation in hi-tech trade.

It mentioned that China-Europe ties "inspire global confidence" and that during Xi Jinping's visits to Italy and France "consensus on global governance, Iran nuclear issue, trade, Belt and Road cooperation have been reached". On differences between China and Europe regarding Hong Kong and Xinjiang, China had "urged some European countries to take prudent actions about China's territorial integrity since Hong Kong and Xinjiang are crucial areas in China". Noting that China-Japan relations are warming up, it called for more efforts and discussion on China-Japan- Republic of Korea (ROK) economic cooperation, the Regional Comprehensive Economic Partnership (RCEP) and the Belt and Road Initiative (BRI).

Discussing China's relations with its neighbours, the report asserted that "Northeast Asian stability matters greatly for China" and that "a new dawn is coming" thanks to China's proposals on denuclearisation and the peace mechanism. Noting that Kim Jong Un had visited China four times, it said that during Xi Jinping's visit to Pyongyang in June 2019, he had assured that China "would play a constructive role in long-term peace and stability on the peninsula". At the same time, it noted China's efforts to promote trilateral cooperation between China, Japan and South Korea and that it had hosted a trilateral summit in Chengdu in December 2019. Describing the South China Sea as a "sea of peace, friendship and cooperation", it said "China urged Hanoi to back away from its legal threat to pursue international arbitration". Asserting that "regional rules are crucial", it said, "China and ASEAN have agreed on a single draft negotiating text for the South China Sea code of conduct. The US' excessive involvement is unwelcome". It observed too that China's Navy had "expelled" a US destroyer which had come "within 12 nautical miles of a new island built by China".

A separate sub-paragraph of the report's section captioned "Neighbour Countries", declared that "peace and stability in South Asia is in China's interest". It said, "India's unilateral move to change the legal status of Kashmir could deal a lethal blow to India-Pakistan relations". China accused New Delhi of undermining its own and Pakistani territorial sovereignty and national interests, but urged India and Pakistan to settle disputes amicably. Afghanistan was mentioned, with the report observing that "Russia, China, the US and Pakistan agreed that negotiation is the only road to peace in Afghanistan". The report said that China had stepped up efforts to mediate since September 2019.

On global governance, the report identified building "a community with a shared future" as a call for world progress and the BRI connectivity as providing momentum for a sustainable world economy. It enumerated China's efforts in organising the 2019 Beijing International Horticultural Exhibition, the Conference on Dialogue of Asian Civilisations in May 2019, the 2019 Military World Games and as well as China's participation in the G-20 and Brazil, Russia, India, China, and South Africa (BRICS) Summits. It assured again that "China maintains an UN-centered international order" and "looks for settlement of major regional hotspot issues, such as the Korean peninsula nuclear issue, the Iranian nuclear issue, Afghanistan, Myanmar, the Middle East, Syria, and South Sudan". South Asia was not mentioned.

The section captioned "Protect Sovereignty against Foreign Intervention" began with the statement that "outsider intervention has undermined Chia's sovereignty and territorial integrity in 2019". Asserting that the Taiwan question concerns China's sovereignty and territorial integrity, it said, "China-US gambling has exacerbated robust, unofficial Taiwan-US relations, but 'One China' is what people want". Taiwan, it said, has lost seven diplomatic allies since 2016. It said that the US, which is Taiwan's only ally, is using Taiwan to "balance China's rapid rise as a regional power". The report listed the numerous steps the US has taken to bolster Taiwan and said, "China urges the US to abide by the one-China principle and the three China-US joint communiques, and not to interfere in China's domestic affairs". It emphasised, "China deters Taiwan's attempt to split the state sovereignty" and reiterated that Taiwan has no right to participate in international organisations like the United Nations (UN), World Health Organisation (WHO) and International

Civil Aviation Organisation (ICAO). It accused the US and UK of "being behind the pro-democracy protests" in Hong Kong and named Canada and Germany as the other countries. The report reiterated China's rejection of foreign criticism in its internal affairs.

The CICIR report described the National Day Celebrations as demonstrating "the achievement, confidence and responsibility of China in the new era". Emphasising that "China stood up under Mao Zedong, became rich under Deng Xiaoping, and became strong under Xi Jinping", the report asserted that China is now economically and militarily stronger than ever and Xi Jinping has called on the people to make more efforts for a brighter future. It recalled Xi Jinping's declaration on October 1, 2019, "There is no force that can shake the foundation of this great nation, ... No force can stop the Chinese people and Chinese nation forging ahead".

The final section entitled "A New Era" spoke of the historic changes in relations between China and the world. Listing the principles being advanced by China's diplomats, it said that the "five principles of peaceful coexistence, peaceful development, and a community with a shared future for mankind" contribute to international peace and justice. The report stressed that "relations with major powers are crucial for China to expand the strategic space". Saying "Chinese diplomacy is seeking common ground while reserving differences," it pointed out that China has "built friendship and partnership with neighbouring countries". It said that China maintains UN-centred international mechanisms and that the BRI has fostered the growth of countries along it. It asserted, "Chinese diplomacy is essential to sovereignty, territorial integrity and national dignity and for mutual understanding". The report made specific mention that a strong Chinese Communist Party (CCP) leadership in diplomatic affairs ensures success, including in the Chinese being independent and excluding foreign interventions in China's pursuit of socialism. It said China's non-alliance has prevented it from getting involved in the confrontations and conflicts between political blocs. The report stated, in conclusion, that pragmatism and prudence are best for dealing with the "enduring challenges from the US."

*(This article was published by the Centre for China Analysis and Strategy, New Delhi, on July 24, 2020.)*

# 38. China Debates Policy Towards US as Biden's Administration Takes Over

China's leadership echelons have been very apprehensive about anti-China actions that the Trump Administration might take in its last days. Zhou Li, a former career diplomat, who is presently senior researcher at the Chongyang Institute of Financial Research of Renmin University and Director of the China Russia Humanities Exchange Research Centre, had, in mid-2020, warned that China must prepare for the deterioration and "full escalation of the struggle" in Sino-US relations. He anticipated a string of punitive actions by the Trump Administration, adding that "decoupling" is ultimately inevitable and that the "difficulties and challenges China will face will be unprecedentedly complex and unprecedentedly severe". As expected, the outgoing Trump Administration has put in place a number of legislations and executive orders. These authorise arms sales to Taiwan, assert that the Dalai Lama has a determining role in the identification of his reincarnation, and impose sanctions on Chinese Communist Party (CCP) cadres and officials and limit the stay of CCP members in the US. All three, incidentally, cross what Beijing considers its 'red lines'!

Since the US-China trade war began, prominent CCP cadres, academics and strategists have blamed Xi Jinping for the deterioration in Sino-US relations. Saying that declaring China's ambitious goals at the 19th Party Congress and adopting a tough stance towards the US was a miscalculation and premature, they argue that China is nowhere near strong enough to take on the US. They have been calling for reverting to Deng Xiaoping's policy of 'hide your strength, bide your time'. As the trade war intensified and US pressure on China increased, some well-known Chinese strategists and cadres proposed areas of possible convergence in a bid to arrest the slide in bilateral relations.

Between April and May 2020, three Chinese think-tanks analysed different aspects of US-China relations and affirmed China's need for good ties with the US. In addition, two prominent Chinese gave interviews to the Hong Kong media and identified areas of compromise with the US. Qiao Liang, a retired Major General of the People's Liberation Army (PLA) and co-author of the best seller *Unrestricted Warfare* who is a 'hawk' with a huge following inside China, suggested that reunification of Taiwan with the Mainland need not have a deadline. The second was Wu Shicun, a senior CCP cadre and President of China's state-backed National Institute for South China Sea Studies and Chairman of the Board of Directors of the China-Southeast Asia Research Centre on the South China Sea. He hinted that China would not precipitate matters in the South China Sea. Wu Shicun also heads the Hainan Provincial Overseas Chinese Affairs Office and the Hainan Provincial People's Association for Friendship with Foreign Countries (PAFFC).

After the failure of the trade talks led on the Chinese side by Vice Premier Liu He, Chinese President Xi Jinping did not offer any compromise solution. On the contrary, he has been obliquely, but consistently, critical of US policies of 'protectionism' and its withdrawal from the climate change agreement. Despite domestic criticism of the deleterious effects of the downslide in relations with the US, Xi Jinping has not wavered and has persisted with his aggressive foreign policy and hardline stance with the US. He has taken steps to reinforce 'ideological education' to counter US efforts to weaken the CCP. His congratulatory message to US President-elect Biden was also delayed and issued only on November 25. In that, he hoped both sides would be able to manage and control differences, and focus on cooperation to advance relations.

With the new US Administration due to take office on January 20, 2021, many in China, including the leadership, see it as an opportunity to improve the relationship with the US. Inner-Party debate on China's policy towards the US has recommenced. While there has been criticism since early 2018 of Chinese President Xi Jinping's assertive foreign policy and hardline response to the US trade war, this has been muted in the past few months. However, comments by US President-elect Joe Biden and his nominees for the senior positions of Secretary of State and National Security Advisor, Antony Blinken and Jake Sullivan respectively, indicating that they would prefer talks to confrontation with China, have revived discussions on how Beijing should engage with the Biden Administration. Sullivan recently co-authored an article with former Assistant Secretary of State Kurt Campbell for *Foreign Affairs* magazine, titled "Competition without Catastrophe".

Beijing's response has been cautious, but positive. Several Chinese officials and academics, including Mme. Fu Ying, China's former Vice Foreign Minister who is presently Vice Chairperson of the Foreign Affairs Committee of the 13th National People's Congress (NPC) and Director of the Centre for International Security and Strategy and adjunct Professor at Tsinghua University, called for improving ties with the US. In an op-ed in the *New York Times* (November 24), Fu Ying made a strong pitch for "cooperative competition". Careful not to fault China, she emphasised that "China does not want to replace US dominance in the world. Nor does China need to worry about the United States changing China's system". She did add though that "China finds it offensive when the United States points a finger at the Chinese system or takes action against Beijing for its policies on domestic matters" and that "the United States should be respectful of China's sense of national unity and avoid challenging China on the issue of Taiwan or by meddling in the territorial disputes of the South China Sea".

China's Foreign Minister Wang Yi and Ambassador to the US, Cui Tiankai have similarly in recent weeks reiterated the need to repair Sino-US ties, treat each other with "respect" and together address common issues like the pandemic and climate change. They, and other Chinese interlocuters, at the same time advised the US not to interfere in China's internal affairs or slander the CCP. While calling for improving bilateral ties, they avoided any criticism of the policies followed by Chinese President Xi Jinping and held firm to Beijing's position where differences exist.

An editorial in China's official English-language *China Daily* (December 3) observed that the current Trump Administration is doing what it can to cement in place its tough China policy, which has already caused some damage that is "simply beyond repair". It warned, however, that a new US Administration "in no way warrants the kind of optimism some have displayed. Not only has the US President-elect indicated that he wants to rally the US against what he sees as a less than friendly China, but the recent deterioration in bilateral ties has fundamentally changed the political atmosphere for the China policies of the US. So much so that containing China has become a bipartisan consensus". A subsequent *China Daily* editorial (December 24) focussed on the need for repairing ties and recounted the mutual benefits of good ties. It highlighted the CCP's unique role and position in China as a ruling party, and said, "The top priority for the two countries now is to sit down, have a comprehensive, candid and in-depth dialogue, clarify the strategic intentions of both sides, and rebuild mutual trust".

A number of prominent Chinese academics, strategists and CCP cadres have commented on the change in the US Administration. They generally perceive it as an opportunity for China to engage and see how it can reduce US pressure. The majority, though, anticipate that Biden's China policy will be an "iron fist in a velvet glove". They assess too that there is consensus in the US to contain China and "the evolution of Sino-US relations might follow a trilogy: trade war - decoupling - full-scale cold war". One analyst warned that the US is likely to pressure its allies to undermine the Regional Comprehensive Economic Partnership (RCEP). The focus of Chinese strategists and international relations experts is to prevent America from delinking from China while China builds its strength.

Reputed Chinese strategist and Dean of the Institute of International Relations at Beijing's Tsinghua University, Yan Xuetong cautioned against "wishful thinking" about the incoming Biden Administration. Predicting that Biden's China policy would shift from the trade war into frictions in the political realm, he forecast that Biden will "take a harder line and invest more resources in these issues, resulting in more serious conflicts". Nevertheless, Yan Xuetong said, China should reach a consensus with the US that competition was at the core of their relationship, which would give the two powers a common ground for pragmatic discussions on how to manage and prevent it from escalating into war. Zheng Yongnian, Dean of the Shenzhen-based Advanced Institute of Global and Contemporary China Studies who attended a symposium hosted by Chinese President Xi Jinping in August to advise on China's long-term strategy, asserted that China should not miss any opportunity to mend relations with the United States, but neither should it assume that relations with the US would return to how they were before Donald Trump's rise to power. In fact, he suggested that Trump could return in the next elections! Professor Zhu Feng, Dean of the School of

International Relations at Nanjing University said, "China's goal is very clear: what it desires now is to continually strengthen and develop its economy and technology. If it enters into a new Cold War with the US, then this will not be to its benefit." Zhao Minghao, a researcher at the Institute of International Studies of Fudan University, said, "There is no reason to believe that Biden's Administration will automatically improve Sino-US relations, but there is no reason to abandon the window of opportunity". Emphasising that China should not underestimate its own strength in guiding and shaping Sino-US relations, he suggested infrastructure construction, data use and protection, anti-money laundering, anti-tax evasion, and anti-terrorist financing as areas of cooperation. He recommended strengthening crisis management to avoid direct military conflicts between China and the United States in the Taiwan Strait and South China Sea.

Efforts are being made by both sides to defuse tensions. Hong Kong's *South China Morning Post* (November 13) disclosed that after the US presidential election, China and the United States restarted their stalled behind-the-scenes diplomacy. Professor Wang Xiangsui of the Beijing University of Aeronautics and Astronautics revealed that several people close to Biden had contacted the Chinese and discussed with Chinese think-tanks how to restart Sino-US relations. Wang Xiangsui said the message from the Biden camp is "positive". The message sent by Democrats visiting China is that China and the United States should avoid a Cold War or direct conflict. Both parties must learn to manage their differences and find ways to coexist. He disclosed that a Chinese government adviser had earlier met Kurt Campbell and Jake Sullivan from the Biden camp and that in the past few years, some former Democratic Party officials visited Beijing many times.

Equally substantive is the *Wall Street Journal* (December 4) report that the US Justice Department is talking to representatives of Meng Wanzhou, Chief Financial Officer of Huawei Technologies Co. and daughter of its founder, that could see her freed to return home from Canada after her detention in December 2018, in exchange for signing a deferred prosecution agreement.

Amid these below-the-radar contacts, however, China's official media published two unusual and hard-hitting articles. These confirm that intense debate is underway on whether and how flexible Beijing should be while engaging with the US. While many Chinese analysts favour the opportunity to mend fences, the more hardline ones will resist any yielding of ground. The high-level Beidaihe conclave in August reportedly endorsed a hardline policy against the US. Both articles specifically addressed the domestic audience and targeted those who they said lacked adequate confidence in China and were advocates of compromise.

Huanqiu, the Chinese-language version of *Global Times*, on December 20, published an editorial captioned "Do your own thing well and not be constrained by the US and the West." Assessing that "the international environment China will face next is not optimistic", it warned that "China is facing the challenge of international anti-China forces trying to isolate, overwhelm and subvert us" and it must take preventive measures. Emphasising the need to maintain "strategic confidence", the editorial stressed that "China has accumulated strong national power after decades of development. Any attempt to crush China is wishful thinking". It asserted that China's status as a major trading nation is rock solid, and claimed that "except for the high-tech decoupling promoted by the United States, the most substantive content of Sino-Western relations has not been significantly affected". It maintained, "The total volume of Sino-Western economic and trade cooperation is unlikely to shrink". Stating that "the most fierce conflict between China and the United States and China and the West occurs in the ideological field", it added that "the vast majority of countries do not want to oppose China" as they consider protecting actual economic interests more important. The editorial advised that China "must adhere to our own political, economic and social agenda, free from external attitudes, and resolutely" oppose the United States, but while supporting what is beneficial to China.

China's authoritative Xinhua news agency published an 826-character sharply-worded commentary by "Xin Zhiping"—a pseudonym for a Xinhua media platform dedicated to promoting Xi Jinping thought—on December 16. It was aimed at Chinese citizens critical of China's assertive stance towards America. Titled: "The 'Worshipping America' and 'Kneeling to America' Soft-bone Disease must be Cured!", the commentary backed Xi Jinping's tough foreign policy. It bluntly criticised those advocating a compromise with the US and castigated those who are "spreading all sorts of arguments about 'worshipping America' and 'kneeling to America', who envy American 'democracy' and 'freedom', or tout the current situation of human rights in the United States". It accused some as going so far as to praise the "anti-epidemic ability" of the United States". The Xinhua commentary charged: "The people who 'worship America' and 'kneel to America' are often the ones who will praise the United States and disparage China" and added that they do their utmost to denigrate and slander their own country and believe that "the moon in a foreign country is rounder than that in China". The commentary said such people naively believe that compromise to seek self-preservation and China not hitting back "can be exchanged for peace and quiet". It declared, "We must resolutely struggle against them, pierce their painted skin, eliminate their influence, and not let wrong values confuse people". In conclusion, it asserted: "The Chinese people are not afraid of trouble, in front of any difficulties and risks, our legs will not shake, our waist will not bend. In the face of big winds and big waves, as long as we have confidence and determination, and steadfastly do our own thing, there is no hurdle that cannot be overcome. A self-reliant, civilized and progressive China is the best cure for 'soft-bone disease'."

There is apparent consensus in China that while the US will persist in trying to prevent China's rise and weaken the CCP, nevertheless China has an opportunity to reduce US pressure. The surge in anti-China sentiment globally will make it difficult for China, but many Chinese experts hold the thinly-concealed view that Beijing's considerable influence among the US power elite will be revived. There is confidence that big American companies like McDonalds, Gap, Hilfiger, Adidas, Nike, Coca-Cola, etc., which, during the previous Administration had little influence, will now be able to influence the Biden Administration's China policy.

Renmin University's International Relations Professor Di Dongsheng spoke candidly of China's influence at an event in Shanghai on November 28. He said "It's because we have people at the top. At the top of America's core inner circle of power and influence, we have our old friends." Di Dongsheng clarified that these friends are mostly investors in Wall Street, who have "had a very profound influence over America's domestic and foreign affairs since the 1970s". "We used to heavily rely on them, but the problem is that after 2008, the status of Wall Street has declined and more importantly, after 2016,

Wall Street couldn't fix Trump". He also touched on the President-Elect's son Hunter's ties to Beijing: "Trump has been saying that Biden's son has some sort of global foundation. Have you noticed that? Who helped [Hunter] build the foundations? Got it? There are a lot of deals inside all this." The book *Year of the Rat* published by Bill Triplett III in 1998 details the extent of China's financial ties to the Democrats.

Recent US media reports mention that China is establishing contacts with persons close to the Biden camp. Chinese Ambassador Cui Tiankai has generally been active in Washington. China also has longstanding financial links to the Democrats, including with Joe Biden's son who was recently served a summons by a Delaware court. Chinese President Xi Jinping and Joe Biden have a personal connection too. Xi Jinping will try and engage with the new Biden Administration, but will not compromise on issues of national interest. He has already initiated steps to guard against US efforts to stall China's rise and weaken the CCP.

Zhou Li, former Vice Minister of the CCP CC International Liaison Department and current member of the Chinese People's Political Consultative Conference (CPPCC), on June 22, anticipated six probable scenarios, and China has already begun preparations in some cases. These are: (i) A deterioration of Sino-US relations and the full escalation of conflict. (ii) A decrease in external demand and the disruption of industrial supply chains. (iii) Adjusting to the new norms under COVID 19 and the long-term coexistence of viruses and humans. (iv) Detaching from the dominance of the dollar and disconnecting the Chinese yuan from the dollar. (v) The outbreak of the global food crisis. (vi) China facing unprecedented challenges, and reference to Xi Jinping's speech stating that the CCP must "adhere to bottom-line thinking and be mentally and physically prepared to deal with changes in the external environment."

*(This article was published by the Centre for China Analysis and Strategy, New Delhi, on December 27, 2020.)*

# 39. China: Conference on Peripheral Diplomacy

In addition to the Collaborative Innovation Centre of the Ministry of Foreign Affairs (MoFA), the Contemporary World Research Centre of the Chinese Communist Party Central Committee's (CCP CC's) International Department and the Peripheral Diplomacy Research Centre of the Institute of International Relations of Yunnan University, other centres participating in the conference on "Diplomacy Around China in the Context of the Coronavirus" included Fudan University's Institute of International Studies; Jinan University's School of International Relations; Xiamen University's Chinese Overseas Chinese Research Institute; Nanyang Research Institute's School of International Relations; The Diplomatic Institute's Asian Institute; and Lanzhou University's School of International Relations.

The first and keynote session entitled "Challenges and Opportunities Facing China" was chaired by Lu Guangsheng, Dean of the Institute of International Relations of Yunnan University. The speakers were: Li Dingxin, Director of the Centre for Contemporary World Studies of the CCP CC's Central Liaison Department, Wu Chongbo, Vice Dean of the School of International Relations, Xiamen University, and Li Chenyang, Vice President of Yunnan University.

Li Dingxin assessed that the spread of the pandemic around the world may affect China's relations with some neighbouring countries and cause pressure on China's peripheral diplomacy. However, he believes that the challenge is shortlived. He suggested that the concept of a "shared destiny for mankind" will become more popular after the epidemic, and that there will be greater acceptability and "respect" for the concept of socialism. He recommended that in future, China should cooperate with neighbouring countries in the post epidemic era through the promotion of think-tank cooperation and local forums.

Wu Chongbo said that the outbreak had caused global trade to stagnate, the international supply chain was interrupted, and the tourism and financial sectors were hit hard, causing economic losses that would exceed those of the financial crises of 1998 and 2008. Under these circumstances, he recommended that China should promote the "East Asian Model" to the world and actively help some countries in Southeast Asia to fight against the epidemic.

Yunnan University Vice President Li Chenyang said that the borderless nature of the virus contributes to the enhancement of the awareness of the "Common Destiny", the awareness of cooperation, the enhancement of interdependence between neighbouring countries and China, and enhancement of the public health mechanism between China and the neighbouring countries. He advised that under such circumstances, China should adopt a country-by-country approach to provide assistance in epidemic prevention to neighbouring countries in order to wean them away from the Western influence. Stating that China had correctly controlled and guided domestic opinion and the public opinion of neighbouring countries, he said a comprehensive plan for the 'community of common destiny' between China and the neighbouring countries should now be fully designed.

The first session of the conference titled "Southeast Asia and China's Surrounding Diplomacy under the New Crown Epidemic" was chaired by Yang Yang, Deputy Dean of the Institute of International Relations of Yunnan University. Speakers included Lu Guangsheng, Zhang Chun, Professor at the Institute of International Relations of Yunnan University, and Li Yuqing, Assistant Researcher at the International and Regional Institute of Tsinghua University.

Lu Guangsheng spoke on "The Peripheral Diplomacy Under the Epidemic Situation: Taking the Mekong Subregion as an example". He said that the new problems facing China's surrounding areas mainly include the epidemic situation which may trigger other non-traditional security issues. He said that the risk of an economic crisis has increased and the public opinion in China's neighbourhood has deteriorated. He recommended that China should consider undertaking high-level peripheral diplomacy, establishing a joint defence and joint control mechanism for the epidemic situation, and initiate regional health diplomacy.

Zhang Chun spoke on "Adjustment of Thoughts on the Interconnection between China and the Peripherals under the Impact of the Epidemic Situation". He emphasised the need for China to connect virtually with states on its periphery, especially during an epidemic. Asserting that for this, digital interconnectivity is particularly important, he said that when building a public health control system in Southeast Asia, for example, data interconnectivity should be at the forefront.

Acknowledging the geopolitical situation, Zhang Chun said China's digital interconnectivity needs to take into account the needs of a developing China. The public health prevention and control system should be further improved during the epidemic. After the epidemic, China can focus more on how to increase exchanges and cooperation on poverty alleviation with neighbouring countries. Pointing out that China will win the battle against poverty and achieve the goal of building a well-off society in 2020, he said China's experience will benefit poverty alleviation in neighbouring countries. It is also in line with the elimination of some forms of poverty in the UN 2030 Agenda for Sustainable Development. He said China has already launched cooperation projects on poverty alleviation with many neighbouring countries but, in the future, it is necessary to strengthen data monitoring and data analysis in order to target poverty alleviation more effectively.

Li Yuqing spoke on "Public Opinion in the Post-Cold War Era with Sino-Thai Relations after the Coronavirus". Examining the assessments of online public opinion by the Chinese and US Embassies in Thailand, as well as opinions expressed by Thai netizens during the epidemic, she concluded that although the United States has been trying to influence Thailand's attitude toward China, most of the Thai media have till now stayed neutral. She recommended that China should step up use of multi-level diplomacy and multi-dimensional discourse for shaping global public opinion.

The conference's second session on "South Asia and China's Surrounding Diplomacy under the New Crown Epidemic' was chaired by Hu Xiaowen, Associate Researcher of the Institute of International Relations of Yunnan University. The speakers were Zhang Jiadong, Director of the South Asian

Research Centre of Fudan University, Wang Shida, Deputy Director of the South Asian Institute of the China Institute of Modern International Relations and Liu Shu, Deputy Director of the Institute of International Relations of Yunnan University.

Zhang Jiadong spoke on "Sino-Indian Relations under the Epidemic Situation". He said that the globalisation process will not stop because of the epidemic and that globalisation and regionalisation will proceed in parallel. China and India have not deviated from the basic principles of following neutral policies in their respective areas of concern throughout the epidemic. According to him, both China and India have considered each other's sensitivities on issues of concern. He suggested that China should provide humanitarian assistance within its capacity to relevant countries, including India.

Wang Shida's speech was titled "The New Challenge of the Epidemic Situation to China's Diplomacy in South Asia". His analysis touched on India, Pakistan and Afghanistan. He assessed that India's economy will be sluggish, and inadequate and that its outdated public health infrastructure will pose serious challenges. He recommended that China provides appropriate humanitarian assistance to India. He observed that Pakistan will face a severe financial crisis and that the normal development of the China-Pakistan Economic Corridor during the epidemic will also face severe challenges. He believed that China should help Pakistan promote the Health Silk Road and cooperate in building its health infrastructure. Wang Shida anticipated that in Afghanistan, the epidemic will accelerate the US withdrawal and the war will come to an end. He anticipated that a stable Afghanistan will help China promote its plan for a Silk Road corridor. He said that the development of China-Afghanistan relations will be a test for China to demonstrate that it can be a responsible major power.

Liu Shu spoke on "The impact of the Epidemic on Sino-Indian Relations. Can the Supply Chain be Cut?" He expressed the view that Indian companies had resumed work and observed production better than expected. He said that after the epidemic, global dependence on India's supply chain may be reduced, but it will be impossible to cut, and suggested that it would be beneficial for China to transfer some industries, including raw materials, to India and

Myanmar. He assessed that reducing excessive dependence on China's supply chain will not affect Sino-Indian relations.

The conference's third session on "Diplomacy Around China in the Post-Epidemic Era" was chaired by Li Tao, Deputy Dean of the Institute of International Relations of Yunnan University. The speakers were Zhang Zhenjiang, Guo Yanjun and Chen Xiaoding.

Speaking on the "New Epidemic Situation and New Opportunities for China's External Relations", Zhang Zhenjiang said China has achieved positive results in the fight against the epidemic and set a good example for the world. After controlling the epidemic, China has also actively participated in the international rescue and carried out active diplomatic actions. Stating that the epidemic has made people realise the ill effects of globalisation, he said China must now focus on regional blocs. He said this focus on a periphery strategy will be a breakthrough for China's diplomacy in the future. He added that since Japan, South Korea, and Southeast Asia agree more with China's anti-epidemic methods, they could become the starting point for China's future diplomacy.

Guo Yanjun spoke on "International Order in the Post-Epidemic Times and East Asian Cooperation". He assessed that the epidemic situation will have a very far-reaching impact on the international order, especially at the institutional and regulatory levels and that the war between the big powers may further intensify. Stating that the East Asian region can shape the international order, he said a lot, however, depends on how China can handle this region. Saying that only successful handling will determine whether China can shape the international order or not, he urged China to establish people-centred diplomacy, promote multilateralism, and focus on building regional organisations.

Speaking on "The Trend of Regional Development in Peripheral Relations in the Post Epidemic Times", Chen Xiaoding observed that while the pandemic had not changed the basic role of peripheral relations in China's diplomacy, the complexity of peripheral relations is expected to increase greatly. He said that in the post-epidemic era, China should promote regionalism and supply goods to build a more effective strategy.

The experts and scholars at this conference examined China's peripheral diplomacy in the context of the global spread of the epidemic and suggested ways for China's peripheral diplomacy to move forward in the post-epidemic era. There was consensus at the conference that by strengthening cooperation with the neighbouring countries in the fight against the epidemic, China could project itself as a responsible power. It was also suggested that to overcome the differences in political systems and the diverse cultural concepts of the neighbouring countries, China should encourage more people-to-people contacts.

*(This article was published by the Centre for China Analysis and Strategy, New Delhi, on July 20, 2020.)*

# 40. Xi Jinping Launches Campaigns to Entrench the Chinese Communist Party Among the People

Chinese President Xi Jinping has been under considerable pressure since he began his second term at the 19th Party Congress in October 2017. The US-China trade war and the COVID-19 pandemic have considerably enhanced the pressure. The Trump Administration's efforts to target the Chinese Communist Party (CCP) so that the ideological commitment of its members would waver would have especially disconcerted Xi Jinping. He has in recent months redoubled efforts to refresh the commitment of Party members to the Communist ideology and enlarged the scope of the campaigns to include students in an attempt to ensure the CCP's monopoly on power in China over the longer term.

Domestic dissatisfaction has spread in China, particularly among students, academics, intellectuals and the privileged group of 'princelings', who have their own networks of influence. The US-China trade war and the COVID-19 pandemic have adversely and severely impacted the economy, contributing to the sharp rise in unemployment and the uptick in prices and the cost of living. The pandemic has, additionally, aroused an unprecedentedly high level of anti-China sentiment globally, which potentially poses a serious problem for China's economic revival. Chinese economists point out that until the US and Europe come out of the COVID-19 pandemic and their economies recover, China's businesses and industries will not receive orders and the US and European Union (EU) markets will be closed. Thereafter too, as countries seek to diversify sources of supply, China is unlikely to regain the former levels of trade. These pose a serious threat to domestic stability.

The Trump Administration's actions on the trade front aimed mainly at China's hi-technology have hit China's technology industry hard. They have set back by at least 5-10 years China's ambitious 'Made in China-2025' plan for catching up with the world's most advanced technologically developed nations by 2025 and almost crippled China's two technology 'champions', namely Huawei and ZTE. They could similarly impact China's effort to modernise and 'intelligentise' the People's Liberation Army (PLA). The US actions have, additionally, revealed to the Chinese leadership the vulnerabilities in their technology sector. The ambitious strategic geoeconomic Belt and Road Initiative (BRI) has also been impacted by the turbulence. All three are among the areas where Xi Jinping has focussed personal attention.

Notwithstanding these pressures and his dented personal image, Xi Jinping has, in keeping with his character, not yielded ground to either domestic opponents or pressure from the United States. On the contrary, he has expanded Party controls and surveillance, imposed more stringent security policies which mandate the growing use of facial recognition technology, and is continuing with the roll out of the Social Credit Management system, all of which have angered Chinese citizens who view these as an intrusive invasion of their privacy. Ignoring foreign protests, he has progressively tightened Beijing's grip on the Hong Kong Special Administrative Region (HKSAR) and kept Taiwan under sustained pressure.

More importantly, Xi Jinping has doubled down on efforts to further consolidate the CCP's grip on China. Keeping in view the international environment and domestic political imperatives, Xi Jinping has, over the past few months, initiated a number of new, major ideological education campaigns across China. These have been accompanied by a publicity blitz through the official media. The campaigns are designed to inculcate Marxist theory and "Xi Jinping Thought on Socialism with Chinese Characteristics in the New Era" in the people, and the Army, with special focus on the academia and the youth who are considered more susceptible to "liberal Western thought". The campaigns follow through on Xi Jinping's 16-character slogan: "The Government, the Military, Society and Schools, North, South, East and West—the Party leads them all!" The slogan was incorporated in China's Constitution in October 2017.

In early July 2020, the CCP launched a new ideological campaign requiring Party members and college and school students to study the "Four Histories." These refer to "the history of the CCP, the history of new China, the history of the reform and opening up, and the history of socialist development"—in other words, the history of the Chinese Communist Party! Cadres were told a "key task" is to promote the contents in classrooms at colleges and universities. Teachers reinforced the campaign with the instruction to students to "firmly keep in mind the contents of the 'Four Histories.' There will be exams when the new semester begins." Many universities were reported to have incorporated the campaign's study materials in their course work. The East China Normal University in Shanghai, for example, incorporated the campaign material in the school's seminar series so that the students could learn and preach its message to people outside the campus.

The focus of the "Four Histories" campaign was elaborated by Lu Yanqin, Deputy Secretary of the Party Committee of Zhejiang Jiaxing University. Writing in the *China Education Daily* (August 13) he emphasised that it is necessary to "inherit the Red Gene, cultivate new generations, unite, educate, and lead the young pioneers to be the successors of the cause of communism." He described the "Red Gene" as the "life code of the Chinese Communists". He said, "It contains the nature and purpose of a Marxist party. It is embedded with the ideals and beliefs of the Communists to fight for. It gathers the great revolutionary spirit of the Communist Party of China; the original intention and mission of the Communist Party of China". He stressed, "To strengthen ideological and political education for young people, it is necessary to carry on the Red Gene well, and strive to cultivate socialist builders and successors who develop comprehensively in the new era of morality, intelligence, sports, and art". The "Four Histories" education, he said, will "help young people understand why the leadership of the Communist Party of China is the people's choice and history's choice". He urged that it be "integrated into the teaching of ideological and political courses and related professional courses, so that young people have a deep understanding of the hard-won New China's red regime and the hard-won socialism with Chinese characteristics, recognise the great significance of the Chinese nation to get rich and strong, and deeply understand the major contribution of socialism with Chinese characteristics to the world socialist movement, and let the Red Gene flow in the blood of young people". He pointed out, "To inherit the Red Gene, we must guide young people to understand the Party's purpose. ... the Party has always put the interests of the people first". Lu Yanqin quoted Mao Zedong, Deng Xiaoping and Xi Jinping—significantly omitting mention of any other Chinese leader! Xi Jinping was quoted as saying, "Our ideological and political courses should allow young people to fully understand the purpose of the Party from the centuries-old history of the Communist Party of China, and guide young people to establish a firm belief in listening to and following the Party". The article concluded that the "Red Gene" was important for "realizing the great rejuvenation of the Chinese nation".

In a related message, the CCP's leading theoretical fortnightly journal, *Qiu Shi* (*Seeking Truth,* August 31) reprinted Chinese President Xi Jinping's speech (of March 18, 2019) at a symposium for teachers of ideological and political theory classes in schools. Xi Jinping regretted that some schools still did not understand the importance of ideological and political courses and there were shortcomings in the selection and training of teachers and the ideological and political courses. He emphasised, "As China increasingly opens up and moves closer to the centre of the world stage, influences from other countries have deepened, and the struggles facing the ideological field have become more complex. .... the destiny of the nation and Party are closely connected. Schools are, therefore, at the forefront of ideological work, and can't be thought of as ivory towers or 'peach blossom gardens'". He said teachers must have knowledge beyond Marxist theory, strict self-discipline, and positive personalities. He exhorted Party Committees to take the lead and stressed that the Party's leadership over ideology and political education courses is the key to their success.

Xi Jinping listed eight "unifications" to promote the reform of ideology and political theory courses:

- Unification of politics and academic rationality: While political guidance is the purpose of these courses, they should not come across as political propaganda. They must "guide students with the power of the truth" and "stand up to students' questions of 'why?'"
- Unification of values and knowledge: The courses cannot simply preach values without the support of "scientific knowledge."
- Unification of "constructiveness" and "criticalness": While the task of these courses is to transmit ideology, they must also inspire a critical spirit, an essential characteristic of Marxism.
- Unification of theory and practice: Political theory should have practical

applications.

- Unification of universality and diversity: While ideology and political theory courses have universal teaching objectives and materials, they should still adapt to local conditions.
- Unification and guidance and subjectivity: Courses should maintain a balance between the teacher's guiding role and empowering students through class discussion and debate.
- Unification of indoctrination and inspiration: While indoctrination is essential to Marxist political education, students should also be inspired by the story of the Chinese nation, the Chinese Communist Party, socialism with Chinese characteristics, reform and opening up, and the new era.
- Unification of explicit and implicit education: While some people advocate hiding ideology and political theory courses within other courses, it is important to be confident in teaching these courses in the open. At the same time, there are ideology and political theory resources in other courses that should be tapped.

Meanwhile, there are signs that some Party cadres want to further expand the scope of the campaigns. An article in *China Education Daily* (September 17) by Jia Hongxia, Associate Professor at the Beijing Open University, stressed that pre-school education is the foundation stage of basic education and life-long education. Stating that "ideological and political elements are the shaping of the personal and national value system", he proposed that children's thinking needs to be guided from the pre-school stage to help them gradually form values that adapt to their own and social development.

Xi Jinping's emphasis on frequent ideological campaigns in the Party to increase indoctrination of CCP members in the last two years is partly a response to US efforts to target CCP members. Inclusion of the youth and school children in these campaigns is intended to ensure that the CCP retains its monopoly on power in China in the decades to come. The incessant ideological indoctrination campaigns also hint that the commitment of CCP members to ideology is weak.

*(This article was published by the Centre for China Analysis and Strategy, New Delhi, on December 14, 2017.)*

# 41. China's 19th Party Congress Indicates No Change in China's Policy Towards Tibet

The week long (October 18-24, 2017) 19th Congress of the Chinese Communist Party (CCP), which was held in Beijing, concluded as anticipated, with Xi Jinping emerging considerably stronger. For those watching the Congress for clues as to Xi Jinping's policies towards China's ethnic minorities and especially Tibet and Xinjiang, however, there appears little prospect of any relaxation of controls. An indication was the sharp drop in the number of ethnic minority cadres elected to the new 19th Chinese Communist Party (CCP) Central Committee (CC).

In fact, the emphatic assertions during the Congress that China will safeguard its sovereignty and territorial integrity were reinforced by a letter publicised a couple of days ago and ostensibly written by two Tibetan village girls to Chinese President Xi Jinping during the Congress. The girls, Zhoigar and Yangzom, had written describing life in Yumai, Lhunze county, China's smallest town. China's official news agency Xinhua reported that Xi Jinping replied asking them "to set down roots in the border area, safeguard the Chinese territory and develop their hometown". Saying, "Without the peace in the territory, there will be no peaceful lives for the millions of families", he expressed the hope "that the family would motivate more herders to set down roots in the border area … and become guardians of the Chinese territory and constructors of a happy hometown". Xi Jinping's reply, which contained the assurance that the Party will look after ethnic minorities, endorsed ongoing efforts by authorities of the Tibet Autonomous Region (TAR) to coopt villagers in guarding the border.

To prevent any protests or incidents like self-immolation that could cause embarrassment during the Party Congress, the already stringent security measures in force in the Tibet and Xinjiang-Uyghur Autonomous Regions had been further heightened. In the months leading up to the 19th Party Congress, China's borders with Nepal and the Central Asian Republics were sealed, foreigners and journalists prohibited from visiting these regions, and Tibetans and Uyghurs especially singled out for searches across China and denied admission in hotels.

While neither Tibet nor the Dalai Lama were specifically mentioned in Xi Jinping's lengthy 32,000-character Work Report presented to the 19th Party Congress on October 18, there were repeated references to "splittism" and "separatism". China's new and potentially tougher policy on the Tibet issue was spelt out in the course of the Congress. China's authoritative official news agency Xinhua reported on October 21, 2017, that at a press conference on the sidelines of the 19th Party Congress on October 21, the Vice Minister of the CCP CC's United Front Work Department and its Executive Deputy Head Zhang Yijiong, who was promoted at the 19th Congress to become a full member of the CCP CC, had reaffirmed China's opposition to the Dalai Lama's visits to foreign countries.

Asserting that "the 14th Dalai Lama is not only a religious figure, but also a political one," Zhang Yijiong made a remark with implications for India. He stated, "After fleeing China in 1959, he established a so-called government-in-exile, whose goal and core agenda is the independence of Tibet and to separate (from) China. For decades, the group headed by the 14th Dalai Lama has never stopped such attempts. As head of the group, the 14th Dalai Lama has never stopped his activities in this regard over the past decades." The statement suggests potentially increasing pressure on India with regard to activities of the Central Tibetan Administration in Dharamshala.

In an apparent toughening of the current policy, Zhang Yijiong warned foreign officials against meeting the Dalai Lama, saying they "can't get away by saying they were meeting the exiled Tibetan leader in a personal capacity as they still represent their governments". Announcing that "any country, or any organisation of anyone, accepting to meet with the Dalai Lama, in our view, is a major offence to the sentiment of the Chinese people," he expressed the Chinese government's "firm opposition" to such meetings, adding, "We consider such visit as a severe insult to the feelings of the Chinese people…".

Interestingly, amidst reports of restrictions imposed by authorities on the movement and teachings especially by Tibetan Buddhist monks and nuns inside China, Zhang Yijiong observed that Tibetan Buddhism was a special religion "born in our ancient China". He claimed, "It's a Chinese religion. It didn't come in from the outside." With this, Zhang Yijiong, who worked in the TAR from 2006-10 as a Deputy Party Secretary, hinted that China's policy towards Tibetan Buddhists would endure. His remark additionally implicitly pointed to the authority of China's 'patriotic associations' that supervise all religions in China and the authority of the Chinese government in religious matters concerning Tibetan Buddhism.

Meanwhile, Xi Jinping has strengthened the CCP CC's United Front Work Department (UFWD), which has expanded its activities. The UFWD with its increased personnel strength and larger budget, has enlarged the Seventh Bureau which looks after matters relating to Tibet and Tibetans. Available information is that since at least 2016, China's 'united front' activities have increased in India, some European countries, Australia, the US and countries along the Belt and Road Initiative (BRI). In addition to targeting Tibetan groups and supporters, the UFWD is reaching out to opinion makers and 'influencers' by offering cash incentives, scholarships through its 'front' organisations and trips to China.

Cadres in the new 19th CCP CC Secretariat and Politburo with a background of Tibet affairs will have substantive inputs on China's policy on Tibet. Wang Huning, who has in the past been a member of TAR delegations to the National People's Congress (NPC) and is now a member of the Politburo Standing Committee (PBSC), heads the CC's Secretariat. The others in the Secretariat are Yang Xiaodu, a 'sent down youth in the Cultural Revolution' and till recently Minister of Supervision who served in the TAR from 1976-2001, and Guo Shengkun who as Minister of Public Security (MPS) is familiar with the Tibet issue and attended meetings of the Leading Small Work Group on Tibet. Three of the Secretariat's members are persons with a background in security or the military, namely, Yang Xiaodu, Guo Shengkun and Huang Kunming, indicating a potential bias favouring progressively tougher Party controls. Among others who will influence the Tibet policy are Politburo member Chen Quanguo, handpicked by Xi Jinping in August 2011 to be TAR Party Secretary and now Party Secretary of the Xinjiang-Uyghur Autonomous Region; 67-year-old Sun Chunlan, who continues as Politburo member and heads the CCP CC United Front Work Department dealing with ethnic minorities and Tibetan affairs; and Zhang Qingli, born in 1951, who is a member of the 19th CC and made the infamous remark describing the Dalai Lama as "a sheep in wolf's clothing and with the heart of a beast".

Interestingly, while there has been a drastic drop in the number of ethnic minorities cadres in the CC, with only 15 ethnic minorities cadres in the 19th CC as compared to 39 in the 18th CC, the TAR has, at the same time, been given increased representation in the CCP CC. TAR Party Secretary Wu Yingjie is a full member of the 19th CC. The number of ethnic Tibetans has also increased by one, with Qi Zhala (Chedak) and Luosang Jiangcun (Lobsang Gyaltsen) both being made full members of the 19th CC. Chedak or Qi Zhala who earlier this year replaced Lobsang Gyaltsen as Chairman of the TAR government and prior to that was Party Secretary of Lhasa municipality, a position usually occupied by a Han cadre, is a first time member of the CC. Lobsang Gyaltsen or Luosang Jiangcun is perhaps the seniormost Tibetan in the CCP and currently Chairman of the Standing Committee of the TAR Congress. He was an alternate member of the 18th CC.

*(This article was published by the Centre for China Analysis and Strategy, New Delhi, on October 31, 2017.)*

# 42. Tibet has been Receiving Higher Priority in Recent Months

High level cadres of the Chinese Communist Party (CCP) do not often travel outside Beijing unless it is to 'Red Revolutionary' historical sites or because of a natural calamity or an important event or meeting. The visits, therefore, in the short span of a month by the second and fourth ranking members of the CCP's Politburo Standing Committee (PBSC)—two among the seven who 'rule' the People's Republic of China—are unusual and significant. At the least, it suggests that the top echelon of the CCP is according new, enhanced priority to the Tibet Autonomous Region (TAR). Chinese Premier Li Keqiang visited the TAR in July while Wang Yang, PBSC member and Chairman of the Chinese People's Political Consultative Conference (CPPCC) which is responsible for China's minority nationalities affairs and religious activities, travelled there a month later in August 2018.

The visits come in the backdrop of a sustained campaign of "patriotic education" for Tibetan Buddhist monks in the TAR, further tightening of controls intended to eliminate the Dalai Lama's influence in the region, and, acceleration since June 2017 in the overall strengthening of the military-security infrastructure. The visit by China's Premier points to sanctions for large financial investments in Tibet, while that by the CPPCC Chairman underscores the elevated priority being given to 'social stability' and reinforcing controls over monks and monasteries and religious activities in the TAR. The China-appointed Panchen Lama's unusually lengthy sojourn in the TAR in July substantiates this. There has been elevated activity by the United Front Work Department (UFWD) since Chinese President Xi Jinping took over as Chairman of its Central Small Leading Group.

In anticipation of the new revised "Regulations on Disciplinary Actions of the Communist Party of China" issued by the CCP Central Committee (CC) on August 26, 2018, the official *Global Times* reported (July 24) that the TAR authorities banned students in Tibet from religious activities during the summer holidays. TAR Party cadres are also confiscating photographs of the Dalai Lama found in residences and, on August 6, a traveller was apprehended at Lhasa's Gonggar airport for possessing the Dalai Lama's photograph. The authorities have begun enforcing the "Regulations on Disciplinary Actions of the Communist Party of China", which include the stipulation that Party members who believe in religion should leave the Party if thought education does not change their beliefs.

Poverty alleviation is an initiative personally steered by Chinese President Xi Jinping. It has been blended in the case of Tibet with the overall objective of reinforcing the military-security infrastructure. The guidelines issued jointly by the CCP CC Politburo and China's State Council on June 1, unveiled an ambitious plan "to lift a further 300 million people out of poverty in the next three years". The CCP CC's United Front Work Department (UFWD), which is responsible for China's ethnic minorities and supervision of religion, posted a lengthy report of China's authoritative official news agency Xinhua (June 1) on it's official website which said the Politburo convened a meeting to deliberate on the "Guidelines for Rural Revitalization Strategic Planning (2018-2022)" and "Guiding Opinions on Three-Year Action on Winning Poverty Alleviation Strategies". CCP CC General Secretary Xi Jinping presided over the meeting. Among other points, the meeting demanded that Party committees and governments at each level must increase their understanding of Party ideology and genuinely implement the countryside revitalisation strategy as a main priority. It ordered that all locales and all departments must integrate the countryside with the cities. The Politburo clarified that different methods must be applied to different locales in order to comply with the sentiments of the villagers.

Interesting and partially explaining the high-level visits to the TAR, was the frank admission at a press conference convened by the State Council in Beijing on August 20, 2018, that because of the high incidence of illness and poverty, achieving the goal of poverty alleviation in the remaining three years "is very arduous". Particularly identified were southern Xinjiang, Tibet and Tibetan areas in the Liangshan prefecture of Sichuan, Nujiang prefecture in Yunnan and the Linxia prefecture of Gansu province. It was stated that in addition to the high incidence of poverty, the areas lacked "basic conditions", were seriously backward in development and had insufficient public services.

During his visit to the TAR from July 25-27, 2018, Chinese Premier Li Keqiang arrived in Lhasa and travelled to Nyingchi and Lhoka (Shannan). He was accompanied on his travels in Tibet by TAR Party Secretary Wu Yingjie and Chairman of the TAR People's Government Choedak (Qi Zala). Pointedly, Li Keqiang travelled to two of the three locations where it was announced on June 8, 2018,after the stand-off at Doklam, that new airports will be constructed in 2019. There is already a recently built airport at Gargunsa-Ali while the earlier one at Shigatse was upgraded with the addition of a new runway in July/August 2017. The airport near Yume village in Lhoka will be additional to that already existing in Nyingchi. Yume village is, incidentally, being developed under the poverty alleviation programme as one of a string of 'well-off border defence villages' along the borders with India and Bhutan—a programme initiated by Chinese President Xi Jinping at the 19th Party Congress in October 2017. Choedak (Qi Zala) had visited Yume village in Lhunze county of Lhoka earlier from May 19-20, 2018.Li Keqiang also inspected the construction site of the Sichuan Lhasa Railway at Nyingchi. Instructions had been issued in the latter half of last year for accelerated completion of this "important" dual-use railway. Li Keqiang's visit focussed on infrastructure development and the economy, but considerable time was also spent on ethnic minority issues and emphasising ethnic unity between Tibetans and the country's Han majority. During this visit, he would certainly have approved large financial investments for poverty alleviation and especially military and dual-use infrastructure projects, including the airports and 'well-off border defence villages' in the TAR.

There was strong focus on ethnic minorities, religious issues and 'opposing splittism' during PBSC member and CPPCC Chairman Wang Yang's visit (August 24—26, 2018) to the TAR. He emphasised or "Xi Jinping's Socialism with Chinese Characteristics in the New Era" and exhorted all the TAR officials to conscientiously implement the General Secretary's and the Party's strategy of managing Tibet and Tibet affairs, "closely focus on safeguarding the 'Motherland's reunification', "oppose splittism and separatism" and strengthen national unity. He emphasised the importance of alleviating poverty and building a well-off society, "deepening anti-separatist movements" and creating innovative but effective temple management systems and fostering long-term stability. While visiting the Sera monastery, he impressed on monastery cadres the importance of religion and religious activities to social and long-term stability in Tibet. He asked monks to be prepared for "menace" and "rain", uphold and follow the "guiding principles" of the Party's religious works and promote efforts to adapt Tibetan Buddhism to socialist society. He also sat in a 'Young Tulku's' class in the monastery. It is pertinent that Wang Yang did not once directly criticise the Dalai Lama by name or refer to the "Dalai clique". Wang Yang was accompanied on his tour by TAR Party Secretary Wu Yingjie, Chairman of TAR People's Government Choedak (Qi Zala), Executive Vice Minister of the United Front Work Department (UFWD) Zhang Yijiong and the Vice President of the Chinese Buddhist Association, Drukhang Khedrup Rinpoche.

There were at least three other interesting events in the TAR during this period which would have been intended to reinforce Wang Yang's message. The first was the visit by the China-appointed Panchen Lama, Gyaltsen Norbu, who, after quite a long interval, spent an unusually long time in Tibet from July 19 till July 31, 2018. In speeches during his stay, he spoke in support of the Party policy. He emphasised the importance of loyalty to Xi Jinping and the Party's religious policies and said, "Tibetans must love the Party and the nation, uphold ethnic unity, and promote social harmony and stability. If someone does not contribute to the harmony and stability of the society, he is not qualified to enjoy the fruits of stable development." He stressed on "the leadership of the Party Central Committee with Comrade Xi Jinping at its core". The China-appointed Panchen Lama also paid a visit to Lhamo Lhatso, the sacred 'oracle' lake of Tibetans and gave religious 'teachings' including a *kalachakra* and visited the Jokhang and Tashilhunpo monasteries. The *kalachakra* ceremony and visits to the monasteries indicate that the Party was continuing its long-term strategy of legitimising Gyaltsen Norbu as the Panchen Lama. At the same time, his extended stay in Tibet suggests a growing acceptance by the Tibetan people.

The other was the visit of the former 10th Panchen Lama's daughter Rigzin Wangmo, along with her children and husband, to the Jokhang and

Tashilhunpo monasteries on June 20. The visit was reported by the state-owned China Central Television (CCTV). Rigzin Wangmo, according to some reports, enjoys a close rapport with the UFWD. The Panchen Lama and Rigzin Wangmo's visits would be a signal to the Tibetans that the CCP acknowledges Tibetan Buddhist religious leaders and keeps a line of communication open to them.

Equally interesting, and possibly presaging a new propaganda campaign to favourably portray developments in Tibet, is the meeting of Chinese diplomats organised in Lhasa on August 21 and addressed by senior TAR cadres and Chinese Vice Foreign Minister Zhang Hanhui. Zhang Hanhui's portfolio of responsibilities includes external security affairs and foreign affairs management.

The visits to the TAR by the two senior central leaders as well as the Panchen Lama, bring into focus the fresh emphasis being given by the leadership to calm Tibet, emphasise ethnic unity and 'social stability' and eliminate the Dalai Lama's influence. It also highlighted the push for completion of major infrastructure projects like new airports, the 'well-off border defence villages' and the strategic Sichuan Tibet Railway. Implicit is that the UFWD would have similar lines of communication open to the Tibetan Buddhist religious leaders in exile.

*(This article was published by the Centre for China Analysis and Strategy, New Delhi, on September 13, 2018.)*

# 43. China Intensifies Efforts to Diminish Dalai Lama's Influence

There has been a visible acceleration over the past many months in the efforts of the Chinese authorities to diminish and undermine the 14th Dalai Lama's influence over Tibetans inside China. Additionally, this year is marked by a number of anniversaries in China's political calendar including the 70th year of the founding of the People's Republic of China (PRC) in October, the founding anniversary of the People's Liberation Army Navy (PLAN) in April as well as the sensitive 30th anniversary of the Tiananmen 'incident' in June and 60th anniversary of the 14th Dalai Lama's flight from Tibet on March 10. The latter two would be cause for the most unease to China's leadership. The current strain in Sino-US relations has added to Beijing's worries.

Despite the investment of billions of dollars in the development of the Tibet Autonomous Region (TAR) and steady tightening of the already stringent security measures in Tibetan populated areas, the Tibetans continue to be restive, with occasional incidents of protest and self-immolation.

Qi Zhala, Chairman of the TAR Regional Government said in his Report on the Work of the Government to the second session of the 11th People's Congress of the Tibet Autonomous Region (TAR) on January 10, 2019, that a total of 180,000 people in Tibet were lifted out of poverty. Emphasising the support to Tibet "by the State and Party", the *Global Times* (January 11) warned people that the "hypocritical" side of the 14th Dalai Lama, who was "regarded as a separatist and fled into exile 60 years ago" should be clearly noted. On March 5, 2019, in his Report on the Work of the Government to the plenary session of the National People's Congress (NPC) at the Great Hall of the People in Beijing, Chinese Premier Li Keqiang too particularly mentioned that special attention had been paid to poverty alleviation in areas of extreme poverty like the "three regions and three prefectures." These include Tibet and the areas of Sichuan, Yunnan, Gansu, and Qinghai provinces with large Tibetan populations.

Wu Sikang, Director of the Policy Research Office of the Shenzhen Municipal Government, penned an 'internal' report last October after a study visit to the US in August 2018, which was particularly critical of the US. He specifically noted that the US had, after a hiatus of some years, increased financial assistance to the Tibetans from this year to US$ 17 million. In reality, though, the overall quantum of US financial assistance has not increased in the past couple of years, but the amount allocated for Tibet related activities in India and Nepal has this year been doubled from US$ 3 million to US$ 6 million. This has certainly aroused Beijing's suspicions and its concern is reflected to an extent in the enhanced attention being paid to Nepal. The announcement (February 22) by Nepal's Transport Minister, for example, that Nepal will use Chinese gauge standards for a planned nationwide rail network, points to China's long-term interest in Nepal. China has for long apprehended that Nepal would be used by "hostile foreign powers" as a launch pad for anti-China activities by the Tibetans inside the Tibet Autonomous Region (TAR). Separately, Hu Shisheng, Director of the Institute of South and Southeast Asian and Oceania Studies in Beijing, touched on US involvement in a remark to the *Global Times* (January 11). He said, "Though some US politicians might continue to play the Tibet card against China in 2019 on issues like human rights, China should ignore those political tricks and focus on exploring a diverse development approach to the region."

The Chinese leadership's attention will particularly be focussed on the Dalai Lama's annual message to the Tibetans on the March 10. This comes in the midst of the 10- day plenary session of the National People's Congress (NPC)—loosely called China's Parliament—underway in Beijing since March 5, amid heavy security. Contributing to Beijing's increased nervousness is the apprehension in the Chinese Communist Party (CCP) leadership echelons that the US has increased support to the Tibetans. Their concerns are reinforced by indicators that the Tibetans in China continue to venerate the Dalai Lama.

The TAR authorities have taken visibly heightened security precautions this year. Tibet has been placed off-limits to foreign and domestic tourists for an extended period this year from January 30 till April 30. On January 29, ahead of the Tibetan New Year 'Losar', the Executive Vice-Chairman of the TAR Party Committee, inspected Lhasa's two best known monasteries of Drepung and Gaden. Here he emphasised that "Tibet's stability is vital to national stability, and maintaining Tibet's security is akin to safeguarding national security." Later, on March 7, large contingents of armed police and armoured personnel carriers paraded through Lhasa and the square in front of Potala Palace.

A special high-level meeting was also convened at the TAR Party School in Lhasa on February 21 to discuss how to prevent "major risks to national sovereignty" and security. Senior TAR leaders attended, including the Chairman of the TAR People's Government, the Political Commissar of the PLA Garrison in Tibet and the head of the TAR's security apparatus. The seminar was addressed by TAR Party Secretary Wu Yingjie. He urged cadres to cooperate with the Party in times of "new problems" and "new challenges" and called on them to intensify the "anti-separatist struggle", proactively take social stability—a euphemism for security measures—initiatives to dilute the "negative influence of religion", carry on the fight against the "Dalai clique" and achieve sustainable long-term stability. He asserted, in this context, the importance of accelerating construction of "well-off" border villages which are conceived as a protective ring around the TAR's international borders. Wu Yingjie has, incidentally, made a direct critical reference to the "Dalai clique" after a long time!

Reflecting the CCP leadership's concerns, the Publicity Department of the TAR Regional Commission for Discipline Inspection on February 1, 2019, released a 46- minute, 4-part video, which was aired on Tibet Television from January 28 to 31. It highlighted that Party officials having religious beliefs or "alleged" involvement in "separatism" or corruption were punished. The report bluntly accused some "two-faced" people in Tibet of claiming loyalty to the Party while secretly sympathising with, and even working for, "separatists". It was not clear how many Party members were exposed and punished and for what specific violations, though the video revealed that a total of 215 people had been punished as of October 2018. Xiong Kunxin, an Ethnic Studies Professor at Tibet University in Lhasa was, however, quoted as saying that the regional government had already identified these people and was strengthening regulations to dismiss them.

CCP cadres are already deployed in each village of the TAR, thus, expanding

Party surveillance. Following the 19th Party Congress in November 2017, the state-run *Tibet Daily* disclosed that more than 20,000 Party cadres had been sent to the villages and to 7,000 monasteries, to preach the Party's message to the Tibetan people. China's official media on February 21, 2019, asserted that 800,000 Tibetans had been 'educated' in the spirit of the 19th Party Congress over the past 18 months and attributed this to holding 9,000 seminars and distributing 70,000 copies of publicity materials across the TAR.

Now in apparent confirmation that it had been decided to embark on a broader programme, the TAR authorities announced on January 22, 2019, that a new training camp had opened in Shigatse in Tibet under paramilitary supervision to "correct" and "mould" the thinking of Party cadres. It has been tasked to carry out political "education" in the broader Tibetan society. It was separately announced that a large 'Tibet Youth Palace' will be opened in Lhasa in May 2019 to strengthen "patriotic education" among young people.

The Chinese appointed Panchen Lama, Gyaltsen Norbu, has also been coopted in this effort. Speaking at a symposium on February 3, on the occasion of the 30th anniversary of the 10th Panchen Lama organised by the China Tibetology Research Centre, Gyaltsen Norbu, spoke of the 10th Panchen Lama's dedication for the Chinese nation. He claimed that "separatist forces"—referring to the Dalai Lama and Tibetans outside China -- were distorting and misusing the speeches of the 10th Panchen Lama and that he had never in his life once lost confidence in the Communist Party. He accused these "separatist forces" of misleading and deceiving the Tibetan people. The head of the CCP Central Committee (CC) United Front Work Department (UFWD) also met Gyaltsen Norbu on February 26, when he complimented him on the progress in his education.

Confirming that efforts to control and regulate the worship of Tibetan Buddhism are part of the planned central policy, the 48-year old Mayor of Lhasa and ethnic Tibetan, Guo Guo, told the Tibetan Deputies to the NPC and journalists in the Great Hall of the People on March 7, "In 2018, Lhasa ... took a clear-cut stand in eliminating the negative influence the Dalai Lama exerted via religion and took great effort in ridding the passive religious influence." He added that the number of days spent observing religious events, and the number of people attending them had both been reduced to less than

10 per cent! Large sections of Tibetans comprising students, government and Party cadres and pensioners are known to have been warned that taking part in religious ceremonies and practices would attract punitive measures. The recent remarks of the Lhasa Mayor suggest that a number of activities of monks and monasteries have been curtailed.

*(This article was published by the Centre for China Analysis and Strategy, New Delhi, on March 9, 2019.)*

# 44. Tibet Autonomous Region's Expenditure on Public Security

Tibetans have till this day not acquiesced to China's occupation of Tibet or large portions of its territory being merged with the neighbouring Xinjiang-Uyghur Autonomous Region and the Qinghai, Sichuan, Gansu and Yunnan provinces to create the Tibet Autonomous Region (TAR) in September 1965. In the process, Tibet was reduced in area from 2.5 million sq km to 1.2 million sq km. Tibetans in exile and the Tibetan Administration in Dharamshala continue to call it *Cholka- Sum*, or Greater Tibet. The Tibet Autonomous Region (TAR), as it was renamed by the Chinese Communist regime in Beijing, has been restive since the People's Liberation Army (PLA) marched into Lhasa and occupied Tibet in May 1951. China has expended considerable sums on maintaining its hold on Tibet, suppressing protests by the Tibetans and persuading them to accept the Chinese Communist Party (CCP). Beijing's policy towards Nepal has also, till very recently, been almost solely driven by its perception that Nepal could be used by "hostile foreign forces" as a launch pad for creating turmoil in Tibet.

After the widespread and violent riots that occurred in Tibet in 1988 and again in 2008, Beijing began devoting greater attention to the Tibet Autonomous Region. Security, or "stability maintenance" as the Chinese Communist Party (CCP) leaders euphemistically refer to it, became a high priority. Expenditure on the security apparatus in the Tibet Autonomous Region (TAR) and its Public Security Bureau (PSB) consequently increased steadily each year after 2008. While Guangdong province continued to receive the highest budgetary allocation for public security, till 2018, the TAR was second, with the troubled Xinjiang-Uyghur Autonomous Region (XUAR) a close third.

Two consecutive TAR Party Secretaries, namely, Zhang Qingli (November 2005–August 2011) and Chen Quanguo (August 2011–August 2016), put in place innovative, new security structures in the TAR. Chen Quanguo was, incidentally, appointed at the express behest of then Chinese Vice President Xi Jinping and as reward for his good work was later elevated to the CCP's Politburo and appointed Party Secretary of the Xinjiang-Uyghur Autonomous Region. The innovative security measures included the "Iron Grid" system (*wanggehua guanli*, 网格化管理) of police stations located at distances of 500 metres from each other and designed to ensure that security personnel reach the scene of an incident within seven minutes of a report; and the "Skynet" (*tianwang gongcheng*, 天网工程), an electronic eavesdropping system to augment other surveillance systems by monitoring all landline, mobile and satellite communications, internet traffic, etc. The "Skynet" was augmented in 2015-16 by the "Bright Snow Project" (*xueliang gongcheng*, 雪亮工程), which expanded "Skynet" coverage by incorporating the TAR's rural areas. Ironically, an unintended benefit for the Tibetans was the four-fold increase—mainly of Tibetans—in recruitment to the TAR Public Security Bureau (PSB) to monitor internet and mobile telephone traffic!

State surveillance in the TAR has since expanded to include that by the CCP, which has deployed one Party cadre to each village. This January, another year-long campaign titled "One Million Policemen into Ten Million Homes", ostensibly to maintain 'zero distance' between the police and the people, was launched.

Under Chinese President Xi Jinping, spending on domestic security during 2013-17, grew 34 per cent faster than total spending. The budget for the Public Security Bureau (PSB), or domestic security, in 2014 was higher than the national defence budget of US$141.45 billion. In 2016, China's national domestic security spending was US$ 175 billion and in 2017, it was US$197 billion. Spending on PSB and police rose by 54 per cent in 2016. The *Wall Street Journal* on March 6, 2018, said spending on domestic security exceeded the defence budget by at least 20 per cent. In 2019, the National People's Congress (NPC) announced a PSB budget of Yuan 178.78 billion or up by 45 per cent. This amount, however, reflects only the central expenditure and not that of the provinces or subordinate administrative divisions. The national defence budget was Yuan 1.19 trillion (about $177.61 billion).

Credible reports indicate that domestic security spending in the Xinjiang Uyghur Autonomous Region (UAR ) increased from RMB 5.45 billion in

2007 to RMB 57.95 billion in 2017, reflecting annual increases of 2 to 3 times the national average and even higher than the increases in the TAR. Increases were noticed in the TAR's PSB budget too, which increased by 28 per cent each year since 2007. Spending on the TAR PSB and the police rose by 54 per cent in 2016.

The upward trend in the TAR's public security budget has continued this year. The budget for public security for the TAR for 2019 approved by the NPC in March 2019 was Yuan 2579 billion. The allocation for 2018 was Yuan 1,991.10 billion and for 2017 it was Yuan 1,886. 75 billion. The real figures are, however, considerably higher! Not included in the TAR Public Security Department's budget are the expenditures towards the Anti-Terrorist Special Reconnaissance Team, Special Service Bureau, Border Inspection Headquarters, Civil Aviation Bureau of the Tibet Regional Bureau, Tibet Police Officer College, and Tibet Autonomous Region Traffic Management Bureau.

Official TAR documents show that the TAR PSB's budget includes expenditure only on the Public Security Department Office, Political Department, Police Security Department, District Discipline Inspection Commission, Public Security Department's Discipline Inspection and Supervision Team, Party Committee, Police Inspector Corps, Economic Crime Investigation Corps, and Public Security Department's Management Corps, Supervisory Management Corps, Criminal Investigation Corps, Exit and Entry Management Corps, Network Security and Security Corps, Legal Corps, Command Centre, Anti-drug Corps, Science and Technology Information Corps, Audit Office, etc. The TAR PSB has more than 20 department-level agencies, 14 sub-departmental agencies, and 74 bureaucratic departments within the entire agency.

Though there are offices of the Ministry of State Security (MoSS) in TAR, the expenditure on national security in the TAR is listed separately and in 2018 totalled Yuan (RMB) 11,069.51billion.

The TAR Public Security Department is under the jurisdiction of the TAR Party Committee and TAR People's Government. A similar arrangement prevails at the level of the administrative districts and below where a Deputy Party Secretary of the district or county is in charge of public security and chairs the Political and Legal Affairs Commission.

The total budgetary revenue of the TAR Public Security Bureau for the year 2018 was RMB 240.8067 million, an increase of Yuan 32.2587 (15 per cent) million over the 2017 budgetary revenue of Yuan 208.5480 million. Out of RMB 240.8067 million, Yuan 8.1262 (3.43 per cent) was allocated as expenditures for projects in TAR, which was RMB 580,100 less than the RMB 8.7963 of 2017 for the same. The reduction from RMB 8.7963 (2017) to RMB 8.1262 (2018) which equals Yuan 580,100 was reportedly due to the reduction of training fees for the civilian police officers.

The main reasons given for the increase in budgetary revenue and expenditure of financial appropriations are the increase in the salary of the police, and the increase in personnel. The decrease in project funding compared to the previous year was reportedly due to the decrease in training fees for public security department agencies.

Yuan 231.409 million was budgeted for administrative operations, Yuan one million for general administrative affairs and Yuan 7.2162 million for other public security expenditure. Administrative operations expenditure increased by Yuan 31.8696 million over the Yuan 199.5394 million of 2017 due to increment of staff wages and increase in daily public funds. The budget allowed for general administrative affairs was the same for 2018 as well i.e. Yuan one million.

The basic public expenditure of the TAR Public Security Department for 2018 totalled Yuan 231.409 million while the personnel budget was Yuan 189.4067 million. The latter included basic wages, subsidy allowances, bonuses, social security, other wage and welfare expenses, housing accumulation funds and subsidies for individuals and families. Yuan 42.0023 million was accounted for public expenditure which included printing fees, post and telecommunications charges, travel expenses, conference fees, welfare fees, daily maintenance fees, special materials and general equipment purchase fees, office space utilities, office heating costs, and official use, vehicle maintenance costs and other expenses.

**Breakdown of the TAR Public Security Bureau Budget**

Total Budget: Yuan 240.8067 [239.6252 General Public Budget Appropriation Revenue (99.51 per cent), 1.1815 (0.49 per cent) million carried over or balance from 2017].

- Administrative Operations (Public Security) amounted to Yuan 231.5006 million, accounting for 96.13 per cent of the expenditure.
- The General Administrative Affairs was Yuan one million, accounting for 0.41 per cent of the expenditure.
- Other Public Security Expenditures comprised Yuan 8.3061 million, accounting for 3.48 per cent of the expenditure.
- In 2018, the financial budget of the Public Security Bureau's operating expenses was Yuan 42.0023 million, an increase of Yuan 7.2092 million compared to the Yuan 34.7931 million in 2017, or an increase of 20.72 per cent. This was mainly due to the increase in personnel and the increase in the daily public budget.

**Government Procurement**

In 2018, the Public Security Department arranged a civilian government casualty insurance government procurement project with an amount of Yuan 440,300, an increase of Yuan 13,700 compared to Yuan 426,600 for the civilian police casualty insurance budget in 2017, an increase of 3.21 per cent, mainly due to the increase in personnel.

**Description of the Use of State-Owned Assets**

As of the end of 2017, the Public Security Department had a total of 268 vehicles. Among these were: one provincial level leader's car, 48 general official vehicles, 18 general law enforcement duty vehicles, two special technical vehicles, and 199 other vehicles. In 2018, the Public Security Department did not allocate any budget for the purchase of vehicles in its departmental budget.

The available breakdown of the public security budgets of the six TAR Administrative Districts as discerned from a scrutiny of official media reports is as under.

**In Million USD/RMB**

Lhasa PSB: US$ 133.12 (Yuan 894.441) in 2019.
Lhasa City PSB: US$ 17.95 (Yuan 120.606) in 2019.
Shannan PSB: US$ 157.04 (Yuan 1,055.16) in 2019.
Nyingchi PSB: US$ 18.90 (Yuan 127.0157) in 2018.

Chamdo PSB: US$ 35.58 (Yuan 239.077) in 2018.
Shigatse PSB: US$ 173.27 (Yuan 1,164.235) in 2018

Expenditure incurred on the large deployments of the People's Armed Police Force (PAPF), now directly under the PLA, in the TAR is not included. Expenditure on the continuous intensive campaigns in the TAR launched by the TAR Communist Party's United Front Department, including to win over Tibetan Buddhist monks and nuns, etc., is excluded from the TAR's security budget. Together, however, all these expenditures contribute to Beijing's efforts at 'stability maintenance'.

*(This article was published by the Centre for China Analysis and Strategy, New Delhi, March 2020.)*

# 45. China's *Xiaokang* (Well-Off) Border Defence Villages in Tibet Autonomous Region

Since the 19th Party Congress in October 2017, Chinese President Xi Jinping has signalled that extra attention would be paid by the Chinese Communist Party (CCP) leadership to building a more comprehensive security structure in the Tibet Autonomous Region (TAR). The new architecture strengthens the present security apparatus already in place and combines it with Chinese President Xi Jinping's new initiative of 'model *xiaokang* (well-off) border defence villages'. It is part of his nationwide push for poverty alleviation spelt out at the 19th Party Congress. The *xiaokang* (well-off) border defence villages are also intended to create a buffer inhabited by people loyal to the CCP and the nation. They will act as watch posts along the border, help prevent infiltration by "pro-Dalai Lama elements" and "hostile forces", facilitate the China-appointed Panchen Lama's acceptance among Tibetans and position him for the traditional role of 'tutor' to the reincarnate Dalai Lama. The pace of these activities, along with China's efforts to detect and weed out "double-faced" officials in the TAR i.e. those professing loyalty to the Party and China while being secretly loyal to the Dalai Lama, has accelerated in the past couple of years.

Xi Jinping's personal letter written on the eve of the 19th Party Congress to the two sisters resident in Yumei village in the TAR's Nyingchi prefecture, whose administrative boundaries in official Chinese maps include the Indian state of Arunachal Pradesh, initiated a new and important security programme centering on the borders. Since then, vast sums have been allotted for the development of so-called 'model *xiaokang* (well-off) border defence villages' from the budgets of the TAR's departments of public security, border defence, poverty alleviation and civil affairs. Some 628 'model well-off border defence villages' are under construction in 21 border counties along the TAR's frontiers, stretching from Ngari (Ali) district, across the Indian Union Territory of

Ladakh, to Nyingchi (Linzhih) opposite India's eastern province of Arunachal Pradesh. They are to be constructed within three years or by 2021.

Zhuangyan, Deputy Party Secretary, TAR Executive Chairman and Chief Commander of the Construction Work Headquarters of Xiaokang Villages, said in March 2018 that the aim of building the border villages is to ensure consolidation of border areas and border security. It is to "align a high sense of political responsibility and historical mission with the masses of the border region" and the Party Committee. An article in China's *Agriculture Economics* on December 18, 2017, gave details of the 'model well-off border defence villages'. Describing Tibet as the "forefront of the national security barrier and the Tibet border as the most impoverished area in China", it said that 628 'model well-off border defence villages' are to be constructed in 21 border counties along the TAR's frontiers stretching from Ngari (Ali) district across the Indian Union Territory of Ladakh to Nyingchi (Linzhih) opposite India's eastern province of Arunachal Pradesh within three years. It disclosed that the original plan provided funds of Yuan 30.1 billion for the 'border well-off village' and that the plans call for raising an additional tens of billions of yuan to invest in construction of infrastructure such as the road network, power grid and internet to ensure the economic growth rate and per capita disposable income in the border areas. It disclosed too that the status and salaries of these village-level cadres will be higher than the average level of those in other villages of the TAR. A villager in a model *xiaokang* (well-off) border defence village' was quoted by the *Tibet Daily* as saying that he receives a border subsidy of Yuan 5,000 per year in addition to an annual ecological subsidy of Yuan 8,871 annually and that, together with all other subsidies, receives Yuan 30,000 each year! The article said Tibet's well-off border defence villages will involve 62,160 households with a total of 240,000 people. They will be provided with ten amenities, namely, water, electricity, road, communication, network (broadcasting network, postal network and financial service network), teaching, science, literature, health and insurance (social security, housing security). All well- off border villages will be accessed by metalled roads.

The Tibet Autonomous Region Border Work Conference held on December 8, 2017, resolved that by promoting poverty alleviation of the border people and closely 'integrating guarding the border with a strong border' by 2020, the rate of solving hardships of border towns and administrative villages in Tibet will reach 95 per cent and 55 per cent respectively. It resolved too that by 2020, the per capita disposable income of the border people would be doubled from the current level and general farmers and herdsmen would have higher per capita incomes than others in the TAR.

These 'model well off border defence villages' appear to have been selected for their remote location, very sparse population, potential location for facilitating trans-border movement, and poor conditions. An important role of the residents in these villages is to keep an eye on the movements of the population and activities across the border. Populations in the 'well-off border defence villages' where local villagers presently number one or two households, will be mixed, with the original number of households being augmented by 15-20 additional households relocated from Tibetan villages from other administrative districts of the TAR. The new 'model well-off border defence villages' being established are planned to finally comprise approximately 20-30 households each with consequently enlarged village land areas and attached grazing grounds. Each border defence village will have at least a Party member, if not Party cadre, positioned in the village.

In addition to the passive security role assigned to them, official Chinese media reports disclose that these 'well-off border defence villages' have other roles as well. They are outposts for keeping a look-out for "secessionist" elements and countering infiltration attempts by "pro-Dalai Lama sympathisers and elements". The official media has indicated a psywar role, suggesting that the well-constructed houses, paved roads, electricity, TV and internet in these villages would be attractive to people living on the "other side" of the border. Party officials posted in these villages would be able to do "political work" in the neighbouring area where people share customs, traditions and often ethnicity with the Tibetan villagers. Related to this are the references since 2018 in China's military literature to the expanded role of Political Commissars of People's Liberation Army (PLA) units, suggesting their tasking includes work across the border in areas of likely operations of PLA formations. It has been noticed, for example, that Party cadres and researchers have been doing extensive work among the various tribes in Arunachal Pradesh.

Analysis of the Chinese media indicates that a total of 358 border defence villages have so far been constructed in four border areas in Nyingchi, Ngari, Shigatse and Tsona. The following illustrate the nature of locations of some of the completed *xiaokang* border defence villages:

**Nyingchi**: Dekyi Dongsar village, Lilong town, Minling county; Bamdrong village, Minling county; and a village in Buji town, Drakyab (Bayi) county.

**Lhokha (Shannan)**: Ninety six *xiaokang* border defence villages have been built according to the Lhokha Municipality Development and Reform Commission. Preparatory work on 40 has commenced and nine new projects have been begun with an investment of Yuan 656 million. Work on the construction of eight *xiaokang* (well-off) border defence villages (including Gongzu and Sangyul villages) with an investment of Yuan 89 million has begun in Lhodrak county. Lhokha has allotted Yuan 1.32 billion for the construction of the *xiaokang* (well-off) border defence villages.

**Tsona**: Lhuntse county has rebuilt one village and started construction of four new *xiaokang* (well-off) border defence villages, including Zhongna and Samba Star villages, with an investment of Yuan 120 million. One hundred and ninety-six members of 56 families would move to their new houses on the National Day on October 1, 2019, in Yulmai village. In Langkazi county, construction is underway on six villages with an investment of Yuan 107 million. In Tsona county, construction of two villages has resumed and work on three new villages (Quna, Khatak and Yama Rong) has started at a total cost of Yuan 340 million. Ma Ma Monpa Nationality Township in Tsona, referred to as "southern Tibet" in the Chinese media, appears to be getting special attention. The Director of the Lhokha Propaganda Department said the Ma Ma Nationality Township is being given Yuan 88.58 million in funds by "aid Tibet", Lhokha and Tsona county for the *xiaokang* well-off border defence village. Forty households will be relocated to 62 new houses and 15 houses will be reconstructed. A hotel is also being built and is estimated to yield Yuan 40,000 annually in tourist income.

**Shigatse**: Model *xiaokang* (well off) border defence villages are being built in Yadong (Dromo), Zhongba, Saga and 9 other counties.

**Ngari (Ali)**: a total of 37 '*xiaokang*' (well off) border defence villages are underway in the counties of Muir, Puland, Rito and Zanda in addition to the construction in 32 'front- line' villages and five 'second-line' villages. The total investment is Yuan 2.14 billion and 21,353 people will be settled.

The sites of some of the border defence villages are illustrative. The village of Men Chu Ma, for example, in Lhakang township, Lhodrak county, Shannan (Lhoka) district of the TAR is in a disputed area between China and Bhutan, on the border with Bhutan. In Bhutan, it is under the Kurtoe Lhuntse district. In the past two years, the Men Chu Ma border defence village has expanded from two households to almost 20 households, with the village head asserting that they can now use their "traditional" grazing grounds which they have till now been unable to and which are said to lie in Bhutan! Similarly, there is little doubt that gradually taking advantage of the thinning population in the border areas and villages on the Indian side, these newly settled villages on the Chinese side could 'nibble' and occupy Indian territories with minimal chances of detection.

Construction of these *xiaokang* border defence villages', which will augment the security measures already in place in the TAR, has probably been accelerated since the beginning of this year. It was in January 2019 that Chinese President Xi Jinping warned cadres that "hostile foreign powers" are trying to provoke a "colour revolution" in China. The ongoing trouble in the Hong Kong Special Administrative Region (HKSAR) will be seen as confirmation of the apprehensions of China's senior leadership. The Chinese authorities will consequently pay attention to Tibet's border with Nepal where, on the Nepalese side, people of Tibetan origin reside.

*(This article was published by the Centre for China Analysis and Strategy, New Delhi, on September 16, 2019.)*

# Appendix

## Illustrative List of Border Well-Off Villages In Tibet Autonomous Region

**A) Lhokha City** 山南市

— **Tsona County** 错那县

1) Quna Village, 错那县曲拿村
2) Yama Rong Village, 错那县亚玛荣村
3) Khatak Village, 错那县卡达村

— **Lhodrak County** 洛扎县

1) Lhakhang Township, 洛扎县拉康镇
2) Gongzu Village, 洛扎县贡祖村
3) Sangyul Village, 洛扎县桑玉村
4) Lagyab Township, 洛扎县， 拉郊乡， 拉郊村

— **Lhuntse County** 隆子县

1) Zhongna Village, 隆子县仲那村
2) Yulmai Border Well-off Village 隆子县玉麦小康示范乡
3) Dakri Township 隆子县扎日乡
4) Douyu Lopa Township 隆子县斗玉珞巴民族乡
5) Sanlin Township 隆子县

**B) Shigatse City** 日喀则市

— **Dromo County (Yadong)**

1) Guru Village , 亚东县古如村

— Gampa County

1) Jiru Village, 岗巴县吉汝村

**Ngari Prefecture** 阿里地区

1) Jagang Village, Risom Township, Ruthok County, 阿里地区日土县日松乡甲岗村

**Nyingchi City** 林芝市

— **Metok County**

1) Dhamo Village, Lopa Ethnic Township, 墨脱县达木珞巴民族乡达木村
2) Guthang Township, 墨脱县格当乡

**—Minling County** 米林县

1) Dekyi New Village, Lilong Township 米林县里龙乡德吉新村

# 46. China and US Could Emerge as Adversaries over the Tibet Issue

China's Communist authorities appear to have reached the conclusion approximately 18 months ago that the time for selecting the reincarnation of the 14th Dalai Lama is drawing near. Since then, they have stepped up efforts to capture the hearts and minds of the Tibetan people and adapt Tibetan Buddhism to "socialism with Chinese characteristics". China's official media has recently begun to often refer to "Chinese Buddhism"! Blatant indication of the effort to project Buddhism as Chinese is the article authored by the Chinese Ambassador to India Sun Weidong and published in an Indian newspaper in November last year. The article claimed that "Buddhism was introduced into Tibet from the Tang Empire" completely ignoring that Padma Sambhava and numerous other sages had travelled from India to Tibet and China carrying Buddhist religious texts.

Beijing's central objectives are to undermine the influence that the 14th Dalai Lama wields over Tibetans inside China and around the world and ensure that they accept the reincarnation of the Dalai Lama who will be selected by the Chinese Communist regime. This is essential for Beijing to legitimise and secure its hold over Tibet. The Dalai Lama has, meanwhile, declared he will live till he is at least 113 years old and made explicit that his reincarnation will not be found within the jurisdiction of an authoritarian regime and, specifically, China. He has, additionally, raised doubts as to whether he will be "reincarnated" or opt for the procedure that allows him to select an "emanation". Beijing has since then insisted that the next Dalai Lama must be reincarnated!

An equally important objective for Beijing is dissipating the anti-Chinese, or more specifically the anti-Chinese Communist Party (CCP), sentiment among the Tibetan Buddhist monks and nuns. In addition to persuading them to adapt the teachings of Tibetan Buddhism to "socialism with Chinese characteristics", they are simultaneously being given "patriotic education" to make them loyal to the Communist regime in Beijing. The efforts have accelerated over the past year and coincide with the CCP's effort to promote acceptance among Tibetans and Buddhists worldwide of Gyaltsen Norbu, appointed by the Chinese in 1995 as the legitimate Panchen Lama. The Chinese-appointed Panchen Lama's initial brief visits to Tibet, interspersed with long intervals have, since last year, yielded to him staying for extended periods in the Tibet Autonomous Region (TAR). More importantly, he has, for the first time, begun venturing outside Shigatse and travelling to other places and regions in the TAR like the Labrang Tashikhyil monastery in the Labrang area of eastern Tibet (Amdo), Nyingchi, opposite the Indian state of Arunachal Pradesh, and Ngari (Ali), opposite India's Ladakh. The aim is to have him accepted as the second highest-ranking religious personage in the *gelug* school of Tibetan Buddhists and facilitate his assumption at the appropriate time of the traditional historical role as the reincarnate Dalai Lama's Tutor.

Other measures are also being implemented. Beijing has directed the Police Headquarters in the TAR to launch a new propaganda campaign entitled "One Million Policemen into Ten Million Homes" ostensibly to maintain 'zero distance' between the police and the people. The year-long campaign, launched on January 14 and scheduled to end by December 2020, envisages grassroot civilian police units entering all aspects of a community, including pastoral areas, monasteries, nunneries, campuses, markets, construction sites, homes, and border areas to 'mingle' closely with the common people. Township police units have been asked to enter virtual WeChat groups. On receipt of these instructions, policemen have started visiting families and giving them edible oil, rice, flour, vegetables, etc. This is in addition to the policy of deploying one Party cadre in each village in the TAR.

Similarly, the TAR People Congress decided in late January this year to establish a 'National Unity Affairs Office' in the TAR. This requires all levels of government, companies, community organisations, villages, schools, military groups and religious activity centres to work on ethnic unity and "integrate ethnic unity" into their culture. Monks and nuns have been asked to treat "national unity" as their personal objective and contribute to "maintaining harmony and stability in the religious field." The measures augment other efforts already underway to control monasteries and nunneries through "model patriotic" monks and a cadre of "monastic monks" who supervise and administer monasteries.

Threatening to upset China's plans is the 'Tibet Policy and Support Act' passed by the US House of Representatives on January 28 with a landslide majority of 392-22, amending the Act of 2002. Since the Tibet issue has wide bipartisan support, the bill is likely to soon be passed by the Senate and will then be forwarded for the US President's signature. The amended 'Tibet Policy and Support Act' is more direct in its support for the Dalai Lama and incorporates potential punitive measures.

Especially important are its recommendations that the Chinese authorities resume talks with the Dalai Lama or his representatives or democratically-elected leaders of the Tibetan community without preconditions; provision for sanctions against Chinese officials who interfere in the 'reincarnation' process of the next Dalai Lama; and visa sanctions, freezing of US assets of those sanctioned and suspension of business transactions between the Chinese officials and US citizens and companies. It additionally opposes any effort by Chinese authorities to identify, select, educate or install Tibetan Buddhist religious leaders, including any future Dalai Lama, in a manner inconsistent with the Tibetan Buddhist faith and community. It adds too that the US Administration should not authorise China to establish any additional Consulate in the US till a US Consulate is established in Lhasa. These new recommendations seek to pressure China into changing its policy on Tibet.

China's consistent position has been that the negotiations are intended only to address the Dalai Lama's personal concerns and are not with the Tibetan administration-in-exile. Talks have, therefore, been thus far restricted to between the Dalai Lama's envoys and representatives of the CCP Central Committee's United Front Work Department (UFWD). It has consequently declined to entertain "democratically-elected leaders of the Tibetan community". The reference to "without preconditions" points to the US Congress wanting to broaden the scope of discussions to include discussion of issues also in the post- 14th Dalai Lama period.

The proposed sanctions give teeth to the Act. Though China's official *Global Times* newspaper quoted Diao Daming, Associate Professor at China's Renmin University, as saying this "long-arm jurisdiction" actually has a limited impact on Chinese officials, the newspaper ignored that many Chinese cadres travel to the US, have relatives residing abroad and children studying in US colleges. They could all potentially be adversely impacted.

The visa sanctions have a precedent. In 2013, Spain's National Court had issued an arrest warrant against five former Chinese leaders, including former Chinese President Jiang Zemin, former Prime Minister Li Peng and Chinese President Hu Jintao on charges of "genocide" in Tibet. The case against them was brought by human rights groups under Spain's 'recognition of universal jurisdiction'—the principle that crimes against humanity can be prosecuted across borders. Before the subject came up for trial, Spain's National Court, reportedly under pressure from China in 2014, introduced changes in the Spanish law. The amendment restricted Spanish judges to only investigate crimes of genocide and crimes against humanity if those indicted were Spanish citizens or foreigners who had their habitual residence in Spain at the time when the crimes were committed.

The US Congress also authorised grants from 2021 till 2025 totalling over US$ 9 million to the Tibetan administration-in-exile, Tibetan communities in India, Nepal and the TAR as well as to Radio Free Asia and Voice of America. While the amount is the same as last year, it confirms continuing US support to the Tibetans and this financial support will cause discomfort to the Chinese authorities.

The bill passed by the US House of Representatives bolsters the Dalai Lama's negotiating position with the Chinese. Once signed by the US President it will give an additional lever to the US. Interesting around this time is the 16-point Joint Press Statement issued at the end of Chinese President Xi Jinping's visit to Myanmar on January 18. It declared, "The Myanmar side reiterates its firm commitment to the One China Policy and supports the efforts of China to resolve the issues of Taiwan, Tibet and Xinjiang, which are inalienable parts of China", possibly hinting that the Tibet issue remains unresolved! Xi Jinping's warning in Kathmandu last October that "anyone attempting to split China in any part of the country will end in crushed bodies and shuttered bones...And any external forces backing such attempts dividing China will be deemed by the Chinese people as pipe-dreaming!" now assumes more relevance.

*(This article was published by the Centre for China Analysis and Strategy, New Delhi, on March 6, 2020.)*

# 47. China's Seventh Tibet Work Forum, August 29-30, 2020

The Seventh Tibet Work Forum was held in Beijing on August 29-30, 2020. The Forum heralds a tougher regime for Tibetans in China, where the Chinese Communist Party (CCP) will penetrate into each village and hamlet in the Tibet Autonomous Region (TAR). There will be renewed emphasis on adapting Tibetan Buddhism to 'socialism with Chinese characteristics' and countering 'separatism' and the 'Dalai clique'.

The entire Politburo Standing Committee (PBSC) including Li Zhanshu, Wang Huning, Zhao Leji and Han Zheng attended the Forum. Chinese Premier Li Keqiang presided over the Forum. Chinese People's Political Consultative Conference (CPPCC) Chairman and PBSC member Wang Yang summed up the proceedings. Chinese Premier Li Keqiang described Xi Jinping's speech at the Forum as "a guiding document on Tibet-related work in a new era".

Though held at irregular intervals, the Tibet Work Forums are important meetings where the CCP's top leadership reviews past plans and performance of the Tibet Autonomous Region (TAR) Party and government, and sets out and approves long-term development and security plans for the TAR. The Tibet Work Forums have been held in 1980; 1984; 1994; 2001; 2010; 2015 and 2020. This is the second Tibet Work Forum in Xi Jinping's term.

Around 300 persons normally attend the Tibet Work Forums. Official Chinese media reports said that among those attending the Seventh Tibet Work Conference "were TAR Party and government officials, the 'principal comrades' in charge of the Party and governments of various cities and provinces, officials in charge of the Party and government of Sichuan, Yunnan, Gansu, and Qinghai provinces and principal officials of the Party and governments of the Tibetan Autonomous Prefectures". Also attending would have been members of the CPPCC, responsible officers of relevant military units, financial institutions, State-owned Enterprises (SoEs) and retired officials with experience of Tibetan affairs. Former Chinese President Hu Jintao, who has served as TAR Party Secretary, might have been invited.

Curious this time, though, is that the official Chinese media did not specifically mention Wu Yingjie's presence at the Tibet Work Forum, although reports reveal that he, along with TAR Chairman Che Dalha (Qizhala), was in Beijing from August 28–30. On August 29 afternoon, Wu Yingjie signed an agreement at the Ministry of Human Resources and Social Security for the establishment of a Technicians Centre in Lhasa.

During the Forum, the 11th Panchen Lama Gyaltsen Norbu was in Medog County from August 29 to 31. The coverage of the state-owned China Central Television (CCTV), China Global Television (CGTV) and Xizang TV of the Tibet Work Forum did not show the presence of Tibetan monks or persons in traditional Tibetan dress.

Speaking at the two-day seventh central Tibet Work Forum, Chinese President Xi Jinping delivered an "important" speech wherein he called for efforts to build a new, modern, socialist Tibet. He underlined the need to fully implement the CCP's policies on governing Tibet for a new era and called for "efforts to ensure national security and enduring peace and stability, steadily improve people's lives, maintain a good environment, solidify border defense and ensure frontier security". He said, "Efforts must be made to build a new modern socialist Tibet that is united, prosperous, culturally advanced, harmonious and beautiful". Xi Jinping recounted that since the Sixth Forum in 2015, Tibet has made comprehensive progress and "historic" achievements in its various undertakings. It had achieved sustained stability and rapid development in Tibet, making a major contribution to the overall work of the Party and the state. He said since the 18th Party Congress in 2012, policies on governing Tibet for a new era have taken shape. He stressed that the CCP leadership, the system of socialism with Chinese characteristics and the system of regional ethnic autonomy must be upheld to carry out work related to Tibet.

Xi Jinping asserted that work related to Tibet must focus on safeguarding national unity and strengthening ethnic solidarity. More education and guidance should be provided for the public to mobilise their participation in combating separatist activities, thus forging an "ironclad shield" to safeguard stability. Xi Jinping stressed that patriotism should be incorporated into the whole process of education in all schools and called for "continuous efforts to enhance recognition of the great motherland, the Chinese nation, the Chinese culture, the CCP and socialism with Chinese characteristics by people of all ethnic groups". He observed, "Tibetan Buddhism should be guided in adapting to the socialist society and should be developed in the Chinese context".

Xi Jinping stressed the need for more work and said measures and support are needed to consolidate the achievements made in poverty alleviation. He said a number of major infrastructure projects and public service facilities will be completed, including the Sichuan Tibet Railway. Touching on the importance of the environment, Xi Jinping stressed the importance of further scientific research on the Tibetan plateau. He described conserving the ecology of the Qinghai-Tibet plateau as the greatest contribution to the survival and development of the Chinese nation.

Commenting on building the Party in Tibet, Xi Jinping instructed that there is need to strengthen the building of leadership teams at all levels, cadre teams and primary-level Party organisations in order to "improve the capacity to respond to major struggles and prevent major risks". Cadres and workers in Tibet should be cared for, and support policies regarding their income, housing, medical care and retirement, as well as education for their children, should be further improved and well implemented. He emphasised long-term commitment to the policy of the CCP Central Committee (CC) to ensure Tibet has support from the central authorities and assistance from the whole country, adding that continued and increasing support will be offered to Sichuan, Yunnan, Gansu and Qinghai provinces in their Tibet-related work.

A day prior to start of the Forum (August 28), the CCP mouthpiece *People's Daily* front-paged an article under the caption: "The Party Central Committee with Comrade Xi Jinping at the Core is Concerned About the Work in Tibet". It summarised Tibet-related work done by Xi Jinping and the CCP CC since the 18th Party Congress. Noting that work concerning Tibet has been a major focus of the Party leadership since its "liberation" nearly 70 years ago, it also said that "since the 18th Party Congress, the Central Committee, with Comrade Xi Jinping at the core, has focused on achieving a moderately prosperous society and modernizing Tibet together with the whole country and thrown a great amount of [their] heart's blood into developing snow-covered plateaus for a new era." The article primarily focussed on the CCP CC's contributions such as "Xi's Important Discourse on Governing the Frontier, Stabilizing Tibet." The front-page article listed instances showing Xi Jinping's concern for the welfare of the people of Tibet and observed that he had visited Tibet as early as June 1998, for investigation of the work of the counterpart assistance mission in Fujian and in July 2011, had attended the celebration of the 60th anniversary of Tibet's peaceful liberation as head of the central delegation. It concluded that "the people who live on this ancient and magical land believe firmly: tomorrow certainly will be even finer!"

The article cited examples of how economic prosperity in Tibet's villages had increased as had schools and the standards of education. It asserted that "as an important frontier ethnic region in China, Tibet is located in the border areas. Due to the high cold and lack of oxygen, the task of fighting against separatism is arduous". It stated, "Tibet has entered a critical stage of making every effort to build a well-off society in an all-round way and long-term stability. Maintaining Tibet's harmony and stability and realizing Tibet's prosperity and progress are the ardent expectations of the cadres and the masses of all ethnic groups in Tibet, as well as the common wish of the entire Party and people of all ethnic groups in the country. General Secretary Xi Jinping has profound thoughts on how to govern Tibet in the new era, to further promote Tibet's long-term development and long-term stability, and to realize the yearning of the people of all ethnic groups in Tibet for a better life". It emphasised, "To govern the country, we must govern the border, and we must first stabilize the Tibet."

Focussing on Party-building the *People's Daily* article stated, "It is necessary to fully and correctly implement the Party's ethnic and religious policies, strengthen national unity, and continuously increase the recognition of the people of all ethnic groups with the great motherland, the Chinese nation, Chinese culture, the Communist Party of China, and socialism with Chinese characteristics". It added, "The central government's concern and national support must be closely integrated with the hard work of the cadres and masses of all ethnic groups in Tibet, and the work in Tibet must be done well in the overall planning of domestic and international issues; and it is necessary to strengthen the building of Party organizations and cadres at all levels to consolidate the Party's foundation for governance in Tibet".

The state-owned CCTV in its 8 pm "Focus" programme on August 31, said that at the Seventh Tibet Work Forum Xi Jinping had evaluated there had been "all-round progress, historic achievement" in Tibet since the Sixth Tibet Work Forum. He said that under the strong leadership of the Party Central Committee and with the strong support of the people of the whole country, the cadres and masses of all ethnic groups in Tibet have united and worked hard, and solved many long-term problems that they had wanted to solve but had been unable to. CCTV said that the "five years since the Sixth Central Tibet Work Forum have been an extraordinary five years in the history of Tibet's development" adding that this was because the Party Central Committee has always attached great importance to work in Tibet. It said that since the 18th Party Congress, after summing up the successful experience of the Party leading the people in governing, stabilising, and rejuvenating Tibet, the Party's strategy for governing Tibet has been formed in the new era.

It highlighted that at the Seventh Tibet Work Symposium, Xi Jinping had explained the Party's strategy for 'governing Tibet in the new era' with the Ten "Musts": (i) We must uphold the leadership of the Communist Party of China, the socialist system with Chinese characteristics, and the system of regional ethnic autonomy. (ii) We must adhere to the strategic thinking of governing the country and governing the border, and stabilising Tibet first. (iii) Maintaining the unification of the motherland and strengthening national unity must be the focus, and the focus of Tibet's work. (iv) We must adhere to the important principles of governing Tibet according to the law, enriching the people and rejuvenating Tibet, building Tibet for a long time, uniting people's hearts, and laying a solid foundation. (v) The overall domestic and international situation must be coordinated. (vi) Improving people's livelihood and uniting people's hearts must be taken as the starting point and goal of economic and social development. (vii) We must promote the exchanges and integration of all ethnic groups. (viii) We must adhere to the direction of the Sinicisation of religion in China and manage religious affairs in accordance with the law. (ix) We must insist on ecological protection first. (x) We must strengthen Party building, especially political building.

Xi Jinping had expounded the Party's strategy for governing Tibet at the Sixth Central Tibet Work Symposium in August 2015, and put forward the "Six Musts". China's official media described the progression from the "Six Musts" to the "Ten Musts" as indicating a "more comprehensive and profound" exposition of the Tibet strategy.

Within days of the conclusion of the Seventh Tibet Work Forum on September 4, retired People's Liberation Army (PLA) Maj Gen Cheng Xizhong, who as Senior Colonel was posted as Defence Attache to India and later in 2014 to Nepal and is now Distinguished Professor of the Southwest University of Political Science and Law, wrote an article on the Tibet Work Forum in the China Tibetology Research Centre's magazine *China-Tibet Net*. Describing Xi Jinping's speech at the Forum as "important", he highlighted that the "Ten Musts" summarise the Party's strategy for governing Tibet in the new era. Mentioning that he had worked in South Asia, including India and Nepal for 20 years, he said that while in Nepal, "I deeply felt that Tibet's stability and development are of great significance to the security and stability of our surrounding areas and to the long-term stability of our country".

Maj Gen Cheng Xizhong noted that by December 2019, all 74 poverty-stricken counties (districts) in Tibet had achieved remarkable results in poverty alleviation. Citing Milin county, Nyingchi city, as an example, he said currently 67 villages had achieved 100 per cent coverage of electricity, roads, communications, and networks. The Tibetan Buddhist community had "shown a strong sense of social responsibility and mission" and worked with other sections of society in prevention and control of the epidemic thus embodying "patriotism, protection of the country, obedience to the overall situation, and mutual assistance". He said this reflected the current social status, ethnic unity and religious harmony in Tibet.

Observing that Xi Jinping had emphasised the necessity of promoting the construction of a number of major infrastructure and public service facilities, he referred to the 1,742.39-km-long Sichuan-Tibet railway presently under construction with an investment of more than Yuan 300 billion. Describing it as an "unprecedented project of the century", he said that once completed, railway travel time from Chengdu to Lhasa will be reduced from 36 to about 12 hours. This is the second railway to Tibet after the Qinghai Tibet Railway and meets not only the expectations of the Tibetan people, but also the aspirations of the people of the whole country. He noted that it is of great significance for the development and construction of the frontier and ecological protection and especially for the stability of the frontier region and the maintenance of national security. Tibet, he said, is gradually improving the construction of a "two vertical and two horizontal" railway networks.

He sought to publicise the benefits of Chinese assistance to Nepal, calling it "a huge centripetal force for neighboring countries and the vast number of overseas Chinese". He recounted that a number of Nepal Army officers visiting China in recent years had remarked that Kathmandu and Lhasa had witnessed transformational changes in the past ten years! In a transparent reference to Tibetans abroad, he added that while he was working in India and Nepal, many "friendly overseas Chinese" had appealed to him saying,"We were tricked out of the country when we were young and wandered abroad for so many years. Now that we have grown up, we especially miss our parents and brothers and sisters. We want to go home."

Another article by Lian Xiangmin, Deputy Director General and Researcher of the China Tibetology Research Centre, was also published by *China-Tibet Net* on September 4. Saying that Xi Jinping's "important" speech was of "a strong political, ideological, and theoretical nature", he called it "a programmatic document that guides Tibet work in the new era". Recounting the evolution of the Tibet Work Forums, Lian Xiangmin said they are of "great significance as a link between the past and the next" and have integrated "the guiding ideology and governance strategy." He said that the Forums have generated a number of innovative results and greatly improved theory. He observed that many things never change, like "maintaining the unification of the motherland and strengthening ethnic unity" and "upholding the Party's leadership".

Lian Xiangmin emphasised that to promote the rapid development and long-term stability of Tibet and realise the aspirations of people of all ethnic groups in Tibet for a better life, the most essential feature comprises the leadership of the Communist Party of China, and the greatest advantage of the socialist system with Chinese characteristics is the leadership of the Communist Party of China. He asserted, "Our Party plays the role of the decision-making core and command center for various undertakings ... and all policies related to the overall development of the Party and the country are under the overall planning of the Party Central Committee" He urged Party organisations at all levels, localities and departments to fully implement the party's strategy for governing Tibet in the new era.

Within days of the Tibet Work Forum, the TAR authorities began disseminating the "spirit" of CCP General Secretary Xi Jinping's "important" speech and the message of the Forum. The TAR'S National Security Council (NSC), for example, held a meeting to implement the "spirit" of the Tibet Work Forum. Separately, the TAR Party Committee convened a meeting on September 4, where TAR Party Secretary Wu Yingjie said the Tibet Work Forum demonstrated the "strategic importance of Tibet" and that it had approved a "blueprint for a new socialist modernisation of Tibet". More such meetings were expected to be held across the TAR.

Xi Jinping's speech indicates that a tougher new regime will be imposed in the TAR. The emphasis will be on Party building and inducting more Tibetans in the CCP to expand its reach. A pronounced uptick in efforts to 'educate' monks and nuns to become 'patriotic' and adapt Tibetan Buddhism to 'socialism with Chinese characteristics' can be anticipated. 'Patriotic education' in schools and campaigns against 'separatism' and countering the influence of the Dalai Lama will intensify. Dual-use infrastructure connectivity projects will be accelerated.

*(This article was published by the Centre for China Analysis and Strategy, New Delhi, on September 2020.)*

# 48. China's Third Central Xinjiang Work Conference

On the eve of the 65th anniversary of the establishment of the Xinjiang-Uyghur Autonomous Region (XUAR) and after an interval of six years, the Chinese Communist Party (CCP) held its Third Central Xinjiang Work Symposium in Beijing on September 25-26, 2020. The conference was held in the midst of negative international media attention, which highlighted the instances of discrimination and reported incarceration of millions of Uyghurs in 'reeducation' or 'vocational' centres constructed across the XUAR. Earlier, in a bid to address international concerns, China's State Council had issued a White Paper on Xinjiang on September 16.

As per past practice, the entire CCP Central Committee (CC) Politburo Standing Committee (PBSC), Politburo, Secretary of the CCP CC Secretariat, leading comrades of the National People's Congress (NPC) Standing Committee, State Councillors, President of the Supreme People's Court, Chief Prosecutor of the Supreme People's Procuratorate and leading comrades of the CPPCC attended the conference. Chinese Premier Li Keqiang presided and CPPCC Chairman Wang Yang summed up the proceedings. Chinese President Xi Jinping made an "important" speech which set out the long-term policies for Xinjiang. Prominent were the emphasis on "unity" and "stability", the change in tasks for the Xinjiang Production and Construction Corps (XPCC or Bingtuan), and the sharp increase in Xinjiang's security budget.

Xi Jinping's speech was reported by Xinhua on September 26. In his speech, Xi Jinping observed that there had been steady improvement in Xinjiang's economic development between 2014 to 2019, with a sound economic momentum and an average annual Gross Domestic Product (GDP) growth rate of 7.2 per cent. The people's living standards had improved significantly with an average annual 9.1 per cent growth in residential per capita disposable income, and more than 2.92 million out of 3.09 million people had been lifted out of poverty. More than 10 million people moved to new homes and the social security system and basic public services in urban, rural and pastoral areas had become better with free health check-ups for all people. The 'standardization' rate of township hospitals and village clinics had reached 100 per cent, with 99.7 per cent of the residents being covered by basic medical insurance.

Stating that support from the central government and assistance from other provinces to Xinjiang were continuously increasing, Xi Jinping disclosed that from 2014 to 2019, the central government's transfer payments to the Xinjiang-Uyghur Autonomous Region and the Xinjiang Production and Construction Corps (XPCC or 'Bingtuan') increased from Yuan 263.69 billion (US$ 38.64 billion) to Yuan 422.48 billion (US$ 61.90 billion), an average annual increase of 10.4 per cent. In other words, during these six years, a sum of more than Yuan 2 trillion (US$ 0.29 trillion) in total was channelled into Xinjiang. Xi Jinping said that the 19 'Aid-Xinjiang' provinces and cities had strengthened all-round counterpart support, invested a total of Yuan 96.4 billion (US$ 14.12 billion) in aid to Xinjiang (including the XPCC), implemented more than 10,000 aid projects in Xinjiang, given over Yuan 1.684 billion (US$ 0.25 billion) as aid to Xinjiang enterprises, and central enterprises had invested an additional over Yuan 700 billion (US$ 102.56 billion).

Xi Jinping expressed satisfaction that "on the whole, Xinjiang social stability is good and people are working in peace and contentment, laying a solid foundation for long-term stability". He attributed this to the "Party's policies on Xinjiang in the new era", which were developed by the 18th CCP CC and "must be adhered to on a long-term basis". He stressed the need to heighten a sense of identity of the Chinese nation to constantly strengthen ethnic unity and suggested that "education on the sense of Chinese identity should be incorporated into the education of officials and the younger generation in Xinjiang" to let the "sense of Chinese identity take root in people".

Noting that development is important for lasting peace and stability in Xinjiang, Xi Jinping stressed that the region's geographical advantages should be leveraged to develop Xinjiang as the centre of the 'Silk Road Economic Belt' and a hub of opening up for the inland and border areas. In this context, he called for efforts for increasing the efficiency of the industrial sector and boosting urbanisation in Xinjiang while protecting the environment. Xi Jinping stressed on the "Six Stabilities" (employment, financial sector, foreign trade, foreign investment, domestic investment, and expectations) and the "Six Guarantees" (job security, basic living needs, operations of market entities, food and energy, stable industrial and supply chains, and the normal functioning of primary-level governments). He called for unremitting efforts to eradicate poverty and promote employment.

There was considerable emphasis on the need for ensuring the loyalty of cadres and the Party's role. While Xi Jinping did say that "cadres of all ethnic groups in Xinjiang are trustworthy and capable of fighting", he also said that "they should be politically motivated" and that "it is necessary to promote the national spirit" and "firmly establish a national ideology" which encourages "cadres at all levels to take root in the border and contribute to the border in the new era". He described doing a good job in Xinjiang as a major achievement for the whole Party and the country.

The leadership of the Party was highlighted and the Central Xinjiang Work Coordination Group was instructed to strengthen its work at the grassroots and "put forward work opinions on major issues" under the leadership of the Party Central Committee. The Xinjiang Autonomous Region Party Committee, Xi Jinping said, "is on the front line and must fulfil its main responsibilities and implement its work well". He also called on all provinces, autonomous regions and municipalities in the interior of China to do a good job in Xinjiang related work, strengthen coordination and cooperation and support Xinjiang's stability and development. Importantly, he called for "the building of stability maintenance capabilities"—an euphemism for the state security apparatus—and enhancement of the organisational advantages and mobilisation capabilities of the Xinjiang Production and Construction Corps so that it could "better play its special role".

In his speech, Chinese Premier Li Keqiang said that Xi Jinping's "important speech comprehensively summarized the major achievements of Xinjiang work" and clarified the policies and strategic measures for promoting social stability and long-term stability in Xinjiang. He observed that it had a strong political, ideological and theoretical nature and that Xinjiang's work must be "guided by Xi Jinping's thoughts on socialism with Chinese characteristics in the new era, strengthen the 'Four Consciousnesses', strengthen the 'Four Confidences', and achieve the 'Two Safeguards'".

Concluding the symposium, CPPCC Chairman Wang Yang described Xi Jinping's "important speech" as "profound in thought, and rich in content" and a "programmatic document guiding Xinjiang work in the new era and a powerful ideological weapon". He too stressed the need to "focus on deep-seated issues related to long-term stability" and the necessity of strengthening organisational leadership and coordination, carrying out a variety of publicity activities and penetrating the grassroots to get deeply rooted in the hearts of the people.

The US-based China-owned *Duowei* news outlet gave an interesting insight into the sharp rise in China's expenditure on security in the Xinjiang-Uyghur Autonomous Region (XUAR). Claiming that it had been tracking security expenditure for some years, it said the expenditure on public security in Xinjiang increased significantly after 2014, from Yuan 22.22 billion in 2014 to Yuan 57.95 billion in 2017, a cumulative increase of 161 per cent, especially in 2017 compared to 2016. Stating that an increase of 92.6 per cent was surprising, it suggested that a considerable part may perhaps be used for the operation of the reeducation conversion training centres.

A *People's Daily* article (September 30) on the Xinjiang conference publicised that Xi Jinping's speech had been widely welcomed throughout Xinjiang. Interesting were the remarks by Qi Xinping, Secretary of the Party Committee of the 6th Division of the Xinjiang Production and Construction Corps (XPCC) in Wujiaqu city of Xinjiang, which confirmed that the XPCC had been assigned an additional new role, which explained Xi Jinping's reference in his speech to the need for enhancing the organisational and mobilization capabilities of the XPCC. Qi Xinping said the XPCC needed to strengthen its "capacity for maintaining stability and continuously improve its organizational advantages and ability to mobilize Xinjiang residents". He called for forging the XPCC into a "top militia force in defense of the border line of China", improving its capabilities related to stability maintenance and contingency response, and establishing a "strong force that helps maintain the security along the border".

The sharp rise in the XUAR's security budget, pronounced emphasis on stability maintenance and call to firmly establish a national ideology clearly indicated that the CCP will intensify 'deradicalisation' measures and 'reeducation' to more effectively absorb Uyghurs into the Han culture. The expanded role of the XPCC will see its greater involvement in security functions and its presence along Xinjiang's borders with the Central Asian Republics and Russia. Xi Jinping's acknowledgement of the good work done between 2014 and 2019 is also implicit recognition of XUAR Party Secretary Chen Quanguo's efforts. Chen Quanguo, who was handpicked for appointment as Tibet Autonomous Region (TAR) Party Secretary at then Vice President Xi Jinping's instance, was moved to Xinjiang on promotion as Politburo member in recognition of the good work done in the TAR. Born in 1955, Chen Quanguo will be just 65 years old at the 20th Party Congress in 2021 and will be in the running for elevation to the PBSC.

*(This article was published by the Centre for China Analysis and Strategy, New Delhi, on October 2, 2020.)*

# 49. Inner-Party Differences on Hong Kong Issue Pose Problems for Xi Jinping

China's leadership will have been incensed by the photographs and videos of protestors in Hong Kong carrying American flags and chanting "America please take over Hong Kong" on September 9, in an apparent escalation of the protests against Chinese rule by millions of Hong Kong residents that have continued over fifteen weekends in the adverse glare of international media publicity. It would have underscored the concerns of senior and veteran leaders at the annual gathering in Beidaihe of a 'colour revolution'.

On September 10, protestors in Hong Kong 'adopted' a new 'anthem' for Hong Kong, which attracted over 700,000 views overnight and is being spontaneously sung by crowds in public places. The following day, the state-owned *China Daily* posted a notice on its official Facebook account warning that protestors in Hong Kong have secret plans to escalate protests from September 11 with "massive" terrorist attacks, including blowing up gas pipelines in Hong Kong and attacks on non-Cantonese speaking people.

Xi Jinping's apparent hesitation in taking action to quell the protests in Hong Kong is suggestive of differences within China's top leadership, namely the Politburo (PB) and Politburo Standing Committee (PBSC). Xi Jinping is reported to have remarked in mid-August that the person responsible for the trouble in Hong Kong should resolve it—hinting at the seventh ranking PBSC member Han Zheng who is responsible for Hong Kong and Macau affairs.

The tenor of reporting by Chinese-owned news outlets affiliated to different leadership factions in the Chinese Communist Party (CCP) provided other indications of differences in China's top leadership echelons. The US-based *Duo Wei News* (*DW News*) and *HK01* in Hong Kong, both owned by Yu Pinhai who owns a lot of theatres in China, are controlled by Xi Jinping's group. The US-based *Boxun* is affiliated with former Chinese President Jiang Zemin.

In a subtly critical report *HK01* pointed out that PBSC member Han Zheng directly manages Hong Kong affairs and that his visit to Shenzhen on June 30 was the first by a senior Chinese leader since the protests started in Hong Kong on July 1, which "reflects the attention that Beijing is paying to Hong Kong". It added that whenever there was a big event in Hong Kong in the past, some top CCP leader would be present in Shenzhen to 'supervise' the work. Clashes between Hong Kong protestors and police have, incidentally, occurred since June 1. On July 5, it reported that Han Zheng had returned to Beijing, and work to handle the situation in Hong Kong had begun. *HK01* said the top leadership had been caught unawares by the developments in Hong Kong!

Separately, *Epoch Times* (July 20) quoted a 'princeling' in Beijing as saying that some top CCP officials had tried to force Chinese President Xi Jinping to make mistakes. They had suggested the use of force and the military, or that the military take control. He said that Xi Jinping was, however, very clear that there would be no bloodshed and another June 4 event would be avoided at any cost. Maj Gen Chen Daoxiang, Commander of the People's Liberation Army (PLA) stationed in Hong Kong, was reported to have personally conveyed to David Helvey, Principal Deputy Assistant Secretary of Defence for Asian and Pacific Security Affairs, US Department of Defence, on June 13 that Beijing would not use the military. This was confirmed by the official *The Paper*, though it added that Chen Daoxiang had "strongly condemned the series of recent incidents of extreme violence in Hong Kong and expressed his attitude with the "Seven Resolutes."

The protests revealed that despite Hong Kong's reversion to China over twenty years ago, neither its citizens nor Beijing yet trust each other and neither have the 'one country, two systems' been able to adjust to each other. The Hong Kong and Macao Affairs Office and Xinhua, China's long-time outpost in Hong Kong, were obviously unaware of the extent of public anger. So also were pro-Beijing newspapers like *Ta Kung Pao, Wen Wei Po, Sing Pao Daily News, Oriental Daily News, Sing Tao Daily* and others. The CCP, which has over the decades penetrated all sections of Hong Kong, similarly, failed. This despite large numbers of Hong Kong businessmen being close to it, at least 15 pro-Beijing groups and associations linked to Chinese provinces, and the CCP controlling the Hong Kong Federation of Trade Unions, the largest in Hong Kong. Reports reveal that since the end of July, more than a dozen officials from Beijing's offices who are stationed in Hong Kong, including the CCP Liaison Office in Hong Kong and the State Council's Hong Kong and Macao Affairs Office, have been punished and some even dismissed.

Initially, China banned all reporting on the protests by its official domestic media, but later instructed them to focus on the "violence" and describe the protests as foreign-funded. Conscious of international opinion, Beijing used social media platforms like Facebook, Twitter, etc. To mobilise favourable public opinion, it organised rallies by pro-Beijing students and prominent personalities abroad and persuaded Hong Kong businessmen and firms to issue advertisements condemning the violence. China's media publicised that overseas Chinese organisations in the UK, Southern California, Bangladesh, Hungary, Madagascar, Madrid, etc had criticised the interference in China's internal affairs.

Beijing's position has visibly hardened in recent weeks. Servers of the Hong Kong based online discussion forum, LIHKG, used by the protestors to mobilise and organise their actions, have come under unprecedented Distributed Denial-of-Service (DDoS) attacks. LIHKG said, "There is a power, or even a national level power behind the attacks as botnets from all over the world were manipulated in launching this attack." Cathay Pacific, whose employees participated in the protests, was issued a "significant aviation safety risk warning" by the Civil Aviation Administration of China, causing a sharp drop in its shares. Reports and photographs of the People's Armed Police (PAP) and People's Liberation Army (PLA) conducting manoeuvres outside neighbouring Shenzhen implied a hint of military action.

Prompted by its apprehension of the past couple of years of the West's intentions, further accentuated by the US-China trade war, China quickly labelled the protests as inspired by foreign forces and part of the West's efforts to provoke a "colour revolution"—a term used to describe the movements to topple governments in Eastern Europe and Egypt, but not often used in China since 1990-91 till January this year by Xi Jinping. Hong Kong's *Ming Pao News* reported (August 17) that at their annual gathering at Beidaihe, veteran CCP cadres reached a consensus to define the anti-extradition protests in

Hong Kong as a 'colour revolution' "led by military and political intelligence agencies from multiple nations and regions", with the CCP as the target. *Ming Pao* claimed that the Hong Kong government may not be capable of handling the protests within a limited time and Beijing can, under the law, provide all needed "assistance." Among those who attended were former Chinese Presidents Hu Jintao and Jiang Zemin.

Yang Guang, spokesman for the State Council's Hong Kong and Macao Affairs Office, said on September 3, that the protests have "clear features of a colour revolution" and the goal is to paralyse the Hong Kong government, seize the power for governing the Special Administrative Region (SAR) and make "one country, two systems" an empty concept. Separately, Zhang Dinghuai, a Professor of Hong Kong and Macao Studies at Shenzhen University, listed the elements of colour revolutions, adding that the protests in Hong Kong included many of these features and defied China's Constitution.

Speaking at his pro-government "Our Hong Kong Foundation" on July 31, former Hong Kong Chief Executive Tung Chee-hwa said, "Looking at the political storm closely—its severity, scale, and organisation—it's reasonable to believe that it's fanned by someone from behind. Various signs are pointing at Taiwan and the US". Claiming that foreign politicians and anti-China forces have tried to incite fear of the Chinese Communist Party and turn Hong Kong into a base to resist the central government, he asserted that "a small number of people" are trying "to damage the relationship between the central government and the SAR", and such acts are unacceptable.

In the backdrop of continuous threats that Beijing will reunify Taiwan with the Mainland by force if required, Taiwan is monitoring the developments very carefully. The protests have boosted Taiwan President Tsai Ing-wen's popularity ahead of the upcoming elections in January. Interesting was her response to media reports of Hong Kong protestors arriving in Taiwan. She said, "These friends from Hong Kong will be treated in an appropriate way on humanitarian grounds."

Other indications of Beijing's toughened stance include an article in the Chinese language official *Global Times* (August 17) hinting that the 'leaders' of the movement would be punished. It listed: (i) Jimmy Lai for meeting with Pence, Pompeo, and Bolton in July and publishing anti-extradition statements in the *New York Times*; (ii) Martin Lee Chu-ming for meeting with Pompeo in May and Julie Eadeh, US Consulate General, in Hong Kong in August; (iii) Anson Chan, for meeting with Pence, Pelosi, and representatives from the National Security Bureau, for appealing and calling on the US to put pressure on Beijing in March as well as meeting with Julie Eadeh in August; (iv) Albert Ho Chun-yan for attending the protest in Yuen Long in July and meeting with a male foreigner in August; (v) Joshua Wong Chi-fung for meeting with Julie Eadeh in August; and for inciting violence during the protests; (vi) Nathan Law Kwun-chung for making up rumours to endanger the police force, for calling on the public to participate in the protest through social media, and for meeting Julie Eadeh in August; and (vii) Alex Chow Yong-kang for his speech in the US in March in which he stated that there is no democracy and freedom in Hong Kong, for calling on the US House of Representatives to further study the development of Hong Kong democracy, and for participating in protest activities in front of the Chinese Consulate in New York in August.

On August 21, Zang Tiewei, spokesman of the Legislative Affairs Commission of the Standing Committee of China's National People's Congress, dismissed the possibility of acceding to the demand for universal suffrage and reiterated, "Recently, some illegal criminals in Hong Kong have openly attacked the legislature, violently attacked the police, and wilfully beat innocent people. These acts are serious crimes in any country under the rule of law and will be punished according to the law." The protests have damaged Hong Kong's economy, lessening its importance to China. Large numbers of businessmen have moved their wealth out and the number of visitors to Hong Kong has fallen since June. Official data released on August 16 showed that Hong Kong's Gross Domestic Product (GDP) growth for the second quarter dipped to 0.5 per cent year on year, the lowest in more than seven years and the value of goods exported and imported via Hong Kong in the first half of 2019, fell 3.6 per cent and 4.5 per cent year-on-year respectively. Hong Kong officials assess that Hong Kong is on the verge of recession amid social unrest and the escalating trade war.

The continuing protests have undoubtedly severely embarrassed China's leadership and become a test case for legitimacy of the CCP. Chinese President

Xi Jinping cannot allow them to drag on without hurting his position. Though international opinion is important, Beijing will be more sensitive to the potential fall-out of the protests inside China and on Taiwan. Beijing will probably try and use Hong Kong's forces to deter others and restore calm in Hong Kong. China would not like to have its 70th founding anniversary celebrations on October 1 marred by disorder.

*(This article was published by the Centre for China Analysis and Strategy, New Delhi, on September 12, 2019.)*

# 50. DPP's Win in Taiwan Elections will have Repercussions

The results of Taiwan's national elections announced on January 12, confirmed assessments that Taiwan President Tsai Ing-wen's popularity ratings had received a substantial boost, partly because of China's threatening posture but mainly because of the unceasing protests in Hong Kong that have now entered their ninth month without losing popular support. The results will impact China. Beijing—and Chinese President Xi Jinping—now confront the prospect of the 'China Dream', envisaging China's 'reunification' by 2021 or even 2049, becoming a distant prospect. The results could have wider repercussions in the region.

Discouraging for Beijing will be the fact that it will now have to view the pro-independence Democratic Progressive Party (DPP) as one with a sizeable following that contests China's "one country, two systems" policy and has overtly challenged its claims of sovereignty over Taiwan. Taiwan President Tsai Ing-wen has, in fact, assiduously sought to build Taiwan's defence capability with Taiwan's defence budget expected to reach US$ 11.9 billion in 2020. Beijing would need to accept that 'Taiwan identity' and nationalism have both acquired a prominent salience for the people of Taiwan.

With the mandate for a new four-year term, the DPP will seek to consolidate its position and project itself as representing the youth, who by some estimates, accounted for almost half the total number of votes polled by the DPP. By being unwavering in her policy of not yielding to China on issues of independence and sovereignty while, at the same time, trying to avoid hostilities with it, Tsai Ing-wen has shown Taiwan that such a policy can be viable. She has shown too, that its appeal overrides that of the better economic prospects anticipated from a compromise with Beijing. Beijing would now need to try and 'befriend' political parties other than the Kuomintang (KMT), as well as sections of Taiwan society, apart from China-dependent businesses. It will undoubtedly step up its 'united front' activities.

Initial official Chinese media reactions suggest that Beijing has been grudging in its acceptance of the DPP's win, and does not yet feel the need to change its policy towards Taiwan. China's state-owned China Global Television Network (CGTN) newscasts did not mention the clear trends of a DPP victory till 6 pm on January 11. The authoritative, official news agency Xinhua published an article that reluctantly acknowledged Tsai Ing-wen's victory, while the more nationalistic but official Beijing-based *Global Times* cautioned (January 12) that the US "will get up to more little tricks on the Taiwan question in the coming years", but that "China should firmly maintain the one-China principle and .... We should strive to hold the initiative of the Taiwan Straits in our own hands". Asserting that "first, we must strengthen the right to define the situation of the Taiwan Strait" and that it should not be decided by the US and "Taiwan authorities", it warned, "We can ignore some of the messages that they want to highlight, and we can harshly stop the acts that they want to slip through unpunished". It said China should maintain the "one-China principle" and "should encourage Tsai to ease her cross-Strait policies and not to further antagonize the Chinese Mainland". It bluntly reiterated that China must meanwhile "plan to crack down on Tsai's new provocative actions, including imposing military pressure, which is an unbearable option for Taiwan authorities". It emphasised, in conclusion, that "the comprehensive strength of the Mainland has been increasing, we have enough ability to contain 'Taiwan independence.' This is a fact that even those 'Taiwan independence' forces believe firmly".

There have been adequate indications that as China becomes militarily stronger, the People's Liberation Army (PLA) increasingly feels that an offensive against Taiwan would be successful. Chinese President Xi Jinping has said he would not like to leave the 'reunification' to successor generations. In February 2019, the PLA Air Force (PLAAF) released a music video called "My War Eagles are Circling the Treasure Island" featuring aerial footage of Taiwan and, in April and August, PLA fighter jets, for the first time in 20 years, crossed the median line in the Taiwan Strait. The PLA Navy's (PLAN's) aircraft carriers *Liaoning* and *Shandong* similarly broke with precedent and sailed through the Taiwan Strait in June and December 2019. In September a Chinese government-backed Twitter account replied to a post by Taiwan's President saying: "Once we have dealt with Hong Kong, we will settle the scores with Taiwan, military unification is unavoidable, we'll keep the island but won't keep the people except for [Taiwanese pop star] Jay Chou". Enoch Wu, a member of Taiwan President Tsai Ing-wen's last National Security Council, recently observed, "We can debate whether it's 2020 or 2022, but we know it's not 2049." Taiwan's military capabilities are limited with mountain tunnels at two air bases providing safe shelters for more than 200 aircraft, but it is developing advanced sea mining capabilities, building fast attack craft and hoping to get meaningful assurances from the US. Thus far, though, Beijing has kept to psychological warfare, it will try and intensify diplomatic pressure on Taiwan, including by shrinking its diplomatic space.

The election victory of DPP leader Tsai Ing-wen has come at an inopportune time for Chinese President Xi Jinping. It coincides with the protests in the Hong Kong Special Administrative Region (HKSAR), where 23 years after reverting to China, the people have challenged Beijing's right to govern Hong Kong and the legitimacy of the Chinese Communist Party (CCP). It coincides too with the growing US-China friction and clear signs of the beginnings of disengagement between the two. Beijing's failure to resolve these problems could make it difficult for China to realise its declared ambition of a 'peaceful reunification' and the 'China Dream' by 2021. Whether the developments will give an impetus to the resistance in Xinjiang and Tibet is unclear, but Beijing has repeatedly warned against attempts by the US and the West at instigating "colour revolutions".

As Tsai Ing-wen commences her second term, it is possible that US President Trump and she will initiate 'quiet' contacts to shore up Taiwan's position and that will put pressure on China. The latter's comment on the congratulatory message from the White House to Tsai Ing-wen indicates how China would view this. China will react to increased overt US-Taiwan interactions. Given Chinese President Xi Jinping's and the Chinese security bureaucracy's suspicions about "colour revolutions", vigilance has already been stepped up throughout the country. On November 28, Guo Shengkun, who is head of the Chinese Communist Party's (CCP's) Political and Legal Affairs Commission, published an article in the *People's Daily* calling for the firm defence of "national political security," which is "the lifeline of the Party's and the nation's security, and an unshakable bottom line." He vowed "resolutely and severely to prevent and crack down on" the infiltration of hostile forces. In the article, Guo Shengkun exhorted the whole country and entire population to enhance their awareness, be "on high vigilance, take resolute precautions, and severely punish" the hostile forces' infiltration and their destructive and subversive, activities to promote secession, thus "building a solid copper and iron wall for national security."

But the delay in diffusing the problem in Hong Kong remains unexplained and points to differences within the Politburo. It was only in late July, a month after the protests began, that Chinese President Xi Jinping publicly commented on them. Another couple of months passed before he and Politburo Standing Committee member Han Zheng separately met HKSAR Chief Executive Carrie Lam. These meetings took place after the important annual meeting of Party veterans and senior cadres at the seaside resort of Beidaihe, where the protests in Hong Kong were labelled a "colour revolution". Subsequently, in mid-December 2019, another report hinting at inner-Party sniping surfaced. It alleged that a 'princeling' of a high-ranking military family and current member of the Politburo Standing Committee (PBSC) had access to substantial wealth abroad. The report in the *Epoch Times*, which is owned by Falungong, a cult proscribed in China, gave enough specifics about the 'princeling' to suggest that the newspaper is aware of the individual's identity and perhaps intends to divulge it later. The situation is tenuous with the potential to put Xi Jinping under greater pressure.

As Tsai Ing-wen commences her second term, it is likely that she will re-energise her 'Southbound Policy' to reduce economic dependence on China and counter its efforts to diminish its space. The evolving cross-strait situation and political developments in China present India with an opportunity. India should actively consider initiating economic and commercial contacts with Taiwan in the slipstream of these developments in select areas. A visit by the Union Commerce Minister or Secretary would be welcomed by Taipei and, given China's extensive commercial and trade ties with Taiwan, cannot be objected to by Beijing. For India, it would result in foreign investments in sectors that will upgrade Indian industry and job creation.

*(This article was published by the Centre for China Analysis and Strategy, New Delhi, on January 15,2020.)*

# 51. CPEC and Challenges for Pakistan

China's 'One Belt, One Road' (OBOR), which was first proposed in September 2013 and combines the twin initiatives of the Silk Road Economic Belt and 21st Century Maritime Silk Road, is a grand concept that envisions China girdling the globe. Potentially covering 55 per cent of the world Gross National Product (GNP), 70 per cent of the global population, and 75 per cent of known energy reserves, it is essentially a plan for a China-built land and sea transportation artery to link China's production centres with markets and natural resource centres around the world. At the same time, it will harness much of China's hitherto idle economy, manpower and infrastructure-technology reserves to get much needed returns. The initiative blends geopolitical and diplomatic objectives and has a strong domestic agenda.

The 'Belt Corridors' run along the major Eurasian Land Bridges, through China-Mongolia-Russia, China-Central and West Asia, China-Indochina Peninsula, China-Pakistan, Bangladesh-China-India-Myanmar. The Maritime Silk Route or "Road" is the maritime equivalent of the 'Belt Corridors' and comprises a network of planned ports and other coastal infrastructure projects that dot the map from South and Southeast Asia to East Africa and the northern Mediterranean Sea.

While Chinese officials and academics emphasise the economic aspects and commercial advantages of OBOR, it includes geopolitical and diplomatic objectives. Implementation of OBOR will augment China's economic influence in the participating countries. The strategy of disbursing them large sums as loans and aid will enhance the financial power that China already exercises through its trading relationships.

Huang Yiping, a Professor of Economics at Peking University's National School of Development, assessed in February 2015, that OBOR represents a sea-change in China's international profile. According to him, OBOR has ended the phase of low-profile diplomacy based on Deng Xiaoping's advice to "hide your capabilities and bide your time" and transformed China into "a new great power" which "is trying to supplement the international economic order". Huang Yiping sought to justify China's more active role as an attempt to redress the limited role given to developing countries in international institutions and in line with US President Barack Obama's demand that China take on more responsibility for providing international public goods. A Renmin University report similarly asserted the need to "supplement, not challenge" the existing order because of the "zero-sum thinking" which ensured that OBOR projects were greeted with scepticism including in China's immediate neighbourhood. Taking note of the challenges ahead, Huang Yiping conceded: "One Belt, One Road is a good international economic strategy, but for now it is certainly not an easy one".

The most publicised bilateral commitment to OBOR was the investment pledged for the China-Pakistan Economic Corridor (CPEC) by Xi Jinping during his two-day visit to Pakistan in April 2015. The CPEC is the first leg of OBOR to be operationalised and is China's flagship venture. It traverses a distance of approximately 2,000 km from Kashgar in China's Xinjiang region till the port of Gwadar in Balochistan. When launched, it was a $45 billion economic and development package that could grow to around $60 billion. Of the $45 billion, energy sector projects accounted for around $34 billion whereas the infrastructure sector accounted for approximately $10 billion.

The CPEC will include the construction of industrial parks, agricultural farms, railways, airports, roads, a fibre-optic network, energy-generating projects including one of the world's largest solar farms, and a high-speed train between Karachi and Peshawar that will travel over 160 km per hour. All these projects will be built according to Chinese plans, with Chinese labour, and will be connected to Chinese businesses. The project will also build a new telecommunications network linking Pakistan with China and, through China, to Europe.

The CPEC includes a number of initiatives in Pakistan that are not only economic in nature, but have cultural and civic implications. The Safe Cities initiative, for instance, is primarily designed to safeguard Chinese workers from Pakistani terrorists, but will also transform many of Pakistan's cities. The Safe Cities project includes building new, safer buildings in urban centres, training local police and military in anti-terrorist and bomb detection techniques, and the use of lighting and cameras to create safe zones in all Pakistani cities. It is also preparing to protect the CPEC inside Pakistan. A secure fibre-optic link has been laid connecting Kashgar, headquarters of China's People's Liberation Army's (PLA's) South Xinjiang Military District with the Pakistan Army General Headquarters (GHQ) at Rawalpindi, highlighting the close military coordination between Pakistan and China. The PLA's Western Theatre Command, established in 2016, is also tasked to safeguard Chinese workers, investments and projects in the CPEC in addition to protecting China's land frontiers. China, at the same time, informed Islamabad that it is creating a division-strength "private army" for deployment in the areas covered by the CPEC. Chinese security organisations have begun functioning in Pakistan. China has already put in place a domestic legal basis for the deployment of Chinese troops and security personnel to protect Chinese investments and workers abroad. The operational tasks assigned to the PLA's Western Theatre Command represent the first of such arrangements.

While this project will no doubt create safer cities, many are concerned that much of the traditional areas of some of these historic cities will be destroyed to build newer, albeit safer, neighbourhoods[1].

### Disadvantages to Pakistan

Assessments of the the CPEC's benefits to Pakistan vary considerably, but a study by DeLoitte[2] is interesting. Pointing out that the volume of trade between Pakistan and China had increased to US$ 16 billion by 2014–15, the study alluded to the impending benefits. It estimated that if all planned projects were implemented, their value would exceed all Foreign Direct Investment (FDI) in Pakistan since 1970 and would be equivalent to 17 per cent of Pakistan's Gross Domestic Product (GDP) in 2015. It further estimated that the CPEC will create some 700,000 direct jobs during 2015–30, adding up to 2.5 percentage points to the country's growth. Importantly, it noted that the Karakoram Highway between Rawalpindi and the Chinese border will be completely reconstructed and overhauled, and Pakistan's railway network will be extended to eventually connect to China's Southern Xinjiang Railway in Kashgar. Almost 80 per cent of China's oil is currently transported over 16,000 km from the Strait of Malacca to Shanghai, but once

Gwadar becomes operational, this distance would reduce to less than 5,000 km. The CPEC will simultaneously open immense economic opportunities for Pakistan, and physically connect China to its markets in Asia, Europe and beyond. According to the *China Daily*, the energy projects would provide up to 16,400 MW of energy altogether with over 10,400 Mega Watts (MW) of energy generating capacity developed between 2018 and 2020 as part of the corridor's fast-tracked "Early Harvest" project.

The assessment of the Deloitte study is not mirrored in the numerous comments and articles by Pakistani politicians, journalists and academics. While they are appreciative that the CPEC has brought a massive influx of much needed infrastructure aid and investment to Pakistan, they are apprehensive that Pakistan risks losing sovereignty to China. The study fails to take into account the high energy production cost of these power plants. With fuel mandated to be imported from China's Xinjiang Autonomous Region, the cost per unit of electricity generated by the new power plants would be double the present, imposing a very high burden on the consumers. Early indicators suggest that the time and production estimates are exaggerated. Politicians in Pakistan's provinces have complained for the past year that locals are not getting employment in the CPEC projects and are not even being allowed access as the sites are 'protected' by 10-foot-high perimeter walls. Pakistan media reports claim that around 9,800 locals were hired for the construction of the 392-km highway from Multan in Punjab to Sukkur in Sindh. Similarly, the Suki-Kinari hydropower project in Khyber Pakhtunkhwa is expected to create more than 4,000 jobs. In terms of jobs actually created, it is reported that the China Machinery Engineering Corporation's (CMEC's) Thar lignite mining and coal-fired power plant in Sindh has created over 1,000 jobs so far, while the Sahiwal power plant, southwest of Lahore in Punjab province 'hired 3,000 locals'. The actual figures of employment are at great variance with the predicted figure of 700,000.

On the other hand, there has been a huge influx of Chinese labour. Chinese restaurants, grocery stores, guesthouses and language centres have opened across Pakistan, aimed mainly at the country's growing population of Chinese citizens. The supermarket shelves are lined with products manufactured in China[3]: everything from noodles to hardhat construction helmets, sea kelp to stationery, spice mixes to industrial meat grinders. Consequently, there has been no benefit to Pakistan's economy as no money is coming in through the service sectors as well.

Politicians, academicians and journalists have voiced serious concerns about Pakistan's mounting debt to China and the anticipated high cost of electricity from the new energy projects. Expressing concern about the viability of the CPEC, Ali Malik, a researcher at the South Asia Programme at the Hudson Institute in Washington DC, on January 4, 2017, pointed out that "most of Pakistan's urban centres are located in the east, not the west and that inter-provincial resentment and differences have flared, with the western provinces accusing the centre of being partial to the country's eastern portion, where the majority of Pakistan's economic bases are located".

There are other questions about the economic viability of the CPEC, for which the bulk of financing has come in the form of loan-based financing, and not unconditional grants from the Chinese government. Though the loans are given to individual construction companies involved with the projects, there are significant risks to the government. Many of the power projects are under sovereign guarantees, thus, making the Pakistani government responsible if these companies fail to meet their debt obligations. Pakistan's current liabilities (debt), both private and public, have reached a staggering 75 per cent of the GDP (Rs. 22.5 trillion).

According to a *Financial Times* (FT) report, Pakistani officials feel that lending money to Pakistan also favours China, as it does not wish to disclose details of the loans that are part of the CPEC project[4]. "The Chinese are not keen on Western institutions learning the minute details of [financing of] CPEC projects," an unnamed official in Islamabad was quoted as saying. "An IMF programme will require Pakistan to disclose the financial terms to its officials." According to the FT report, prior to the April 2018 loan of $1 billion, Pakistan had borrowed almost $1.2 billion from Chinese banks since April 2017. Pakistani Prime Minister Imran Khan and Chinese Premier Li Keqiang met in November 2018 after which China agreed to provide aid for Pakistan's deteriorating economic situation. On the other hand, some people have alleged that China's generosity may worsen Pakistan's financial difficulties.

Additional worries are that the CPEC's success depends entirely on Pakistan's ability to export goods and services and show a strong rise in exports.

Pakistani analysts warned that these sectors of the economy would have to compete with the influx of cheaper Chinese imports that have the potential ability to strangle the domestic market. Chinese imports have, incidentally, already grown from 4 per cent in 2010 to 9 per cent in 2015. Economists say that if this downward trend of exports and increase in imports continues, Pakistan will face a serious balance of payments crisis. Others suggest that Pakistan is already on the verge of experiencing a crisis, as debt servicing will increase to between 30 per cent and 60 per cent by 2020 because of the CPEC and Pakistan's purchase of Eurobonds. There is a general view that in order to safeguard its economic future, Pakistan must be cautious in how it implements and administers completion of the CPEC. More importantly, they assert that the central government must be honest about the nature of Chinese investment as Pakistan risks losing its sovereignty, being beholden to China, and exploited by it for its natural resources and geostrategic location.

For China, however, the centre-pieces of the CPEC are the Gwadar port and the area of the Karakoram in the north. It has eyed Gwadar for years and agreed to fund its development only after Pakistan agreed to grant it "sovereign guarantees to the port facilities" in 2007. Gwadar is important for China's maritime ambitions. As China enlarges its Navy and retains a permanent presence in the Indian Ocean, its aircraft carriers, other surface warships and submarines will require a base. The importance of Gwadar for China is emphasised by the inclusion of Gwadar International Airport and other major development works of Gwadar port in the CPEC's first phase with completion targeted for 2017. A total of 9 projects valued at approximately US$ 1 billion, each intended to augment China's commercial and military capacity, are planned in and around Gwadar. China is reported to have established electronic eavesdropping posts at Gwadar.

The CPEC's first phase also includes expansion of the Karakoram Highway, connecting Pakistan's railway network to China's Southern Xinjiang Railway to Kashgar, and placing of a secure fibre-optic line between Kashgar and Rawalpindi, all projects of military significance. What is really interesting is that when tensions rose early last year because of Pakistani complaints about the rising costs and the slow pace of work, China sought to assuage Pakistan and said many of the projects around Gwadar would be grants! The security of Gwadar is a source of continued concern for the Chinese and has imposed a heavy financial burden on Pakistan. In January 2016, the Pakistan Navy decided to deploy two additional Marine Battalions to provide round the clock security at Gwadar. On 21 September 2016, in the wake of the deterioration in Indo-Pakistan relations over Kashmir, Chinese Premier Li Keqiang publicly expressed reservations and told Pakistan's former Prime Minister Nawaz Sharif that he "hoped" Pakistan could continue to provide protection to the CPEC and Chinese personnel in Pakistan. The official Chinese newspaper *Global Times* similarly warned that "the increasing cost of security is becoming a big problem in efficiently pushing forward the project." In November 2016, during the inaugural Kashgar-Gwadar cargo run and subsequent transfer of the containers to waiting vessels at Gwadar port, Pakistani officials went to great lengths to allay Chinese concerns and the Pakistan Navy deployed ships and aircraft to provide security cover to ensure safe and secure transit.

Since Gwadar became operational, the role of Pakistan's maritime forces has increased and the Pakistan Navy has been assigned special responsibility to protect the Gwadar seaport project and the more than 500 Chinese nationals working there from offshore threats. Pakistan has set up a Special Security Division (SSD) under a Major General solely for protecting CPEC construction sites. With China refusing to provide any financial assistance towards the security expenses of the CPEC, the Pakistan government on September 24, 2016, decided to meet such expenses by adding 1 per cent more to the cost of all central energy projects and recovering it from consumers through the National Electric Power Regulatory Authority. This cess is to help the Pakistan Army meet expenses incurred on the SSD. The Senate Standing Committee on Planning Development and Reform has protested over the billing of Pakistani citizens for providing security to Chinese nationals in Pakistan.

Pakistani politicians are already complaining about the US$ 12 million a year expenditure on the SSD, which is now expected to double. The success of the CPEC and Gwadar port depends on having a safe and secure maritime environment in the Arabian Sea and Indian Ocean region in general. Envisaging attacks by militant groups or insurgents on seaports and vessels, and use of the container vessels to smuggle weapons, drugs etc., Pakistan has strengthened maritime security capabilities. This includes: intensifying security patrols and coastal exercises; creation of Coastal Watch Stations; establishing a Joint Maritime Information Coordination Centre (JMICC); establishment of the Force Protection Battalion of the Pakistan Marines; and more robust maritime security activities jointly by Pakistan and China. Collaboration in building Navy craft has been stepped up. China and Pakistan have agreed to jointly construct the F-22P frigate in addition to the Azmat and Jalalat class fast-attack craft and corvettes for the Pakistan Maritime Security Agency.

In June 2015, Pakistan's Ministry of Defence Production signed a contract with M/s China Ship Trading Company for the construction of seven maritime patrol ships, four of which are being built in China and the others at the Karachi Shipyard and Engineering Works. The China Shipbuilding Industry Corporation (CSIC) is to also provide Pakistan's Navy with eight attack submarines. Pakistan has to pay for these vessels. Other serious issues threatening the development of Gwadar have surfaced, with Pakistani analysts implying that China has undue interest in Gwadar port. Gwadar is described as an "island isolated in an arid landscape, with roads and railways linking it to the rest of the nation." The city's water supply dam has dried up following three years of drought. The existing desalination plant does not work and there is no more water. Unless Gwadar gets its full road and rail connectivity, the port cannot flourish. Gwadar additionally symbolises the sense of alienation felt by many in Balochistan, who suspect that most of the benefits of the CPEC are going to outsiders.

However, the non-flexible and strict terms and conditions imposed by Beijing have led to unsuccessful negotiations on some projects between Islamabad and the Chinese government. In November 2017, Pakistan backed out from the Diamer-Basha Dam project due to its "unrealistic" terms and conditions and as China taking ownership of the entire project was stated to be unacceptable by the former Prime Minister Shahid Khaqan Abbasi. The Diamer-Basha Dam is excluded from the list of CPEC projects and the Pakistan government is now funding the project on its own after some changes in the project's design. The new Pakistani government has also rejected China's proposal to build a US$60 billion coal-fired power plant under the CPEC. The Pakistani newspaper *Dawn* reported that Prime Minister Imran

Khan, who took office in August 2018, officially informed Beijing that the country is not interested in building the Rahim Yar Khan power plant.

Besides this, the Chinese influx is creating fissures in the feudal Pakistani society. A recent scandal was unearthed in Pakistan about Chinese men, with the help of collaborators in Pakistan, marrying young Pakistani women after making cash payments to their families, and taking them to China. The human trafficking issue gained widespread attention in April, 2019 when Pakistani television broadcaster ARY News raided a compound in Lahore, where several Chinese men were discovered with six Pakistani wives, two of whom were 13 years old. ARY News reported that the men paid Rs 400,000 ($2,820) to each of the women's families, who were also promised Rs 40,000 in monthly payments and a Chinese visa to a male relative of the bride. One of the women who were forced into a marriage, contacted the broadcaster, which led to the expose. The Chinese Embassy in Pakistan issued a statement on April 13, 2019 conceding that while some unlawful match-making centres earned illegal profits from brokering cross-national marriages by victimising Pakistani and Chinese youth, it termed the reports of organ sales as "misleading and groundless."

### Challenges for CPEC in Pakistan

The major problems that the CPEC faces in Pakistan are the regional and ethnic differences and conflicts. Created in 1947 as a country for the Muslims of the Indian subcontinent, Pakistan is, in fact, composed of several, not always friendly, ethnic enclaves. Pakistan's four provinces and two autonomous areas generally, but not perfectly, represent these groups. These ethnic groups include the Punjabis, who make up almost 45 per cent of the national population and dominate the national government; the Pashtuns, a conservative tribal group, who live in the Khyber Pakhtunkhwa province and make up about 17 per cent of Pakistan's population; the Sindhis, who live in large feudal estates in Sindh province, including the city of Karachi, and constitute about 14 per cent of the country's population; the Balochis, who live in the relatively poor area of Balochistan and make up less than 4 per cent of Pakistan's population; and the Muhajirs, who are the descendants of the refugees who fled India in 1947 and do not have a province of their own, but reside in Karachi and areas around that city and make up about 8 per cent of the country's population. Other groups include the Kashmiris, the Brahuis, and the Saraikis from Multan.

Regional and ethnic rivalries and feuds have played a major role in Pakistan's short history. For instance, although the official language of Pakistan is Urdu, (and English), it is spoken as a native language by only about 8 per cent of the population. Urdu, in fact, was the language spoken by the Muslims in the Indian subcontinent, but not by the people who lived in the area that is now Pakistan.

These ethnic and regional rivalries represent not only differences in culture or language, but also bitter rivalries for national political and economic dominance. This clash of cultures is particularly exhibited in the tension between the military, dominated by the Pashtuns, and the Punjabis who control the apparatus of the national government. The military has stepped in several times since 1947, declaring martial law and replacing incompetent and corrupt national governments.

Balochistan, which has a potentially pivotal role in the CPEC, is another province in ethnic turmoil. Balochistan is the largest province and has many natural resources. However, the Balochis have the lowest standard of living of any ethnic group in Pakistan and feel alienated from the Pakistani power structure. Because of this, in part, a number of militant Baloch separatist groups have emerged and have been causing trouble.

The fear among many Pakistanis is that the CPEC will only enrich the Punjabis (some have suggested that the "P" in CPEC stands for Punjab), since the Punjabis control the national government, while leaving the rest of Pakistan relatively poor. This is especially a concern of the Balochis and the Pashtuns, who have already seen many of the CPEC programmes directed away from their provinces and towards the Punjab or Sindh province. The obvious case is of the new highway being built as part of the initiative between Kashgar and Gwadar. One of the routes in the original plan, referred to as the Western Route, was to go through the Khyber Pakhtunkhwa province. However, the route was changed by Islamabad to avoid that province. The route is now planned to run largely through the Punjab and Sindh provinces. True, a large section of the route will be through Balochistan, but largely in the remote areas of the southern section of the province, and will, therefore, not benefit Balochistan much. Both the provincial governments of the Khyber Pakhtunkhwa and Balochistan have voted against the CPEC and have petitioned the national government in Islamabad to include more projects in provinces other than the Punjab[5].

The fate of the project in Balochistan is the key to the ultimate success of the CPEC since the use of the port of Gwadar is one of the project's key elements. Increasing calls in Balochistan for the creation of a separate state and ensuing armed conflict pose an enormous challenge to the corridor. Baloch nationalists oppose the project as the demographic balance could ultimately turn against them, making them a minority in their own province with other ethnic groups moving into the province. Even presently, the Baloch people only make up about 55 per cent of the population of Balochistan. This anger towards the CPEC has increased to the point that Chinese citizens have been kidnapped and killed by Baluch militant groups.

On May 13, 2017, gunmen killed 10 Chinese labourers working on the CPEC project in Gwadar. The attack was carried out by the Baloch Liberation Army (BLA) a group reportedly fighting for an independent homeland for the Baluchis. A spokesperson for the BLA said[6], "This conspiratorial plan, CPEC, is not acceptable to the Baloch people under any circumstances."

In addition, the CPEC, and with it China's cultural and economic incursion into Pakistan is reminiscent to many of the British rule in the Indian subcontinent from 1858 to 1947. China's influence in Pakistan is not of the same nature—China does not officially claim to govern the country—but there are similarities which many in Pakistan have noticed and this could trigger considerable ethnic and regional pushback against the projects.

**Militant Islam**

Pakistan was created in 1947 as an avowedly Muslim country. As a result, Islamic doctrines, laws, and institutions have been a part of Pakistan since the beginning. However, though Islamic political parties have always been active, in the last couple of decades, a new kind of Islamic militancy has emerged. These orthodox militant parties include homegrown groups such as the Tehreek-e Taliban and Lashkar-e Jhangvi, which are local or regionally based organisations with specific agendas internal to Pakistan.

One target of these groups comprises the religious minorities in Pakistan, including the small Christian minority and the Shia Muslims whom they consider heretics and idol-worshipers. These groups strongly oppose foreign intervention, including by the Chinese, and will constitute a challenge to the CPEC.

Other militant Islamic groups are connected to, or supported by, transnational Islamic movements. These include the Lashkar-e-Tayyeba (LeT) and the Harkat-ul-Mujahideen (HuM). Also, increasingly active in Pakistan are elements of the Islamic State, Al-Qaeda, and Afghan Taliban. These groups have been responsible for a number of terrorist attacks in Pakistan. Militant Islamic movements have deep roots and can be traced back to the beginning of Pakistan. They received a fillip in the 1980s when the United States and Saudi Arabia, among others, poured considerable amounts of money into creating *madrasahs* on the Afghan-Pakistan border to recruit and train Afghan Mujahideen to fight the Soviets. The Pakistani military and powerful Inter-Services Intelligence (ISI) participated in this effort and continue to retain their links and nurture them. These Islamic militant groups are useful to the Pakistani military establishment in many ways and especially to wage the low-intensity conflict against India in Kashmir. But these militant Islamic groups also harbour a profound and deep hatred of the West, and especially the United States and favour orthodox Islam.

These militant Islamic groups would, therefore, potentially be particularly dangerous for the Chinese projects in Pakistan. China does not have a good image in the Islamic world and its treatment, especially of the Uyghurs in Xinjiang province, has generated resentment. An indication was when Hafez Syed of the LeT warned then Prime Minister Nawaz Sharief against Pakistan's "new best friend" and asked him to enquire about their treatment of Muslims in Xinjiang during *Ramzan*. This resentment will fester. The presence of thousands of Chinese workers and their habits and customs will offend the orthodox Muslims residing in rural Pakistan where the CPEC projects are sited. Attacks on Chinese citizens in Pakistan have already taken place and will continue. Although the Chinese will create safe places for their workers, there will be a continual threat of violence against Chinese citizens in Pakistan.

In conclusion, it is clear that the CPEC will confront many problems in Pakistan. These will include the threat to Chinese workers and personnel from the rural Muslim population of Pakistan and the Balochis who apprehend being marginalised in their home province. Other difficulties will centre on the Pakistani reappraisal of the CPEC and China's financial agreements on CPEC projects. Allegations that they are heavily skewed in China's favour are gaining ground. The International Monetary Fund (IMF) and World Bank too, at the US' instance, have insisted that Pakistan provide detailed accounts for the CPEC projects. A Pakistan whose economy is in dire straits and is seeking loans from them will have fewer alternatives. The accusation that Pakistan risks losing sovereignty to China is emotive and has the potential to spread. It could get aggravated with the presence of Chinese security personnel in Pakistan, which has already triggered local tensions and fights. China will, however, not want to jeopardise its huge strategic investment in Pakistan and will want to keep the relationship in good repair. It additionally has important military ambitions of acquiring Gwadar port and securing a large chunk of Pakistan occupied Kashmir (PoK) and adjacent areas.

It is difficult for China and Pakistan in the longer term to resolve their widely differing objectives. Their objectives are quite different and almost at cross-purposes—while China has a larger strategic objective and views the corridor more as an essential stepping stone towards global leadership, Pakistan sees it just as a solution for its economic difficulties.

## Notes

1. A. Corr (2017), *China Will Suppress Terrorism, Diversity, and Democracy in Pakistan.* (Online) Forbes, Available at: https://www.forbes.com/sites/anderscorr/2017/05/15/china-will-suppress-terrorism-diversity-and-democracy-in-pakistan/—662cb4db5cd6. Accessed April 20, 2019.
2. "How will CPEC Boost Pakistan's Economy?" https://www2.deloitte.com/pk/en.html
3. Asad Hashim, "Pakistan: A Slice of China in Islamabad". Accessed at https://www.aljazeera.com/indepth/features/2017/08/pakistan-slice-china-islamabad-170830081303813.html on April 25, 2019.
4. "Pakistan Seeks More Loans from China to Avert Currency Crisis ".Accessed at https://www.ft.com/content/1256ceaa-802c-11e8-bc55-50daf11b720d on April 24, 2019.
5. R. Shah (2017), "China's Trouble with Pakistan's Turbulent Democracy" (online) *The Diplomat*, http://thediplomat.com/2017/01/chinas-trouble-with-pakistans-turbulent-democracy/. Accessed April 20, 2019.
6. "Gunmen Kill 10 Labourers in Balochistan's Gwadar", https://www.aljazeera.com/news/2017/05/gunmen-kill-10-labourers-balochistan-gwadar-170513111330168.html. Accessed on April 21, 2019.

## References


1. Abdul Manan, "12 Sites Proposed for Special Economic Zones in Balochistan, K-P", https:// tribune.com.pk/story/1026167/12-sites-proposed-for-special-economic-zones-in-balochistan-kp/, January 12, 2016.
2. Asad Hashim, "Pakistan: A Slice of China in Islamabad". Accessed at https://www.aljazeera.com/indepth/features/2017/08/pakistan-slice-china-islamabad-170830081303813.html, on April 25, 2019.
3. A. Corr, (2017), "China Will Suppress Terrorism, Diversity, and Democracy in Pakistan", (Online) *Forbes*, Available at: https://www.forbes.com/sites/anderscorr/2017/05/15/china-will suppress-terrorism-diversity-and-democracy-in-pakistan/—662cb4db5cd6. Accessed April 20, 2019.
4. "CPEC Mess: Chinese Company Building Gwadar Port Operating in Pakistan Illegally, Lawmakers Told", March 14, 2018. Available at http://zeenews.india.com/world/cpec-mess-chinese-company-building-gwadar-port-operating-in-pakistan-illegally-lawmakers-told-2089425.html
5. "Chinese to Outnumber Baloch Natives by 2048", http://nation.com.pk/national/29-Dec-2016/ chinese-to-outnumber-baloch-natives-by-2048/amp, December 29, 2016.
6. Falak Arreba, "Angry Balochis Oppose China Pakistan Economic Corridor". October 22, 2017. Published in the *Sunday Guardian* and available at https://www.sundayguardianlive.com/world/11369-angry-balochis-oppose-china-pakistan-economic-corridor
7. "Gunmen Kill 10 Labourers in Balochistan's Gwadar", https://www.aljazeera.com/news/2017/05/gunmen-kill-10-labourers-balochistan-gwadar-170513111330168.html, accessed on April 21, 2019.
8. Kiyya Baloch, "Can China's Gwadar Port Dream Survive Local Ire?", http://thediplomat.com/ 2014/12/can-chinas-dream-of-a-pakistan-port-survive-local-ire/, December 17, 2014.
9. "Pakistan Seeks More Loans from China to Avert Currency Crisis". Accessed at https://www.ft.com/content/1256ceaa-802c-11e8-bc55-50daf11b720d on April 24, 2019.
10. Saibal Dasgupta, "China to Seal Border with Pakistan to Curb Terror", *The Times of India*, January 11, 2017.
11. Sattar Khan, "Gwadar—Pakistan's Impoverished Colony or an Economic Hub?", http:// www.dw.com/en/gwadar-pakistans-impoverished-colony-or-an-economic-hub/a-19185999, April 14, 2016.
12. R. Shah (2017), "China's Trouble with Pakistan's Turbulent Democracy", (Online) *The Diplomat*. Available at: http://thediplomat.com/2017/01/chinas-trouble-with-pakistans-turbulent-democracy/. Accessed April 20, 2019.
13. FM Shakil, "Pakistan Seeks Bailout from China and Saudis Instead of IMF", April 4, 2018. Available at http://www.atimes.com/article/pakistan-seeks-bailout-china-saudis-rather-imf/
14. http://www.cpecinfo.com/home (Official website of CPEC)


*(This article was published by the Centre for China Analysis and Strategy, New Delhi, on August 1, 2017, and Pugwash India, April 2020.)*

# 52. Brief Analysis of Chinese Propaganda During India-China Face-Off at Doklam, June 16-August 1, 2017

An analysis of China's propaganda effort and its state-owned media's coverage between June 16 and August 1, 2017, during the ongoing face-off between Indian and Chinese troops on the Doklam plateau, yields some interesting insights. The main features are: (i) China showed little concern for the long-term damage it would do to the India-China relationship; (ii) China's anti-India propaganda offensive diminished whatever little trust existed between the two countries; (iii) Beijing took a deliberate decision to reduce the room for negotiations by insisting that Doklam is Chinese territory and accusing India of "invading" China and launching a "surgical strike" against it; and (iv) there appears to have been a stiffening in China's position in the past week. The Indian establishment is likely to keep these in mind while proceeding with the relationship with China in the future.

Noticeably, while the face-off commenced around June 16, 2017, Beijing went public with the incident only on June 26, or almost 10 days after the face-off began, with a statement by its Ministry of Foreign Affairs (MoFA) spokesman at a press briefing. In the interim, two border flag meetings including one on June 20, failed to ease the tension. During this period, China would have weighed its options before deciding to confront India. Undoubtedly, the seriously strained India-China relationship and India declining to attend the 'One Belt, One Road' Forum in April 2017, have been factors and this was corroborated in the subsequent 'warnings' and 'threats' issued by China's propaganda apparatus.

On the ground though, Commanders of the People's Liberation Army's (PLA's) Western Theatre Command who planned and approved the road building activity were clearly caught unawares and unprepared. They had not anticipated India's swift and robust response. They would have been expecting that in view of the already strained India-China relationship, New Delhi's desire to persuade Beijing to relax its opposition to India's entry to the Nuclear Suppliers Group (NSG), India's past responses, etc., India would restrict itself to nudging Thimpu to lodge a diplomatic protest and, at most, follow with a protest note of its own. It is discernible from China's propaganda that in this interval of 10 days before China reacted publicly, there would have been a series of discussions at the higher echelons of the Central Military Commission (CMC) and the Party as to the next steps that China should take. The strained relationship would have been prominent in these discussions as also the views of the PLA. Senior officers of the PLA's Western Theatre Command must be smarting after having been stymied by the Indian Army and would want to retrieve their dented prestige. Specifically, the Commanders of the Western Theatre Command and Shigatse Military Division, both officers with excellent records and assessed to be on the fast track for promotion, would want to redeem their military reputations.

In contrast to the shrill stream of anti-India criticism by the Chinese media and numerous, though restrained, MoFA statements, India displayed quiet confidence and refrained from reacting, thereby indicating its desire not to escalate matters. Bhutan's Foreign Ministry issued a statement on the incident on June 29, and India's Ministry of External Affairs (MEA) similarly followed with a solitary statement on June 30, 2017.

By going public and consistently asserting that India had "invaded" China, Beijing has sought to use its propaganda machinery along with comments by MoFA spokespersons to push the dispute between China and Bhutan over the Doklam plateau into the background and, instead, emphasise that Doklam is Chinese territory. It reinforced this by accusing India of "invading" China and conducting a "surgical strike" against China—protesting that China is not Pakistan or Myanmar. It insisted that Indian troops must first "unconditionally" withdraw. Beijing's effort to build a case to support its claim over this territory in the Doklam plateau is unmistakable and a classic part of its 'Three Warfares' (propaganda, legal and psychological) strategy.

China also attempted to divide the Indian political class. China's Ambassador to India, Luo Zhaohui, quite unusually met leaders of opposition parties, including Rahul Gandhi of the Congress, West Bengal Chief Minister

Mamata Banerjee, Kerala Chief Minister Pinarayi Vijayan and former Assam Chief Minister Tarun Gogoi and his son Gaurav. He also met former National Security Advisor Shivshankar Menon and another former Indian Foreign Secretary. Luo Zhaohui's wife, a Counsellor in the Chinese Embassy in Delhi, Dr Jiang Yili, contributed to the effort and flew to Bhutan and called on the royalty there, including the Queen Mother. Meanwhile, New Delhi-based Chinese diplomats met their interlocutors and think-tanks to propagate China's views.

Pertinent in this context was the Chinese Embassy posting on its website the news of Congress leader Rahul Gandhi calling on the Chinese Ambassador. The post was quickly deleted after, as anticipated, it attracted notice and became an issue of political debate. The object of reporting the meeting on the embassy's website was questionable as was the Chinese Ambassador's visit to Darjeeling at this juncture.

Pro-China 'intellectuals', journalists and columnists seemed to have been activated with many expressing doubts about the wisdom of the government's decision to take a stand, and its direction to the Indian Army to block the PLA building the road through the Doklam plateau. Doubts were raised about India's interpretation of the Convention of 1890, referred to by China, and whether India's security would actually be jeopardised, with China building the road till Gyemochen. Concerns have been expressed too about the Indian Army's preparedness to confront the Chinese.

Between June 26, 2017 and August 1, 2017 alone, 36 articles on the stand-off at Doklam were noticed in the English-language state-owned *Global Times*. The *PLA Daily*, which caters to China's armed forces, published six articles in English. In addition there were 33 in the official English-language *China Daily*. The official Chinese Communist Party (CCP) mouthpiece *People's Daily* published 21 articles in English while the authoritative official news agency Xinhua issued 6 despatches in English.

In an indication that popular opinion was being sensitised to the tension at the Doklam plateau, there was a greater number of articles in Chinese-language newspapers on the Doklam issue. The Chinese-language edition of the *People's Daily* published 49 articles, the *PLA Daily's* Chinese-language version published 31 articles and the Hong Kong-based China-owned newspapers namely the *Wen Wei Bo* and *Ta Kung Pao* published 30 and 20 articles each respectively. The official news agency Xinhua restricted itself to issuing two despatches in Chinese.

The tenor and content of the articles differed considerably though, with the *Global Times* publishing the maximum number of provocative articles warning India of dire consequences. Despite disingenuous remarks downplaying the importance of the *Global Times*, it is pertinent that the *Global Times* is a subsidiary of the CCP's mouthpiece *People's Daily* with a former Deputy Editor-in-Chief of the *People's Daily* as its Editor-in-Chief. The *Global Times* is equally subject to the vetting and 'advisories' of the CCP Central Committee's Propaganda Department as other official Chinese media. The articles appearing in the *Global Times* cannot have been published without high-level clearance from the CCP's Propaganda Department. One reason for *Global Times* having been chosen as the propaganda vehicle of choice would be the awareness that Indian journalists do not speak Chinese and would, therefore, readily republish reports from the *Global Times* and disseminate them to a wider Indian audience. It is significant that New Delhi-based Chinese diplomats in their briefings to think-tanks and others in New Delhi used the same arguments that were repeated a day or two later by the *Global Times*!

Of concern is the fact that the threats and warnings issued by the *Global Times* have not yet been denied or contradicted by any Chinese official. By late July, the state owned *Global Times* had published nearly 20 articles. In addition to warning India of a repeat of the 1962 War and an image of a *People's Daily* edition of 1962 being posted on the *People's Daily's* website and circulated on the popular Chinese sites Weibo and WeChat on July 12, 2017, each of the articles sought to prick India on sensitive issues and has a background. The threat about China's intention to reverse its recognition of Sikkim as part of India, repeated by Chinese diplomats in New Delhi, underscores the remark by a Chinese Vice Foreign Minister to the visiting Indian External Affairs Minister in 2008 that the issue of Sikkim remains unsettled. The warning about promoting insurgency in the northeast, after Deng Xiaoping reversed Mao's policy of "exporting revolution" in 1979, has a backdrop of the persistent reports about weapons purchases by northeast insurgent groups from China and the clandestine links maintained by Chinese intelligence over the years with these groups. The warning can impact the proposed Bangladesh-China-India-Myanmar (BCIM) Corridor. China, incidentally, has a Consulate in Kolkata though it has refused to permit India to reopen one in Lhasa. The article attempting to draw a parallel between India's action in Doklam in support of Bhutan and mentioning the possibility of a Chinese intrusion in Kashmir ostensibly at Pakistan's instance, brings into focus China's links with Kashmiri separatists and the growing collusion between China, and Pakistan and the pronounced military content of the China-Pakistan Economic Corridor (CPEC). These articles as well as the statements by official Chinese spokesmen reveal the thinking in the CCP's senior echelons about India.

The *Global Times* has also not hesitated in 'personal attacks' on Indian personages including External Affairs Minister Sushma Swaraj. On July 21, it called her a "liar". Another article attacked Prime Minister Narendra Modi and ascribed the "rise of Hindu nationalism" as one of the reasons for pushing India and China into another war. The *Global Times* stated, "Nationalist fervor that demands revenge against China has taken root in India since the border war. The election of Indian Prime Minister Narendra Modi has fuelled the country's nationalist sentiments. Modi took advantage of rising Hindu nationalism to come to power.... The border row this time is an action targeted at China that caters to the demand of India's religious nationalists." Later, another article described Ajit Doval as the "main schemer" who planned the incident and said his visit will not "sway Beijing".

Articles in the Chinese media have been noticeably consistent in asserting that "India's withdrawal from the Doklam area is the precondition for talks", that China will not budge from this stand and that "the longer the stand-off, the more disadvantageous India's position will be". They have declared too that "China will make no concessions over the territorial issue nor will it yield to anyone when it comes to national security". Similar statements have been made by Chinese MoFA spokesmen. On July 25, on the eve of National Security Advisor (NSA) Ajit Doval's visit to Beijing for the meeting of Brazil, Russia, India, China, and South Africa (BRICS) nations' NSAs, Chinese Foreign Minister Wang Yi elevated the level of the Chinese demand and became the seniormost Chinese official to blame India for triggering the military standoff at Doklam and asked it "to withdraw its border troops". A disingenuous statement in Chinese issued by the MoFA quoted Wang Yi as telling reporters in Thailand that the "problem was very straightforward" and "even Indian officials publicly said that Chinese soldiers didn't enter the Indian territory. In other words, Indian side admitted (crossing) into Chinese territory."

There were other articles too questioning the wisdom of boycotting Chinese goods. In this context, one lauded Prime Minister Modi for following an "open policy" of trade. A Xinhua commentary published immediately after Doval's bilateral meeting with Yang Jiechi, however, struck a conciliatory note. It said, "Instead of being rivals, India and China have much more common ground, common interests and common aspirations. Both, as developing countries, need to work together on important issues like fighting climate change, protectionism and the financial privileges of Washington. Hopefully, wisdom will guide both countries to common prosperity. There is more than enough room for them to coexist and thrive in Asia and in the world. Both China and India need to enhance communication and nurture trust between them, first by recognizing that the two are not born rivals and that harboring ill will against each other is dangerous." This was the first time an article published by China's official media had used a conciliatory tone and not asked India to withdraw first.

Interesting are the posts and blogs that have appeared on the People's Liberation Army (PLA) owned or maintained websites. While the face-off at Doklam did not seem to dominate the military social media, the posts and blogs on the subject were noticeably firm and categoric. Some of them merit attention and are indicative of the thinking in sections of the PLA. At least one post authored by a serving and 'informed' PLA officer, stated that August would be the crucial month for military hostilities as the weather would become too inhospitable thereafter. Another military 'expert' recommended that the best time for China to strike India is in August, arguing that "from September, weather conditions in the theatre of combat will change and not be conducive for soldiers to survive and fight at such high altitudes". He said if the two countries are able to prevent the situation from worsening and escalating till September, then the possibility of an armed confrontation could reduce substantially as both countries would have to withdraw troops in September.

Other posts on these military sites listed the advantages for China of "teaching India a lesson", asserting that this time around, China should not make the same mistake as in the past and should "recover" the whole of "southern Tibet", or Arunachal Pradesh. One recommended that China should block the flow of river waters to India and especially cited the need to accelerate building the planned dams on the Tsangpo (Brahmaputra) river. None of the postings and blogs referred to any statements on the face-off that might have been made by higher PLA Commanders or CMC Chairman Xi Jinping.

A few posts on the military's social media did, however, express concern at the possibility of outbreak of hostilities with India. Some said the PLA was inadequately prepared and not equipped to undertake such a venture, while others argued that differences should be resolved through diplomatic channels.

The PLA's stated position was stiffened by the remarks on July 30, of retired PLA Maj Gen Yao Yunzhu, presently Director Emeritus at the PLA's prestigious Academy of Military Science (AMS) Centre on China-America Defence Relations and whose remarks usually reflect the official Chinese 'line'. Describing the face-off as of "unprecedented nature" that could make Beijing look for a strong resolution, she claimed the CCP and the PLA are under "huge pressure" to take strong action against the "invasion". Yao Yunzhu was quoted as saying, "China and India are unlikely to go to war, depending on how you define war. If it is very small, if it is a limited-scale military operation against an aggression, it is possible. So, we are talking about very specific military operational issues. What I want to say is that for this Doklam (Donglang) event, Indians have intruded, invaded Chinese territory. That is something that has to be corrected. That is what I have been stressing." She added "trespass" is "intolerable". She said that this is "not going to be talk about war or military operations, limited or unlimited without a context. The context is this—not only India, any country that has invaded China (or) Chinese territory and stayed on, would have to be dealt with whatever means we have, because we cannot accept Chinese territory to be invaded and occupied." She also said, "Let us be specific. We are talking about the Doklam (Donglang) incident, not generally along the border. Because on the border, we have other mechanisms (to resolve disputes). We should analyse them case by case. But Doklam is a unique case, it is an established border line, uncontested territory. I will not say surgical operation, or missile strike or whatever. I will not specify ... with whatever means, it has to be corrected ... you have an invasion, you have to defeat that invasion." She added, "We are stronger. The Chinese military is stronger compared to the Indian military—not only in numbers of aircraft, warships, artillery pieces, tanks, we have a much stronger defence industrial base."

China's propaganda offensive against India during the period (June 26-August 1, 2017) of the face-off at Doklam appears to have been particularly critical. Such public warnings have not been seen in the past three to four decades and clearly reflect the level of tension in the India-China relationship. Posts on the PLA websites have been firm in expressing the resolve to defend China's sovereignty and territory. Inherent in China's propaganda offensive is undoubtedly a high level of psywar but China, which has projected itself as a major world power, will not want this image dented. Xi Jinping has also, since he took over in November 2012, used ideology and nationalism to consolidate the Party's and his personal power. With the crucial 19th Party Congress scheduled two months hence, he cannot afford to appear weak. Other factors including the recent tension between the US and North Korea could, however, prompt Beijing to defer action against India.

*(This article was published by the Centre for China Analysis and Strategy, New Delhi, on August 1, 2017.)*

# 53. Different Facets of the Doklam Face-Off: An Overview

The 73-day face-off between India and China at Doklam that ended on August 28, 2017, marks an important juncture in India-China relations. The nature of the military deployments, kind of Chinese propaganda offensive not witnessed in over 40 years, and actions of the Chinese Foreign Ministry and Chinese Embassy in New Delhi, set it apart from earlier stand-offs. It was also for the first time since 2007 when China began projecting its strength that its policy of aggressive territorial expansion had been successfully challenged by any power. Importantly, the face-off revealed the Chinese Communist Party's (CCP's) leadership's intentions and thinking about India. For these reasons, the face-off at Doklam requires a closer look.

**The Backdrop**

India-China relations have, at least since 2015, been at a crucial and very uncertain juncture as they enter a new phase in readjusting their relationship. Since late 2007, China opted for an assertive and expansive foreign policy, which included enlarging territorial claims and testing its neighbours as it pushed to dominate and 'recover' claimed territory. With specific reference to India, China became more assertive in restating its claim on Arunachal Pradesh, particularly Tawang, while expanding its territorial claims to depict the entire state of Jammu and Kashmir (J&K) as disputed and include the region of Ladakh. Intrusions by China's People's Liberation Army (PLA) increased in depth and aggressiveness. The extended intrusions in the Depsang plains in 2013 and later in the Chumar area in 2014, both in Ladakh, were unusual and almost coincided, or overlapped, with the first visits of Li Keqiang and Xi Jinping to India as Chinese Premier and President respectively. The intrusions were premeditated and deliberate.

In May 2014, the Bharatiya Janata Party (BJP) led by Narendra Modi formed a new government. It won the elections with a resounding popular mandate that allowed it to formulate and pursue a foreign and strategic policy unfettered by domestic constraints or politics. Signalling the initiation of a firmer, definitive foreign policy that underscored national interest and territorial integrity, at his swearing-in ceremony itself Prime Minister Modi outlined the geographic perimeter of areas of India's strategic interest. This was discernible from the list of invitees to the swearing-in and visits by Modi soon thereafter to countries in India's neighbourhood. In the process, areas where India's and China's interest potentially overlap were indicated. India very soon energised and began further consolidating relationships with Japan and the US, among other countries, with noticeable emphasis on their strategic content, in the process acquiring enhanced strategic manoeuvrability. Modi simultaneously clearly indicated to China a desire for a collaborative relationship and enhanced economic interaction. At the same time, he did not hesitate to raise outstanding and, at times, contentious issues, like the border and terrorism, with the Chinese leaders at each meeting. It was now for Beijing to respond.

Bilateral relations soon came under strain, however, when Xi Jinping during a visit to Islamabad in April 2015 announced the China-Pakistan Economic Corridor (CPEC), valued by the Pakistanis at an estimated US$ 46 billion and later enhanced to US$ 62 billion. By doing so, the Chinese Communist Party (CCP) leadership ignored India's sensitivities on issues of sovereignty and territorial integrity; discarded the ambiguity Beijing had maintained for decades on the status of Pakistan occupied Kashmir (PoK), Gilgit and Baltistan; and overtly highlighted the potential fusion of Chinese and Pakistani military power, thereby directly increasing pressure on India. The CPEC initiated the process of attempting to unilaterally bend India's borders with Pakistan, which moved to fully integrate Gilgit-Baltistan to 'protect' the huge Chinese investment in these areas. This it did by getting Gilgit to send 'observers' to the Pakistan Parliament with the stated plan of later having it 'elect' members to the Pakistan National Assembly. The CPEC represents China's commitment and enduring support to Pakistan. Within days of announcing the CPEC, Chinese officials began describing Pakistan as China's "only friend and ally"!

Significantly, China's commitment to Pakistan was made clear during Prime Minister Modi's visit to Beijing later in April 2015—within weeks of Xi Jinping announcing the CPEC in Islamabad. It was conveyed then, and in subsequent months to delegations visiting China for one and a half or two track dialogues, including a delegation of Indian think-tanks, that "India must ease tensions with Pakistan, resolve the Kashmir issue and then look to improve ties with China". This position holds till now and was reiterated at an interaction in early November 2017.

However, in mellower language, Yao Wen, Counsellor in the Chinese Ministry of Foreign Affairs (MFA) on October 18, 2017, on the sidelines of the 19th Party Congress, "invited" India to join the 'One Belt, One Road' (OBOR) now renamed the 'Belt and Road Initiative' (BRI). Stating that "India has expressed its concerns on the CPEC because they believe CPEC passes through territory they believe is their own", he listed the "Kashmir conflict" as a "top priority along with the Korean peninsula, the South China Sea and the instability in Afghanistan".

There are other visible indicators of Beijing's unstinted support to Pakistan. Beijing has consecutively vetoed India's requests at the UN Sanctions Committee, thus, supporting Pakistan's harbouring of internationally acknowledged terrorists and terrorist organisations like Masood Azhar (of the Jaish-e-Mohammed), Syed Salahuddin (of the Jamaat-ud-Dawaa), Hafez Sayed (of the Jamaat-ud-Dawaa) and Zaki-ur-Rahman (of the Lashkar-e-Tayyeba). China defends Pakistan against criticism claiming that it has itself suffered enormously from terrorism and should be lauded for combating it. Beijing is additionally assisting Pakistan to develop tactical nuclear weapons and helping it frustrate US pressure to give these up. China also, in a break from past practice, did not hesitate to come to the forefront to deny India admission to the Nuclear Suppliers Group (NSG) in order to prevent it gaining enhanced international stature. In addition to trying to demonstrate the limits of American power, it linked India's admission with that of Pakistan, ignoring Pakistan's dubious record as a nuclear weapons proliferator. Beijing and Islamabad continue to actively collude in blocking India's effort to get permanent membership of the United Nations Security Council (UNSC).

In addition, China is insistent that India endorse the BRI and come on board the CPEC. During his visit to India in September 2014, Xi Jinping publicly recommended that India dovetail its 'Act East' and 'Sagarmala' initiatives with China's BRI and Maritime Silk Route (MSR). There was particular interest in obtaining India's endorsement for the BRI, Xi Jinping's flagship project, with enormous pressure—including through the Indian media—till even a day before the BRI Forum in Beijing in April 2017, with efforts to persuade India to send a representative, even if from its embassy in Beijing. India declined. These strains imposed on India-China relations saw the steady deterioration of ties.

Incorporation of the BRI in the CCP Constitution at the 19th Party Congress in October 2017 implies that the initiative will be pushed harder. The BRI was specifically mentioned in the communiqué issued after the Russia-India-China Trilateral Meeting of Foreign Ministers in Delhi on December 11, 2017.

**The Face-Off**

The operation at the Doklam plateau in May-June 2017 was a 'localised' operation probably largely planned by the PLA's Western Theatre Command and Shigatse Military Division with limited objectives. Both Commanders involved, namely 63-year-old Gen Zhao Zongqi and Maj Gen Fang Jianguo, have sterling military records with the latter commended as among the PLA's most promising and "outstanding" Commanders. As per the PLA's standard practice, the annual plans (which include patrols, exercises, intrusions, etc.) of the erstwhile Military Regions—now Theatre Commands—are approved by the Central Military Commission (CMC). Particularly vetted are plans involving neighbouring countries. In the case of the intrusion in the Depsang plains of Ladakh carried out by troops of the PLA's Ali Military Sub-District in April 2013, for example, the plans are understood to have been discussed and approved by the CCP Central Committee's (CC's) Politburo (PB). In the case of resumption of the road construction by PLA personnel at Doklam, which meant unilateral violation of the agreement concluded between India and China in 2012 and intrusion into Bhutan, the plans would certainly have been vetted by the CMC and PB.

The plan's limited objectives were to exert pressure on Bhutan to get it to agree to establish full diplomatic ties with China; acquiesce to handing over the Doklam plateau to China, possibly in exchange for two portions of land claimed by China elsewhere in northern Bhutan; and build the road through the Doklam plateau to Gyemochen to reinforce China's claim that Gyemochen—and not Batang la—is the trijunction and that the boundary between India and China should be drawn eastwards from there, thus, placing Arunachal Pradesh within Chinese territory. India's swift and robust military response to the Chinese intrusion caught the Chinese unawares and by surprise. They probably anticipated a diplomatic protest note from Thimpu, followed at most by one from India. The Indian Army's action stymied Chinese plans and blocked China's territorial expansion.

The 10-day lull before China made the stand-off at Doklam public on June 26 was pertinent. Undoubtedly, in this interregnum, the situation on the Doklam plateau and how to counter India's action were discussed at length within the PLA and CCP and between the two. The PLA, and particularly the Commanders of the Western Theatre and Shigatse Division whose military reputations were at stake, would have recommended a military response. A section of senior CCP cadres had also for many months felt that India needed to be "punished" as it was opposing China and not endorsing the BRI. There was, additionally, a feeling that India was only "asking" for things, namely settlement of the border, admission to the UNSC, lifting of veto on its requests at the UN Sanctions Committee, entry to the NSG, etc.

From June 26 onwards, China's propaganda apparatus mounted an intense vitriolic offensive comprising over 150 articles. This included personal attacks on Prime Minister Modi, External Affairs Minister Sushma Swaraj and National Security Advisor (NSA) Ajit Doval. The English-language state-owned *Global Times* published articles on each of the 73 days threatening India. Each of the threats had a historical background. In addition to warning India that it risked a repetition of the 1962 debacle, the articles threatened that China would revive insurgency in India's northeast, reverse its position on Sikkim and foment internal strife there, launch an international campaign to disrupt the close India-Bhutan ties and, as India had done at Doklam, send PLA troops to Kashmir ostensibly at the behest of Pakistan. The *People's Daily*, the CCP's official newspaper, on August 14, 2017 stated that "as of press time, China has laid out its position 67 times, with the country's Ministry of Foreign Affairs reiterating its firm stance on the issue for 54 times, while the Ministry of National Defense has issued 4 announcements regarding the incident". There was also a large number of posts by Chinese 'netizens' and PLA ex-servicemen advocating war and that India 'be taught a lesson'. The kind of language used by the Chinese media has not been seen in more than 40 years. Delhi-based Chinese diplomats adopted a similarly belligerent stance and in conversations with interlocutors repeatedly threatened "war".

This propaganda offensive would have been launched with the twin objectives of buying time for Chinese leaders as they deliberated on the best course of action open to them, and getting India to blink and back off. China's propaganda offensive was certainly orchestrated by the CCP CC's Propaganda Department, which keeps a tight grip on China's official and other media, supervised at the time by Politburo Standing Committee member Liu Yunshun. Pertinently, Liu Yunshun was also (till his retirement at the 19th Party Congress in October 2017) the seniormost member of the CCP CC Secretariat that reports directly to Xi Jinping and which, in Xi Jinping's term, has grown to become more powerful than in the past. There is no doubt that the threats and statements of the Chinese media during this period reflect the views and intent of the CCP leadership towards India.

Meanwhile, Xi Jinping assumed leadership of the Central Leading Small Group on United Front Work in mid-2015 and strengthened the CCP CC's United Front Work Department (UFWD). With its increased personnel strength and larger budget, the UFWD, since at least 2016, has increased its activities in India, some European countries, Australia, the US and countries along the Belt and Road Initiative (BRI). The Chinese Embassy in India became noticeably more active since 2016 in projecting China and has been trying to 'win over' journalists, columnists, academics, think-tanks and opinion makers by offering all expenses-paid trips to China, cash inducements and scholarships through 'front' organisations. The embassy has sought to publicise China's stand through the Indian media and create divisions in the Indian media, the strategic community and politicians.

During this time, China moved additional troop reinforcements along with missiles to the Doklam area. Chinese fighter aircraft, Unmanned Aerial Vehicles (UAVs) and missiles were deployed at various airfields. By early August 2017, People's Liberation Army Air Force (PLAAF) aircraft were deployed at the airbases at Shigatse, Lhasa, Nyingchi, Changdu-Bangda, New Xining, Golmud, Chengdu and Chongqing Baishiyi. Far from seeing India yield ground, China met with an Indian response. At the same time, India, which refused to engage in a tit-for-tat war of words with China or pay heed to China's demands that India first withdraw its troops from Doklam before negotiations could begin, consistently maintained that diplomacy was the only way to defuse the situation, and kept channels open for negotiation.

With the passage of time, it became increasingly difficult for either country to withdraw without loss of face. China had for years projected an image as a strong and powerful country intent on establishing its dominance in the region and 'recovering' territories 'lost' because of the imposition of 'unequal treaties' by imperialist colonial powers. It had challenged countries as it expanded its territorial claims in the South China Sea and East Sea and on its periphery. Moreover, Xi Jinping had initiated the most extensive and far-reaching reforms intended to make the PLA one of the world's strongest armed forces. China was also trying to extend its influence in South Asia while undercutting India's. The momentum that China had built without being challenged by any power for decades was now stalled by India! The stakes were high for India too. Having opted to take a firm stance on issues of sovereignty and territorial integrity, it could not buckle under Chinese pressure. Its stand vis-a-vis China would affect its relationships with neighbours like Pakistan, Nepal, Bangladesh, Sri Lanka, etc. Equally importantly, the domestic political cost would be very high.

The Brazil, Russia, India, China, and South Africa (BRICS) Summit and 19th Party Congress scheduled from October 18–28, 2017, provided a time limit for the defusing of tensions. Indian Prime Minister Modi not attending the BRICS Summit would have been an embarrassment but, more importantly, tension continuing at Doklam during the 19th Party Congress would have made Xi Jinping—who had effectively been using large doses of ideology and nationalism to boost the legitimacy and prestige of the CCP—very vulnerable. Wang Dehua, head of South Asia Studies at the Shanghai Institute for International Studies, said on August 30, 2017, that "China understands the importance of creating a favourable atmosphere for the success of the summit and the all-important Party Congress." Indications that the Party Congress would be held in October had become available by mid-June. In a surprise, but welcome, development India's Ministry of External Affairs and China's Ministry of Foreign Affairs on August 28, 2017, announced the simultaneous disengagement of troops involved in the by now 73-day long face-off on the Doklam plateau. Later that afternoon, India confirmed that bulldozers and other road building equipment had been removed by the Chinese.

### The Withdrawal

Throughout the face-off, India had repeatedly said a diplomatic solution was the only way to defuse the situation, but China had been insistent that India first withdraw its troops before talks could begin.

In all probability when India did not yield ground despite sustained Chinese propaganda using language and threats not seen in over 40 years, and mobilisation of PLA forces, Chinese President Xi Jinping concluded that the PLA would not be able to achieve a decisive victory against India and agreed to the withdrawal of troops without insisting on the precondition that India withdraw its troops from Bhutanese territory before negotiations could commence. The state of morale of the PLA—which by March 2017 had seen more than 4,883 officers including 86 officers of the rank of Major General and above arrested and dismissed—could have been a factor. Most important was that anything short of a decisive victory would have been a humiliation for China, the Chinese Communist Party (CCP) and Xi Jinping, especially before the 19th Party Congress.

Finally, with war not an option, quiet backdoor negotiations offered an acceptable solution. But suspicion remains and military personnel of both sides remain in a state of watchful wariness at a distance of 300 metres from each other, with reinforcements and weaponry in the immediate vicinity. Recent reports indicate that China is reinforcing logistics in the area.

### The Aftermath

Reluctance to accept the decision for disengagement has been apparent in China. On August 30, Yue Gang, a retired Colonel of the PLA's General Staff Department and frequent commentator on military matters, quite significantly said, "Despite Beijing's deliberate ambiguity, China has apparently made substantial concessions in order to end the dispute. India has got exactly what it has wanted. It was a humiliating defeat for China to cave in to pressure from India despite all the tough talk." There were numerous comments on China's social media as well and their not being deleted suggests a degree of tacit official support. Netizens asked why there had been no "apology" from India; whether China had given up "legitimate rights such as building the road" and "whether India's withdrawal was unconditional." Meanwhile, a rumour spread in China claiming that it had purchased India's acquiescence to the withdrawal by giving it a loan of US$20 billion! Revealing the Chinese leadership's discomfiture, separate denials were issued by the spokesman of China's Ministry of National Defence Col Ren Guoqiang, spokesperson of China's Ministry of Foreign Affairs (MFA) and the CCP's official mouthpiece, *People's Daily*. In a widely circulated video clip, the Editor-in-Chief of the *Global Times*, He Jixin, declared the people were unhappy with the 'withdrawal'. The *Global Times* of September 12, published a significant article by serving PLA Maj Gen Qiao Liang, who justified the withdrawal as "strategic positioning". Arguing that "only doing the right thing at the right time is correct", he added that entering into a military conflict with India at this point of time would only harm China. Within a couple of days of the announcement of the disengagement, Chinese Foreign Minister Wang Yi asserted that Doklam was sovereign Chinese territory and that China would build the road to Gyemochen. He was the seniormost Chinese official to make such a statement.

In Delhi, Chinese diplomats led by Chinese Ambassador Luo Zhaohui hosted journalists, politicians, academics and others to receptions and seminars, suggesting that there was scope for "reconciliation" and "cooperation". Posts on the official Chinese Embassy website displayed pictures of the invitees to seminars hosted by the embassy. A disconnect was apparent, however, with the People's Liberation Army (PLA) and China's powerful propaganda apparatus adopting a stance different from that of China's diplomats. China's official media continued to publish articles critical of India. Unlike prior to the face-off at Doklam, PLA border personnel exchanged no pleasantries or visits with Indian counterparts on China's National Day on October 1. Neither did

China propose dates for the annual 'Hand-to-Hand' exercises between the two Armies.

**Future Trend**

The Doklam face-off was undoubtedly an important event which would colour India-China relations for a long time. Despite the passage of three months, China appeared unwilling to set it aside and move ahead. The PLA's sharp reaction to the Indian drone crashing inside China in the Doklam area on December 7, 2017 reflected this. The official news agency Xinhua quoted Zhang Shuili, Deputy Director of the PLA's Western Theatre Command Combat Bureau, as saying, "India's move has infringed upon China's territorial sovereignty, and we are strongly dissatisfied with and opposed to this. We will fulfil our mission and responsibility and defend China's national sovereignty and security resolutely." The Western Theatre Command said it did not accept the Indian Defence Ministry's statement that the accident was due to technical reasons, adding that the statement contained no apology and China would decide what to do with the drone. It said India had learnt no lessons from Doklam.

In a further incremental toughening of tone, Chinese Foreign Minister Wang Yi referred to the stand-off at Doklam after the Russia-India-China Trilateral Foreign Ministers Meeting in New Delhi on December 11, 2017. He stated, "China is also firm in upholding its sovereign rights and interests and territorial integrity. We handled the Indian border troops' trespass into China's Dong Lang area in our national interest, on just grounds and with restraint. Through diplomatic means, we engaged with the Indian side and it withdrew its equipment and personnel". He also asked India to drop its opposition to the BRI, which was separately recommended by Russia's Foreign Minister. The same day, the Chinese Foreign Ministry website reported on Wang Yi's meeting with NSA Ajit Doval. It quoted Wang Yi as observing that "China-India relations are at a crucial moment at present, and both sides need to make the correct choice regarding the future development of bilateral relations".

Days after the 19th Party Congress the state-owned *Global Times* warned: "If, for whatever reason, the nation's peaceful development is thwarted by external influence, China will not hesitate to strike back with sharp strategic force, or if necessary, prepare for a full-scale showdown." The reference to the BRI was implicit.

A new uneasy phase in India-China relations, which could be interspersed with periods of tension, has begun. What little trust there was in the bilateral relationship has dropped to negligible levels. It appears that China's leadership, urged by the military leadership and especially the Western Theatre Command which are smarting at being blocked by India, will look for ways to salvage what it feels is hurt pride as both countries also seek to find new accommodation.

*(This article was published by the Centre for China Analysis and Strategy, New Delhi, on December 16, 2017.)*

# 54. Composition and Implications of Chinese Defence Minister Wei Fenghe's Visit to India

India and China have planned to exchange a few important visits in the remaining months of this year. An Army Commander from India is scheduled to travel to China in a few weeks, the first visit by an Army Commander since 2015, followed by National Security Advisor (NSA) Doval and possibly another high level visit. Chinese Defence Minister Gen Wei Fenghe, who was on a four-day visit to India from August 21, is the first of the important visitors from China. He is to be followed in a couple of months by China's Minister of Public Security Zhao Kezhi, who has worked closely with one of Chinese President Xi Jinping's closest associates and current right hand man Li Zhangshu.

The visits are part of efforts to portray an emerging cordiality in the relationship, a reason why no other country was included in the itinerary of the Chinese Defence Minister's delegation. The Chinese also took care to ensure 'appropriate' coverage of the Chinese Defence Minister's visit by selecting only the authoritative official news agency Xinhua, the state-owned China Central Television (CCTV) and the official Chinese Communist Party (CCP) newspaper *People's Daily* to cover the visit. Chinese journalists were instructed to provide only "correct" coverage. Significant, however, will be the assessment of the two Chinese visitors of India's political and economic situation including the state of India's armed forces, which will be important inputs for Xi Jinping in determining China's policy towards India. Both Gen Wei Fenghe and Zhou Kezhi have direct access to Xi Jinping.

The visit of Gen Wei Fenghe, who led a 27-member Chinese military delegation which included six Lieutenant Generals and Major Generals, is important for its timing and interesting composition. Coming days after Imran Khan took over as Pakistan's new Prime Minister, the Chinese Defence Minister predictably pointed to Imran Khan's public comments about wanting to improve ties with India and urged India to take advantage of this. Especially since Chinese President Xi Jinping announced the China-Pakistan Economic Corridor (CPEC) in April 2015, China has been insistent in official, Track-II and other interactions that India ease tensions with Pakistan and resolve the Kashmir issue preceding any improvement in ties with China. China is, additionally, concerned that India is involved in efforts to derail the CPEC.

At least four members of the Chinese delegation are reported to have arrived a few days earlier and would have held working level discussions. According to the Indian government's press release, the Defence Ministers discussed a new Memorandum of Understanding (MoU), more joint exercises, issues relating to border management and decided on greater interaction at the working level to ensure maintenance of peace and tranquillity. The Chinese-language edition of *Global Times* on August 21 said that the Doklam incident would also be discussed. The most important issue of operationalising a hotline—a proposal pending for nearly a decade—is yet to be agreed upon. While both sides agree on the need for a hotline, differences persist as to whether this would link the Director General (Military Operations) in the Indian Army Headquarters (HQ) with China's Central Military Commission (CMC) in Beijing or the Western Theatre Command. The Chinese continue to insist on the latter. Till now, however, tensions have been noticed to have been defused only after intervention by Beijing.

The Chinese People's Liberation Army's (PLA's) Western Theatre Command, which has operational responsibility for the Chinese side of the entire 4057-km-long border with India, was represented in the delegation by one Lieutenant General and two Major Generals. Pertinently, the Western Theatre Command's tasks include protection of the CPEC. The second ranking member of the delegation, Lieutenant General Chang Dingqiu is Deputy Chief of Staff in the Joint Staff Department of the Central Military Commission (CMC) and is from the PLA Air Force (PLAAF), which is getting an increasingly important and growing role in the Tibetan plateau, and is the most likely to succeed the current PLAAF Commander when he retires. The delegation has considerable expertise on Sino-Indian border issues and three of its senior members have direct experience of the border areas across Ladakh and the northern areas of Pakistan. In addition, Defence Minister Gen Wei Fenghe, as a member of the CMC and till March 2018, Commander of the PLA Second Artillery and PLA Rocket Force—China's strategic missile force—is privy to high-level operational and other military decisions and is himself familiar with developments along the Sino-Indian border.

Of particular interest is the inclusion in the delegation of Maj Gen Li Haiyang and Maj Gen Kuang Dewang. Both have served for decades in the South Xinjiang Military District, which has operational responsibility for the area across Ladakh and Pakistan occupied Kashmir (PoK). They were in position during the major intrusions in April 2013 in the Depsang plains just before Chinese Premier Li Keqiang's visit to India, and in September 2014 in Chumar in Ladakh, during Chinese President Xi Jinping's visit. Maj Gen Li Haiyang continues as Major General of the South Xinjiang Military District and Kuang Dewang, who till 2017 commanded the Hetian Miltary Sub-District (MSD)—responsible for the area across the Depsang Plains and subordinate to the South Xinjiang Military District—has been promoted as Major General and Deputy Chief of Staff of the Tibet Military Region. Similarly, though not part of this delegation, Liu Geping, Commander of the adjoining Ali MSD, subordinate to the South Xinjiang Military District and responsible for the areas across Chushul, Pangong Lake, Demchok, Chumar and Shipkila Pass, was also promoted from Senior Colonel to Major General! Their promotions and inclusion in the delegation confirm that the intrusions in 2013, 2014 and thereafter were authorised and these officers continue to retain responsibility for the area.

Inclusion of officers from the South Xinjiang Military District and Western Theatre Command attracts notice because the ongoing intrusion in Demchok, for which they have direct operational responsibility, has now lingered for nearly three weeks despite India's efforts to defuse it. This casts substantial doubt on the reported decision by the two leaders at the Wuhan Summit to give "strategic guidance" to the "respective militaries to strengthen communication". This was not included in the Chinese statement issued after the Wuhan Summit and neither has a single reference to this been noticed since in the official Chinese media.

In fact, the 73-day stand-off at Doklam remains a sensitive issue in China. The Chinese people and the PLA remain dissatisfied with the decision to "disengage". The sustained propaganda of nationalism and ideology administered by Xi Jinping since taking over in November 2012, has contributed to inculcating strong sentiments among the people and the feeling that China should have administered India a 'sharp lesson'.

This is reinforced by the noticeable increase in the number of military exercises on the Tibetan plateau and accelerated pace of development of military infrastructure post-Doklam. China's military press divulged that a new PLA Air Force (PLAAF) Base was established in Lhasa in March 2018, that construction will commence in 2019 of three new airports in Tibet across the borders with India, and that a new Special Warfare Battalion has been inducted into the Tibetan plateau. PLAAF Aviation Assault Brigades have also been carrying out paradrop training and "integrated joint operations" exercises with helicopter pilots for "low altitude deep penetration" operations in the high-altitude Tibetan plateau.

The continuing intrusion at Demchok during the visit of a high-ranking Chinese military official conveyed an additional subtle message. Viewed along with the intrusions at the Depsang plains in April 2013 and at Chumar in September 2014, it signals that regardless of high-level visits by government, Party or military officials, the PLA will remain unwavering in its stated mission of safeguarding China's sovereignty and territorial integrity and retrieving territories claimed to have been lost by the imposition of "unequal treaties".

*(This article was published by the Centre for China Analysis and Strategy, New Delhi, on August 26, 2018.)*

# 55. Chinese State Councillor and Public Security Minister Zhao Kezhi's Visit Yields Little Tangible Results

Chinese State Councillor and Minister of Public Security Zhao Kezhi arrived in India on October 22,for visits to Delhi and Mumbai, at the head of a 20-member security delegation. It included 13 officials of China's Ministry of Public Security (MPS) and three from the Ministry of Foreign Affairs (MoFA). He later travelled to Bangladesh where too he had high-level meetings, including with Bangladesh Prime Minister Sheikh Hasina. India and Bangladesh are both, coincidentally, headed into national elections in the coming months.

The visit followed by that of Chinese Defence Minister Wei Fenghe to India in August and is obviously part of efforts to portray that relations are improving after the meeting between Prime Minister Modi and Chinese President Xi Jinping in Wuhan in April this year. Notwithstanding this and highlighting their territorial claims, Chinese troops intruded into Arunachal Pradesh just days prior to Zhao Kezhi's arrival. During the Chinese Defence Minister's visit too, a similar intrusion by Chinese troops in Demchok in Ladakh was vacated weeks after his departure. Important for Chinese President Xi Jinping will be Zhao Kezhi's discussions on the issues of Tibet and the Dalai Lama and his assessment of the likely results of India's upcoming national elections.

In addition to meeting his host Home Minister Rajnath Singh, 64-year-old Zhao Kezhi was received by India's National Security Advisor (NSA) and Prime Minister. That India did not genuflect to avoid giving imaginary offence to China and Kiren Rijiju, Minister of State for Home and Member of Parliament from Arunachal Pradesh attended the meetings, is encouraging. Perhaps to add apparent substance to the visit, a security cooperation agreement was signed between India and China. The agreement covers areas like intelligence sharing, exchange programmes, sharing of best practices, and cooperation in disaster mitigation besides others. In material terms, though, there is likely to be negligible, if any, cooperation in these areas.

Actually, there is no possibility of substantive cooperation in counter-terrorism as long as China remains protective about Pakistan and seeks to insulate it from accusations by other countries. The intelligence agencies of both countries have very close, long-standing ties. China's interests and its relationship with Pakistan are far too strategically important for any change in China's policy towards Pakistan and the current uncertainties regarding the China-Pakistan Economic Corridor (CPEC) will serve only to strengthen Beijing's commitment to Pakistan. Confirming that talks on terrorism made no headway, China's stand on cooperation in counter-terrorism was made public at the routine Chinese Foreign Ministry press briefing in Beijing on October 23, barely a day after the Indian and Chinese delegations met in New Delhi. In response to a question about Beijing's position regarding Pakistan harbouring internationally acknowledged terrorists like Masood Azhar, Hafez Sayeed, etc., the official Chinese spokesman Hua Chunying emphasised that there was no change in China's position, which it has made known on a number of occasions. The presence of the MPS Director General of Counter-Terrorism, An Weixin would have been cosmetic.

On the contrary, the Chinese delegation would have again pressured India to reopen talks with the new government in Pakistan and resolve the Kashmir issue. It would have also emphasised the importance of the CPEC and the need to ensure its security.

Beijing's immediate concern about Uyghurs transiting through Pakistan into China's Xinjiang-Uyghur Autonomous Region (XUAR) are, it feels, currently being adequately met by Pakistan's security forces. Chinese agencies also have a free hand inside Pakistan. China and Pakistan are additionally cooperating and furthering each other's interests in Afghanistan.

The other issue troubling China is that of the Rohingyas who, according to Beijing, are being radicalised by Al Qaeda. Beijing is concerned that these elements will cross into China through the porous borders with Myanmar. The delegation, which arrived in the Bangladesh capital, Dhaka, on October 26, would have had this on their agenda. China has earlier suggested that India should cooperate in this area. On the other hand, Zhao Kezhi's delegation is very unlikely to have offered any material information regarding Indian northeast insurgents visiting Yunnan province and its capital Kunming to purchase arms from Chinese suppliers there.

The Tibet issue undoubtedly ranked high on the Chinese delegation's agenda and would have been pushed hard. It is likely that they sought to exchange views on the Dalai Lama and urged curbs on the Dalai Lama's set-up in Dharamshala, accusing it of infiltrating and carrying out anti-China activities inside Tibet. The Chinese have an interest in the situation surrounding Uyghen Thinley Dorje, recognised as the Karmapa by the Chinese authorities and the Dalai Lama, and who 'escaped' from Tsurphu Monastery in Tibet, particularly in the backdrop of the numerous news reports—many inspired—in recent months. These reports mentioned that he was unhappy and felt constrained in India and that he had acquired the passport of the Dominican Republic. The statement jointly issued on October 11 by Uyghen Thinley Dorje after his recent meeting with the other claimant Thaye Thinley Dorje, earlier backed by Shamar Rimpoche, would have further perked Chinese curiosity. Reliable reports suggest that China made conciliatory overtures to Uyghen Thinley Dorje while he was in New Jersey.

There is a large number of Kagyupa adherents in Tibet and the Himalayan border belt and they have a dominating presence in Sikkim and Bhutan. Clear pointers to the importance of Tibet-related issues are the inclusion in the delegation of Zhang Hongbo, Director of Public Security of the Tibet Autonomous Region (TAR) and Ms Hou Yanqi, of MoFA who has served in its Department of External Security Affairs which also looks after matters relating to Tibetans outside China and Wu Wei, Counsellor in MoFA's Department of External Security Affairs.

Zhang Hongbo, an ethnic Han who was born in Sichuan and joined the Chinese Communist Party (CCP) in 1985,has been working in the TAR since at least 1982, indicating that he is either an 'Aid Tibet' cadre from Sichuan or that he grew up in Tibet. He has extensive experience in security work and his last appointment was as Mayor of Shigatse, one of the TAR's two largest cities and also the traditional seat of the Panchen Lama, till July 2018, when he was appointed Director of TAR Public Security. He will have detailed knowledge of Tibetan issues including the interactions between the Chinese authorities and Tibetan Buddhist monks in India and elsewhere.

Similarly pertinent is the inclusion of 1970-born Ms Hou Yanqi, Deputy Director General of Asian Affairs in MoFA. An Urdu-speaking specialist in Pakistan and Afghanistan affairs—her husband works in Afghanistan—she was awarded the 'Tangha-i-Pakistan' by Pakistan President Zardari in March 2013. She has served in the Department of External Security Affairs of China's Ministry of Foreign Affairs which would have given her insights into issues concerning the Tibetans and Uyghurs. She is backed by Wu Wei, Counsellor in MoFA's Department of External Security Affairs.

Other issues like, cross-border movement of Uyghurs, complaints by Chinese businessmen about limited duration visas, and India's objections to the issue by China of stapled visas for residents of Arunachal Pradesh and Jammu & Kashmir (J&K), etc. would have been on the agenda.

Zhao Kezhi would have raised trade issues and expressed the hope that India does not follow the US and impose restrictions on Chinese telecom, Information Technology (IT) and other companies operating in India. An offer to try and redress the imbalance in trade may have been suggested.

An important aspect of Zhao Kezhi's visit will be the assessment he provides to Chinese President Xi Jinping after in-house discussions with the Chinese Ambassador and others when he would meet. His briefing will be important as it coincides with the building election tempo in India. In addition to being Minister for Public Security, Zhao Kezhi is also a long-time confidant of Xi Jinping.

*(This article was published by the Centre for China Analysis and Strategy, New Delhi, on October 27, 2018.)*

# 56. Can the Second Xi-Modi Summit Tackle the Really Difficult Issues

In just around a fortnight in mid-October, Chinese President Xi Jinping is scheduled to arrive in India for his second 'informal' meeting with Indian Prime Minister Narendra Modi in the ancient coastal town of Mamallapuram near Chennai. Xi Jinping is likely to combine it with a visit to neighbouring Nepal where China has in recent years acquired considerable influence, the pace of which has accelerated since the installation of the Communist government initially under Prachanda. Developments over the past months, however, make any meaningful progress at the summit unlikely.

China was keen that the visit takes place as soon as possible after India's national elections so that Xi Jinping would be the first foreign leader to have a summit with Indian Prime Minister Narendra Modi and the two would be able to build on their first 'informal' meeting held at Wuhan in China. Developments in the interregnum centering especially on India's robust punitive response to terrorist attacks sponsored by Pakistan and the air strike against the terrorist training camp at Balakot inside Pakistan have, however, dimmed the prospects for the upcoming summit. China's support to Pakistan has been overt. Curious too is the fact that Chinese State Councillor and Foreign Minister Wang Yi has not yet visited India. It is unusual for a Chinese Foreign Minister not to personally visit and approve arrangements prior to the Chinese President's visit. Wang Yi has, additionally, on two recent occasions —the latest on September 27 at the UN General Assembly— made specific reference to the issue of Kashmir and UN Security Council Resolutions on Kashmir. This raises doubts about how serious Beijing is about the visit. Chinese and Indian security delegations have, meanwhile, visited Mamallapuram and Chennai.

Around the same period Wang Yi travelled to Islamabad for the trilateral Afghanistan-Pakistan-China meeting where he held talks with Pakistan's Prime Minister, Army Chief and President. India-Pakistan relations and

Kashmir were discussed, with Wang Yi assuring Pakistan of China's support and stressing that the Kashmir issue should be resolved in accordance with the UN Security Resolutions. Reports state too that there has been a marked increase in the number of Chinese military personnel travelling to Pakistan since early this year.

This was followed by Wang Yi's visit over September 14-15 to Kathmandu to prepare for a possible visit by Xi Jinping which, if it materialises, will be the first by a Chinese President to Nepal since 1996! In Kathmandu, Wang Yi is reported to have expressed concern at the large Muslim population and the possibility of their staging embarrassing pro-Uyghur demonstrations during Xi Jinping's visit. The demonstration by the Tibetans protesting Wang Yi's visit added to his concern.

Importantly, Chinese President Xi Jinping's meeting with Prime Minister Modi takes place at a time of mounting difficulties for the Chinese leader. Dissatisfaction with Xi Jinping and his policies is spreading inside China. The country's economy is shrinking and growth has slowed despite measures to halt the slide. Hundreds of small private enterprises have shut down adding to rising unemployment and the number of protests by laid-off workers has doubled over the previous year. Demobilised and retired military personnel also staged public protests in Beijing last year demanding reemployment, better benefits and 'respect'. The cost of living has also been rising. Students and academics are disgruntled and respected prominent academics, quite unusually and at personal risk, have gone public with their criticism of Xi Jinping's policies. The anti-corruption campaign continues to fell hundreds of senior Party, military and government officials, widening the circles of the discontented.

The US-China trade war has accentuated Xi Jinping's problems and seriously set back China's technology sector. US restrictions on the sale of critical components, like laser micro-chips, etc., to Chinese hi-technology and telecommunications companies highlighted to China's leadership how dependent China continues to be on the import of hi-tech components. Despite initial claims that they are equipped to weather the crisis, Chinese companies like Huawei and ZTE are in distress and laying off employees. Chinese President Xi Jinping's goal of achieving the 'China Dream' by 2021 and 'Made in China-2025' within the time-limits declared at the 19th Party Congress now appears difficult.

Adding to these problems is the continuing turbulence and sporadic violence in Hong Kong, which has challenged the legitimacy of the Chinese Communist Party's (CCP's) rule. Apart from describing the protests as a "colour revolution" instigated by the US and the West and making a few token concessions, China's leadership has thus far taken no substantive action to quell the protests. There are indications of inner-Party differences in the highest echelons of the CCP, which suggest a weakening of Xi Jinping's authority.

China's overt support to Pakistan and recent actions have imposed additional strain on its relations with India. Beijing's call for a meeting of the United Nations Security Council (UNSC) in support of Pakistan to discuss the amendment of Article 370 by India—an avowedly internal matter clarified as having no repercussion outside the boundary of the state—was avoidable. This was compounded when a Chinese diplomat disingenuously insisted that the meeting had criticised India's action in a statement, which was swiftly denied.

China's official media reactions since Article 370 was amended on August 5, have been uniformly critical and, additionally raised China's claims on Tibet and specifically Ladakh. Stating that India "will divide the areas of Aksai Chin and other areas of China's Xinjiang", they quoted the Chinese Foreign Ministry spokesman as clarifying "that this practice in India seriously violates China's territorial sovereignty"! Stressing that it is by no means India's internal matter, the Chinese media said, "It is a violation of China's territorial sovereignty and damages China's interests. It violates the relevant agreements between the two countries on maintaining peace and tranquillity in the border areas, and the leaders of the two countries on the proper control of disputes". The articles insisted that the relevant areas "are completely located in China's Tibet and Xinjiang, and … These areas have always belonged to China, and under the actual control of China, they are an inseparable part of Chinese territory".

Reiterating China's claim, the official media said, "Ladakh has been Chinese territory since ancient times". Stating that India has "continuously penetrated into the western section of the Sino-Indian border to infiltrate and create and expand disputes" seriously affecting bilateral relations between the two countries, the articles warned: "If the Indian side does not learn the lesson" it will worsen the border situation, aggravate the border dispute and endanger the peace and tranquillity of the border area". The articles threatened that "the Chinese side will certainly not sit idly by".

China's official media has published articles asserting China's claim over Ladakh earlier too, for example, in May 2013 and more recently in May 2019. China also continues to offer India gratuitous "advice" to ease tension with Pakistan and resolve the Kashmir issue. Most recent was that proffered by China's Ambassador Sun Weidong who, noticeably, dropped reference to the UNSC Resolutions in his interview to an Indian newspaper.

There have been other hints of military implications. Earlier in August, China and Pakistan held their largest yet Air Force exercise, the Shaheen-VIII. Official Chinese military media reporting of the exercise specially highlighted that the People's Liberation Army Air Force (PLAAF) had for the first time sent its fourth generation J-16 fighter to help train the Pakistan Air Force (PAF) take on the Rafale fighter aircraft being acquired by India. A report suggests that the air base for the exercise, surrounded by high mountains and jungles, was in China's Gansu province within the operational jurisdiction of the People's Liberation Army (PLA) Western Theatre Command. This Shaheen exercise was held after the Indian Air Force (IAF) strike on the *jihadi* terrorist training camp at Balakot in Pakistan.

Possibly reflecting ongoing discussions within Chinese military circles another official Chinese military media report on September 28 discussed the deployment of PLAAF aircraft. It suggested that a certain number of the PLAAF's "newly introduced" JH-7-II electronic warfare aircraft can be deployed along the Sino-Pakistan border so that in the event of a conflict, they could be "quickly loaned" to Pakistan. It added that this would also be the best option for "cash-crunched" Pakistan to meet its urgent needs and tilt the balance in an air war in Pakistan's favour. Interesting is the uptick in China's military media highlighting the aspect of collusive cooperation between the Air Forces of the two countries. Pertinent in this context is a remark made earlier in July this year by an officer of the PLA Western Theatre Command, who said that the intensified training by formations in this Command is focussed "on building its global combat capabilities"!

On the other hand, Indian Prime Minister Modi will be meeting Xi Jinping for a one-on-one 'informal' summit after obtaining a huge victory in the national elections. The mandate was forcefully reinforced in Parliament during the passage of the amendment to Article 370, which passed with a two-thirds majority in both Houses of Parliament. Modi has also just returned from a successful high-profile public event in the US where US President Trump shared a platform with him and Modi unequivocally signalled that there would be no talks with Pakistan till it took substantive action to stop terrorism against India and dismantle the terrorist infrastructure. India's Home, Defence and External Affairs Ministers have separately reiterated this and added that in case there are talks, then discussions would centre on Pakistan-occupied Kashmir (PoK), Gilgit, Baltistan and Aksai Chin!

The 'informal' summit meeting between the leaders of the two largest Asian nations takes place in this backdrop, which limits the potential for substantive progress. If there is some agreement on keeping the borders quiet and limited moves to reduce the trade deficit, that will be a good outcome.

*(This article was published by the Centre for China Analysis and Strategy, New Delhi, on October 2, 2019.)*

# 57. Implications of the Ongoing Tension with China Along the LAC

China has accused India of crossing and violating the Line of Actual Control (LAC) . On May 5 the Chinese media reports said: "On the May 18, a reporter from the *Global Times* (in Chinese) learned from sources that the Chinese border guards have strengthened control over the Galwan Valley area and resolutely responded to the infringement of the Sino-Indian line to build facilities. According to relevant sources, since the beginning of May, the Indian side crossed the line into the Chinese territory and entered the Chinese territory, began to construct barriers, and blocked the normal patrol of the Chinese border defense forces. They deliberately provoked the incident and tried to unilaterally change the status of border control. The Galwan Valley region is China's undisputed territory. The above actions of the Indian side seriously violated the relevant agreements on the border issue between China and India".

China's People's Liberation Army (PLA) troops crossed the LAC and entered Indian territory some time in late April 2020 in north Sikkim at Naku La; at one point at Hot Springs and two locations to its northwest at Patrolling Points 14 and 15; and at three points on the Galwan river in the Galwan valley where they are reported to have pitched close to a hundred tents; and at a point called Gogra. They are now reported to be digging defences, preparing bunkers and moving in heavy vehicles. They have moved up artillery guns and reinforcements from the rear to their side of the LAC. Efforts by local Commanders, including Brigadiers from higher formations, have not resulted in defusing the situation. One press report said that the PLA has reportedly stopped responding to Indian requests for flag meetings under the mutually established protocol termed the "Border Management Posture" (BMP). These are indications that the PLA troops are preparing for either a long stay or to build near permanent defences while protracted negotiations continue.

From the time these reports surfaced, there have been clear indications of premeditation and preparation by the Chinese. First, the involvement of the large number of troops, almost 250, is very unusual as routine patrols are normally between 10-30 people in strength. Reports also said that the PLA troops were carrying batons with metal studs which is odd, but suggests they had planned to, if possible, avoid the firing of weapons which would lead to immediate escalation. The quick arrival of Chinese helicopters, of which the PLA has a large number, deployed with the South Xinjiang Military District and Ngari (Ali) Military Sub-District, at the point of confrontation on Pangong Tso (near Chushul) points to a high state of readiness of the PLA.

The actions would certainly have been authorised and coordinated at the highest level. The entire 4,057-km length of the India-China border is under the overall operational jurisdiction of the PLA Western Theatre Command. It is the largest of China's five Theatre Commands. The areas opposite Ladakh come under the operational jurisdiction of the South Xinjiang Military District (MD), subordinate to the Xinjiang Military Region and directly under the Ngari (Ali) Military Sub-District (MSD) subordinate to it, which exercises jurisdiction over the areas across Ladakh and up to the border with Himachal Pradesh. The area opposite Sikkim, including the area of Doklam (or Dolum), comes under the operational jurisdiction of the Shigatse Military Sub-District (MSD) subordinate to the Tibet Military Region. While there has been a changeover of Commanders at both these MSDs, the PLA has posted their predecessors to higher positions in the Military District/Military Region. Care has been taken to ensure that continuity of local experience has been retained at the more senior level thereby facilitating coordinated planning. Pertinent is that among the PLA Western Theatre Command's tasks is also the safeguarding of Chinese assets and nationals of the China–Pakistan Economic Corridor (CPEC).

There are many reasons why China has triggered this tension at this time: (i) Chinese President Xi Jinping is under increased domestic pressure, including unprecedented demands for him to step down, because of his policies and in the wake of mishandling of the COVID-19 outbreak in Wuhan, and wants to divert attention, including when the 'Big Two' [Chinese People's Political Consultative Conference (CPPCC) and National People's Congress

(NPC)] plenary sessions are underway. (ii) Chinese President Xi Jinping's promise of achieving the China Dream includes the 'rejuvenation' of China by the hundredth year of the founding of the Chinese Communist Party (CCP) in 2021. This implies reunification of all territories claimed by China. The protests in Hong Kong, reelection of the pro-independence Democratic Progressive Party (DPP) in Taiwan, resistance in the South China and East Seas have all created the impression inside China that the leadership is unable to deliver the 'China Dream'. Here, in order to strengthen his position and that of the CCP, Xi Jinping has since February adopted a noticeably tougher policy with Hong Kong, Taiwan and the areas of transgression are within Indian territories claimed by China. (iii) China sees India getting visibly closer to the US, especially after the COVID-19 pandemic. (iv) China perceives the timing as opportune since India and other countries, like the US, France etc., are preoccupied with tackling the COVID-19 pandemic. (v) China has major economic and strategic interests in the larger Aksai Chin area—the Karakoram, CPEC, etc. After India issued its revised map showing the correct extent of its territories, China feels its interests are threatened and wants to 'dig in' and secure territory it considers its own. It wants to keep the dispute in the area 'open'. (vi) China has not accepted these territories—where the intrusions have occurred—as Indian territory but as disputed. Now that it is much stronger and India and the world are preoccupied and grappling with the Covid-19, China could be wanting to grab larger slices of the territories claimed by it. China has, incidentally, over the years been 'nibbling' away Indian territory. (vii) China's moves would, additionally, be welcomed by Pakistan. The possibility that Pakistan made some contribution to these moves cannot be entirely ruled out considering that since March this year, an Inter-Services Intelligence (ISI) Colonel is posted at China's Central Military Commission's (CMC's) Joint Staff Department.

Noticeably, the official Chinese media has been quiet on these incidents. The CCP-owned *Global Times'* solitary initial article on the incidents at Galwan valley contained strong language not perhaps seen since 1962, but it has been silent on the subject thereafter. Chinese Foreign Minister Wang Yi made no reference to this in his press conference on May 24 on the sidelines of the NPC session, though he criticised the United States. There have, however, been reports on the Chinese social media platform Baidu. Interestingly, articles justifying China's so-called historical claims on Ladakh, the Galwan valley and Sikkim, apparently from an official source, appeared on May 5, 6 and 9 to coincide with the incidents at Ladakh, Galwan valley and Sikkim.

Little noticed has been the strong and tough response (May 20) from the spokesman of the Chinese Embassy in New Delhi to US Assistant Secretary of State Alice Wells' recent statement showing support for India. His statement was stronger than that by the Chinese Foreign Ministry spokesman at the weekly press conference in Beijing. Chinese Embassy Counsellor Ji Rong said: "We are firm in determination to oppose separatist activities and safeguard China's national sovereignty and territorial integrity. We are firm in determination to oppose foreign meddling in China's internal affairs. We are firm in determination to realise final reunification".

His statement appears to have inherent warnings against any attempt to rake up the issue of the Dalai Lama; on drawing close to the US; and opposing Chinese actions on the border.

While reports indicate that there has been no progress in the negotiations thus far, it seems that China is prepared for negotiations. Beijing probably intends for these negotiations to be protracted so that it remains in de facto physical control of the areas now occupied. The PLA troops being armed only with metal-studded batons is one such sign as is the silence at the official level. China's end game would be for the PLA troops to not withdraw from the regions now occupied and possibly try to negotiate for a larger area to be handed over. Their rhetoric, articulated since April 2013, staking a so-called historical claim on entire Ladakh and other areas should not be ignored and we should be prepared for the Chinese expanding their presence in other areas of strategic importance to them.

But in 2019, the year when Prime Minister Narendra Modi and Chinese President Xi Jinping met at Bishkek and Mahabalipuram, there was also a 75 per cent surge in Chinese transgressions in Ladakh — 497 as against 284 transgressions in 2018. Nearly three-quarters of the transgressions, data since 2015 show, have taken place in the western sector of the LAC, which falls in Ladakh. The eastern sector, which falls in Arunachal Pradesh and Sikkim, witnessed almost one-fifth of the Chinese transgressions.

## Appendix

| Incidents on Line of Actual Control | | | | |
|---|---|---|---|---|
| **Year** | **West** | **East** | **Mid** | **Total** |
| 2019 | 497 | 138 | 28 | 663 |
| 2018 | 284 | 89 | 31 | 404 |
| 2017 | 337 | 119 | 17 | 473 |
| 2016 | 208 | 71 | 17 | 396 |
| 2015 | 342 | 77 | 9 | 428 |
| *(Western Eastern, Middle Sectors)* | | | | |

*(This article was published by the Centre for China Analysis and Strategy, New Delhi, on May 26, 2020.)*

# 58. China Probably has a Larger Hidden Agenda

Since the beginning of May this year, China has created an arc of sustained military pressure along India's northern borders. This presently stretches from Daulet Beg Oldi in Ladakh, to Naku La over a thousand kilometres to the east in north Sikkim, and possibly on to Bhutan. China's action appears to blend military, civil and diplomatic instruments.

Confrontations between Indian and Chinese troops, or Chinese military activities, have been reported from a number of places, including around Daulet Beg Oldi, Gogra, Galwan valley, Chushul, Pangong, Demchok, Shiquanhe, Rudok and Naku La in north Sikkim. Such a military build-up takes planning and preparation. At least three Military Sub-Districts (MSD), namely Hetien, Ngari and Shigatse, subordinate to the Xinjiang and Tibet Military Regions are involved in this military build-up. Both Military Regions come under the PLA Western Theatre Command (WTC), which exercises operational jurisdiction over the Chinese side of the entire 4,057-km-long border with India.

Among the WTC's tasks is safeguarding Chinese nationals and assets at the China-Pakistan Economic Corridor (CPEC). Such an operation involving multiple MSDs, as also induction of additional troops, heavy equipment, tanks, vehicles, artillery, aircraft, etc to reinforce the WTC and MSDs, will have required careful planning and coordination, including between the WTC and the Central Military Commission (CMC) chaired by Chinese President Xi Jinping in Beijing. It would certainly have been approved, if not initiated, by Chinese President Xi Jinping who is also the Chairman of the CMC and Commander-in-Chief of the People's Liberation Army (PLA).

There is also potential for additional tension on the Tibet-Bhutan border opposite Drowa village in Lhodrak county, Shannan, Tibet Autonomous Region (TAR), where a report indicates that the PLA is constructing, or upgrading, a Military Training Base (Base No 32) since May 8. Four fighter jets and 21 military buses were reported to have been sent from Gongga

Airport to the construction site of Base No 32 on May 14. Another 100 Army buses are expected to reach the site this month. Coincidentally, the Men Chu Ma village, which is a disputed area between China and Bhutan, and has been developed as one of China's 'model well-off border defence villages' is also in Lhakang township, Lhodrak county, Shannan, Tibet Autonomous Region (TAR), or Bhutan's Kurtoe Lhuntse district.

Additionally, related civilian activity by the TAR and Rudok county administrations, pointing to long-term interest in the Pangong lake has been noticed. On April 21, Dorjee Tsedup, Deputy Chairman of the TAR People's Government and Head of Pangong Lake Governance travelled to Ngari's (Ali's) Rutok county to inspect the Pangong lake and its environment. He was accompanied by the Deputy Commissioner of the Ngari Municipal Administrative Office and other senior officials of Rutok and the Pangong lake district. Interestingly, Dorjee Tsedup's instructions hinted at long-term plans for Pangong lake. He told assembled officials that "Pangong lake, being an international lake, must receive special care and attention for maintenance and improvement of the lake's ecological environment." He emphasised that law enforcement and protection of the lake "is important for long-term work". Days later, Rutok county's Judicial Bureau and the Ngari Regional Customs and Commerce Bureau officials conducted propaganda campaigns in the border villages of Deru and Jaggang also known as Chagkang village, not far from Demchok in Ladakh, India. They explained the alignment of China's border. In late May, the Ngari Municipal Public Security Bureau revealed that all public security personnel in Ngari had received "three-stage intensive real combat training".

Simultaneous with this activity, Beijing has seemingly encouraged Nepalese Prime Minister KP Oli to open another front of pressure on India. Oli owes his continuance as Prime Minister to the efforts of China's Ambassador to Nepal, Ms Hao Yanqi's and Chinese President Xi Jinping's 40-minute telephone conversation with Nepal's President. China's action has the potential to be a long-term problem for India.

A number of factors have contributed to China's actions. In addition to the steady slide in bilateral relations over the years, is Chinese President Xi Jinping's bold operationalisation of the geostrategic 'One Belt, One Road'

(OBOR) in the region with the China-Pakistan Economic Corridor (CPEC) in April 2015. Since then, Chinese leaders have been telling India at every interaction, whether at the official level, Track 1.5 or Track 2 meetings, interactions with think-tanks, etc., that India must resume talks with Pakistan to ease tensions, resolve the Kashmir issue and then look to improved relations with China!

Beijing maintains this pressure on India with the aim of safeguarding its huge strategic and financial stakes invested in the larger Ladakh area, including Aksai Chin, Gilgit, Baltistan and Pakistan occupied Kashmir (PoK). The Indian Army's surgical strikes in PoK and subsequent air strike on the Jaish-e-Mohamed (JeM) terrorist training camp at Balakot in Pakistan, together with the rapid improvement of defence logistics infrastructure on the Indian side and revocation of Article 370, have raised China's apprehensions. China has consequently raised the Kashmir issue in the United Nations Security Council (UNSC) on four occasions thus far in coordination with Pakistan. China's large stakes in the region leave open the possibility of Beijing resorting to a military option.

There is also serious domestic pressure on Chinese President Xi Jinping. The growing discontent caused by various factors like the abolition of term limits on appointments of cadres to senior posts, criticised by cadres as a return to the 'one-man rule' of Mao, rising popular dissatisfaction because of increasingly restrictive and stringent security policies, and expanding intrusive Party surveillance, have provoked wide criticism. The economic downturn, accentuated by the US-China trade war and burgeoning unemployment, estimated this March at between 70-80 million, has broadened the pool of popular dissatisfaction. The initial mishandling of the outbreak of the coronavirus pandemic at its epicentre in Wuhan, sparked a widespread surge of anger. Almost unprecedented for China was that the popular criticism was directed at the Chinese Communist Party (CCP) and Chinese President Xi Jinping personally.

At the same time, the developments in Hong Kong, Taiwan and the adverse impact of the US-China trade war on China's already slowing economy, gave rise to the popular perception that Chinese President Xi Jinping's assertive foreign policy was not working and the 'Two Centenary' goals ('China Dream' by 2021—the hundredth year of the founding of the CCP—and making China a 'major power with pioneering global influence' by 2049—the centenary of the founding of the People's Republic of China) was slipping from the leadership's grasp. A think-tank of China's Ministry of State Security recently cautioned that global anti-China sentiment was growing exponentially and could even lead to conflict. The *PLA Daily* (May 5) warned that the socio-economic situation was "bleak" and at a "high explosive situation" and foreign powers could accelerate a recession and create social upheaval. Xi Jinping has, since February, adopted a series of tough measures to retrieve his and the CCP's credibility. These include the pressure on Hong Kong, Taiwan and now, India. There have also been regular critical references to India in China's military media over the past year and, most recently, at the National People's Congress session that concluded on May 28.

Viewed in this backdrop, the activity at multiple points along India's borders is different from earlier intrusions and certainly tests our military preparedness and political responses. It suggests a larger objective—reflected again on this occasion with reiteration of China's claims on the whole of Ladakh and Galwan valley—either immediate or in the near future. It also raises the question of whether Xi Jinping can yet again risk denting his credibility by withdrawing his forces without showing some gains.

*(This article was published by the Centre for China Analysis and Strategy, New Delhi, on June 17, 2020.)*

# 59. Chinese Thinking on the India-China Border Issue

Recent utterances on the situation along the India-China Line of Actual Control (LAC) by Chinese officials—though infrequent—reflect the sentiment within China of strategists and academics specialising in international relations. While there has been negligible coverage of the developments by the main print or TV channels, except in the *Global Times* which has been prolific, views have been expressed in articles and comments on China's social media. These uniformly maintain that India has violated China's sovereignty and territorial integrity in Ladakh, that it is building up forces in the Sikkim sector, and that China must respond effectively. The sentiments were echoed in the recent statement by Chinese Foreign Minister Wang Yi and the statement issued (September 7) by the People's Liberation Army (PLA) Western Theatre Command. Two recent articles published by the Shanghai-based official *Paper* also reflect this. All emphasise that China will not give up even an inch of its territory and that China must respond effectively. At the same time they speak of retaining commercial ties with India.

Illustrative of Chinese views after the incident of September 7, were those of Xu Liping, researcher at the Institute of Asia-Pacific and Global Strategies, Chinese Academy of Social Sciences and Director of the Southeast Asian Studies Centre. He observed that it was a very serious and provocative incident and 'surpassed the bottom line'. Lin Minwang, researcher of the Institute of International Studies of Fudan University and Deputy Director of the South Asian Studies Centre, described the situation as "relatively severe" and said India's firing of gun shots opens the Pandora's box and poses a "great threat to our border guards". He cautioned that if China continues to exercise restraint, it will "actually pose a great threat to our security" and China must have some new ideas about whether it should comply with the border control mechanism'.

Chinese Foreign Minister Wang Yi's remarks on August 30, at the French Institute for International Relations in Paris, though made before an international audience and, therefore, modulated, are interesting. Omitting the usual platitudes or use of words like 'good-neighbourliness' or 'friendship' that he used immediately earlier while replying to a question on relations with Japan, his comments on the situation along the LAC were matter of fact. Affirming that China will "safeguard our sovereignty and territorial integrity", his formulation that "such situations are bound to occur till the boundary is not settled" suggests that China is prepared for the recurrence of such crises. Worth note, though he was addressing a foreign audience, was Wang Yi's comment that China will "not take the initiative to complicate and expand the situation".

Writing in *Global Times* (September 8) its Editor-in-Chief Hu Xijin too commented, "If the Indian Army fires the first shot at the PLA, the consequence must be the annihilation of the Indian Army on the spot". This hints at a possible intention of keeping the conflict confined to a specific area.

Of interest is the official version of Wang Yi's remarks released (September 2) by *Zhejiang Ribao* which quoted him as stating: "China has always been committed to maintaining stability in the Sino-Indian border areas. We will not take the initiative to complicate and expand the situation. Of course, we must also firmly safeguard our sovereignty and territorial integrity. The border between China and India has not been demarcated, so there will always be problems of this kind. We are willing to manage various problems through dialogue with the Indian side. At the same time, these issues should be placed in appropriate places in bilateral relations".

Pointedly, neither Chinese President Xi Jinping, who holds the posts of General Secretary of the Chinese Communist Party (CCP) Central Committee (CC), Chairman of the Central Military Commission (CMC) and, since April 2016, of Commander-in-Chief of the PLA's Joint Operations Command, nor any of the 25 members of the CCP CC Politburo have till now commented on the situation publicly. It was, however, on the agenda of the high-level 'Safe China (*Ping An*) Construction Coordination Group Political Security Task Force' on June 6, revealing that it is being discussed at the highest levels of the CCP leadership.

After the onset of tensions on May 5, Chinese Foreign Minister Wang Yi has so far publicly commented on the situation only twice earlier. Once after the bloody clash at Galwan on June 16 and, the second time, after the incident on August 29/30. Wang Yi did, however, pay a rare visit to the Tibet Autonomous Region (TAR) on August 14, where he briefed officials in Lhasa on the current international situation and stressed that Tibet's security and stability is closely related to the overall development of the country. His visit possibly indicated some nervousness among CCP leaders about the situation inside Tibet. He was reported to have visited "border areas", which could have included border counties in the Ngari (Ali) and Shigatse Administrative Districts. Dromo county in Yadong bordering China and Nepal could have been one.

The absence of comment by China's leadership and tight control over the propaganda apparatus indicates that the planning of this military operation, which has been underway for many months and certainly since 2018-19, has been done in secrecy, with few in the CCP aware of its details.

The statements issued after the meeting between the Defence Ministers of both sides reiterated the respective positions on territorial integrity. The joint statement issued on September 11 after the meeting of Foreign Ministers is devoid of specifics. It leaves progress in deescalation to negotiations between the Commanders of the forces at the border, though it calls for avoiding any action that escalates matters. There is no indicated timeline for disengagement of forces, or whether Chinese forces will withdraw to the pre-May positions.

Relevant in this context are two papers presented by Chinese scholars and published by the official Shanghai newspaper *Paper* on August 29, which give an idea of the hardened position on India-China relations inside China. The papers were presented by Dr. Tongyu Tao of the School of International Studies at Peking University and Dr. Zhu Chao, China Boundary and Ocean Research Institute, Wuhan University respectively. Summaries of their presentations are given in the succeeding paragraphs.

In his paper captioned "From Donglang to Galwan River Valley: Beware of Three Changes in the Sino-Indian Border Issue", reproduced in the *Paper* on August 29, Dr. Tongyu Tao stated there would be frequent clashes on the border between India and China because the balance of power between the two in the border area has changed. He said India has undertaken construction of roads and camps. Observing that there had been two serious confrontations in three years, Tongyu Tao said, "China must pay sufficient attention to possible changes in the Sino-Indian border issue". The confrontations at the Donglang region and East Ladakh region essentially reflect the changes in the Sino-Indian border issue. These changes have a significant impact on the 'status' of the Sino-Indian border issue and development of Sino-Indian relations. He accused India of trying to change the 'status quo' in recent years as the Indian government hopes "to change the balance of power in disputed areas" and said that "the recent confrontation in East Ladakh was caused by India's infrastructure construction in the actual control zone. In the Galwan area, the dispute was the construction of the Daulat Beg Oldi (DBO) road in India". Saying studies based on satellite imagery of the border areas show that India has set up military bases along the highway, he said, "China should firmly oppose this". In a significant observation he said, "In the past few decades, India has built a large number of facilities on the Sikkim section of the Sino-Indian border, deployed a large number of troops, and even built military installations such as bunkers in some places, constantly changing the border areas status quo".

Attributing accelerated border infrastructure construction to the Bharatiya Janata Party (BJP) government led by Modi coming to power, he asserted that "the reality that needs to be faced is that India's material capabilities on the side of the actual control line have been significantly improved. In the future, as the comprehensive national strength of China and India increases, infrastructure construction activities in border areas will inevitably increase". He underscored that "the two sides have huge differences on the actual line of control. Delineating the actual line of control is not easier than delimiting the formal boundary line. Therefore, there is no solution to the actual line of control for the time being".

Recounting that China and India had signed five border agreements, Tongyu Tao acknowledged that the "treaties have played an extremely restraining role in the recent border stand-offs. Even in the East Ladakh stand-off, before and after the casualties on the evening of June 15th, the two sides were able to conduct dialogue in accordance with the relevant treaties".

He cautioned that if restrictions on the use of weapons by the Indian Army in the border areas are lifted, then the 1993 and 1996 treaties will essentially be broken, with attendant huge risks, and border issues will become increasingly uncontrollable. He warned that as India's military deployment and infrastructure construction increases, India may depart from some treaty restrictions and create a *fait accompli* that benefits India in the border areas. He assessed that the border issue may become the core issue of China-India relations for some time to come. He anticipated that after the current situation and based on actual political interests, India will be less active on other issues of Sino-Indian relations. While presently India's approach is to gradually dilute the border conflict and resolve it peacefully, on other strategic issues India may adopt a more negative attitude towards China. He said that as long as the Sino-Indian border issue is unresolved, it will be the core issue affecting the entire Sino-Indian relationship and negatively impact other areas of China-India relations.

Tongyu Tao additionally drew attention to India's policy towards Pakistan, describing it as "increasingly radical and extreme". Stating that India is willing to risk a full-scale war with a nuclear country and implement cross-border military strikes, he cautioned China to be vigilant of India's behaviour against Pakistan and advised it to effectively deter Indian military actions in the border area, and "resolutely counter-attack any form of force".

Commenting on Sino-US relations, he said that though cooperation between India and the United States is deepening, "it cannot be judged that India has completely fallen to an alliance that 'contains' China. However, after the Galwan incident, whether it will make India more strategically inclined to the United States deserves close attention".

He said that the East Ladakh stand-off has become an obstacle to the positive development of China-India relations, but hoped that after it ends, India will return to the right track and put the Sino-Indian border issue at an appropriate position and avoid border issues.

Dr Chu Zhao's paper captioned, "Looking at 'Modi Logic' from the Main Actions on the Indian Border in the Past three Years" was also published by the *Paper* on August 30, 2020. Dr. Chu Zhao observed that India has launched four major operations in the northern border zone since 2017, and each has caused tension in the border area. He listed them as the China-India confrontation in 'Donglang'; cancellation of the special status of the Indian-controlled Kashmir region; the Ladakh region military exercise; and the conflict in the Galwan valley. Assessing that these border incidents 'provoked by India' have profound domestic and international backgrounds, Chu Zhao elaborated on each.

He asserted that the confrontation between China and India in the Donglang area had been caused by "Indian border guards", crossing into "Chinese territory at the Sikkim section of the China-India border" on June 18, 2017, in violation of the 1890 "Sino-British Conference Tibet-India Treaty". He claimed that India's actions were because it felt China had obstructed pursuit of its dream of becoming a great power. For example, the attempt to join the Nuclear Suppliers Group (NSG) in 2016, failed due to China's opposition; India failed to have the "leader of a religious army in Pakistan" listed as a terrorist in the UN because of China; and the riots in the Darjeeling region, which 'undoubtedly' posed a challenge to India's national unity and stability. India felt that if its Army crossed the border and infringed China's sovereignty, it could divert attention from domestic conflicts and reduce pressure. He said this confrontation would have an adverse effect on the settlement of the Sino-Indian border issue and undermine the development of bilateral relations, but not fundamentally change the status quo: China-India relations will be normal like relations between major powers and be neither intimate nor deteriorate to the extreme.

Stating that revocation of Article 370 on August 5, 2019, by the Modi government, had a major impact domestically and internationally, and generated anxiety among the people of Kashmir, he assessed that the main impact internationally had been felt by Pakistan. Pakistan's Ministry of Foreign Affairs strongly condemned it in a statement on August 5, calling Jammu and Kashmir "an internationally recognized disputed area" and that unilateral measures by India cannot change disputed facts. Pakistan cut off trade and communications with India, downgraded diplomatic relations, "expelled" India's Ambassador and recalled its diplomats. Pakistan also decided to refer the Kashmir issue to the International Court of Justice.

Among the motives ascribed to the cancellation of Kashmir's special status were that it was on the election manifesto of the BJP; the BJP's belief that its revocation was necessary for integrating Kashmir with the rest of India; and that it was a way to divert the people's attention as Modi's government came under criticism for the growing unemployment and its economic policies.

Chu Zhao additionally claimed that it was done to ease tension with the United States and cater to the US' intention to contain China; India took actions in the Kashmir region leading to regional tension; since China and Pakistan are all-weather partners and have close relations and China and India are two of the most important economies in the world and share extensive common interests, India-Pakistan tensions could compel China to choose sides, putting it in a dilemma; the more tense India-Pakistan relations are, the more uncomfortable China will be and, therefore, if India creates tension to the west of China, it will certainly help the United States' calculations; and, that India wanted to cater to the US' intention to contain China in an all-round way.

He said that on September 19, 2019, India held its first large-scale military exercise in the Ladakh region where the infantry, mechanised troops, paratroopers, T-72 tanks, artillery, and drones were deployed. He said the exercises were aimed at alleviating the pressure generated by the cancellation of Kashmir's special status and resultant divisions and fragmentation in society which could threaten India's stability; and for creating a good atmosphere for Modi's visit to the United States as the exercises would inevitably cause certain pressure on China. According to him, military exercises in Ladakh adversely affect regional stability since "the Ladakh region is not only the border zone between China and India, but also close to the disputed Kashmir region between India and Pakistan". They affect maintenance of the status quo between China and India.

The conflict in the Galwan valley, Chu Zhao said, occurred because Indian troops unilaterally built roads, bridges and other facilities in the Galwan valley area since April 2020, ignoring Chinese protests. On May 6, Indian border guards crossed into Chinese territory in the Galwan valley region by night, constructed barriers, blocked the normal patrols of the Chinese border guards, deliberately provoked incidents, and tried to unilaterally change the status quo of border control. The Chinese border troops had to take necessary measures to strengthen on-site response and border area control. To ease the situation, China and India have maintained close communication through military and diplomatic channels. "At the strong request of the Chinese side, the Indian side agreed to withdraw the cross-line personnel and remove the cross-line facilities". Dr Chu Zhao claimed that India provoked the conflict in the Galwan valley to divert attention from the negative impact caused by the epidemic and the locust disaster. It was also intended to "secretly" help the United States.

Explaining the "Modi Logic" in these actions, Dr. Chu Zhao claimed that in each of these four actions, the intention was to divert domestic attention and cater to the US' checks and balances. In the case of the cancellation of Kashmir's special status and the Ladakh military exercise, India chose to exert pressure on China without directly aiming the spearhead against it.

Dr Chu Zhao offered two suggestions for China's response: (a) India will surely continue to pose challenges in the border areas in the future, and China should be fully prepared; and (b) China should increase its troop strength on the border and use exercises and other methods to deter India. The ultimate goal is to send India the signal: "Actions must be modest, and patience is limited!'"

*(This article was published by the Centre for China Analysis and Strategy, New Delhi, on September 11, 2020.)*

# 60. China Appears to have Initiated a Phase of Deception along the LAC

Though China's statecraft and diplomacy have evolved after the establishment of the People's Republic of China (PRC), camouflage, psywar, deception and deceit remain integral to the Chinese Communist regime's diplomatic practice.

Recent developments along the Line of Actual Control (LAC) between India and China show that despite the meetings in Moscow recently between the Defence and Foreign Ministers of India and China, there has been no easing of tension. There are adequate indicators that the imminence of war has not receded. On the contrary, the Chinese have initiated a phase of deception in which uncertainty and tensions remain high and which is likely to last as Chinese President Xi Jinping weighs his options.

Indicators of this phase of deception include the announcement by the Lhasa city authorities on September 14 evening of an air raid alert practice on September 19; China's state-owned official media continuing to report the induction of military hardware and aircraft into the Tibetan plateau; reports of high-altitude para-jump training in the Tibetan plateau by People's Liberation Army (PLA) Paratroop Brigades for operations behind enemy lines on two occasions so far and training by PLA recce battalions; the Chinese not having given a date and time till September 18, for the next meeting of border Commanders; the differences in the joint press statement issued at Moscow and that issued by the Chinese Foreign Ministry almost simultaneously; some markedly opaque comments and an article by the otherwise 'hawkish' Hu Xijin, Editor-in-Chief of the Chinese Communist Party (CCP)- owned *Global Times* and supporter of Xi Jinping; and the continued silence on the subject from the top echelons of the CCP.

China's plans for conflict are known to envisage a localised war wherein it brings in heavy firepower and secures a swift decisive victory. It is presently clear, however, that any conflict with India will be neither swift nor decisive, but bloody and protracted, with damage to both sides. Xi Jinping needs to decide whether damage to the Chinese Communist Party (CCP) and him personally will be greater if his forces disengage and withdraw, or if the PLA suffers a bloody nose in battle. There will, in any case, be no decisive victory. As Xi Jinping ponders over his decision, China will use this phase to try and put India's armed forces and political leadership under strain. It will test them to assess whether there is any weakening of resolve and whether Beijing can extract major concessions. While negotiating the latter, China's objective will be to humiliate the current political leadership.

An article in the *South China Morning Post* (September 9) observed that in the weekend (September 5-6) edition of the *Global Times*, the latter's Editor-in-Chief Hu Xijin had asked that as China faces mounting criticism, including over its aggressive diplomacy and initial handling of the coronavirus outbreak, and its rift with the US worsens: "How come the whole world is China's enemy? Why is China so isolated?" At the same time, Hu Xijin dismissed the widespread criticism as misperceptions and Western bias against China, but did admit that Beijing had a "public opinion dilemma" in many parts of the world over the South China Sea, Hong Kong, Xinjiang, Tibet and the border row with India. He then stated: "China must decide whether to try to get its way as an unencumbered major power, prevailing by dint of its sheer weight and economic strength—but at the risk of strong pushback," or "Alternatively, China could ... accept that the world now has higher expectations of it." The statement appeared to indicate that China's options were still open.

The article by Hu Xijin in the *Global Times* of September 11, is especially curious. His comment that "Chinese society must, therefore, have real courage to engage calmly in a war that aims to protect core interests, and be prepared to bear the cost", suggests that China is preparing militarily and morally on all fronts to defend China's sovereign territory. At the same time, it suggests an apparent unwillingness to engage in war and says, "As long as the outside world can feel such true will from China, it might in turn help us avoid a war". It additionally introduces a so-called 'moral' perspective by saying, "Of course, after all, wars cannot be fought casually, and we must win if we are to fight. Such winning has two meanings: First, it means defeating the opponent on the battlefield; second, it must be morally justified. This is particularly true for China, because China is not the strongest power in the world". In reality this means that China should not appear to have initiated the conflict. A subsequent comment hints at Taiwan and India as potential targets. It says, "We are confident to win on the battlefield if conflicts are fought with neighbouring forces that have territorial disputes with China. Similarly, if there is a war with the US near China's coastal waters, we also have a good chance of victory".

In the backdrop of the situation at the LAC, however, the article seemingly lays the ground rules for conflict with India and stipulates: "Before engaging in war with a neighbouring force, China needs to do the following: First, we must make it clear that the other side, not China, is the one that breaks the status quo. Second, we also need to make it clear that the other side is the provocateur in a complex situation. Third, we must make the international community see that China has made hard diplomatic or political efforts to resolve tensions before the war. Fourth, the first shot is fired by the other side, not China. The international community should be fully aware of this. Fifth, only in extreme situations, if we need to fire the first shots, we must deliver an ultimatum in advance so that a just war can be started in an upright manner. If we can satisfy these conditions, I believe China can be free to engage in a war if it has to. This means that even if the US then tries to smear China, the international community will understand: China is not a country that bullies the small, but instead it had no option but to go to war".

Hu Xijin underscores that "China must not fight an impulsive war. We must be fully prepared militarily and morally".

Finally, retired Indian Army Generals invariably refer to Sun Tzu while talking of the tactics and likely battle plans of the PLA. It will, however, be prudent to remember that PLA officers are not wedded to this classical text, but have invested considerable time, money and effort in studying the latest methods of warfare. It will be especially prudent to remember that the PLA has very intensely studied the US campaigns during the two Gulf Wars in 1991 and 2003 and the operations of the UK's Royal Air Force against Libya where cyber capabilities were effectively used to disable the Libyan command's communications. Relevant in this context is that the Chinese leadership, in the middle of last year, deployed a squadron of its latest J-20 aircraft to the Western Theatre Command and has moved units of the PLA Rocket Force up to the Tibetan plateau. While the comment in the *Global Times* article that "if the Indian Army fires the first shot at the PLA, the consequence must be the annihilation of the Indian Army on the spot", hints at the possibility of conflict being confined to a specific area, that may not be the case.

*(This article was published by the Centre for China Analysis and Strategy, New Delhi, on September 18, 2020.)*

# 61. Chinese Publication Asserts Aksai Chin is "Illegally Occupied by India"

A lengthy over 23,548-character (Chinese) article reasserting China's claim on Aksai Chin and Ladakh and authored by Zeng Hao, Associate Professor of the Law School of Hunan University as part of the phased research of a major National Social Science Fund-2018 project titled "Research on Major International Law Issues in Sino-Indian Relations", was published in the *South Asian Studies* (Issue 3/2020) of Sichuan University. Incidentally, Sichuan University was designated the nodal university for research on South Asia in 2017 by Chinese President Xi Jinping and allotted considerable funding. This issue of *South Asian Studies* was released on September 24, 2020.

The article asserts that China effectively occupied the Aksai China region and exercised administrative control over it since the middle of the 18th century in the period of the Qing dynasty. It says these are the two criteria which determine the legal right of a country's claim over a territory. Stating that Aksai Chin is "illegally occupied" by India, it says China must further strengthen the control of disputed areas between China and India. It recommends that China take counter-measures and coercive steps such as retaliation and even self defence to "effectively" defend national sovereignty and security.

Earlier, an article in the *Zhongguo Qingnian Bao* (*China Youth Daily*), a paper of China's Communist Youth League (CYL), which has a higher circulation than the *People's Daily*, the official mouthpiece of the Chinese Communist Party, had published an article highlighting the cultural, linguistic and other similarities between the people of Tibet and Ladakh and said that Ladakh's ancient Turbo dynasty owed allegiance to the Chinese Emperor. This article was published within days of the Chinese intrusion in the Depsang plains which occurred shortly before the first visit of Li Keqiang as China's Premier to India in April 2013.

More recently in the course of the ongoing stand-off along the Line of Actual Control (LAC) including in Ladakh since May this year, China's claims over Aksai Chin and areas of Ladakh have been reiterated in the statements of the Chinese Foreign Minister Wang Yi and the People's Liberation Army'a (PLA's) Western Theatre Command. This article too specifically mentions that Chinese border guards have since November 7, 1959, been effectively controlling the seven posts of: (i) Gul Lake; (ii) Khurnak Fort (库尔纳克堡/ (Kù ěr nà kè bǎo)/ 33.7667°N 78.9877°E); (iii) Kongka Pass (or Kongka La 空喀山口/ (Kongke Shankou)/ 34°20′ 06″ N 79°02′ 07″ E); (iv) Shenxian Bay (神仙湾 (Shenxianwan)/ 35°34'10"N 77°50'45"E); (v) Chip Chap River Valley ( 奇普恰普河 (Qipuqiapuhe) 35.275N, 78.186E); (vi) Hot Springs in the area of Kongka Pass (Kyam)/ 贡嘎山 温泉 (Kongga Shanwenquan) 34.30°N 78.95°E); and (vii) Niyagazu north of Bangong Lake.

It anticipatedly stressed too that the Qing dynasty had unified Xinjiang in 1759 and that Aksai Chin, which is located in the southern part of the Hetian region of southern Xinjiang, was included in the Chinese territory. Moreover, in order to set up a military system of government, the Chinese government in 1759 set up a Minister of Khotan in Yiliqi (now Hotan), which governed the Aksai Chin region.

This article is an effort to build a detailed legal and administrative case to reinforce China's claim and occupation of Aksai Chin. Briefly, the article states that the Chinese government officially incorporated the Aksai Chin region into its national territory and from the middle of the 18th century "obtained the original source of sovereignty over the region". Over the next 200 years, the Chinese government has effectively maintained its territorial sovereignty over this area. On August 21, 1958, India formally claimed sovereignty over "China's Aksai Chin region", which the Chinese government rejected on November 3, 1958, leading to a "conflict of legal opinions or interests" regarding Aksai Chin's sovereignty. It said that judging by the weight of evidence of countries exercising administrative jurisdiction over the region prior to the critical date of November 3, 1958, "we can find that India has never exercised administrative jurisdiction over the Aksai Chin region, and the evidence it enumerated cannot be used as proof of its territorial sovereignty over the Aksai Chin region". In contrast, China has exercised "long-term, sustained, peaceful and adequate administrative jurisdiction over Aksai Chin with the intention of occupation" and it can be fully concluded that Aksai Chin's sovereignty belongs to China. Insisting that "India's claim of sovereignty against Aksai Chin is illegal and invalid", it asserted too that the Indian government's declaration of "sovereignty" over "China's Aksai Chin" is not "Indian internal affairs", but an internationally illegal act that violates China's sovereign rights and interests and undermines the status quo of the Sino-Indian border. It reiterates that the Chinese government has the right to take corresponding counter-measures against "India's internationally wrongful acts" in accordance with international law.

It listed India's passing of the "Jammu and Kashmir Reorganisation Act of 2019" to include "China's Aksai Chin" in the so-called "Ladakh Territory"; comprehensive additions and announcements of Indian regional names for "southern Tibet"; and the establishment of administrative divisions in disputed areas between China and India illegally occupied by India; as additional violations by India. These, it said, necessitate effective counter-measures.

Publication of this article at this time clearly indicates that China will not relent on its claims and will probably neither withdraw from the areas it has already occupied. Its publication shows also that China began building its case to justify its future actions as part of the "Three Warfares" (propaganda, psychological and legal) in 2018! As can be discerned from China's social media and the very few articles published in its mainstream media, which portray India as the aggressive power, nationalist sentiments on the issues of sovereignty and territory with India, as well as the Taiwan issue, are high in China. They point to popular support for military action to take over the claimed areas.

NOTE: Place names and locations at Para 4 have been identified by the Centre for China Analysis and Strategy (CCAS).

*(This article was published by the Centre for China Analysis and Strategy, New Delhi, on September 26, 2020.)*

# 62. An Authoritative Chinese Assessment of how China Views India

Far from any sign of an end to the military stand-off between India and China, or that tensions between the two will ease, China's mood towards India is hardening. There are indications that China sees the current confrontation as the beginning of a period of sustained, protracted pressure on India. The military confrontation in the Himalayas is likely to escalate, with a high possibility of clashes occurring periodically commencing from spring this year. These could include sharp, swift military actions.

China has meanwhile stepped up domestic publicity, though yet limited, of its narrative on the military stand-off in Ladakh. Predictably, China's official media describes China's actions in Ladakh as a counter-offensive provoked by India's aggressive "forward policy" and as infringing on Chinese sovereignty. China's official media anticipates that further military build-up, accompanied by the possibility of clashes, will commence as conditions ease in April-May.

Important are two recent articles by Hu Shisheng, Director of the Institute for South Asian Studies at the China Institutes of Contemporary International Relations (CICIR). He is probably the institute's leading expert on South Asian affairs, especially India and Pakistan. The CICIR is one of China's most influential institutes and is directly under the Ministry of State Security (MoSS), China's external intelligence establishment. Most recently Yuan Peng, President of CICIR and an Americas expert, addressed the 26th 'study session' of the Communist Party of China Central Committee (CCP CC) Politburo on December 12, to offer suggestions on how China should engage with the United States.

Hu Shisheng co-authored a 33-page article titled "The Behavioural Logic behind India's Tough Foreign Policy Toward China", in the latest (Sept-Oct) issue of *Contemporary International Relations* (CIR), the CICIR's official publication. In it, Hu Shisheng was categoric that the "conflict was not incidental", but the "inevitable" result of the "high risk, high yield" policy followed by the Modi administration. He attributed this policy to "a desire to seek revenge" prompted by "India's long-term pursuit of absolute security and dominance in the regional order" and the Modi government's ambition to "overtake China by taking advantages of India's favourable external strategic environment".

The CICIR article was published in Chinese as well as English. The intention is obviously to ensure wider publicity for China's views of its relations with India and the problems in the relationship.

India's international environment, Hu Shisheng said, has generally improved since Prime Minister Modi came to power. He assessed that "India's geo-value" has risen to its highest since independence because of the demands of the US and the West to contain China, particularly in the context of intensifying China-US confrontation. This has given the Modi administration "more courage and confidence to be tough on China".

Hu Shisheng projected a pessimistic view for China-India relations explaining that "Indian conservatives already held deep strategic mistrust and apprehension about China due to the structural problems existing between the two countries". He described the Rashtriya Swayamsevak Sangh (RSS) as a conservative, right-wing, hardline political organisation opposed to foreign investment. Pointing out that important leaders in the government and the majority of those in the Bharatiya Janata Party (BJP) came from an RSS background, he stated that India's political orientation was steadily shifting to the right. He gauged the RSS' increasing influence from the number of *shakhas* which had grown from about 40,000 when Modi first came to power in 2014, to 84,000 in 2019. He assessed that the rise of conservative forces had shrunk the space of the liberal groups—traditionally comprising diplomatic and business elites—and "even done away with the strategic culture of swinging between the sides of China and the US". He said that Modi had, additionally, tried to downplay popular opposition by being increasingly tough on China and building his image as a leader tough on security issues. Hu Shisheng emphasised that "staying in power is the most important political strategy for a leader in a democracy".

Discussing the confrontation on the border, Hu Shisheng asserted that "it was India that provoked the conflict by launching a surprise attack on the Chinese-controlled area in the middle of the night, seriously wounding Chinese border guards, while China took a posterior action to fight back inflicting great casualties on Indian border troops". He said, "The Modi administration has become increasingly tougher in its policy toward China, hence, building up antagonism between the two countries and putting China-India relations on a downward trend". He stated that this "first major large-scale border conflict with widespread casualties since 1975 indicates that the development of China-India relations has come to a structural bottleneck, and the time has arrived for the two countries to restructure their relations, otherwise their relationship can hardly be resumed". He added that since Modi came to power, China-India relations have every year "witnessed a benign beginning and a sad ending".

Hu Shisheng assessed that India had provoked the border conflict at the Galwan valley because "China's border infrastructure building activities in that region were thought to pose serious threats to the Darbuk-Shyok river-Daulat Beg Oldi highway, which is an important strategic route for India to ensure effective control of the Siachen glacier, which is not only the strategic high grounds to monitor the China-Pakistan Karakoram highway, but also the world's highest battlefield where Indian and Pakistani military troops confront each other".

Describing the conflict at the Galwan valley as "anything but the end", Hu Shisheng said the contest over the border is highly likely to move from "reconciliation through dialogues" to a new stage featuring "contention for control with real power". This will inevitably give rise to border stand-offs and clashes. With the Indian government authorising its border troops to tackle border incidents, he felt the probability of conflict escalating from "cold weapons to firearms" is likely to increase. Hu Shisheng anticipated that in the course of time "the bottom line of tolerance will become a red line lying between the border troops of both countries".

In other words, the two sides will continue to advance their control in the frontier areas to their respective perception of the border. While there is a hint that both would try to avoid full-scale conflict, there is acceptance that occasional fire-fights could well occur. This could, he assessed, eventually lead to a mutually accepted border, or defined line of actual control.

Stating, "Today, the Indian military has basically controlled most of the commanding heights along the eastern and middle section of the China-India border", he shifted the blame onto India saying, "Since Modi came into power, India's border troops have focused on promoting the Forward Policy along the western section of the China-India border". The incidence of border confrontations, he claimed, has consequently increased in the western section. "In 2019, for example, India trespassed China's line of actual control 1,581 times, of which 94 per cent occurred in the western section of the China-India border". When China responded strongly, border confrontations and even clashes occurred. This, he said, is why "China and India have always been caught in yearly vicious cycles of "starting high and ending low" since Modi assumed power in 2014".

Moving to broader issues that bedevil bilateral relations, he candidly assessed that India and China "were doomed to have a serious collision of interests or even military conflict from the very beginning of their independence and since establishing frontier and regional order". He asserted this was inevitable, "as one newly-born state is a denier of the colonial order, while the other one is its successor". He clarified this as China resenting humiliation by foreign colonial powers while India, on the contrary, had accepted colonial rule and felt it had benefitted from this. Explaining that India perceives itself as a "successor" to the colonial power and continues to pursue its policies, he said that because of this, "Tibet-related issues and border disputes between China and India continued to intensify and even today, from time to time, these two problems still threaten the stability of China-India relations". He pointed to the conflict at the Galwan valley as the latest example.

Touching on the broader aspects of the relationship, Hu Shisheng asserted that more complicated than border issues are the contention for influence and dominance and "order in the region involving relations among China, India and their neighbors". As the respective national strengths of India and China grow, "the two major regional powers, would have an increasing overlap of interests in the same area".

In this context, he claimed, "Unfortunately, the Monroeist policy currently pursued by the BJP has collided with the advance of China's Belt and Road Initiative". With an increasing number of India's neighbours actively participating in the Belt and Road Initiative (BRI), competition between the two has intensified to involve the regional order in South Asia and the northern Indian Ocean. He described India's tendency to "overreact with respect to China's South Asian policy" as the most significant external factor that triggers domestic political unrest in India's neighbouring countries. As examples, he listed the blocking of Nepal's border (from September 2015 to January 2016), "dividing the pro-China regime in Sri Lanka (from December 2014 to January 2015)", "strongly curtailing the pro-China tendencies in Bhutan's internal politics by intervening in its national elections (in 2013 and 2018)", and "toppling the pro-China government in Maldives (2019)".

Hu Shisheng encapsulated that "Sino-Indian relations have been disturbed deeply by the five 'T' issues, referring to the Tibet issue, territory disputes, the third-party factor, trade unbalance and trust deficit". He claimed, "Different issues have different impacts on their bilateral relations at different times".

In conclusion, Hu Shisheng said that since both countries face issues like food shortages and are determined not to be vassals of major powers, they need "to design a stable and far-reaching path for the future development" of relations. Pointedly avoiding any mention of close and friendly ties, he suggested that "both countries have to build a relationship resembling two cars driving in parallel lanes, each sticking to its own respective lane" to avoid accidents. If this is done, the China-India relationship will be smooth for the next 70 years, he observed.

Another article by Hu Shisheng, this time published in the *Global Times* (December 17), suggested a more negative and obstructive view of India. Publication of this article in a CCP owned publication will have the required high level approval.

The article stated that India's multilateral diplomacy has become "more pro-West and Sinophobic" and that India had abandoned a balanced approach. Hu Shisheng said India is less interested in multilateral mechanisms in which China plays a leading role, elaborating that "India tends to disrupt China's agenda in multilateral mechanisms" to prevent them from boosting China's rise. He criticised India for not promoting internal unity in the Brazil, Russia, India, China, and South Africa (BRICS) and Shanghai Cooperation

Organisation (SCO), but trying to dismantle them from within. He attributed India's withdrawal from the Regional Comprehensive Economic Partnership (RCEP) to India being unable to play a dominant role there.

He said India wants to be the leader of the developing world. However, as the gap between India and China widened, differences between them grew on matters such as regional and global governance and "the favorable atmosphere for China-India cooperation" gradually faded.

The Indian Ocean was identified as another area where India wants to be the net security provider, but since it cannot do this alone because of the BRI, it is trying to align with the US Indo-Pacific strategic framework. Stating that Indian political elites tend to stand with the US and the West to launch ideological offensives against China, Hu Shisheng said they emphasise their connections with American and Western value systems. In India's view, China is its top geopolitical competitor and China-India cooperation on development and international issues cannot change this fact. Hu Shisheng said in conclusion that India is no longer interested in small-scale multilateral mechanisms where China plays an important role and is instead more interested in promoting multilateral mechanisms with the US and the West.

Another article by an anonymous author, but posted on a PLA-maintained website on December 24, claimed the Indian Army is "waiting for an opportunity to cause trouble next year" and "the conflict may be worse than this year". It claimed that China and India "have prepared for a long-term confrontation in the disputed border area". Reiterating that China does "not want to be an enemy of India, but this does not mean that China will compromise on sovereignty issues", it added, "China will at best cool down but will not withdraw". It claimed that because of the "Indian party's strong Hindu nationalist ideology" and elite strategic thinking, along with the United States' aim to control China, "the confrontation is expected to continue for several years".

It anticipated that military confrontation will resume as conditions improve in April and the Indian Army again becomes active before May. "The goal of the Indian Army is not to launch a full-scale war, but to try to control a part of the strategically important hills through infiltration and sneak attacks while preparing for a full-scale war to optimize its confrontation". The article added, "It is very likely that the two sides will further expand the scale of the battle" which will make the situation more difficult to control by mid next year.

In conclusion, it said "India has chosen to confront China, then we must also be prepared. It is just that in this long-term game, India must be the one that pays the greater price. India will waste decades on the misjudgement of Modi's and Jaishankar's strategy".

The publication of these articles gives an insight into China's view of its longer-term relationship with India. Publication of Hu Shisheng's candid and detailed assessment in CICIR's official magazine is important and will reflect the view, at the least, of China's intelligence establishment. It also implicitly confirms Beijing ambitions.

*(This article was published by the Centre for China Analysis and Strategy, New Delhi, on December 31, 2021.)*

# Index